Autism Works

People with autism are being left behind today, with only 16 per cent in full-time employment. This inspiring book addresses the lack of understanding of the wonderful contributions people across the autism spectrum can make to the workplace, drawing attention to this vast untapped human resource. Employers who create supportive workplaces can enhance their companies by making use of the talents of people with autism while also helping to produce a more inclusive and tolerant society, and people with autism can themselves benefit materially and emotionally from improved employment opportunities.

Packed with real-life case studies examining the day-to-day working lives of people across the autism spectrum in a wide variety of careers, this book provides constructive solutions for both employers seeking to improve their workplaces and for individuals with autism considering their employment options. It dispels popular myths about autism, such as that everyone is good at IT, and crucially tackles the potential job opportunities available across the spectrum, including for those who have no language at all. It also highlights the neglected area of gender differences in the workplace and the costs of autistic females' ability to 'camouflage' their condition.

This book is a must-read for parents, employers and adults with autism, and for anyone interested in the present and future of people with autism in the workplace who will benefit from the positive message that employing autistic people is not an act of charity but one that makes sound economic sense.

Adam Feinstein is an internationally recognised autism historian and researcher. His globally acclaimed previous book on autism, *A History of Autism: Conversations with the Pioneers*, was called 'a treasure trove' and 'a terrific book' by Professor Simon Baron-Cohen, director of Cambridge University's Autism Research Centre, and has since been translated into a number of languages. Feinstein has given numerous lectures on autism around the world, including Mexico, Argentina, the United States, Russia, China, India, Spain, Italy, Germany, Switzerland and the Netherlands. His presentations in the UK include talks at Cambridge and Oxford Universities and at the Royal Society in London.

Autism Works

A Guide to Successful Employment across the Entire Spectrum

Adam Feinstein

Routledge
Taylor & Francis Group

LONDON AND NEW YORK

First published 2019
by Routledge
2 Park Square, Milton Park, Abingdon, Oxon OX14 4RN

and by Routledge
711 Third Avenue, New York, NY 10017

Routledge is an imprint of the Taylor & Francis Group, an informa business

British Library Cataloguing-in-Publication Data
A catalogue record for this book is available from the British Library

Library of Congress Cataloging-in-Publication Data
Names: Feinstein, Adam, 1957– author.
Title: Autism works : a guide to successful employment across the entire spectrum / Adam Feinstein.
Description: 1 Edition. | New York : Routledge, 2018. |
Includes bibliographical references and index.
Identifiers: LCCN 2018010058 | ISBN 9780815369318 (hb : alk. paper) |
ISBN 9780815369486 (pb : alk. paper) | ISBN 9781351252348 (eb)
Subjects: LCSH: People with disabilities–Employment. |
Discrimination in employment. | Autistic people–Employment.
Classification: LCC HD7255 .F45 2018 | DDC 331.5/95–dc23
LC record available at https://lccn.loc.gov/2018010058

ISBN: 978-0-815-36931-8 (hbk)
ISBN: 978-0-815-36948-6 (pbk)
ISBN: 978-1-351-25234-8 (ebk)

Typeset in Gill Sans
by Out of House Publishing

Contents

Acknowledgements

First and foremost, my profound gratitude must go to Dame Stephanie Shirley, without whom this book would never have seen the light of day. Steve, as all of us who know her well call her, entrusted me with the responsibility of tackling this most important, and sensitive, of topics (just as she did with my previous book in the field, *A History of Autism: Conversations with the Pioneers*) and, once again showed enormous generosity in sponsoring me during the writing process. Steve also read through the typescript and made many valuable suggestions.

My profound thanks also go to the other members of the Steering Group – Professor Elisabeth Hill, Eileen Hopkins and John Carrington – who worked with Steve to see the book through to its completion.

I have encountered wonderful examples of good practice, all of whose employment schemes – up and down the United Kingdom, as well as internationally – have emphasised the positive contributions so many autistic individuals can make to the workplace and to society as a whole. They are, of course, far too numerous to thank in their entirety here, but I would like to express my immense gratitude to Thorkil Sonne, the founder of Specialisterne, Viola Sommer at Auticon UK, David Perkins at AS Mentoring, Jane Hatton at Evenbreak, Nick Llewellyn and Alex Covell at Access All Areas, Judith Kerem at Caretrade, Anne O'Bryan at Project Search, Philip Bartey at Autism Plus, John Phillipson at the North East Autism Society, Laurel Herman at ASPIeRATIONS, Sue Hope at IWork4Me in Scotland and Sharon Didrichsen of Specialisterne Northern Ireland. Ian Iceton, of Network Rail, and David McNeill, also offered me helpful information.

Other smaller (but in their way, just as important) British organisations, and their energetic founders and leaders, also deserve my deepest admiration and thanks. Once again, space precludes a comprehensive list, but the names must include Kathy Erangey, at Autism Oxford (and her team of very talented autistic public speakers and trainers); Claire Cordell and everyone at the remarkable Little Gate Farm; Jackie Renfrey at the equally extraordinary Poetry in Wood, a social enterprise that has demonstrated that even non-verbal people with autism can earn a living wage; Pino Frumiento and Mark Williams, the founders of the innovative Heart n Soul, (as well as its general manager, Sarah Ewans), which celebrated its thirtieth anniversary while I was writing this book; Shaz and Mona Shah of Harry Specters: Emily Hayward at the Paddock School Café and Andrew Billings at miLife.

I appreciate the invaluable assistance of a range of people in guiding me through the latest research findings relating to autism and employment. They include Professor Martin Knapp, of the London School of Economics, Dr Beatriz López at the University of Portsmouth, Anne Cockayne at Nottingham Trent University, Professor Cathy Lord at Cornell University in New York. My conversations with Dr Sarah Bargiela, of

University College London, and Dr Kevin Pelphrey, of George Washington University in Washington DC, illuminated their own significant new studies on females with autism. My good friend, President Simon Baron-Cohen, director of Cambridge University's Autism Research Centre, was, as usual, a source of great support as well as information – not least when we spoke together on neurodiversity in the workplace at the Latitude Festival in 2017. I also thank Dr Thusha Rajendran and Dr Peter McKenna, of Heriot-Watt University in Edinburgh, for details of Alyx, their new robot aimed at helping autistic employees negotiate their way through the social 'minefield' of the workplace.

It should go without saying that there were countless examples of people on the autism spectrum who, during the writing of this work, inspired me with their experiences, their creativity and their optimism and determination in the face of considerable challenges. Many of them formed the basis of the case studies in this book. My gratitude, in this regard, goes to Jon Adams, Dean Beadle, Jules Robertson (and his mother, Kathy Lette, who allowed me the time to share my passion for tennis with him), Cian Binchy, Derek Paravicini (and his teacher, mentor and coach, Adam Ockelford), David Harris (and his cousin, Lynn Hart), Thomas Madar, Jamie Knight, Tilley Milburn, James Christie, Ryan Tebbit, Luke Jackson, Richard Macguire, James Cordless, Angela Dellow, Patrick Birmingham and David Chegwidden (all Little Gate Farm success stories) and Oliver Wiltshire (and his mother, Natalie).

Dinah Murray has been exceptionally helpful in emphasising the need to apply an inclusive concept of employment – to embrace unpaid work and self-employment, among other key, under-investigated areas of discussion. I thank Dinah profoundly for these and other crucial observations raised during the writing of this book, and for her invaluable contributions to a deeper understanding of autism in general through her own writings and activities.

I am grateful to Damian Milton for providing astute comments, both about his personal experiences in the workplace and relating to the insights acquired from his own research into the issues involved.

Jonathan Andrews, the lawyer and poet with Asperger's syndrome, has been immensely helpful in exploring various areas, notably transition into work, demolishing the well-meaning but misguided stereotypes about autism and discussing LGBT issues, for which he is also such a powerful advocate.

I am very grateful to Mark Lever, Carol Povey, Jane Asher, Emma Jones and Louisa Mullan, of Britain's National Autistic Society, all supplied valuable information and observations, as well as suggesting further contacts, for which I also thank them.

Further afield, in the US, the views of Temple Grandin, the world's most famous woman with autism, helped to shed new light on the best ways of making use of the 'autism advantage' in the workplace. Dr Darold Treffert described his work on special skills in employment, moving beyond the sheltered workshop to part- or full-time employment in the regular workforce using programming, electronic, mechanical or farming skills. I also have to thank Stephen Shore, at Adelphi University in New York, both for the moments of laughter we have shared in many parts of the world and for his insights into finding a successful path into employment for himself and for many others on the autism spectrum. I welcome the crucial emphasis that Randy Lewis, former vice-president of Walgreens, placed on the sound business sense of employing people with autism (rather than doing so out of charity). I appreciate this message from a fellow father of an autistic son, as well as his support for this book.

I am naturally extremely grateful to Russell George, Lucy Kennedy and Alex Howard at Routledge for their constant and exceedingly patient support at all stages of writing this book, and to Jennifer Hinchliffe and Gail Welsh in the final copy-editing phase, ensuring a smooth transition from typescript to publication.

Last but by no means least, I must thank my family and especially my autistic son, Johnny, of whom I am inordinately proud. He lost his language at around three but his non-verbal sense of mischief and fun have been a constant source of inspiration to me, as they have to so many others.

Foreword

Figure 0.1 Dame Stephanie Shirley

Autism is a developmental disorder which affects communication, forming relationships and how people make sense of the world. It affects over one in 100 people. The UK's national cost is some £34bn, mainly in lost employment.

Autism Works describes both the theory and practice of people with autism at work. Work – the physical or mental activity required to achieve a result – can be for remuneration or an activity in its own right.

The Shirley Foundation has its focus on pioneering strategic projects in the field of autism spectrum disorders. Its trustees initiated the study underpinning this book in 2014.

The project was driven by a volunteer steering group consisting of Professor of Neurodevelopmental Disorders Elisabeth Hill from Goldsmiths, University of London; Autism Consultant and Executive Director, Ai-Media, Eileen Hopkins; and me – all chaired by businessman John Carrington.

I knew and admired the author, Adam Feinstein, from the portal site AutismConnect, Autism Cymru and his History of Autism, three previous Shirley Foundation projects. He personally developed the case studies incorporating the views of employers and family.

He and I share the searing experience of our autistic sons being also profoundly learning disabled. *Autism Works* includes this part of the autism spectrum in a practical and realistic way. Adam's family and professional history make him an excellent and practical advocate.

I also recognise the Danish parent, Thorkil Sonne of *Specialisterne*, who first conceived the idea of autistic people in the labour market. His innovative, indeed disruptive, ideas have made a strategic difference. People are now adapting to the autistic personality rather than the conceitful reverse: expecting the autistic individual to be like everyone else.

Dame Stephanie Shirley CH

Introduction

On 7 July 2017, the British daily, the *Guardian*, published a powerful and poignant anonymous 'Letter to my boss'. It came from an employee on the autism spectrum:

'When you offered me the job, it seemed perfect. You said I blew the competition away and you wanted me to start as soon as possible. You beat my current pay and promised a family-style atmosphere where emphasis was on the "right personality". As someone with autism, I wasn't looking for special treatment. If anything, telling you about my condition has made my job worse. Now, rather than being seen as "cutely eccentric," I am "the one with the developmental disability". I didn't complain about the fluorescent lighting, or when you moved me from a quiet office to a busy one, or when you cancel our meetings and then lean in the doorway and regurgitate your weight loss goals to me.

If I mention that these things make me panic, want to vomit, make my ears ring – you tell me to get it together. Then you ask me for my personal input on autistic patients. I am not here to tick boxes on an equal opportunities form. When I told you I needed support in the workplace, you immediately extended my probationary period, knowing that this new insecurity around job safety was directly related to a disability.

Yes, I can hear you whispering two offices away through closed doors. Just like I can hear washing machines three doors down on my road or my partner opening a plaster. Yes, I know my eye contact is poor, but don't bully me into making it. And do not touch me. It makes my skin burn so I'd rather you didn't. Yes, I do have very rigid routines and travelling alone is difficult, but I manage.

I need you to understand that these things may seem crippling to you, but actually I have a pretty good life. A couple of good friends, partner, planned holiday and a mix of interests. I wish I could tell you this is the first job where I have felt disabled. You remind me weekly of my special needs. That time you shouted at us in a meeting, I began shaking because the volume of your words made me feel sick. And afterwards, everyone else was asked if they were OK, but I was avoided. You told people to leave me alone and whispered that I just couldn't cope.

I wish I could tell you how confused I was when you encouraged me to make a statement against a discriminatory member of staff and said you'd back me. When your boss was there and told me I shouldn't be pursuing it, you said nothing. Later, you told other staff that you thought I was trying to catch out the company for my own personal gain. HR policies state I should take this up with your boss, but the one time I told them about it, I wasn't allowed back in the meeting.

When you say: "Don't you worry that if you have kids they'll be autistic?" I need you to know that only you feel shame and worry about my disability. For me, my autism isn't a problem.[1]

This book aims to speak for that autistic employee and for all others. It is also directed at employers and at professionals working in the field. I am in no way proceeding in adversarial fashion or condemning employers for their lack of understanding. Far from it! I hope to show that some employers are showing an increasing willingness to address the complexities of autism and to acknowledge the commercial advantage of employing people on the autism spectrum, realising that this is in the interests of the company, and is not an act of charity. As Randy Lewis, formerly senior vice-president of Walgreens — the second largest pharmacy store chain in the United States — and the father of an autistic son, told me:

Although progress is slow, I continue to see signs that employers are opening up to the idea of employing people like our children who are on the spectrum. But it is not fast enough and people like you and me need to keep pushing.[2]

At least 1 per cent of the world's population is on the autism spectrum, which equates to some 70 million people. Autism is a heterogeneous neurological condition which can be associated with difficulties with social relationships, communication, adjusting to unexpected change, dealing with ambiguity, anxiety and sensory hypo- and hyper-sensitivity. But increasingly, among those with those 'negative' issues, we are coming to understand the very positive advantages of the different perceptual, cognitive and learning style, which can lead to creativity of thought — including, of course, in the workplace. Many people on the autism spectrum demonstrate a preference for detail, and develop unusually narrow interests, and an unusually strong preference for facts, patterns, repetition and routine.

Indeed, back in 1979, Hans Asperger wrote:

It seems that for success in science or art, a dash of autism is essential. For success, the necessary ingredient may be an ability to turn away from the everyday world, from the simply practical, an ability to re-think a subject with originality, so as to create in new, untrodden ways, with all abilities channelled into the one speciality.[3]

The other great pioneer in the field of autism, Leo Kanner, in a 1971 paper, pointed out that a person's 'fixations' can be extremely motivating and may lead to careers.[4] We know how Temple Grandin, the world's most famous woman with autism today, acquired her interest in designing cattle ranches: her mother sent her to stay at her aunt's ranch one summer (something to which she was not looking forward, because her aunt had no television set!) and it turned out that she loved observing the cows. She is now one of the most successful designers of cattle ranches on the planet — she designed a third of all such ranches in the US, including John Wayne's.

Everyone needs to work. As Dame Stephanie Shirley reminded her audience at the North East Autism Society's employment conference in Gateshead in 2016, Picasso called work 'the ultimate seduction' and Thomas Carlyle believed it was 'the grand cure of all the maladies'.[5] People with autism have this same drive to work and derive the same pleasure and boost to their self-esteem from meaningful employment as the rest of us. But employment is more than just paid work. Temple Grandin puts it tellingly: 'Without work, no matter how big or small the job, life would become small and unsatisfying.'[6]

There was a graphic example of this drive to work in 2017: Jason Polyik, a 27-year-old British man with autism, was jailed for 10 months after hacking into the UK retail giant Sports Direct's website because he wanted the firm to employ him. The site went down for 30 minutes, costing the company around £50,000. Polyik was probably searching for a vulnerability on their site in the belief that, just as Google and Amazon have been known to hire people who have successfully identified flaws in computer systems, Sports Direct would also offer him employment. His lawyer, Joe Harvey, was quoted as saying: 'He is a talented graphic artist, but no one wanted to work with him because of his social issues. He is socially awkward and on the autism spectrum. He has honed and shaped his skills over a number of years.'[7]

Self-esteem

Work brings satisfaction, fulfilment and, above all, self-worth. But it is not an infallible panacea. It is extraordinary, in fact, how profoundly lack of self-esteem can affect even the most gifted of individuals on the autism spectrum. Luke Jackson is a brilliant photographer with Asperger's syndrome. Yet he still says he wishes he were exceptionally good at something, even though his mother, Jacqui – who has three other children on the spectrum – tells Luke several times a day what a talented photographer he is. As well as an articulate and inspirational public speaker, 'to him, if there is more to learn about his specialist subject, then he is not good at it'.[8]

I was given an intriguing insight into a surprisingly positive spin-off to low-esteem in the workplace. James Hoodless, a young man with Asperger's syndrome who works as a presenter for Autism Oxford but is also successfully employed at a toy shop in High Wycombe, told me:

> It is almost impossible to shift low self-esteem – that is the default position. On the other hand, strangely enough, this means that I strive even harder to be helpful to customers or audiences, because I feel they are superior to me and deserve the best treatment.[9]

James's Autism Oxford colleague, Richard Maguire, another man with Asperger's syndrome who is in great demand as a speaker and whose excellent memoir, I Dream in Autism, was published in 2014, told me: 'My low self-esteem stems from the fact that I was told by everyone that I was wrong when I was growing up, that I was a faulty version of humanity.'[10]

The 'autism advantage'

One of this book's aims is to help people on the spectrum find fulfilling, meaningful employment – and to help employers to understand just why accepting autistic workers into the workplace will benefit the company as well as the employees. The autism advantage is there for us all to see: individuals with autism tend to be extremely reliable, conscientious, focused. Their unusual ability to 'think outside the box' is invaluable. As Francesca Happé and Dame Uta Frith have shown, weak central coherence (or, to employ the more positive terminology, local processing bias) is a common trait in people on the autism spectrum: they tend to see the parts rather than the whole.[11] This can be a problem in some settings but a terrific attribute in others, especially in certain professions – for example, if you are looking for unique cells (as a lab technician), deep space anomalies (as an astronomer), differences among species (as a biologist) or particular qualities of objects (as a gemologist, an antiques appraiser or an art historian).

As Anne Cockayne, of Nottingham Trent University, has written:

> Someone with high predilection for spotting detail is very likely to be able to see errors and oddities in a situation or document that others simply do not. If overused, such a characteristic can be a weakness, and may lead to people with autism being described as pedantic by colleagues. But a fine eye for detail in the right context is a strength, for example lawyers poring over heavy text and proof-readers checking websites for spacing inconsistencies and inaccuracies.[12]

There is a basic misunderstanding about autism. Because it is often associated with cognitive inflexibility, the mental leap is then to assume that this equates to lack of creativity. Nothing could be further from the truth. An important study from the University of Stirling, in Scotland, in 2015 showed that people with autism displayed higher levels of creativity than previously believed. The researchers found that people on the spectrum were far more likely to come up with unique answers to creative problems, despite having traits that could be socially crippling and make it difficult to find jobs.[13] The co-author of the study, Dr Catherine Best, said it revealed a link between autistic traits and unusual and original ideas: 'We speculate that it may be because they are approaching things very differently. It goes a way towards explaining how some people with what is often characterised as a disability exhibit superior creative talents in some domains.'[14]

Pattern recognition, attention to detail and persistence are all traits typically associated with those on the spectrum. As Emma Jones, Partnerships and Employment Training Manager at Britain's National Autistic Society, puts it:

> Without generalising too much, an autistic employee is very methodical in their approach, they offer a different way of thinking ... they help challenge the way we are doing things and often it is the person with autism who notices a fault in the process and questions why we are doing it like this.

If an employer can get the workplace adjustments right, they are almost guaranteed a more productive, loyal and reliable employee, she adds. And yet many are still neglecting to tap into this market.[15]

Right across the spectrum

Crucially, this book – as its subtitle indicates – will demonstrate, with uniquely illuminating case studies, that there are jobs for people right across the autism spectrum, not just on the so-called 'higher-functioning' end. Creativity comes in all shapes and sizes. My own autistic son, Johnny, now aged 25, lost his language at around three. But being non-verbal does not necessarily equate to being unemployed. To cite just a sprinkling of very exciting examples: in Whitechapel, east London, non-verbal employees with autism earn a living wage producing wooden objects at the wonderfully named charity, Poetry in Wood. The Little Gate Farm in Rye, the only provider of supported employment in East Sussex, aims to be supporting 30 adults with learning disabilities and autism in paid employment by 2018. The organisation Heart n Soul, based at the Albany in Deptford, in south-east London, celebrated 30 years in 2017 of working creatively with hugely talented people with autism and individuals with learning disabilities.

Unlike other books, this volume will also dedicate considerable space to self-employment, which can work for some people on the spectrum but which requires its own specific set of organisational skills. There are several advantages: the troublesome interview process is eliminated, as is the 'hidden social curriculum' of the workplace, and it permits a more controlled structuring of the environment. There are, of course, records to keep, marketing to be conducted and clients to keep satisfied. But the rewards may be considerable – and so are the non-office-based options: public speaking, gardening, freelance designing, musical performance.

There will also be a major focus on the hugely neglected area of gender differences in the workplace. We have become increasingly aware over the past few years that females are being under-diagnosed with autism because of their ability to 'camouflage' their autistic symptoms. How does this relate to employment? Could it imply, for example, that in more cases than in males, females might be able to avoid disclosing their condition to prospective employers in the CV and interview stages of a job application? At the same time, the costs of camouflage can sometimes be crippling: exhaustion, depression, distress. This book features unique new research and case studies in this area. And although this book will focus largely on the United Kingdom, the author has had access to relevant information in seven languages to provide an international perspective.

Through the author's numerous interviews with autistic adults who have made a success in computing, acting, singing, etc., after suffering bullying, the reader will be given an informative and entertaining primer to the considerable strengths of people on the autism spectrum in the workplace, as well as the very real challenges they confront, and how to make the most of the 'autism advantages'.

Never has this book been more relevant. The prevalence of autism spectrum conditions is reported to be as high as one in 68 by the US-based Centers for Disease Control and Prevention. That would mean there are more than 600,000 people with autism in Britain. Data from other countries consistently show that fewer than a third of autistic adults are employed. Even among those achieving work, employment is likely to be part-time or in low-skill, low-paid occupations.

In the UK, only around 25 per cent of autistic individuals progress to further or higher education in the UK. And according to the National Autistic Society's 2016 report, 'Autism Employment Gap', just 16 per cent of autistic adults are in full-time work in Britain and only 32 per cent are in any kind of paid work at all. The NAS says these figures have remained the same for the past decade, indicating that people on the autism spectrum are not benefiting from Government employment programmes.[16] Professor Patricia Howlin, of London's Institute of Psychiatry, who is one of the world's leading autism authorities, agrees. Howlin, co-author of a 2013 study on the cost-effectiveness of supported employment for adults with autism in the UK, told me: 'Governments pay lip service but they do not want to put money where their mouth is.'[17] And yet, a study led by Professor Martin Knapp, of the London School of Economics, estimates that autism costs the UK at least £34 billion per year in treatment, lost earnings, care and support for children and adults with autism. Autistic people have a strikingly low employment rate – only 24 per cent of working age are in employment. This is the lowest of all disabilities, and almost half the average employment rate for all disabled people, which stands at 46.3 per cent.[18] Part of the reason for this is that autism is a hidden disability, and people with hidden disabilities in general have lower employment rates than those with visible disabilities. But people with autism also have a lower employment rate than people with other hidden disabilities.

The vast untapped resource

There is a vast untapped human resource. The NAS report, 'Autism Employment Gap', found that over three-quarters (77 per cent) who were unemployed said they wanted to work, while four in 10 say they have never worked. Of the individuals asked by the NAS for the single biggest thing that needed to change to help autistic people acquire work, over 50 per cent replied support, understanding or acceptance. Meanwhile, 60 per cent of the employers questioned declared that they were worried about getting support wrong and they did not know where to go to obtain information about how to support autistic employees. Roughly half of respondents (48 per cent) reported experiencing bullying or harassment in the workplace or other discrimination or unfair treatment (51 per cent) due to their autism. Shockingly, the discrimination figure has increased since 2012, when a third of adults responding, who had worked, reported bullying, unfair treatment, or discrimination at work because of their autism. In a YouGov survey of businesses of various sizes, carried out between 31 May and 3 June 2016, 60 per cent of employers said they were concerned about getting support for an autistic employee wrong, and an equal number said they did not know where to go for advice. Over a third (35 per cent) of the autistic employees questioned by the NAS for their 2016 report claimed that the support or adjustments made by their current or most recent employer were either 'poor' or 'very poor'.[19]

The NAS report claimed that autistic job seekers were also being let down by the system. Six in 10 (61 per cent) of people with autism questioned rated their experience of the British government's Jobcentre Plus as 'poor' or 'very poor'. More than half (56 per cent) offered the same assessment of the government's Access to Work Programme, introduced in 2011.[20]

Up to 85 per cent of the population with Asperger's syndrome (AS) are without full-time employment, despite the fact that many have above-average intelligence – and Asperger's syndrome comes with no learning disability. (Although Asperger's syndrome was removed as a separate category from DSM-5 in 2013, we will continue to use the term in this book, as it is so widely recognised. It is, nevertheless, totally misleading to call AS 'mild autism', since it can be associated with serious social and sensory problems and severe depression). At present, of this more able group, many of those in work do not have jobs that match their intellectual abilities. Despite graduate-level skills, they fail to get or keep jobs – even ones (typically in retail, care or administration) that do not represent their formal qualifications. And yet they have so much to offer.

In 2009, after a series of campaigns and inquiries, the British Parliament passed the Autism Act. This was the first ever disability-specific law in England and included the development of an adult autism strategy, published in 2010. One of the five aims of this strategy was to help adults with autism to find jobs. However, as Professor Elisabeth Hill has written: 'A great aim, but perhaps little more than a dream. With little funding supporting this aim, it is not surprising to hear that since 2010, little has changed for adults with autism in terms of employment.'[21] For this reason, Hill and her team at Goldsmiths, along with other organisations who promote and support autistic employees, joined up as the Autism Employment Alliance to develop and promote support for both autistic adults seeking and in work, as well as for employers.

Emma Jones, at the NAS, believes there has been a definite shift in employers' attitudes over the past few years: 'Employers are coming to us and saying that they recognise the strengths of people on the autism spectrum.'[22] Yet Professor Simon Baron-Cohen, director of Cambridge University's Autism Research Centre, told the United Nations in New York in March 2017 that the basic human rights of autistic people — including the right to employment — were not being met, despite the adoption of the UN Convention on the Rights of People with Disabilities in 2006:

> People with autism account for a significant minority of the population worldwide, yet we are failing them in so many respects. This creates barriers to their participation in society and to their autonomy that must be addressed ... The right to work should extend to everyone, whatever support they might need. Unemployment is another well-known risk factor for depression.[23]

In his UN speech, Baron-Cohen commended some enlightened employers, like the Danish company, Specialisterne, and the German firms, SAP and Auticon, for setting an example around the world in how to help people with autism into employment and how employers can make reasonable adjustments for people with autism. But much work needs to be done.[24]

One of the world's leading pioneers in the field of autism employment, Thorkil Sonne, founder of Specialisterne, likes to use the dandelion analogy. As Sonne told me:

> Kids love dandelions. But as you become an adult, this love turns to hate. The dandelion has become a weed. It destroys the order of your garden and you want to get rid of it. But the flower is the same. Something else has changed. Your own norms have been replaced by society's norms. But what is a weed? A weed is a flower in an unwanted place. If you put the dandelion in a wanted place, it turns into a herb. I know this because I visited a farmer who makes a living out of growing dandelions. He harvests them for nutritional purposes. They give you back so much if they are treated well. It's the same with people – if they're made to feel welcome, you have access to values. So what we're trying to do is make autistic people welcome in the workplace so that employers have access to all the values.[25]

The Specialisterne Foundation, which was founded in Denmark in 2004 and now operates in more than a dozen countries worldwide (see Part V: Neurodiversity in the workplace), has the global aim to ensure that there are a million jobs for people

Figure I.1 Thorkil Sonne (left) with Adam Feinstein

on the autistic spectrum by 2020. It works with autistic individuals' strengths. At Specialisterne, autism is the norm rather than the exception among employees. They report, for example, that their IT consultants are on average 10 per cent better at checking software code for errors than their non-autistic peers, a clear example of where an employer would prefer to employ someone known to have autistic characteristics.

This book aims to open minds and doors. As Baron-Cohen told me:

> Creating employment opportunities for autistic adults could be one of the most transformational interventions in the field of autism that we have seen to date. Given that we know that unemployment is a well-established risk factor for mental

ill-health such as depression, employment may contribute to better mental health for autistic adults. Employment could also contribute to a greater sense of social inclusion and acceptance of difference. Finally, employment gives individuals control over their lives by having an income, and makes individuals feel valued and have purpose and meaning in their daily lives, which we all need. We need research to test for such benefits but even in advance of such research, we should accelerate the opportunities for employment for autistic adults. Naturally, such opportunities need to include reasonable adjustment for their disability, but this is a legal requirement for all employers. It is encouraging that companies such as Auticon, Specialisterne, and SAP are pioneering these initiatives. If other employers follow this example, this could be a game-changer and would have added benefits for wider society, in changing our views to make space for neurodiversity in the workplace.[26]

Of course, certain jobs tend to make much less successful matches for people on the autism spectrum, including those that involve multi-tracking, high levels of socialising and sensory overload, such as cashier, airline ticket agent, waiter or receptionist. Yet the suggestion that a shift away from manufacturing industries towards service industries represents a problem for people on the autism spectrum – because the service industries, by definition, require greater social interaction – is, once again, over-simplistic. I know of very successful waiters with autism. There are heart-warming examples in this book of autistic employees thriving in positions which require direct contact with customers. To cite just one: David Harris, a man with Asperger's syndrome, has been an extremely successful employee on the information desk opposite Platform 1 on London's Paddington Station for many years. I have seen him dealing resolutely, but resourcefully with some extremely angry passengers wanting to know why there was a delay on the train to Oxford. David simply remained calm and explained the facts.

Demolishing the stereotypes

It is important to emphasise that people with autism – like those without autism – cannot be easily categorised. It should be recalled that Temple Grandin's first professional job was one which required using words, not images: she worked on a print journal, the *Arizona Farmer Ranchman*. And yet she famously 'thinks in pictures', of course. Similarly, the late Donna Williams, Australia's most famous woman with Asperger's syndrome, was a poet as well as a painter. So these generalisations, while well-meaning, are like all generalisations: misleading and over-simplistic. The same applies to other overarching views of potential employees with Asperger's syndrome: that they are all great at IT and that they are all happy to do mundane repetitive tasks. These are well-intentioned but misguided stereotypes which present a grossly distorted picture. There are plenty of people with Asperger's who do not know one end of a computer from another. And it is a mistake to assume that someone with autism will necessarily enjoy loading and unloading lorries day after day. Some may, but others will find the task horrendously tedious. One woman with Asperger's syndrome, identified only as N., told the University College London researcher, Sarah Bargiela:

> I hate getting bored ... If I'm left to think, things can spiral out of control to a very dark pit. I've done dead end jobs where I'm just left to think and I just end up getting even more and more depressed. Whereas some people find it's nice and relaxing not to have to think about things all the time, my brain just wants to think, think, think.[27]

Alex Lowery, a successful public speaker with Asperger's syndrome, says he did try working in an office environment (with his father) – basic jobs like stamping post, printing and indexing – but found it 'boring and repetitive'.[28]

As this book will make clear, the autism spectrum incorporates a broad range of abilities. Many people on the spectrum are very successful at work. Other people may have difficulties in the workplace and some people may remain unemployed. Because of this 'spiky' profile, the hierarchical structure of the workplace may suit some and not others. For Janine Booth, a trade unionist with Asperger's syndrome,

> workplaces are generally organised in very hierarchical, authoritarian ways, with the focus on maximising profitable production rather than recognising and including the diversity of the workforce. This presents particular barriers to autistic workers throughout the employment cycle, from recruitment to redundancy. Barriers arise in key areas, such as the sensory environment, communications, training, social interaction, workplace change, how work is organised, harassment and bullying. On top of this, the current economic situation in the UK, and the austerity policies that have come with it, have intensified pressures on autistic and other workers and have seen a big increase in insecure employment – for example, temporary, agency and zero-hours contracts. This is very disabling for people who prefer routine and security.[29]

Jolanta Lasota, chief executive of the UK charity, Ambitious about Autism, said:

> There are many misconceptions and myths about autism, the biggest including being antisocial and having a lack of empathy. However, what people with autism struggle with is fitting their feelings of sympathy and caring into everyday interactions. While it is true that some people with autism can have very specific interests and may struggle with abstract concepts, this research helps to highlight the fact that seeing the world in a different way can be a positive trait too. We find time and again that many of our pupils in our TreeHouse School and Ambitious College are very creative, whether that be through art, music, film or photography. It is great to see research continued in this area to help dispel more autism myths.[30]

There are a number of other well-meaning myths about autism which continue to cloud the employment picture. One is that everyone with autism has the type of 'savant' skills demonstrated by Dustin Hoffman's character, Raymond Babbit, in the 1988 movie, *Rain Man*. As Jonathan Andrews has pointed out, this myth

> has encouraged employers to invest in people with autism due to their 'unique' abilities. It does more harm than good, however. It ignores the fact that many

autistic people are multi-talented, and not only good at one thing. It's true that a key diagnosis trait for autism is 'restricted, repetitive and stereotyped patterns of behaviour, interests and activities'. But note the plural 'interests' – several people with autism have a number of things they enjoy and are good at. In that regard, they're not too different from non-autistic people – very few people are good at everything, after all. Most are better at some things than others. Also, since autism is a spectrum, not everyone with an ASD will have this trait. And it risks pigeon-holing autistic people. Anything they do well risks being seen as their 'one thing', and people then assume that they're poor at everything else – when it's probable they have other skills too. This is especially damaging for a person with autism who wants a change in career – people will assume they cannot move outside one field.[31]

Of course, the myth that autistic people are all geniuses and/or hugely talented in one area can quickly lead to the presumption that autism does not count as a 'real' disability and that autistic people need no support either achieving employment or adjustments once employed. This is far from the case. Take the example of Daniel Lightwing, a brilliant mathematician with Asperger's syndrome whose story was told in the 2007 BBC documentary, *Beautiful Young Minds*, and then turned into an impressive film, *X+Y*, directed in 2014 by Morgan Matthews. When Daniel worked as a web designer at Google, he was not happy: 'I have a problem with office culture, I ate lunch by myself to avoid people talking about things that were not work-related. The more I did stuff like that, the more people rejected me.'[32]

The obstacles are still there for all to see. As Lucy Kenyon has written:

We live in a world where many organisations are struggling to understand and fulfil their legal obligations to people with disabilities. Fitness for work poses significant professional challenges for occupational physicians in a litigious society keen to point the finger when something goes wrong. Equally challenging are the pressures felt by employers to implement advice at any cost or to let an employee go on the grounds that it is not reasonably practicable to make adjustments for them. A consequence of a poorly managed case is reluctance to risk a similar situation in future, which can potentially lead to discriminatory practices. In recent decades, workplace environments have increasingly become open-plan, with more distractions and the demand for emotional intelligence, flexibility and adaptability. New demands for flexibility have also affected employers with a shift from prescriptive legislation to framework regulations and guidance (Health and Safety at Work Act, 1974). This brings specific challenges for people with autism, including distraction, unpredictability and uncertainty. It is also likely that, if you have employees born before 1990, a significant number of them will not have received a diagnosis of autism spectrum disorder (ASD), but could display behaviours and emotions that affect their ability to cope with the work environment.[33]

Carly Jones, a prominent British autism advocate, filmmaker and speaker (she was the first British woman with autism ever to address the United Nations), says the problems begin much earlier than the interview room or the rejection letter: 'It's true that employers are not seeing the "autism advantage" and that even those fully qualified struggle to get a job. But this is due to inequality in exams, as well.'[34]

She explains:

> Increasing autistic employability starts with addressing inequality in educational settings and exams. Ask yourself: If people knew you had a high IQ and a special interest/expertise, but you had no way of showing your abilities in an exam situation, would you be considered a respected professional – or an eccentric obsessive? I have been researching the UK General Certificate of Secondary Education (GCSE) papers, and find the questions loaded with theory of mind-based exam questions. In 2014, for example, an autistic youth's ability to get an English 'Pass' would be dependent on reading a newspaper article about a tree, then describing in an essay *other people's thoughts* about said tree? In my opinion, this is unethical – it does not work, it is a massive oversight, and is detrimental to the rights of autistic students.[35]

Another area which has been very little studied is the significance of the age of diagnosis for workplace well-being. Tiffany Johnson and Aparna Joshi, of Pennsylvania State University, plugged this research gap with their important 2015 study, in which they suggested that individuals who had received a diagnosis at a younger age and had been socialised as 'autistic' for a longer period of time, might accept the label to a greater extent and also might have been selected into specific employment situations based on a full awareness of their condition.

> In contrast, for those diagnosed later, the encounter with the label is newer and adjustment to the employment context following the diagnosis is, therefore, a salient event. ... We expected that the age at which an individual is diagnosed should negatively predict workplace well-being among individuals with ASD, because older individuals who receive an autism diagnosis are more likely to view membership to this stigmatised group as a threat to their identity.[36]

There is one more, overarching reason why this book is so important: not only do many experts agree that making the workplace suitable for people with autism is likely to make it suitable for everyone, but employing workers on the autism spectrum will produce a more inclusive, diverse and tolerant society as a whole. As Dame Stephanie Shirley told the employment conference in Gateshead in 2016:

> Enlightened employers should be hiring someone *because* of their differences, not in spite of them. Autistic people make good, reliable employees once they're there! The paradox is that, to give the necessary structure for those with autism with their need for predictability, the employer needs to think flexibly.[37]

In Part I, I shall discuss the importance of work – beginning with the transition from education to the workplace.

How do you choose which job is right for you? Part II will assess the many different employment avenues available and – with the help of revealing case studies – will guide employees towards making the decisions most likely to prove successful.

Part III will examine the crucial aspects of applying for a job, from the response to an advertisement and the drawing up of a successful CV through to the frequently nightmarish interview process.

Once you have found a job, how do you keep hold of it? As Part IV amply indicates, there are many hurdles to negotiate in the workplace for employees in the autism spectrum: the sensory bombardment, the use of non-literal language, the problems with executive function (planning ahead, etc.). We will show people on the spectrum just how to negotiate these hurdles – and indicate to employers how to ease the passage through to successful employment.

That last point leads neatly on to Part V, with its analysis of 'neurodiversity' in the workplace and the encouraging increase in companies recognising the value of employing people who display differences in the way they think, see the world around them and process information. Autism, including Asperger's syndrome (as well as dyslexia, dyspraxia, ADHD and Tourette's) are all neurodiverse conditions protected under the Equality Act of 2010.

Part VI tackles the criminally neglected area of gender differences in the work-place, from the autistic point of view. For the first time, a book will investigate, with copious first-hand case studies, the very real day-to-day strengths and challenges involved in being a woman on the spectrum seeking – and holding down – employment.

The emphasis throughout this book will be on what people on the autism spec-trum *can* offer the workplace and society as a whole, not what they cannot. The final section will include a round-up of UK employment schemes helping to turn this posi-tive approach into practice.

A word on terminology: Jesse Saperstein, a man with Asperger's syndrome, avoids the term 'work' because he believes it is associated with less appealing words like toil, labour, hardship, drudgery and grind.[38] He prefers the term 'employment' because 'employ' is related to more positive synonyms, such as 'utilise' and 'keep busy'. I appreciate Jesse's message but I have a different 'take': I believe 'work' can also have a positive connotation, as in the play on the words in the title of this book. It is this book's contention that by focusing on the positives – on the strengths, rather than the deficits – both autistic employees and their employers will not only make the workplace more productive but they will be contributing, to a considerable degree, in forging a society which is generally more inclusive.

Notes

1   See: www.theguardian.com/careers/2017/jul/07/what-i-wish-i-could-tell-my-boss-my-autism-is-not-a-problem (accessed 28 April 2018).
2   Randy Lewis in communication with the author, 30 June 2016.
3   H. Asperger (1979), 'Problems of infantile autism', *Communication*, 13: 45–52.
4   L. Kanner (1971), 'Follow-up study of eleven autistic children originally reported in 1943', *Journal of Autism and Childhood Schizophrenia*, April–June, 1(2), 119–145.
5   Dame Stephanie Shirley, 'The Issues and Challenges around Autism Employment', presentation to the North East Autism Society's 'Employment Futures' conference in Gateshead, UK, 16 September 2016.
6   See Temple Grandin (2008), *Developing Talents: Careers for Individuals with Asperger Syndrome and High-Functioning Autism*. Shawnee, KS: AAPC Publishing, p. xi.

7   *Derby Telegraph*, 19 August 2017.
8   See Dinah Murray (ed.) (2006), *Coming Out Asperger: Diagnosis, Disclosure and Self-Confidence*. London: Jessica Kingsley, p. 194.
9   James Hoodless in conversation with the author, 13 September 2017.
10 Richard Maguire in conversation with the author, 13 September 2017.
11 See F. Happé and U. Frith (2006), 'The weak coherence account: Detail-focused cognitive style in autism spectrum disorders', *Journal of Autism and Developmental Disorders*, January, 36(1), 5–25.
12 See: www.cipd.co.uk/Images/an-investigation-of-asperger-syndrome-in-the-employment-context_2016_tcm18-20003.pdf (accessed 28 April 2018).
13 See C. Best, S. Arora, F. Porter and M. Doherty (2015), 'The relationship between subthreshold autistic traits, ambiguous figure perception and divergent thinking', *Journal of Autism and Developmental Disorders*, 45(12), 4064–4073.
14 Ibid.
15 See: www2.cipd.co.uk/pm/peoplemanagement/b/weblog/archive/2014/11/20/business-is-still-scared-of-autism.aspx (accessed 28 April 2018).
16 See: www.autism.org.uk/get-involved/media-centre/news/2016-10-27-employment-gap.aspx (accessed 28 April 2018).
17 Patricia Howlin in conversation with the author, 10 June 2016.
18 See Valentina Iemmi, Martin Knapp and Ian Ragan (2017), 'The autism dividend: Reaping the rewards of better investment', on behalf of the National Autism Project.
19 See: www.autism.org.uk/get-involved/media-centre/news/2016-10-27-employment-gap.aspx (accessed 28 April 2018).
20 Ibid.
21 See: www.gold.ac.uk/news/comment-autism-spectrum-disorder-and-employment/ (accessed 28 April 2018).
22 Emma Jones, in conversation with the author, 5 October 2016.
23 See: www.cam.ac.uk/research/news/human-rights-of-people-with-autism-not-being-met-leading-expert-tells-united-nations (accessed 28 April 2018).
24 Ibid.
25 Thorkil Sonne in conversation with the author, 6 March 2016.
26 Simon Baron-Cohen, in communication with the author, 3 August 2017.
27 See S. Bargiela, R. Steward and M. Williams (2016), 'The experiences of late-diagnosed women with autism spectrum conditions: An investigation of the female autism phenotype', *Journal of Autism and Developmental Disorders*, 46(10), 3281–3294.
28 Alex Lowery in conversation with the author, 20 May 2016.
29 See: www.janinebooth.com/content/importance-autism-equality-workplace-%E2%80%93-interview-janine-booth (accessed 28 April 2018).
30 *The Observer*, 22 August 2016.
31 See Jonathan Andrews (undated), *Autism and the Workplace: Common Myths and Untapped Talent*.
32 *London Evening Standard*, 19 March 2015.
33 Lucy Kenyon (2015), 'How to manage autism in the workplace', *Personnel Today*, 21 August.
34 Carly Jones in communication with the author 5 June 2016.
35 See: www.thinkingautismguide.com/2016/04/five-ways-to-brighter-future-for.html?m=1 (accessed 25 April 2016).
36 See T. D. Johnson and A. Joshi (2016), 'Dark clouds or silver linings? A stigma threat perspective on the implications of an autism diagnosis for workplace well-being', *Journal of Applied Psychology*, American Psychological Association, 101(3), 430–449.
37 Dame Stephanie Shirley, 'The issues and challenges around autism employment', presentation to the North East Autism Society's 'Employment Futures', conference in Gateshead, UK, 16 September 2016.
38 Jesse A. Saperstein (2014), *Getting a Life with Asperger's. Lessons Learned on the Bumpy Road to Adulthood*. New York: Perigree, p. 154.

Part I

The importance of being employed

Chapter 1

The paucity of research

The period between the ages of 18 and 28 is critically important in establishing a foundation for adult life. For young people on the autism spectrum, these years tend to be especially challenging.

In the United States, about half of young adults on the autism spectrum work for pay at some point after they leave college. But only one in five works full-time, and their rates of employment are lower than those of people with language impairments, learning disability or intellectual disability alone. Young US adults with autism are more likely to work for pay if they are from middle- to high-income households and have reasonable conversational abilities and functional skills. 'I see a lot of people on the spectrum who come out of high school with no work skills,' Temple Grandin told me:

> I think that is really terrible. You've got to get creative to find niches for these people. It is important to get children to use skills that other people will want. There are plenty of jobs for visual thinkers, like industrial design (which I do), car mechanics, photography, animal training. And for those who are non-verbal, there is stacking library bookshelves, or working in a factory. Above all, don't try to de-geek the geek. There are lots of happy geeks – in Silicon Valley, in Hollywood.[1]

One of Britain's leading autism researchers, Elisabeth Hill, argues that more time, money and research need to be invested in autism in employment.

> A lot of research has focused on children living with ASD, and we know that many have good ability and a range of skills that are of huge benefit to society, including excellent attention to detail and technical skills. These strengths emerge out of a different way of seeing and acting in the world. But very little is known about what happens next. What happens when children on the spectrum leave education and enter into the world of employment? Until recently, very little attention had been paid to the adult end of this group, despite the fact that there are more adults than children in the population. Most service provision resources and research funding for ASD focuses in some way or another on childhood.[2]

As Hill notes, a lack of secure employment not only places continuing financial demands on autistic adults and their parents, but also involves costs associated with additional care, such as the benefits system, thus providing a significant economic burden to the nation.[3]

Research related to support for adults with autism tends to be under-developed. As an example, system and service development to support the successful transition to adulthood and meaningful vocation for adults has received relatively little research scrutiny until recently, with practitioners and programme developers lacking evidence-informed approaches guiding service delivery.

For many years, at least in the United States, researchers were not particularly interested in these issues. Partly, this was because autism professionals tended to focus on children. For nearly four decades after Hans Asperger, in 1938, and then Leo Kanner in 1943, introduced the term 'autism' in the sense we understand it today, confusion continued to reign between autism and schizophrenia, with some professionals still referring to autism as 'childhood schizophrenia'. Indeed, this confusion persists, to this day, in Russia and other parts of the Soviet Union. As Igor Shpitsberg, founder of the Our Sunny World institute for autism in Moscow, told me in 2016:

> Usually, when a child with autism reaches the age of 18 years, doctors change his diagnosis to schizophrenia or mental retardation. In this case, even if he manages to find a job later, he will have a different diagnosis and will not be counted in the statistics as a person with autism. This is a huge problem which we have been fighting for many years, because officially, there are still very few adults with autism in Russia. The Minister of Health, Veronika Skvortsova, and the Prime Minister, Dmitri Medvedev, have promised me that this situation will change. I hope they keep their promise.[4]

Even when researchers do begin to investigate the transition to the workplace, they have run into a number of obstacles. One is the shortage of study participants. The autism community appears to be more tightly knit among families with younger children and, once children are older, families may not be as keen to take part in research because they no longer anticipate the kind of 'quick fix' for which they might once have hoped.

Another problem is funding. Funding agencies tend not to be enormously interested in supporting any studies which might help to explain why the years after college are so daunting. This is especially the case for research related to services assisting young people with autism to transition to adulthood. The overwhelming majority of autism research remains focused on children. Funding agencies also tend to prefer research which explores the biological mechanisms underpinning autism – especially those which can be translated into animal models.

Dr Catherine Lord, professor of psychology at Weill Cornell Medical College in New York, has proposed an enlightened method of 'luring' sponsorship by research into transitions. Scientists, she suggests, could interpret the concept of a 'mechanism' more broadly to include the evaluation of therapies which improve conversational skills or other aspects of daily living.[5] There is some evidence that adults with strong adaptive living skills – such as communication and social skills, personal hygiene, cooking, cleaning and ability to use public transport – are more likely to be employed and to be better integrated into their communities than those with poorer skills. Nevertheless, little research has so far investigated adaptive functioning during the transition to adulthood for people with autism.

Lord concedes that one major problem with young adult research is the difficulty in defining what constitutes a 'good outcome' for a young person on the autism spectrum. A bright young woman with autism might find a job which does not match her academic qualifications.'However, should this automatically be deemed poor out-come – even if the woman is happy in her job?'[6]

New research published in the journal *Autism Research* in January 2018 did suggest that many middle-aged adults with autism had little independence. The study, conducted by the University of Wisconsin-Madison's Waisman Centre, derived from Professor Ed Ritvo's mid-1980s survey of autism prevalence in Utah involving 489 people.[7] The Wisconsin researchers contacted the 305 people from that survey who either met criteria for autism as children or would meet current criteria based on their medical records. Of the 305, 162 people or their caregivers responded. Of these, 127 had intellectual disability, and 128 were men. Only 38 had full- or part-time jobs. Others had a 'supported' job or were otherwise considered to have an 'occupation' because they volunteered, attended a day programme or worked for minimal pay at a sheltered workshop. The remaining 30 people (20 per cent), were unemployed. Surprisingly, landing a job did not track with intelligence: of the 38 employed individuals, 10 had IQ scores below 70, and of the 24 unemployed participants for whom the researchers had IQ scores, five scored in at least the average range.[8]

It is important to note that autism diagnostic criteria were stricter in the 1980s than they are today. As a result, the participants were likely to have relatively severe autism features. Nevertheless, the findings appeared to align with the 'everyday reality' of today's adults with autism, according to Dr Shaun Eack, professor of social work and psychiatry at the University of Pittsburgh. He said this was 'one of the first systematic' studies of housing and employment among people with autism in the United States.

The results of the study also indicated that many adults with autism lacked autonomy. For example, 44 per cent had a legal guardian. Only 9 per cent lived in a home they had purchased themselves or in their own apartment. The same proportion lived in an institution. And 35 per cent lived in a group home, supported apartment or other supervised living situation. The remaining 47 per cent lived with family.[9]

> Parents are continuing to provide a huge amount of support, said the study's lead researcher, Dr Megan Farley, a senior psychologist at the Waisman Centre. Parents are ageing, and there is no clear way for them to develop plans for care for their adult sons or daughters when they're not able to care for them any more.[10]

Some researchers warned against using standard measures of job (or relationship) success for people on the autism spectrum. 'What these rating systems generally don't do a good job at is understanding how good the fit is between the person's situation and what that person's ability level is and what their own goals are,' said Dr Paul Shattuck, associate professor at the A.J. Drexel Autism Institute in Philadelphia. People with autism and their families should be allowed to set their own goals – and measure achievement based on those, he added.[11]

There have been a number of studies around the world demonstrating the economic impact of autism spectrum conditions. The largest research study of autism and employment in the UK was published in 2017. Martin Knapp and colleagues, reporting for the National Autism Project (NAP), wrote that, among autistic adults aged 55 or over, 41 per cent had been unemployed for more than 10 years. Among autistic people out of work, 59 per cent did not believe or did not know whether they would ever be employed.[12] Nevertheless, 70 per cent of autistic people without learning disabilities would like to work, as would 65 per cent of people with learning disabilities (including autistic people).

The same 2017 NAP study found that individuals with autism were more likely to be employed if they came from households with a higher family income, higher parental education, if they were male, had higher social skills, an absence of learning disability, higher educational qualifications, had received career counselling in school and received post-secondary vocational training.[13]

The authors of the 2017 report also noted:

> While the challenges of increasing employment are substantial, so too are the potential rewards. Over 60 per cent of autistic adults are financially dependent on their families, and the productivity loss for an autistic adult without learning disabilities has been estimated at £21,797 per annum (2011 price levels). For an autistic adult with learning disabilities, the estimated loss is £25,644. Of course, employment has a positive impact not only on an individual's income, but also and foremost on their quality of life, cognitive functioning and well-being.[14]

Martin Knapp and colleagues observed that, over the past 20 years or so, interest had focused on intervention programmes which offered on-the-job training and support. Many of these interventions shared common features:

- consideration of the individual's strengths and interests when matching employers and employees;
- vocational training involving structured techniques such as behavioural therapies,
- natural support or simulation;
- a job coach to provide individualised training and workplace support;
- involvement of families, partners, carers, employers and colleagues to provide long-term, comprehensive support and follow-up to assist job retention.[15]

Nevertheless, employment support is currently being received by only 10 per cent of autistic people in the UK, whereas 53 per cent would like to have access to it. According to the 2017 NAP study, the only British study to date to have assessed the efficacy of employment support was a pilot investigation of the effects of Prospects (which was a supported employment scheme funded by the then Department for Education and Employment in collaboration with the National Autistic Society). The intervention focused on high-functioning individuals with autism. It was found that, at the end of the two-year study period, those using the Prospects service were significantly more likely to be employed than those receiving the usual services (63 per cent compared to 25 per cent). The supported employment group also spent a greater proportion of time at work (27 per cent compared to 12 per cent) and had obtained higher-level jobs than the control group. When followed up, 13 of the 19 employed adults from the original sample who found employment were still employed seven to eight years later. Overall, two-thirds of young adults had found employment, mostly with permanent contracts and involving administrative, technical or computing work. Those individuals who received employment support experienced a rise in salaries, contributed more in taxation and claimed fewer benefits.[16]

In 2012, Britain's National Institute for Health and Care Excellence (NICE) published a clinical guideline providing evidence-based recommendations. Their systematic review identified only the Mawhood and Howlin study of a supported employment programme[17] as meeting the quality criteria to inform an economic evaluation of the cost-effectiveness of employment support. The NAP survey reported that the economic evaluation carried out by NICE 'assumed that the benefits of employment for autistic people were the same as the benefits for the general population, and concluded that the supported employment intervention was cost-effective'. The cost-effectiveness ratio was calculated to be £5,600 per quality-adjusted life year (QALY), which is well below the NICE threshold for recommending treatments (£20,000 to £30,000 per QALY). Further analysis as part of the National Autism Project extended the NICE analysis, in particular to look beyond the health and social care perspective that NICE always adopts in its analyses. By taking additional account of the productivity gains arising from supported employment (including the types of jobs that people secured) and also from carers' increased productivity, the intervention was found to be even more cost-effective. Indeed, the further analysis showed that supported employment 'was not only more effective but also cost-reducing'.[18] Supported employment schemes take account of individual strengths and preferences, provide individualised training and workplace support through a job coach, and involve a range of stakeholders (including families, partners, carers, employers and work colleagues). The limited research data do appear to indicate that supported employment can be successful, but the outcomes need to be replicated on a larger scale and – where appropriate – to a progressively wider subgroup of autistic people.

Of course, as outlined in the Introduction, employment is important not only from an economic perspective. It also represents an essential cog in the overall mechanism of well-being. Many studies have shown that independence, self-esteem, community engagement and social status are all related to an individual's capacity to work, and employment has a positive effect on physical and mental health.[19] The desire to be employed, and the view that it is an important goal, is common in people with ASD.[20] Furthermore, those who are employed are more likely to experience a better quality of life and improved cognitive and mental health outcomes than those who are not employed.[21]

Two 2016 studies, one interview-based and the other survey-based, both from Pennsylvania State University, indicated that a clinical diagnosis of autism was a milestone event that triggered both positive (silver linings) and negative (dark clouds) responses to work. These positive and negative responses were shaped by the age at which the diagnosis occurred as well as specific work-related contingencies: identity management (disclosing or not disclosing), the importance of the social demands imposed by the job and organisational support policies for autism. The results showed that, compared with individuals diagnosed later in life, individuals who were diagnosed at an earlier age experienced greater organisation-based self-esteem and lower perceived discrimination when they disclosed their disability, worked in jobs that placed lower social demands on them, or were employed in organisations that offered policies to support workers on the autism spectrum.[22]

Cathy Lord pointed me to recent findings indicating that 'school achievement does mean something in terms of employment and living independently, even when you control for IQ and other factors in autism'.[23] A study by Lord's Cornell colleague, So Hyun Kim, of 65 children who were referred for possible ASD at the age of two and who were then followed until the age of 26, found that relative delays in achievement scores in spelling and reading compared to IQ at the age of nine

> were predictive of poorer adult outcomes in employment (p←0.001) and independent living respectively (p←0.05), while controlling for age, gender, maternal education, ASD diagnosis and age 9 IQ. For instance, individuals who had paid jobs or those living independently at age 26 were more likely to have the achievement scores in reading that were either higher than or equivalent to IQ scores at age nine compared to those without paid jobs or those who lived with parents or in group homes.[24]

Studies suggest that individuals with ASD experience difficulties in both finding and maintaining employment. Those with higher IQs generally have better employment outcomes relative to those with ASD and an intellectual disability, although meaningful, stable employment is often still not achieved. As So Hyun Kim's research indicated, many individuals with autism and other pervasive developmental disorders had intellectual disability, yet there was a lack of data about employment needs and outcomes among people with mild to moderate intellectual disability. Furthermore, individuals educated in post-secondary institutions reported employment challenges, including being under-employed relative to educational qualification and tending towards entry-level positions due to previous employment difficulties, thus impeding career advancement.[25]

A new study published in December 2017 indicated that adults with autism who underwent therapy designed to bolster social learning showed cognitive benefits which could increase their chances of employment.[26]

So-called 'cognitive enhancement therapy' combines computer-based tasks to improve problem-solving and memory with structured group sessions that provide practice in reading non-verbal cues, taking someone else's perspective and other social skills.

'Improved cognition seemed to lead to more competitive employment outcomes,' said the study's lead researcher, Dr Shaun Eack, professor of psychiatry at the University of Pittsburgh. 'The cognitive effects weren't unrelated from the employment effects; in fact, they cascaded each other.'

The study was the largest and most comprehensive evaluation of cognitive enhancement therapy for people with autism. Dr Eack and his colleagues gave seven women and 47 men with autism, aged 16 to 45, either cognitive enhancement therapy or supportive counselling for 18 months. In the cognitive group, 29 participants performed tasks on a computer for one hour each week. Some of the tasks were designed to increase processing speed, such as typing certain letters when prompted. Other tasks tapped short-term memory. The individuals also participated in activities designed to train them to act appropriately in everyday situations. For instance, in an 'airport' exercise, participants had to announce via a mock public address system that a wallet had been discovered. They were to do so without revealing information that could lead to the wrong person claiming the wallet. The other 25 participants received one hour of so-called 'enriched supportive therapy' per week. In these sessions, a therapist taught them strategies for coping with their emotions and managing their stress. The same therapist delivered both types of therapy in order to ensure consistency.

The Pittsburgh researchers assessed the participants' working memory, mental-processing speed and other cognitive functions halfway through the programme and at the end. They also measured social skills, such as the ability to understand others' perspectives and feelings, and the ability to manage their own emotions. (A single researcher who was not privy to the treatment type recorded all the scores.) The participants who received cognitive enhancement therapy scored higher on social learning measures than the control group at nine months, but that difference disappeared at 18 months. This result suggested that both treatments were effective, but cognitive enhancement therapy worked more quickly, according to Dr Eack.

However, only cognitive enhancement therapy had a positive impact on employment: of the 29 participants who received it, only seven were employed at the beginning of the study. But after 18 months of therapy, 10 of the 21 who remained in the study had jobs. By contrast, in the other group, employment rates dropped slightly: 10 of the 25 people in the original group were employed, compared with six of the 20 people who completed the study.

Experts not involved in the study said that, although the sample was small, it did show that cognitive enhancement therapy has promise. Dr Terry Brugha, professor of psychiatry at the University of Leicester in the UK, declared: 'The most encouraging thing is that the authors are now undertaking a second trial, which reflects these initially fairly encouraging results.' (Dr Eack and his team are now testing cognitive enhancement therapy in a study of 100 individuals with autism. This work includes brain scans to determine whether changes in brain structure track with the treatment's effects.)[27]

A highly significant new study published in 2018 demonstrated, for the first time, that sleep problems were associated with unemployment in adults with autism. The researchers, led by Emma Baker at La Trobe University in Melbourne, Australia, found that autistic adults with a sleep disorder (under the International Classification of Sleep Disorders–Third Edition) had higher scores on the Pittsburgh Sleep Quality Index and were more likely to be unemployed compared with adults with autism and no sleep disorder. The study authors concluded that further research exploring the direction of this effect was required: do sleep problems which have developed during adolescence make attainment of employment for those with autism difficult, or does unemployment result in fewer restrictions being required for optimal and appropriate sleep timing?[28]

Notes

1   Temple Grandin in conversation with Adam Feinstein, Looking Up, 5(6), 2011, p. 24.
2   See Elisabeth Hill, 'Autism spectrum disorder and employment', www.gold.ac.uk/news/comment-autism-spectrum-disorder-and-employment/ (accessed 28 April 2018).
3   Ibid.
4   Igor Shpitsberg in communication with the author, 14 February 2016.
5   See: www.slate.com/articles/health_and_science/science/2017/04/the_twentysomething_cliff_is_much_worse_when_you_re_autistic.html (accessed 28 April 2018).
6   Ibid.

7   E. R. Ritvo et al. (1989), 'The UCLA-University of Utah epidemiologic survey of autism: Recurrence risk estimates and genetic counselling', *American Journal of Psychiatry*, August, 146(8), 1032–1036.

8   M. Farley et al. (2017), 'Mid-life social outcomes for a population-based sample of adults with ASD', *Autism Research*, 11(1), 142–152.

9   Ibid.

10 See Hannah Furfaro, 'Jobs, relationships elude adults with autism', https://spectrumnews.org/news/jobs-relationships-elude-adults-autism/ (accessed 15 February 2018).

11 Ibid.

12 See Valentina Iemmi, Martin Knapp and Ian Ragan (2017), 'The autism dividend: Reaping the rewards of better investment', on behalf of the National Autism Project.

13 Ibid.

14 Ibid.

15 Ibid.

16 Ibid.

17 Mawhood, L. and Howlin, P. (1999), 'The outcome of a supported employment scheme for high-functioning adults with autism or Asperger syndrome', *Autism*, 3, 229–254.

18 See Valentina Iemmi, Martin Knapp and Ian Ragan (2017), 'The autism dividend: Reaping the rewards of better investment', on behalf of the National Autism Project.

19 June L. Chen et al. (2015), 'Trends in employment for individuals with autism spectrum disorder: A review of the research literature', *Review Journal of Autism and Developmental Disorders*, June, 2(2), 115–127; P. A. Creed and S. R. Macintyre (2001), 'The relative effects of deprivation of the latent and manifest benefits of employment on the well-being of unemployed people', *Journal of Occupational Health Psychology*, 6(4), 324–331; N. T. Feather and G. E. O'Brien (1986), 'A longitudinal analysis of the effects of different patterns of employment and unemployment on school-leavers', *British Journal of Psychology*, November, 77(4), 459–479.

20 June L. Chen et al. (2015), 'Trends in employment for individuals with autism spectrum disorder: A review of the research literature', *Review Journal of Autism and Developmental Disorders*, June, 2(2), 115–127.

21 H.-M. Chiang et al. (2013), 'Factors associated with participation in employment for high school leavers with autism', *Journal of Autism and Developmental Disorders*, August, 43(8), 1832–1842; D. Hendricks (2010), 'Employment and adults with autism spectrum disorders: Challenges and strategies for success', *Journal of Vocational Rehabilitation*, 32(2), 125–134; I. Mavranezouli et al. (2014), 'The cost-effectiveness of supported employment for adults with autism in the United Kingdom', *Autism*, 18(8).

22 See T. D. Johnson and A. Joshi (2016), 'Dark clouds or silver linings? A stigma threat perspective on the implications of an autism diagnosis for workplace well-being', *Journal of Applied Psychology, American Psychological Association*, 101(3), 430–449.

23 Catherine Lord, in communication with the author, 28 August 2017.

24 So Hyun Kim, unpublished research, 2017.

25 Ibid.

26 Eack, S. M. et al. (2018), 'Cognitive enhancement therapy for adult autism spectrum disorder: Results of an 18-month randomised clinical trial', *Autism Research*. March 11(3), 519–530.

27 See Arran Frood, https://spectrumnews.org/news/games-plus-group-therapy-may-help-adults-autism-find-jobs/ (accessed 7 February 2018).

28 E.K. Baker et al. (2018), 'Employment status is related to sleep problems in adults with autism spectrum disorder and no comorbid intellectual impairment', *Autism*. First published online February 18, 2018. https://doi.org/10.1177/1362361317745857.

Chapter 2

Transitioning from education to work

The transition from education to employment is a particularly tricky path to nego-tiate for people on the spectrum. As Luke Jackson, a gifted writer and photographer with Asperger's syndrome, so aptly puts it:

> Education is at least linear in a certain way, and has a definitive beginning and end, but work is a different thing altogether. Work is a strange, often disorienting thing – it's a huge change from education, as a job carries a lot of responsibility ... Messing up a job won't earn you a detention, but you may very quickly find yourself looking for a new position ... The common denominator between high school, college, university and employment is that there is help available. It can be in different ways and can often be more difficult to obtain from one place than another, but it's still there. While obviously funding is always going to be an issue, often the help is rooted simply in people who are willing to understand, or even willing to just try to understand.[1]

Luke adds:

> Unless you decide to work freelance in your chosen field of work (and even if you do, you may find that it still applies to you on occasion), there's a good chance you'll be working as part of a team. Working as a member of a team can include a number of things that people on the autism spectrum can find problematic: social interaction, face-to-face contact and communication of ideas are things I have always struggled with in a group setting. Unemployment in autism is rife, but there are a lot of successful people with ASD who lead healthy, and often wealthy, working lives.[2]

Thorkil Sonne, founder of Specialisterne, agrees that transition from education into the job market is a grey area. 'We will focus a great deal on this over the next few years,' Sonne told me.

> Because if your first interaction with employers happens *after* graduation, it will be very difficult. The recruiters will not understand you, and vice versa. If you provide internships along the way, that helps. My ultimate goal is that one day, we stop talking about autism altogether. Because there may be ten million people with autism in India, but only a tenth have a diagnosis. How do we define a target group without speaking about autism?[3]

As Robert Austin and Gary Pisano note, companies implementing neurodiversity programmes have encountered challenges. 'Although there are plenty of potential candidates, many are hard to identify, because universities – sensitive to issues of discrimination – do not classify students in neurodiversity terms, and potential candidates do not necessarily self-identify.'[4]

In the United States, in response, one company, Hewlett Packard Enterprise, is helping colleges and high schools to set up non-traditional 'work experience' programmes for neurodiverse populations. These involve video gaming, robotic programming and other activities. Microsoft, is also working with universities to improve methods of identifying and accessing neurodiverse talent.

Here is Temple Grandin's advice:

> Some individuals, while they are still in high school, should be encouraged to take courses at a local college in drafting, computer programming or commercial art. This will help keep them motivated and serve as a refuge from teasing. Families with low income may be wondering how they can afford computers for their child to learn programming or computer-aided drafting. Used computers can often be obtained for free or at a very low cost when a business or an engineering company upgrades their equipment. Many people do not realize that there are many usable older computers sitting in storerooms at schools, banks, factories and other businesses. It will not be the latest new thing, but it is more than adequate for a student to learn on.[5]

While a typical young adult may anticipate the freedom and independence that having a job may bring, young adults on the autism spectrum can, on the contrary, experience anxiety and pre-transition distress, especially after leaving a structured school or university environment or family routines.

❖ CASE STUDIES

- KINGWOOD COLLEGE
- AMBITIOUS COLLEGE
- BOVERIDGE COLLEGE
- BATH EMPLOYMENT SPRING SCHOOL FOR AUTISM
- STRATCHCLYDE BUSINESS SCHOOL

The pioneering KINGWOOD COLLEGE, which opened in Reading in 2012, is a residential and training facility providing full-time life skills training and education programmes to a small group of young autistic people aged between 18 and 25.

The college, run by the Autism at Kingwood Trust, offers a transition from school to adult life which involves a huge change for people with autism. By offering life skills and vocational training, they can be prepared and fully equipped for entering into paid work in a variety of occupations, according to their individual wishes and abilities.

In the 2013, Kingwood was awarded more than £95,000 by the Big Lottery Fund to help people with autism find work in Oxfordshire, Berkshire and Hampshire. Autism at Kingwood's then chief executive, Sue Osborn, said:

However profound the disability, organisations can restructure their work to ensure that people with autism can contribute. An example of this is job carving, whereby you create a job for someone by identifying the person's skills and matching them to tasks your organisation needs doing. In my view, with a bit of imagination, any organisation can become autism-friendly. If you look at the high-functioning end of the spectrum, many people with autism have a high level of skills in areas such as IT. It's about giving people the right support and harnessing their skills in order to engage with the working world. This isn't about charity, it's about realising people's potential in society.[6]

In 2016, the first college in London catering exclusively for young adults with autism opened at the Pears Campuses in Tottenham and Isleworth. AMBITIOUS COLLEGE is dedicated to supporting young people between the ages of 19 and 25 with complex autism, helping them to start work and live independently. The institute, run by the charity, Ambitious About Autism, opened temporarily in 2015 and has now found a permanent new home. Its principal, Vivienne Berkeley, said: 'Ambitious College prepares young people with autism for a bright future where they can make a positive contribution to their local communities and develop meaningful employability and life skills.'[7]

The best-selling author, Nick Hornby, whose son, Danny, is autistic, acts as an 'ambassador' for Ambitious College. He said: 'As a parent of a child with autism, I know how difficult it is to secure the right education. I support Ambitious College for giving young people and their families a lifeline that can be trusted.'[8]

BOVERIDGE COLLEGE opened in Cranborne, Dorset, in September 2017 to offer people aged 16 to 25 with Asperger's syndrome, anxiety disorders and mental health issues the chance to gain employment.

The college principal, Kim Welsh, said: 'So many youngsters with Asperger's, autism and other related conditions are unable to find work once they leave education. We want to change that so they can achieve meaningful employment.'[9]

The college, run by the Aurora Group, will include subjects such as agriculture, horticulture, events management and web design. Students will also transform the 16-acre gardens into a working mini farm and kitchen garden to run as a business.

The new BATH EMPLOYMENT SPRING SCHOOL FOR AUTISM (BESSA), which aims to improve job hunting support for graduates with autism, represents a significant collaboration between a British university and a prominent employer.

Launched in February 2018, BESSA – a partnership between the University of Bath's Centre for Applied Autism Research (CAAR) and JP Morgan Chase – will offer 30 university students and recent graduates with autism tailored support in preparing for work and hunting for jobs.

The new school builds on JP Morgan Chase's successful US programme, 'Autism at Work', which aims to help graduates with autism find work which matches their skills and attributes. It also complements the successful Autism Summer School, which has been run since 2013 by the university's Department of Psychology to help younger students with autism transition into higher education.

Dr Chris Ashwin, deputy director for research at CAAR, said:

> We know that graduates with autism have a unique set of highly-attuned skills that can make them incredibly valuable to a whole range of organisations. Yet all too often, barriers are put in their way that prevent them from applying for the right kind of jobs, being successful at interview or transitioning into organisations. This important collaboration between the University of Bath and JP Morgan Chase is about valuing the incredible contributions that autistic people can make and finding new ways to help them find the right kinds of work. We're excited to welcome our first cohort next year and look forward to developing this in the years to come.[10]

For his part, James Mahoney, executive director and head of Autism at Work at JP Morgan Chase, added:

> We're delighted to expand J.P. Morgan's Autism at Work Programme with the help of the Centre for Applied Autism Research at the University of Bath. Through the programme, we're developing better career paths for graduates with autism spectrum disorder (ASD), improving our interviewing techniques to capture strong talent and deploying new training for managers and non-ASD colleagues. We began a pilot programme in 2015 with four people, and it has since grown to dozens of individuals across five countries in a variety of roles across the firm.

Eight young Scots with learning disabilities – including autism – are enrolling at STRATHCLYDE BUSINESS SCHOOL, in Scotland, in 2018. The group will be paired with third-year students for support, and given extensive work placements, in the partnership between the charity Enable Scotland, Strathclyde University and Scottish Power.

In 2017, only 56 pupils with learning disabilities went on to higher education in Scotland (a little over one in 10 of those leaving school), compared with 40 per cent of all Scottish school leavers who go to university. Under the pioneering new Breaking Barriers scheme, eight 18 to 24-year-olds with learning disabilities will study for a Certificate in Applied Business Skills, with eight weeks in the classroom studying digital and social media marketing, people management and customer service, and eight weeks on placement.

Jamie Rutherford, director of employment for Enable Scotland, said it was a ground-breaking development for those with aspirations to attend university: 'Not enough people with learning disabilities think it is possible and not enough people tell them it is possible,' he said. 'Attending university isn't just about learning; it is a passage into adulthood. Young people get the chance to live away from home, have relationships, make life-long friends, maybe even eat beans on toast every day for a month.'[11]

Anthony McGinley, of Glasgow, was born with underlying medical conditions, including a heart defect and hydrocephalus: a build-up of fluid on the brain. It was only after he left school that he was also diagnosed with autism. 'Throughout primary and secondary school, I felt different, had a tough time making friends and never really felt like I fit in,' he said.

> As I watched my class mates discover subjects and activities that they loved, I used to panic that I wasn't doing the same. I had to work so much harder than everyone around me and even with all of that effort, I was still barely treading water. My school work suffered and I suppose eventually I gave up trying.

Now, under the new Strathclyde scheme, Anthony says he plans to 'work hard to prove myself and show people what I'm capable of and that people like me can go to university and make a go of it.'[12]

Professor Sir Jim McDonald, vice chancellor of the University of Strathclyde, said: 'This is the first university-led programme for people with learning disabilities and will help build the skills and enhance the job opportunities of participating students.'[13]

Jonathan Andrews, a lawyer and poet with Asperger's syndrome who chairs the youth council of Ambitious About Autism, actively promotes a campaign that aims to improve the way autistic people move from education into work. He points out that, although the British government introduced reforms to the special educational needs and disability (SEND) system in 2014, families still struggle to receive the appropriate support.[14] Research from the National Autistic Society suggests that 17 per cent of parents appeal to SEND tribunals against their council's decision on their child's education. And government figures show special needs pupils are more than seven times more likely to receive a permanent exclusion than their non-SEND peers.[15]

'There can be assumptions that pupils are "being naughty" and exclusion is the easiest approach. But it should be a last resort. A lot of people are shut out of education and it's very hard to get back in,' writes Andrews.[16]

Many people with autism who have specific skills are not good at selling those skills. Some have low self-esteem, some are unable to communicate their strengths verbally. Parents (and also the siblings, perhaps) can play a crucial role here. The important thing is to exploit special interests creatively and flexibly. For example, one young boy with autism was obsessed, from an early age, with fire safety and dreamed of becoming a firefighter. However, he and his parents both realised that the sensory differences associated with his ASD made this choice of career problematic: he did not like the loud sound of the fire engine sirens and felt claustrophobic wearing the fireman's mask. Moreover, he could not adjust to the lack of a fixed routine: firemen generally work on two-day shifts. However, the boy's strength lay in his attention to detail (he could quickly calculate where a fire had started) and in his much-admired ability to calm people down in tense situations. He eventually became a successful fire inspector.

Supported internships – personalised study programmes based primarily at an employer's premises – have developed in the UK in response to the high rate of young people with SEND who are NEET (Not in Employment, Education or Training) or at risk of becoming NEET. (The ethical issues related to taking on unpaid labour will be addressed in full in Part II.)

Within the SEND cohort, young people with learning disabilities can find the pursuit of qualifications particularly challenging, and this goal may not always be in their best interests. An employment-focused route can be the best way of preventing young people with learning disabilities from becoming NEET. Supported internships are recognised as being an ideal stepping stone for those learners whose primary goal is paid work. For the employer, the internship must meet a real business need, with the potential of a paid job at the end of the programme of study, should the intern meet the required standard. The structured study programme includes on-the-job training provided by expert job coaches, and the chance to study for relevant qualifications, where appropriate. Job coaches are critical to the success of supported internships. They provide in-work support for young people which tapers off as the individual becomes familiar with their role. Job coaches provide support to employers, increasing their confidence of working with interns and helping them to understand the business case for employing a diverse workforce. Job coaches also provide support.

The SEN code of practice from Britain's Department for Education and Department of Health requires that employment be considered in a young person's Education Health and Care Plan. This has prompted local authorities to ensure they have a 'local offer' which includes employment. This, in turn, has begun to raise aspirations around employment among young people with SEND and their families.

Supported internships offer in-work support from a trained job coach. In this respect, as well as the recognition that pursuit of a qualification is not essential, supported internships differ from apprenticeships. Consequently, supported internships have developed as a strong alternative to students whose level of impairment prevents them from undertaking an apprenticeship. Yet ironically, apprenticeships do not yet enjoy the same status, recognition and funding as internships in the UK.

Remploy, Mencap and other British supported employment providers are committed to working with young people with SEND to support them into paid employment on leaving education. However, many employers are not aware of supported internships as a recognised model of good practice, with some assuming that supported internships are similar in their approach to unpaid work experience. Consequently, these employers are reluctant to be associated with a programme which might bring them negative publicity or criticism.

Access to Work, the British government's scheme designed to help people with disabilities into employment, has been opened up to young people with SEND taking part in supported internships, and can be used specifically to fund the job-coaching element of the programme. When used alongside education funding streams, this should allow supported internships to be adequately funded. However, supported internships operate with short-term funding and often do not have the financial stability to run from one year to the next. This, in turn, reduces the attractiveness of the model to employers and other partners.

❖ CASE STUDIES

- OLIVER WILTSHIRE
- RICHARD MAGUIRE

OLIVER WILTSHIRE's early life was medically complicated – he was blind in one eye, suffered from convulsions and an enlarged liver, was short in stature and had mild delayed development. At his pre-school assessment, it was noted that he was clearly bright – indeed, he was ahead of his peers academically – but he showed some 'delay with interaction and social skills'. His mother, Nathalie, recalls that, at this very early stage whilst at a very small pre-school nursery,

> we were asked to keep Oliver at home on the day of the Ofsted inspection 'for everybody's sake'. The fact that I found this mildly amusing and co-operated with the request was as inappropriate a reaction as the request itself, but a premonition, nonetheless.[17]

At five, Oliver began biting his peers as an effective way to clear his personal space: 'In our misguided desperation, his attendance at four different schools in four years complicated, confused and compounded the problem, leaving Ol a sad and lonely young child and back where he started full circle at Dunchurch Infants' School.'[18]

By now, Oliver had been diagnosed with both autism and Semantic Pragmatic Disorder. He was eventually excluded from mainstream education in 2003 and spent nine months being home-schooled. 'We made the decision to send our eight-year-old, psychologically broken little boy away to a residential special school three hours away from home,' says Nathalie. It was Southlands School, part of the Cambian Group.

> I am still reduced to tears that we were faced with this horrendous dilemma and it was a massive gamble. ... The very first thing they did was to tell Oliver what his diagnosis was and what it meant, something we had been encouraged to keep from Oliver up until that point. The team at Southlands did such a good job at empowering Ol that even today he considers it an advantage over the neurotypical person to have a diagnosis of Asperger's! The specialist expertise, the positive affirmation, the routines and the self-awareness Ol received during his time at Southlands have unquestionably set him up for life, and it could be argued that allowing our young people more time to understand themselves, their strengths and limitations is time well and better spent than learning about facts and figures ...
>
> What the years at Southlands also gave Oliver was a voice, and there came the time when he wanted his voice to be heard, and that time came when he shouted loudly that he was ready to move on and didn't want to be at a school with other children with Asperger's any more ... However, what was a little difficult to explain to Oliver was the rather fundamental stumbling block with this transition from specialist school to mainstream school – no one would take him.[19]

Eventually, Oliver was accepted at Sibford School, which was run with a Quaker philosophy. 'Much to our surprise and delight, Oliver relished the Quaker style whole school assembly meetings when the school sat together often in silence. He used to say how calm these periods of togetherness in quietude were.'[20] By 2009, he was appointed the school's Environmental Officer and the environment started to become an ongoing theme in Ol's life. At his next school, Princethorpe, he was Upper Sixth Form pupil who achieved the best A Level results in the School. In his final year, he threw himself (and his family) into University visits, dedicated himself to achieving his Gold Duke of Edinburgh, gained his black belt at Taekwondo and another write-up in the local press. He passed his driving test and took an extra GCSE in Astronomy in addition to his four A-levels. He was rewarded with 3 A*s (Maths, Further Maths and Physics) and an A (Chemistry) at A level. He was also awarded a Scholarship to take a Masters at his first choice, Southampton University, to read Civil and Environmental Engineering.

Oliver eventually found employment as an engineer at John Sisk & Sons, the largest construction and property company in Ireland which is expanding into the UK, mainland Europe and the Middle East. The first week at work, in June 2017, Oliver texted his parents to say:

> I've been doing paperwork this week, looking at concrete cube tests for massive piles going down 400m into the ground. I'm making sure they're all up to the UK standard, and that each pile has a corresponding test to show that the concrete is strong enough. It's been interesting! ... My line manager is very nice ... very sensible and fair. He's told me I can ask him anything, any time. Early starts are a change, but I'm getting used to them. Currently sitting on a plane about to take off to go to Heathrow. Good first week![21]

Oliver told me:

> Growing up, I have always wanted my Asperger's not to be defining of who I am, and thus I don't share the fact that I have it. I have not told Sisk I have Asperger's, and I have not shared it with many of the people I consider friends. Some of those whom I have told have commented that they wouldn't have guessed, which is both a relief, and also a bit of a let-down, due to the perceived beliefs of how those with autism and Asperger's behave.[22]

He says the civil engineering industry is all about clear communication, 'which has helped me feel more empowered to ask for clarification if I don't understand something, and ask for clear instructions for what to do, which is how my brain works!'[23]

RICHARD MAGUIRE, a public speaker and mentor with Asperger's syndrome who works for Autism Oxford under Kathy Erangey, says:

Work is hard to find for autistic people. We are the most under-employed group of adults in the world. Even if paid employment is not available, volunteering is a good away to help build up skills, self-esteem, a CV of commitment and experience for a paid job.[24]

Richard adds:

I remember being 19 and leaving the education system. It was one of the darkest times in my life. I had no idea how I would get on in society and felt a sense of loss and grief at having no perceptible future. Knowing my peers had advanced much further in life was a crushing blow – I was way behind them. Life felt hopeless and not worth living. I was bright and had plenty to offer, but just could not put that to positive use. Instead, I felt convinced that, because of my 'oddity,' I had no real value and did not deserve to exist ... Imagine having lots of potential and not being able to connect with it. Like being a coke bottle all shaken up – full of pressure with the lid still on. Imagine not even knowing the lid is on or not knowing that it could be removed to let the energy inside out ...

Working in mundane jobs, alongside one of my interests (which was cycling) got me through life day by day. If you don't have any hope, you keep going through the motions, unaware events could get better. I had no idea how to proceed, or any hope that these low-paid jobs would work in my favour, but they gave me a reason to get up and do something. They gave me a structure and way of meeting people, a way to feel like a human, with something positive to do.[25]

Richard is now happily married and has a successful career as a public speaker with Autism Oxford.

Notes

1   See Luke Jackson (2016), *Sex, Drugs and Asperger's Syndrome – A User's Guide to Adulthood*. London: Jessica Kingsley, pp. 81–82.
2   Ibid., p. 81.
3   Thorkil Sonne in conversation with the author, 6 March 2016.
4   R. D. Austin and G. P. Pisano (2017), 'Neurodiversity as a competitive advantage', *Harvard Business Review*, May–June, 96–103.
5   See Josie Santomauro (ed.) (2011), *Autism All-Stars: How We Use Our Autism and Asperger Traits to Shine in Life*. London: Jessica Kingsley.
6   See: www.bbc.co.uk/news/uk-england-23317892 (accessed 16 July 2013).
7   *Evening Standard*, 13 September 2016.
8   Ibid.
9   See: www.bbc.co.uk/news/uk-england-dorset-40873621 (accessed 3 August 2017).
10 See: www.bath.ac.uk/announcements/new-autism-school-to-improve-employment-chances-for-autistic-graduates/ (accessed 31 January 2018).
11 See: www.heraldscotland.com/news/homenews/15942254.Students_bag_a_first_as_Strathclyde_University_launches_pioneering_business_course_for_people_with_learning_disabilities/ (accessed 7 February 2018).

12   Ibid.
13   Ibid.
14   See Jonathan Andrews (undated), *Autism and the Workplace: Common Myths and Untapped Talent.*
15   See: www.autism.org.uk/schoolreport2016 (accessed 27 April 2018).
16   See Jonathan Andrews (undated), *Autism and the Workplace: Common Myths and Untapped Talent.*
17   Nathalie Wiltshire in communication with the author, 17 July 2017.
18   Ibid.
19   Ibid.
20   Ibid.
21   Ibid.
22   Oliver Wiltshire, in communication with the author, 27 August 2017.
23   Ibid.
24   See Richard Maguire (2014), *I Dream in Autism.* CreateSpace Independent Publishing Platform.
25   Ibid.

Part II

Which job – and why?

Chapter 3

Choosing a job – an overview (and a demolition of the stereotypes)

Max, the clay protagonist with Asperger's syndrome voiced by the late Philip Seymour Hoffman in Adam Elliot's marvellous 2009 animated movie, *Mary and Max*, has a bizarre CV. It includes jobs as varied as rubbish collector, condom manufacturer, military inventory analyst, Frisbee maker, Underground employee and Communist.

I would venture to suggest that few of these positions would actually be appropriate for someone on the autism spectrum. So how to choose? As Luke Jackson, the photographer with Asperger's syndrome, puts it:

> There are all kinds of jobs, but there is hardly a catalogue you can flick through to find out which one is right for you. There will be certain vocations that you won't have heard of, and others people will try to turn you away from. The problems that being on the autism spectrum can pose in the world of employment can seem all-pervasive. A large number of jobs, especially at entry level, involve face-to-face social interaction, rebranded as 'customer services'. When working full time, this can be absolutely exhausting – 'running an emulator' or 'pretending to be normal' for any length of time takes its toll, so doing this for 30 or 40 hours a week can be too much for someone with an ASD to handle.[1]

In fact, as we shall see, the late twentieth-century switch from manufacturing to service industries does not necessarily spell disaster for everyone on the autism spectrum. Cases like David Harris, the man with Asperger's syndrome working on the information desk at Paddington Station, show that for some, personal interaction is not an obstacle, and indeed the ability to respond calmly, unemotionally and with direct factual information can be a distinct advantage.

John Lewis Holland, an American psychologist and Professor Emeritus of Sociology at Johns Hopkins University, devised the Self-Directed Search (SDS), a self-administered career interest test that asks questions about your aspirations, activities, skills, and interests in different jobs. From the responses, the SDS produces your personal three-letter Summary Code, which you can use to find occupations and fields of study that match well with your personality.

The SDS is based on Holland's theory that both people and working environments can be classified according to six basic types: Realistic, Investigative, Artistic, Social, Enterprising and Conventional. These personality types are known together as RIASEC.

- Realistic: often mechanically inclined
- Investigative: enjoy learning how things work and solving problems
- Artistic: value self-expression and original, creative ideas
- Social: want to help others
- Enterprising: enjoy taking risks and managing others
- Conventional: prefer routine work[2]

How closely can the SDS map on to the aspirations of people with autism? The list is useful, in general, but I frankly believe that autism is far too heterogeneous for this scheme to be meaningful: during the writing of this book, I have met individuals on the spectrum who fit into each of the above categories, or none.

The complexities of autism defy easy stereotypes – but that has not stopped people from trying to introduce such over-simplifications. A hugely damaging myth is that people on the autism spectrum lack imagination and creativity and so are suited only for routine/repetitive work. This is partly the 'fault' of the Triad of Impairments, introduced by Lorna Wing and Judy Gould in 1979. But Wing often emphasised to me that she regretted omitting a crucial adjective from the Triad: what autistic individuals actually lacked, she said, was *social* imagination, meaning that they found it difficult to understand or predict the behaviour of other people. It is true that people with autism can think rigidly and prefer to work in familiar environments. But as the previously mentioned 2015 study from the University of Stirling, in Scotland,[3] demonstrated, they often show far more creativity than we had imagined and have unique and inventive ways of looking at, and doing, things. This can be an immense asset in a business environment – where there is often a focus on finding new and imaginative concepts and methods. In other words, their ability to 'think outside the box' may often prove invaluable in the workplace. If anything, as Jonathan Andrews – a prominent advocate for autism and employment who himself has Asperger's syndrome – has noted, the problem is that people on the spectrum may think *too* creatively and not consider the social aspects, such as how their target demographic might react to their idea. 'But that's not really an issue, since others at the table will be able to add that view.'[4]

Although a diagnostic criterion of autism does indeed remain 'restricted, repetitive and stereotyped patterns of behaviour, interests and activities' (note – as Andrews observes – the plural *interests*), some people with autism have a number of things they enjoy and are good at. In that regard, they are not too different from non-autistic people. Moreover, this attitude risks pigeon-holing individuals with autism. 'Anything they do well risks being seen as their "one thing,"' says Andrews,

> and people then assume that they're poor at everything else – when it's probable they have other skills too. This is especially damaging for a person with autism who wants a change in career – people will assume they cannot move outside one field. And finally, while autistic savants do exist, they are usually severely impaired when it comes to interpersonal skills – so are far less likely to be able to hold down a job than people with more mild autism.[5]

Caroline Hearst, a British consultant with autism who runs post-diagnostic peer support groups for autistic adults, prefers to think of autism as a constellation, rather than a spectrum with abilities on a linear scale. She believes the neat spectrum or continuum does not match the more complex reality – some autistic individuals will find some tasks very easy some days and impossible to do at other times and individual profiles tend to be spiky and changeable.

> The idea of a spectrum implies (for a lot of people) a line that goes from low to high. People talk about low- and high-functioning. I prefer the term 'constellation'. The truth is that when people say 'high-functioning', what they really mean is 'cognitively able' and being cognitively able does not make you high-functioning,

says Hearst.

> We have a lot of autistic people with PhDs who sit in rooms all day and stare at walls. I would not call that high-functioning. I also know a lot of people who prefer the term Asperger's because they are under the illusion that the label means they are more intelligent. For a lot of intelligent autistic people, the one thing that they have been appreciated for is their intelligence, so they feel the need to highlight it, but I believe that's not necessary. Intelligence isn't the only human quality of anybody, and all autistic qualities are human qualities, they are just of a different neurology. So I think the whole concept of neurodiversity is very helpful.[6]

Jonathan Andrews has usefully demolished many of what he calls the 'benevolent' myths surrounding autism. Recent research highlighting the strength of many autistic individuals in identifying visual-spatial patterns indicates that, in addition to being good at pinpointing individual details – the weak central coherence or 'local processing bias' cited previously – they can also 'process large-scale patterns effectively'. So if a task involves something visual – like designing a website, or storyboard, or devising a video – a person with autism will generally be a helpful addition to the workplace.

Another well-meaning but fallacious generalisation has it that all people with autism have a 'special gift', while, their skills elsewhere are severely impaired. In fact, such savant abilities are probably restricted to no more than 10 per cent of autistic individuals – although a 2009 study by Patricia Howlin put the figure at much higher – 30 per cent.[7] Darold Treffert, the world's leading authority on the savant syndrome, told me:

> I stand by the 10 per cent figure, using my definition of savant skills. Savant skill is still a subjective definition, as is my classification of splinter skill, talented and prodigious categories I think we are seeing more savants because we are seeing more people with 'autism', although that, too, is rather a subjective determination, especially as we have expanded that term to 'autism spectrum disorder'.[8]

Jonathan Andrews says the misunderstanding is mostly caused by people confusing savant syndrome with the autism spectrum.

> The two overlap, but are not identical – there are autistic savants, but savants can just as easily have another disability, or have no disability at all … This may be seen as a benevolent myth, which has encouraged employers to invest in people with autism due to their 'unique' abilities. It does more harm than good, however. It ignores the fact that many autistic people are multi-talented, and not only good at one thing.[9]

In fact, Treffert, who runs the Treffert Centre in Wisconsin, told me:

> We are finding success with our adolescent/early adult caseload, especially when special skills are present, and we hope the next expansion of our programme will be with young adults. We have moved beyond the sheltered workshop to part- or full-time employment in the regular workforce using programming, electronic, mechanical or farming skills. Some of these individuals need residential placement or small group settings, but others make it independently. Some mentoring works well for the transition to regular workforce.[10]

Andrews also cites the case of a man with Asperger's syndrome who is doing a menial job and several people see this as a travesty, arguing that he's 'so much better than that'. But the man himself is perfectly happy with the job, and admits he simply doesn't have the (academic) intelligence to rise higher. According to Andrews, what upsets the man more is the attitude of others, namely that he is 'wasting his talents'.

The message here, says Andrews, is that employers should not assume that all employees with Asperger's will be geniuses:

> The vast majority will not, though naturally those qualified for graduate-level jobs will be intelligent. Employers should instead focus on the many real, positive job skills most people with Asperger's possess – such as being dutiful, loyal and honest, being skilled at systemising, and in other areas.[11]

Barbara Bissonnette offers the telling example of a man with Asperger's syndrome who wanted to be an airline pilot – but only because he was keen to wear a uniform! (This story had a happy ending – he eventually found a job as a hotel doorman.)[12]

Sarah Hendrickx, of the Brighton-based charity, ASPIRE, advises jobseekers to ask their family and friends which job they think would be the most suitable and which they would be most likely to be good at – because it can be easier to assess these skills from outside. Then, carefully list all these skills (and interests) in writing.[13]

As Dinah Murray has correctly noted, paid employment represents an exceptionally small part of the overall employment picture for most autistic people. 'It is important to emphasise the thousands of hours of unpaid labour that I, like many autistic people, have put in to making the world a better, juster, more harmonious place,' Murray told me.

> If we aren't politically active, regularly and abundantly volunteering, singing in choirs, playing musical instruments (often professionally if not often lucratively), dancing, attending religious activities or organically cultivating vegetables, we are likely to be acquiring some further education or pursuing research topics relevant to our interests. If it is at all possible, we prefer not to waste our lives (in our own judgement). Do not equate 'being positive' about autistic employment with only the people who have had most paid employment, that is, those who have been 'successful' in a worldly sense. We should all value those other non-money-focused employments and the time devoted to pursuing them.[14]

Murray added:

> It is crucial to apply a very inclusive concept of 'employment'. There is a yawning gap between self-motivated or self-created unpaid work and the sort of internships followed by being thrown on the junk heap that we see so often among job seekers. The former needs to be supported and if it is, it may lead to a satisfying and constructive way of life and positive contributions to the community. The latter is a cruel imposition and almost a guarantee of depression and loss of self-worth. At the moment, there's a huge swathe of people who are longing to contribute, to be valued and earn it through our own worth, will mainly be thwarted by our weirdness, if getting and keeping a job is involved.[15]

Self-employment, as we shall see, may prove a valid option for some. But for those who prefer the workplace environment to the very real challenges – as well as delights – posed by being one's own boss, then pursuing a part-time job may be the most suitable plan.

Jane Meyerding has worked part-time for most of her life. 'If I try to work a full-time job, I needed to spend the rest of my working hours recuperating – literally.'[16] Meyerding adds:

> No doubt, more autistics would be willing and able employees if it were possible for more of us to get along on what a part-time job pays, or if it were possible to combine a job with receiving 'daily living' assistance. Unfortunately, being employed part-time usually eliminates all access to supplemental income (e.g. 'disability') … The theory seems to be that either you are disabled and need both financial and practical support or you can work and therefore need/deserve nothing. For many employed autistics, the result of that dichotomy is steadily accumulating stress which, sooner or later, spills over into the job.[17]

Notes

1   Luke Jackson (2016), *Sex, Drugs and Asperger's Syndrome – A User's Guide to Adulthood*. London: Jessica Kingsley, p. 82.
2   See: www.self-directed-search.com/what-is-it (accessed 27 April 2018).
3   See C. Best, S. Arora, F. Porter, M. Doherty (2015), 'The relationship between subthreshold autistic traits, ambiguous figure perception and divergent thinking', *Journal of Autism and Developmental Disorders*, 45(12), 4064–4073.
4   See Jonathan Andrews (undated), *Autism and the Workplace: Common Myths and Untapped Talent*.
5   Ibid.
6   See: http://learnfromautistics.com/voices-constellation-17-caroline-hearst-neurodiversity-autism-advocacy/ (accessed 27 April 2018).
7   See P. Howlin, S. Goode, J. Hutton and M. Rutter (2009), 'Savant skills in autism: Psychometric approaches and parental reports', *Philos Trans R Soc Lond B Biol Sci*. 27 May, 364(1522), 1359–1367.
8   Darold Treffert, in communication with the author, 2 September 2017.
9   See Jonathan Andrews, op. cit.
10 Darold Treffert, in communication with the author, 2 September 2017.
11 See Jonathan Andrews, op. cit.
12 See Barbara Bissonnette (2014), *Helping Adults with Asperger's Syndrome Get & Stay Hired: Career Coaching Strategies for Professionals and Parents of Adults on the Autism Spectrum*. London: Jessica Kingsley, p. 84.

13 See Sarah Hendrickx (2009), *Asperger Syndrome and Employment – What People with Asperger Syndrome Really Really Want*. London: Jessica Kingsley, p. 99.
14 Dinah Murray in communication with the author, 9 April 2016.
15 Ibid.
16 See Dinah Murray (ed.) (2006), *Coming Out Asperger: Diagnosis, Disclosure and Self-Confidence*. London: Jessica Kingsley, p. 250.
17 Ibid., pp. 250–251.

Chapter 4

Unpaid work – and internships

The ethical implications of employing people on the spectrum in unpaid positions or internships are considerable. While there is no doubt that any form of meaningful employment, paid or unpaid, can increase feelings of self-esteem in these individuals – as in all members of society, autistic or not – claims have been made that such unwaged placements amount to little more than exploitation. As Professor Elisabeth Hill, of Goldsmiths, University of London, told me:

> Unpaid internships can be exploitative across the *entire* population. However, work experience is often a huge benefit when seeking paid employment and huge numbers would be deprived of job opportunities completely if you eliminated such opportunities. These need to be considered carefully.[1]

Mark Lever, chief executive of Britain's National Autistic Society, pointed out that there was initially concern about doing paid work

> because of the battle of getting back into the benefit system. Internships take some of the 'bungee jump leap' from benefits into employment. Although unpaid, internships do assist in 'testing out' a particular job without losing benefits. But making the benefit system easier to negotiate would also help a great deal.[2]

Lever's NAS colleague, Emma Jones, the society's Employment Training Manager, agrees: 'The value of internships depends on how they are set up. They can be a very useful link into getting paid work.'[3]

Are they exploitative? 'Employers are used to paying for work. We should work with employers to ensure that they pay for valuable work,' says Thorkil Sonne, founder of Specialisterne.

> I think it would be an over-simplification to say that it is unethical to ask non-verbal people with autism to work for nothing. My way of thinking with employers is that if someone provides value, employers, by default, find it unethical not to pay for it. But if someone says you can work and we cannot pay you, there may be reasons. And it may be an important step, work experience, a stage towards paid employment. It is very difficult to say what is good or bad in this area. Microsoft want to pay. That's how business works.[4]

Giles Harvey, who was diagnosed with Asperger's syndrome at the age of 22 in 1997, emphasises the importance of doing voluntary work:

Sometimes, employers think the long-term inactive have no willingness or desire to work, so won't hire them. References from voluntary jobs or work placements can speak a thousand words, in that they open doors; they do demonstrate willingness and a desire to work. They may also show successful time management, the ability to do a task and follow instructions ... all the things a potential employer is looking for. Often, placements can turn into jobs, if vacancies become available and the person has been reliable.[5]

❖ CASE STUDIES

- LITTLE GATE FARM
- GWEN GREENWOOD
- FERN ADAMS

LITTLE GATE FARM, in Beckley, near Rye, in Sussex takes in young adults with autism all over the Hastings, Bexhill, Battle and Rye area of southern England and helps them to acquire the skills and confidence to join the workforce. Although these young adults – called 'rangers' – are not paid at the farm, they answer the telephones and complete office tasks such as spreadsheets or filing and very often go on to take up paid employment in the community. For example, Angela Bellow, aged 22, now works at an Italian restaurant in Bexhill, and the restaurant says she makes the best tiramisu in the whole of the region! David, another Little Gate ranger, currently works in a tax office in Battle. When they return from their part-time jobs to work at the farm for the rest of the week, their whole posture reveals a new self-confidence.

The charity, which has been operating since 2014, receives around 50 per cent of its funds from Adult Social Care from East Sussex County Council but it is gradually increasing the amount of earned income from sales of produce and charcoal. But, as The Little Gate's director, Claire Cordell, explains, 'growth is slow, primarily because we always prioritise "ranger learning" over business success'.[6] Little Gate has placed 19 people in paid employment in schools, care homes, cafés, restaurants and offices. The managers of the farm emphasise that employing adults with disabilities is actually good for business and point out that several studies have shown that the workplace becomes more caring and supportive, which in turn means that staff in general are more motivated and committed.

In the coming months, Little Gate will launch its Apprenticeship Scheme. A small group of young adults with autism and learning disabilities will work with an education provider and an employer (NHS Hospital and Care Homes) to learn new skills which will prepare them for paid employment. By the end of 2018, Little Gate plans to be supporting 30 adults with autism and learning disabilities in paid employment. (See more about Little Gate's successful Horticulture Project in Chapter 8, under 'Gardening and Agriculture'.)

GWEN GREENWOOD volunteered with Bradford Autism Support. By her own admission, her mother 'coerced' her into it. 'On the day of my interview at BAS, Mum drove me down in the car,' she recalled.

> I had swapped my usual black combat shoes, corset and thick black eyeliner for a white top, black skirt and natural make-up in an attempt to look more 'professional'. Imagine how foolish I felt when I walked into the office and met my boss – a man wearing ripped jeans, a Cure T-shirt and with messy, Robert Smith-style hair. There's a lesson in that for everyone – always be yourself, because you never know when you might bump into someone who'd love the real you.[7]

Gwen did not disclose her Asperger's syndrome (she had been diagnosed at the age of six) because she herself had not come to terms with it. She knew she was different, separate – in fact, she later wrote a poignant poem about the 'glass walls' around her 'thinner than a single layer of skin'. At BAS, she ran a summer play scheme and the walls of her 'glass box' started growing even thinner. She loved working with the autistic children. On the second play scheme, she found it difficult to get up early enough, especially after taking quetiapine (an anti-psychotic she was taking for her anxiety). But the six-hour working days went past more quickly because they were more carefully structured than first time around. The children 'taught me more about autism than any textbook ever could'. eventually, the glass walls which had surrounded Gwen since childhood fell away completely.

> I saw so many of my own struggles in the children I worked with. But I also saw that they were happy, social, confident and productive. There was no reason why I couldn't be all of those things myself. I just needed to adopt a more autism-friendly approach to life. For the first time, I started to talk openly about my Asperger's with friends and family.[8]

Today, Gwen is officially a paid staff member at BAS. She has led several drama workshops for autistic children and teenagers and spoken at autism training sessions for the social services and the National Health Service.

> Volunteering and working with BAS has undoubtedly been a positive experience for me. It's helped me to come to terms with my own autism, given me lots of opportunities to socialise and I've built a career around it. Despite (and because of) my issues, I am very proud to have Asperger's syndrome. And I am very, very proud of the work I do with others on the spectrum.[9]

FERN ADAMS, a young woman with autism who graduated from university in politics with international relations, had previously volunteered for work in Uganda as a primary school teacher and medical clinic assistant. Fern actually found that her autism helped.

Autism manifests itself outwardly in a working environment through anxiety, lack of grasping social clues, dislike of office talk and inability to sit in an office from 9 to 5, five days a week. Working abroad, however, often makes these challenges easier to deal with and sometimes gets rid of them. Everybody moving to a new country faces nerves, and they often have to learn the social cues, customs and how to fit in. For a person with autism, this has often applied to them within their own country, also. Therefore, they are by no means novices at being the odd one out and having to put effort into what is going on around them.[10]

Fern added:

Similarly, office small talk can become much easier, as you can use this time to find out about the country and culture ... Furthermore, international work provides handbooks in living that your own country might not give you. Going abroad, it is likely you will pick up a country guide which will provide detailed instructions on things such as public transport, customs, etiquette and how to do various tasks. These are things you would just be expected to pick up and know how to do in your own country.

(Intriguingly, Fern says that, although there is very little awareness of autism in Uganda, traits such as hard work, determination and the ability to remember and collect knowledge are valued far more highly than in the UK.[11])

Interestingly, Daniel Lightwing, the British mathematician with Asperger's syndrome, played by Asa Butterfield in the film X+Y, also feels that he can adapt to completely new situations relatively easily,

because I don't have this cultural bias towards the culture I grew up in, because I can't connect to that either. So when I was in China, I thought everything was different, but I felt the same about the UK, too – it was all foreign to me.[12]

Stephen Shore, the hugely successful American speaker with Asperger's syndrome who teaches at Adelphi University in New York, also echoes Fern Adams' comments about a 'culture' of autism: 'As I entered the world of work after earning my Bachelor degrees, I found that all my friends hailed from other countries.' He thinks there is a 'three-part cultural explanation' for this. First, people from another culture may not detect as many differences as someone from one's own culture. Second, people from another culture may attribute behavioural variances to cultural differences. Third, it may be that, because people of another culture are already content with integrating into a new society, there may be 'greater tolerance or even appreciation for differences'.[13] Stephen, by the way, has a Chinese wife to whom he has been happily married for 25 years.

Internship programmes

Project SEARCH

Project SEARCH is a programme designed specifically for young people with learning disability and/or autism spectrum conditions who are in their last year of education. It has developed over 21 years since originating at the Cincinnati Children's Hospital Medical Center in 1996.

Over the past two years, European Project SEARCH has gone on to develop 50 programmes in large prestigious businesses in the UK, Ireland, the Netherlands and Portugal and has achieved 650 full-time paid jobs for Project SEARCH graduates. Approximately 25 per cent of UK Project SEARCH interns and graduates have autism spectrum conditions.

Anne O'Bryan, who is responsible for Project SEARCH's programme implementation and development in Europe and Asia, told me:

> The most important elements of Project SEARCH are partnership working across the host employer, an educator, a supported employment service and a Local Authority. When all of these partners focus on what is best for the interns in and beyond their Project SEARCH year, they can achieve a wonderful paid job for each young person, as well as improved quality of life.[14]

O'Bryan added: 'The second most important element is the development of competent and reliable training and support for each of the young people and their managers. Ambitious goals and skilled expertise are required for each Project SEARCH intern to be successful.'[15]

❖ CASE STUDY

• SUSIE

SUSIE, who has autism, took part in a placement at St George's University Hospital's NHS Foundation Trust in south London from 2014 and 2015. During her time in training and development, logistics, medical records, medical human resources and in the post room, she discovered that she had enormous strengths in attention to detail and in interpreting lists.

She told the NHS that her dream job would be to work for a well-known retail outlet. The NHS contacted the supported employment organisation, Remploy, who arranged for Susie to have a work trial interview, which allowed her to highlight her strengths and showcase her abilities much more easily than in a traditional interview format. She was supported by her Project Search job coach for a six-hour trial which included filling shelves, rotating stock, checking dates, tidying products and using the till. The shop manager observed Susie in all tasks and realised that her strength was date-checking products. The manager suggested that Susie could perform this function as her main role – and employment method known as job carving – and offered Susie the post, which she happily accepted.

To support Susie in her role, the charity, Action on Disability, arranged for Susie to have a job coach, who was provided through the British government's Access to Work fund.

Susie herself says:

> I feel really good about my job. I like my colleagues and working with the customers. I'm a bit more confident talking to the customers and I'm saving to go on holiday to Mallorca – my first time abroad and my first time on a plane.[16]

Internship programme launched by Deutsche Bank, Autistica and Ambitious About Autism

In 2017, Deutsche Bank, together with two British charities, Autistica, and Ambitious About Autism, launched a unique internship programme aimed specifically at autistic graduates. The scheme was due to begin in London and Birmingham in September 2017, marking a major step forward in the battle to improve employment opportunities for those on the autistic spectrum.[17]

The new scheme is based on the success of a small pilot programme last year – the first of its kind in the UK – where eight autistic graduates spent three months working at Deutsche Bank in London. Anna Remington, who led the team evaluating the scheme with her colleague at the Centre for Research in Autism and Education (CRAE), Liz Pellicano, said:

> The Deutsche Bank scheme is a very promising initiative to help autistic people access the labour market. Our study highlights the importance of clear communication, support for managers throughout the internship, and a commitment to embrace individuality in the workplace.[18]

CRAE commented:

> Not being in employment therefore places autistic people at serious risk for problems with their mental, emotional and physical well-being. The few existing studies in this area suggest that work placements and internships might be a key step in the process to easing people on the autism spectrum into paid employment. Yet we don't know much about the experiences of all those involved.[19]

CRAE's 2017 study investigated the experiences of all those involved in the first autistic internship scheme at Deutsche Bank: the interns themselves, their hiring managers, their team members and their buddies (a mentor who was assigned to each intern from outside their own team).

Both the interns, and the staff they worked with, felt that the autistic interns had made meaningful contributions to their teams and had left a lasting legacy at the firm.

In fact, five of the eight interns had their placements extended and continue to work within the bank. One intern said: 'The most useful thing that I've learned is that I am very able and it's made me realise that I can do anything….'

Nevertheless, a number of problem areas were highlighted. One of these was communication between interns and managers. As one intern put it: 'Actually I wasn't all that great with people, the contradictions anyway. It was like, "don't tell people what you feel like", and then "tell people what you feel like".'[20]

The CRAE researchers recommended that, in future internship programmes, employers should

> provide clear expectations about the programme, use straightforward language and be sincere in what they offer. … It would also be beneficial to have a neutral person who could help with communicating concerns, and facilitate discussion between different parties in the event of a disagreement.[21]

Anxiety is experienced by the majority of people on the autism spectrum – and the interns interviewed on this scheme were no exception. One called the experience 'not just acutely daunting for [himself], but also that anxiety affected him slightly more and certainly differently from how it would affect other people in the team'.[22]

Again, the CRAE researchers suggested that more support was needed for staff involved in the internship, for example a helpline or regular meeting with a job coach with expertise in autism to allow managers or colleagues to seek guidance. They also recommended more widespread training to help equip all staff with a knowledge of autism, but also an understanding that each person was unique and must be treated as an individual. One hiring manager declared: 'Everyone has strengths and weaknesses. You need to work out what the strengths are of your candidate and what the weaknesses are and find the right way [to support them].'

The CRAE study concluded that such internships represented 'a very promising strategy to turn around autistic people's exclusion from the labour market – and to offer a competitive advantage to the firms involved'.[23]

Notes

1   Elisabeth Hill in conversation with the author, 1 June 2016.
2   Mark Lever, in conversation with the author, 5 October 2016.
3   Emma Jones, in conversation with the author, 5 October 2016.
4   Thorkil Sonne in conversation with the author, 6 March 2016.
5   See *Asperger Syndrome and Employment* (2008), ed. Genevieve Edmonds and Luke Beardon. London: Jessica Kingsley, p. 29.
6   See report 'Little Gate Farm – July 2017'.
7   See Luke Beardon (ed.) (2017), *Bittersweet on the Autism Spectrum*. London: Jessica Kingsley, p. 27.
8   Ibid.
9   Ibid.
10 See: www.ambitiousaboutautism.org.uk/fern-adams (accessed 27 April 2018).
11 Ibid.
12 See Daniel Lightwing's interview with CRAE (the Centre for Research in Autism and Education, London), 2 April 2015. http://crae.ioe.ac.uk/post/115301526093/ interview-with-daniel-lightwing-who-inspired-the

13 See Josie Santomauro (ed.) (2011), *Autism All-Stars: How We Use Our Autism and Asperger Traits to Shine in Life*. London: Jessica Kingsley, p. 93.

14 Anne O'Bryan in communication with the author, 15 December 2017.

15 Ibid.

16 See 'Susie's journey into employment', by Bethany Madigan and Catherine Pymm, NHS England, 21 March 2016. www.england.nhs.uk/blog/bethany-madigan/#Proj%20Search.

17 See: www.autistica.org.uk/wp-content/uploads/2017/06/Internship-Programe-for-Autistic-Graduates_June2017_FullReport_web.pdf (accessed 27 April 2018).

18 Ibid.

19 See: http://crae.ioe.ac.uk/post/161851143988/sometimes-you-just-need-someone-to-take-a-chance (accessed 27 April 2018).

20 Ibid.

21 Ibid.

22 Ibid.

23 Ibid.

Chapter 5

Self-employment

Luke Jackson has written:

> One of the biggest things to remember when it comes to employment and autism is that there are non-traditional routes to employment ... When I was younger, I used to fret constantly that I'd never find a job in retail, never be able to work in a bar and might never be employed in customer services. It was only when people started to ask me whether I was selling my services as a photographer and when I started to write earnestly, that I realised that thinking laterally can have its pros. Never be afraid to go for non-traditional routes of employment and, more importantly, if you're good at something, don't be afraid to let people know. The line between confidence and arrogance is a fine one and is easily crossed, but if you're good at something, more often than not, work will find you.[1]

Self-employment may be an option in some cases. There are several advantages: it eliminates the 'hidden curriculum' of the workplace and it permits a more controlled structuring of the environment. Nevertheless, there is stress attached: there are records to keep, marketing to be conducted and clients to keep satisfied. As Temple Grandin puts it, 'Freelancing is not for the faint-hearted'.

Self-employment tends, by definition, to be less structured. The British writer and comedian, Alexei Sayle, has expressed this sensation in the following way:

> I am self-employed and find that working from home, setting your own schedule, the days generally blur into each other, with weekends holding no significance, and public holidays, when those who are employed in factories, offices or shops get time off, meaning nothing. I am often surprised to go out and find the streets empty of traffic because it is some national day of observance, such as Christmas, that I wasn't aware of. I find myself puzzled as to why the shops are suddenly full of Easter eggs or pancake batter.[2]

By working freelance, you can organise your own structure and environment. Nevertheless, as Grandin emphasises, 'self-employment can be stressful if it is not handled correctly. There are records to keep, marketing to be done and clients to keep happy. Make sure you are up for these tasks before deciding to go down this route.'[3]

For her part, Dinah Murray told me:

> Self-employment may be highly productive, especially when a keen interest is socially valued. Many autistic people who are unable to succeed in job interviews, or can't cope with workplace politics, are able to at least scrape a living through their own enterprise. Many people will never get paid work of any kind, so considering how their time can be employed most rewardingly and constructively should also be part of your brief, in my view.[4]

Jon Adams, a hugely talented British artist and musician with Asperger's syndrome, dyslexia and synaesthesia, observes:

> I feel you're often stuck between a rock and a hard place, and many autistic people opt for self-employment because they seemingly have more control. Around 80 per cent of autistic people have experienced mental health issues and it's becoming apparent that placing them in a non-adaptive work environment without proper care or attention to understanding the way they experience the world may adversely affect their mental health. It's funny: you either attempt to hold a job down in the face of possible harm to your mental health because of employers' misunderstanding your needs, or you try self-employment, where you receive very little help, if any, whilst spending all your time and energy searching for the few autism-enabling opportunities. This is not a fulfilling or equitable choice for autistic people to have to make.[5]

According to Cynthia Kim, a woman with Asperger's syndrome who has successfully started up several businesses, the two biggest potential roadblocks in self-employment are issues with executive function and uneven social skills. Executive function affects things like planning, initiation of actions, problem-solving and attention switching. Kim writes:

> If you have poor executive function, the lack of accountability inherent in self-employment can be a recipe for disaster. I've developed a lot of systems to keep me on track and impose order on my work day – things like keeping lists, using a day-planner, creating artificial deadlines, setting alarms, making notes to myself, and rewarding myself for meeting goals. No matter what type of business you have (or what type of job you do), executive function is fundamental to staying on track on a day-to-day basis. If you can't master the basics of managing a daily schedule and completing tasks on time, then being your own boss will probably make you more miserable than happy.[6]

As for the other major challenge, social skills, Kim notes:

> While it's possible to structure a business or freelance position so that you have very little contact with others, that isn't always the case. Some common freelance/self-employed positions lend themselves to solitary work and others require a lot of contact with people. For example, a website like Elance makes it possible for freelancers and small businesses to bid on and complete jobs entirely online. I've hired freelancers and got excellent work done without ever speaking with anyone

over the phone or in person. If you're skilled in a field that primarily requires creating deliverables (websites, graphics, text, analysis, code, etc.), you may be able to transact most of your business without a lot of face-to-face interaction (if you prefer). On the other hand, turning your skill into a career may require you to interact with a lot of people on a daily basis. If you're an expert bicycle repair person, you'll have to talk to people about their bikes to find out what work needs to be performed. But – oh wait! I bet someone with a special interest in bicycle repair would love nothing more than talking to people about repairing bicycles![7]

Kim adds:

That's another benefit to turning a special interest into a career. I find business-related interaction to be less stressful than general social interaction. If I'm talking to someone about a project then I'm in my element and can navigate the conversation fairly confidently. I've even been interviewed by writers for articles and books in my industry as an 'expert' and actually enjoyed those opportunities. It was fun to talk about a subject I know well (even if the interviewers had to keep reminding me to slow down so they could understand me).[8]

Kim takes issue with the idea of conducting a SWOT analysis – standing for Strengths, Weaknesses, Opportunities and Threats. The thinking behind this is that, by identifying internal (S and W) and external (O and T) positives and negatives, you can then set realistic objectives for a project or business.

I've found that weaknesses (and sometimes threats) can be just as helpful in achieving an objective as strengths. If you see a weakness as an opportunity to adapt, compensate or innovate your way around a problem, then that weakness is going to be helpful in the long run. For example, because of my weaknesses in executive function, I've created all sorts of organisational systems and fail safes that make me far more organised at work than the average person. Not because I love being organised but because if I wasn't super-organised, I would spend my days going in circles, accomplishing little. Out of necessity, I've taken a weakness and turned it into a super-competency.[9]

Kim points to what she believes are eight of the biggest positives she has found, from personal experience, of becoming self-employed with Asperger's syndrome:

- You make your own rules: 'The beauty of not answering to a boss is that I get to put my better way into action and make that the rule for me. I work more efficiently – and I'm happier – when I'm doing things in a way that makes sense to me.'
- You work alone: 'Navigating the social aspects of the workplace is challenging and demands a lot of energy, energy that many of us would rather expend on doing actual work. I found working in an office with other people distracting and anxiety-inducing, even when I was the boss and could close my door on the rest of the office.'
- You can control your work environment: 'This is critical for individuals who have sensory sensitivities or an unconventional work style. With a little planning and

the right kind of business, you can structure your workday to accommodate your autistic traits in ways that would be impossible in a conventional workplace.'

- You can do what you love: 'The deep knowledge and passion that develop around a special interest are autistic superpowers. Not every special interest can be turned into a marketable skill, but many can, sometimes in very unconventional ways.'
- You can 'leverage' your strengths: 'I think Aspies have at least as many unique strengths as weaknesses. These are mine: detail-oriented, risk taker, persistent, perceptive, consistent, outside-the-box thinker, excellent pattern recognizer, diligent, optimistic, forthright, non-judgemental.'
- You can expand your competencies: 'I hate talking on the phone, but there are times when completing an important business task requires making a phone call. Over the years, I've learned some tricks to make phone calls less stressful (planning ahead, coming up with a script, phrases to signal that I'm ready to end the call).'
- You can put your self-teaching skills to work: 'There are a lot of aspects of owning a business that you can teach yourself, and happily, many autistic individuals are natural self-teachers thanks to years spent pursuing special interests. Among the things I've taught myself are bookkeeping, tax preparation, page layout, database construction, HTML and CSS, basics of Photoshop, and press release writing.'
- You can wallow in the glory: 'Being self-employed can be very validating. You make something or do something and someone else values that thing enough to give you money for it. There is a very direct connection between your skill and the reward.'[10]

On the other hand, like Temple Grandin, Kim strongly advises taking a hard look at potential pitfalls before trying your hand at being your own boss. The pitfalls she identifies are as follows:

- You are responsible for literally every aspect of the business, which can be extremely stressful at times. How good are you in a crisis? How do you handle failure? What is your risk tolerance?
- The hours are long for relatively few rewards. 'Unless you're fantastically lucky, getting your business off the ground will mean working longer hours for less pay than the average fast food worker. There were a few years when I worked full-time hours and paid myself nothing because I needed every last dollar to keep the business afloat.'
- Executive function is essential. 'It's important to know in advance where you are going to face the biggest executive function challenges and to have a plan for supports in place. This is not something you can solve on the fly.'[11]

When Kim set up her own business, she spent a great deal of time studying other businesses, looking for patterns – how they treated their customers, how they promoted themselves, how they priced their products. 'From here, it's a matter of, as Bruce Lee said, "Adapt what is useful, reject what is useless, and add what is specifically your own".'[12]

❖ CASE STUDIES

- LAURA JAMES
- JON MCCULLOCH
- ALEX LOWERY
- DR PATRICK SUGLIA
- AARON SULLIVAN
- RAVI MUNIANDY
- CHRIS TIDMARSH
- JEREMY SICILE-KIRA
- MATT COTTLE
- MATT RESNIK
- JACOB WITTMAN

Figure 5.1 Laura James
Source: Tim James/Mabel Gray

LAURA JAMES is a successful freelance journalist. She found out she was autistic only after she had forged a career for herself, married twice and raised four children. Her 2017 memoir, *Odd Girl Out*, tracks the year after she received the definitive diagnosis of Asperger's syndrome at the age of 45 in 2015. She went freelance soon after interviewing the novelist, Jilly Cooper – and that is the way she has worked ever since.

She has an interesting past. An adopted child, her real-life mother was an underwater ballerina, who would dance with crocodiles. When Laura herself was very young, she did a Saturday job in a hairdressers, making appointments and sweeping up. 'When I got home in the evening, I was too tired to speak,' she told me.[13]

> I like working from my home in Norfolk. There are none of the sensory issues from offices and I can pace myself. Journalism can suit an autistic mind – we can ask difficult questions directly but also we have very inquiring minds.[14]

She freely admits she is not very organised, 'I don't have the executive functioning to make things happen – and I don't have a competitive bone in my body.'

Asked about the unpredictability of the journalistic profession, Laura replied: 'There is some unpredictability in any walk of life. But I'm such a control freak that I manage. I'm not sent anywhere – I take commissions.'[15]

When she tells people about her autism, they immediately point out how unusual it is for someone with a condition characterised by communication difficulties to communicate for a living.

> I've thought a lot about this. It was one of things that made me think twice about asking for an assessment, I love my job. I love the variety, the filling of empty pages, the decisions I have to take, the fascinating people I get to interview. The key to why I find it easy is that there is a structure to everything. Features need to be a set number of words. An interview is not like a social conversation. I get to ask any question that pops into my head and it is not seen as impolite. There is no hedging around a subject and little small talk ... I love interviewing people. I don't feel any different talking to a scientist than I do to a celebrity. It is a huge privilege to be able to ask questions of someone, whether those questions relate to genetics or the latest film they are starring in. Meeting experts is pure heaven for someone autistic. The access I am given to someone's knowledge never fails to make me happy ...
>
> I also think my autism is helpful in some aspects of my job. My ability to hyper-focus can be really helpful when doing something long haul, such as writing a book. Also, being naturally curious and hungry for facts, makes journalism quite a natural choice. It would be a lie to say that I find everything at work easy. I don't. I struggle with things on a daily basis. My desk is in permanent chaos. I write things on pieces of paper and then spend hours upending bins

trying to find those few scribbled words that seem meaningless to anyone else, but are essential for something I need to do.[16]

She says she fears many deadlines.

It's not that I couldn't have met the deadline. Rather, it's that my anxiety at giving up control, of handing something in, will take over and I will become paralysed, taken over by autistic inertia, unable to finish my task and unable to start anything else ...

I like things to go smoothly, because the majority of my socialising is done within my work setting, often on the phone. It matters hugely to me that no one is upset, so often I will find myself agreeing to take on unpaid work or go outside the remit of a contract simply to ensure no feathers are ruffled. I have always felt unworthy and as if, at any minute, I will be found out. I've learned, however, that many neurotypical women feel this way, too. It's not just an issue for autistic women, although we seem to feel it particularly keenly. In part, for me at least, it is anchored in my feeling of not being a grown-up, a proper person. But, as I need to pay the bills, I have learned to keep pretending.[17]

Laura's husband, Tim, used to be a journalist himself but became a freelance photographer. 'My diagnosis helped our marriage. And cognitive analytical therapy really helped me. It gave me an instruction manual for life.'[18]

Cork-based JON MCCULLOCH – also known as the 'evil bald genius' – is one of the leading 'marketing gurus' in the UK and Ireland. He told me that self-employment worked for him because it allowed him control over his own schedule.

I work only when I want. I keep my own hours and live on an isolated farm in a fairly sparsely populated part of Ireland. The only person I see on a regular basis is my wife. If she's away, I can go for a week without seeing a single person, so there's just me and my dog – which suits me fine.[19]

He says he has very strict rules about how people contact him:

Even my lawyer or bank manager don't call me unless they set up an appointment first. This suits an 'Aspie' like me very well, because I don't keep getting surprised by people wanting to talk. Because I run my own company, I can do this. Otherwise, I'd have to join in office politics, which I did for many years.

McCulloch is quick to add:

There are so many ways of setting up a company which would not work. I am very well known in the industry for the concept of 'positioning' – which means how to run a business by setting rules for yourself and your client.

I don't like the term high-functioning, because it is not strictly true. I may appear that way on the outside, and people sometimes doubt whether I have Asperger's at all. But that's because they can't see what's going in inside.[20]

As for the challenges of being self-employed, McCulloch says:

I imagine there are no more problems for someone on the spectrum than for anyone else. You are working long hours on your own, you have to be self-disciplined and you have to create your own structure. I struggle with structure. I tend to move from one thing to another. I have my own issues, as well: three years ago, my daughter tried to commit suicide and I've been looking after her since then. That brought my anxiety to the fore and the medication brought my Asperger's to the fore.

Another issue is, that, if you care what people think of you and have problems socialising, as I do, you may feel cast adrift. You can feel isolated at the best of times. But if you are deliberately isolating yourself, as you are with self-employment, this can get even worse. I manage because the only people I want to spend time with are the people who join. They all know I have Asperger's and they are very accommodating.[21]

ALEX LOWERY is a successful public speaker, author, trainer and autism campaigner who was diagnosed with classic autism at the age of four. He has written a book, *Thinking Club: A Film Strip of My Life as a Person with Autism*. As a teenager, he remembers seeing men with autism in their twenties 'who weren't doing much with their lives. I've seen autistic adults who literally spend their whole time walking around town or just stuck indoors. I remember thinking: "I do not want this to become my future".'[22]

His career began at the age of 17 when he was asked to give a talk to an audience at St John's Ambulance. He was subsequently trained in public speaking by the Welsh charity, Autism Cymru. He became self-employed in 2013 at the age of 19. 'I'm very happy that I now have a job,' he says.

It's like a dream come true. But it's quite clear to me that there is no way I'd be able to do it if I didn't have all the support from my family. My mother is involved with everything and will take me to some of my talks. Although when necessary, I get support from someone who's paid through Access to Work. My father manages the accounts, my sister-in-law built my website and designed all my leaflets and business cards.[23]

Despite his blossoming career, Alex admitted to me that he continued to dislike physical contact and still indulged in 'stimming' (self-stimulation) a great deal and even took his favourite piece of string, which he calls 'Freddy', to his speaking engagements. His bookings are handled by his mother, Sylvia.[24]

Alex says he did try working in an office environment (with his father) – basic jobs like stamping post, printing and indexing – but found it 'boring

Figure 5.2 Alex Lowery
Source: Jane Williams

and repetitive'. He was also not good at hiding the fact that he was bored! He also has dyspraxia and attention-deficit hyperactivity disorder (ADHD), which makes it difficult for him to stay still. He struggles to read and take in information at the same time. In fact, multi-tasking in general is difficult. He still experiences considerable problems with literal thinking. 'Instructions have to be crystal clear. I can't read between the lines.' Interestingly, he notes that he himself can use sarcasm when he speaks, which is a problem because other people tend to take *him* literally! ('It sounds as though I'm being serious and this gets me into trouble.')[25]

For Alex, self-employment can be one of the best options for adults with autism:

> If they have the necessary support, self-employment can work well, because they can go into business doing something which they're good at. Many people with autism have gifts and/or obsessive interests. They will

probably have a really high level of knowledge in their favourite subjects that they may be able to use to their advantage. It can be a good idea to broaden out an obsessive interest or gift into something they may be able to turn into a career. As well as having autism myself, I have an obsessive interest in autism, and I've managed to use my high level of knowledge and insight into the condition to my advantage.[26]

When Dr PATRICK SUGLIA learned as an adult that he was on the autism spectrum, it explained a lot about the problems he encountered at work: complaints from his bosses that he learned too slowly, or needed to be more outgoing. Now, he is in business for himself, and this has resolved many issues.

'Being your own boss means you can make the rules the way they work for you,' says Suglia, who works as a mobile chiropractor and a certified medical examiner for the federal Motor Carrier Safety Administration in Perry Township, Indiana, in the US.[27]

Suglia's wife, Becky, has worked as a licensed clinical social worker and therapist with people of all ages who are on the autism spectrum. She knows the diagnosis will come with challenges in a work environment. Becky lists communication and dealing with change as those that may require the most coping skills for an autistic individual who wants to become an entrepreneur.

'As a businessperson, we often have to reach out to other businesses and create linkages, find new customers and clients,' she says. 'To do that involves communicating with others.' According to Becky, problems with communication can drastically impact business development, potentially wreaking havoc with entrepreneurs on the spectrum.[28]

Becky adds that coping with change might constitute a significant challenge for many people with autism who become entrepreneurs: 'When you're in business for yourself, it's like driving without a map.' However, coping skills can be acquired to help prepare for the unexpected. Moreover, many autistic individuals learn to persevere and become stronger in the face of having to cope with the social and administrative challenges. These are all traits that, in Becky's view, would benefit an entrepreneur. On top of that, becoming their own bosses could give people on the spectrum the capacity to create a job in an environment where they were comfortable working.

Becky has worked with many people with autism who exhibit great amounts of creativity: 'Many of those individuals had a different way of thinking about a problem,' she says. 'They came at solutions from a different angle.'[29]

Patrick's inventively 'out-of-the-box' solution to his marketing challenges is his mobile chiropractic and medical examination care vehicle which allows him to bring his business to his patients, rather than waiting for them to come to him.

He agrees that marketing himself is difficult because of his social abilities not reaching the level of most adults, but he has found ways to compensate. As a medical examiner for the US Department of Transportation, his name is automatically included in a database where anyone needing an exam checks to find an available practitioner. Which meant that he did not need to market that service: 'The phone just started ringing,' he says.

Patrick recommends that entrepreneurs with autism find a mentor who knows their skills and gifts and will spread the word about the business and its services.

And it seems that the word about Patrick's business is extremely positive. Elizabeth Jackson is a regular chiropractic patient of Suglia's. She is full of praise for his healing abilities, and also for his style of communication: 'He's really good,' she says. 'When Pat has something to say, it's usually something that needs to be heard. He's thoughtful about how he speaks his mind.'[30]

Patrick, who has written three books on autism, recommends avoiding any environments with loud noises, bright lights or with job duties which are communication-intensive, such as sales. 'I don't think that way,' he says. 'It's an autistic thing.' He concedes that inflexibility may represent a problem. 'If what you're doing isn't working out, try other things,' he says. 'Maybe you have a gift, and you're a natural at something.'[31]

In his latest book, *Autism, Spirituality and Medical Mayhem*, Suglia writes that it took him years of dedication to build on his strengths in healing rather than attempting to change his weaknesses, and he has grown to have confidence in his abilities, knowledge, education and insights.

'This is the approach someone on the autism spectrum must take if they wish to be successful being their own hero,' he says.[32]

At 17, AARON SULLIVAN decided he wanted to become a spokesman for other people with autism in Sussex whose talents, he said, were not being well represented or supported fully in some educational settings and work environments across the county. He lobbied his local Member of Parliament, Amber Rudd (Britain's former Home Secretary), in a bid to raise funds and awareness for his campaign. That led to Aaron setting up his own business, Aspie Rational Talks, and he now gives motivational presentations to parents, schools, colleges, public services, employers and organisations. 'Our motto is: Raising awareness, Embracing Difference, Inspiring change,' he says.

For the past six years, Aaron has volunteered as an ambassador at both his secondary school and his further educational placement, where he has helped teachers with their training and autism awareness, as well as being a mentor for students in their transition from secondary school into further education.

'I'm really aware of the mental distress felt by many who are overlooked or not considered for work placements that would be ideal for them, just because they are different,' says Aaron.

> Many Aspies are reliable, loyal, hard-working, creative, are analytical and have excellent problem-solving skills, yet these skills are simply not being

recognised by enough employers and that needs to change. I hope through my endeavours, however small, I can make a difference to those like me and in turn, help those with mental health problems that very often have been exacerbated by their exclusion from the working world. Autistic people have a lot to offer to the community and I'd like to help them, and employers, realise what an asset they can be to business and enterprise.[33]

RAVI MUNIANDY, 31, from Southwold, near Suffolk, was diagnosed with Asperger's syndrome and ADHD three years ago. He struggled to find employment after leaving school and became very depressed and anxious after working in the NHS for three years – almost to the point of not being able to function at all. It was then that his parents decided to encourage him to take up work he could do from home.

Ravi started baking bread, which he initially sold to friends locally until his parents converted their garage into a bakehouse. His mother, Liz, said:

> He can bore for Britain about bread! But this gave him the confidence to ask for an assessment and the diagnosis then opened the gateway for social service involvement and the support they have provided has enabled him to now live independently (around the corner). However, the business depends on our considerable involvement and we are now worrying about what happens when we cannot continue – a common issue for parents, I'm sure.[34]

In 2012, Ravi joined the Real Bread Campaign to champion buying freshly made, locally produced bread – rather than picking up a cheap, mass-produced loaf from a supermarket – and opened his bakery that same year. He said:

> It is a brave move to open a bakery in the current climate, but the whole point of doing it is to provide good bread in the local area. I have always been interested in cooking and have done a lot of home baking, but it was my uncle, John Gale, who said I should do it for a living.[35]

He was one of the first 50 bakers in Britain to adopt the Real Bread Loaf Mark as part of the Real Bread Campaign. This provides assurance from the baker that the bread is made without processing aids or artificial additives: the result – artisan bread of the highest quality. He now makes more than a dozen varieties of artisan breads and has extended his range of products to include cakes, biscuits, scones and breakfast cereals – all hand-made to his own recipes with the same quality ingredients. He claims a hand-crafted loaf is tastier, healthier and better for the environment, as all his produce is delivered by bike or on foot.

At present, Ravi sells his bread at Southwold's Country Market on a Friday, and in six local shops in the Suffolk region.

CHRIS TIDMARSH, a 30-year-old man with autism, is the co-founder and co-owner of Green Bridge Growers, a commercial greenhouse in north central

Indiana, in the US, which provides herbs, lettuces and nasturtiums to local restaurants, and sunflowers and cosmos to florists.

Chris set up the company in 2013 with his mother – and co-owner – Jan Pilarski, after a promising job as an environmental researcher ended abruptly because he had difficulties communicating. Jan does most of the administration, including accounting, marketing and sales. He perfects the spacing between rows of kale and spinach, and keeps close tabs on water chemistry and soil acidity. He spends hours researching natural and effective pesticides to deal with aphids.

Green Bridge is projecting revenue of US $80,000 and profit of $30,000 in fiscal year 2018. In fiscal 2020, when an expansion is complete, it expects to reach $220,000 in revenue and $72,000 in profit.

Chris was diagnosed with autism as a child but went on to earn three degrees from Hope College, a small liberal-arts school in Holland, Michigan. After graduating in 2010, he got a job as an environmental researcher. 'I was doing a lot of office work and behind the computer. I'm not the best with that style. They generally communicate verbally, and I'm more of a visual learner,' Chris told the *Wall Street Journal*.[36] He prefers following directions when they are written in emails and texts. It is harder when they are spoken. He lasted just three months in that post.

After that initial blow, Chris interned at an organic farm, became a master gardener and took a class designed to help people become farmers. 'I've been really interested in the environment and Earth for a long time,' he says. 'I decided I wanted to do something related to that.'[37]

He and his mother, who grew up on a farm, visited a software business set up by the family of a young man on the spectrum, and they also visited several farms, including one that used an aquaponics process, where fish waste is used to fertilise plants growing in water, while the plants clean the water to cycle it back to the fish tank.

Jan left her own job in 2012 and applied to a programme through her *alma mater*, Notre Dame, designed to help start up social enterprises, involving local students. Part of the class involved creating a plan that could be entered into a business-plan competition at Notre Dame's Mendoza Business School. When the group presented the plan to the competition judges, Chris spoke about unemployment problems faced by people on the autism spectrum and described his own experience. They won the social impact prize, which provided $15,000.

In 2013, the partners built a prototype for their business, located on a site in South Bend, Indiana which housed an agency serving people with disabilities. As they produced their first crops – basil, cilantro, red Russian kale, lettuce, mint and parsley – they learned the ins and outs of the growing process. They raised money through donors and a crowdfunding campaign, which they added to a $10,000 entrepreneur-of-the-year award won by Chris.

After searching for more than a year, in December 2014, they found a farm with five acres, a house and barn, and bought it for $70,000. Things were progressing until March 2016 – when Jan was diagnosed with cancer. But since then, with her health improving, Chris has found a purpose in life in the business. Not only that: he has also addressed large audiences, speaking in front of advocacy groups and gatherings at Notre Dame and St. Mary's, including graduate speech pathology classes. The goal is to help them understand the difficulties that those on the autism spectrum experience in communicating. He recently moved into a house with a friend who is also autistic.

'I've seen him grow in such a lovely way,' says his mother. Chris himself is optimistic about the future of Green Bridge: 'It does provide hope not just for me, but others on the autism spectrum to find and keep jobs. I think I can see myself doing this for the rest of my life.'[38]

JEREMY SICILE-KIRA's mother, Chantal, is a French-Canadian autism consultant, speaker and author specialising in adolescence and transition planning. Now Jeremy himself has found paid work as a producer of personalised paintings which are used by businesses on their notecards, business cards, and logo backgrounds.

'Although I encouraged Jeremy to try employment or volunteer experiences that seemed like a good fit in high school, I was not holding my breath waiting for any opportunities to show up on the horizon,' says Chantal.

> I am not convinced that that much has changed since 2010 in the job market in regards to hiring people like Jeremy, although I hear about opportunities for those who are able to learn computer programming, testing, data entry. I don't anticipate a huge rush of employers looking to hire my son any day soon. But that doesn't mean I am going to give up on him – or society. We have to educate employers, but we also have to prepare our students better.[39]

Chantal became interested in the concept of self-employment when Jeremy was not offered any work experiences during his first few years of high school, about 10 years ago. The 'workability' woman at the time felt that Jeremy was not ready for any of the job options she had in the community. She deemed Jeremy 'not community-ready', despite the fact that Chantal had him out and learning shopping skills, appropriate behaviour in the library and taking subways and buses in three of the world's busiest cities. However, his excellent teacher felt that everyone, including Jeremy, had potential, and was open to creating a self-employment experience.

> At that time, Jeremy could not communicate as readily as he can now, and so we had to come up with ideas based on observations that people who knew Jeremy made about his strengths and weaknesses, his likes and dislikes, and then ask him 'yes' or 'no' questions

says his mother.

> Jeremy's teacher came up with the idea of starting a sandwich delivery
> service for the teachers, based on Jeremy's strengths and likes, and the
> fact that by the end of the week, the teachers were sick of the on-site
> lunch option – so there was a need for such a service. Jeremy's second
> experience was providing a needed product (selling flowers to peers at
> school where no flowers were available on campus). Then he was asked
> to help with a coffee cart initiative on the school site. A Self-Employment
> Workbook I created was used to help get these different experiences up
> and running.
>
> By actually doing these businesses, Jeremy learned valuable business
> lessons ... [He] also learned that if he could not do all aspects of his job,
> he had to pay someone else to do the parts he could not. In reality, it
> is these kinds of business lessons the all neurotypical teens should be
> learning in the current economy.[40]

Chantal concedes that self-employment is not for everyone and requires
a business support team. The business support team can be made up of a
teacher or parent, a para-professional, a mentor, a friend, someone who has
business experience. For Chantal, each person brings his or her knowledge
to the team. The business team helps to advise in areas where the individual
needs help and also does parts of the business the person cannot, just as in
all businesses.

> Looking at self-employment as an option sometimes leads to an actual
> job. The process of discovering a person's strengths and weaknesses, can
> lead to discovering areas of traditional employment that had not been
> considered for that person previously. Sometimes, it leads to a job offer
> from a business in the local community that the person had visited to get
> more information about his area of interest.[41]

Recently, Chantal discovered that Jeremy was painting portraits of people in
his dreams. He started dictating his dreams to me and his support staff and
decided he wanted to try and paint his dreams in real life. Today, he is paid
to paint people's 'colours' – translating emotions into beautiful portraits. His
paintings also make gifts for birthdays, weddings, housewarmings, bridal and
baby showers.

MATT COTTLE was inspired to start up his company, Stuttering King Bakery,
after watching a culinary demonstration during his senior year of high school.
He realised that culinary school was not an option, because traditional
classrooms were not conducive to his learning style. Matt knew the odds
were stacked against him. However, much like King George VI (a celebrated
stammerer whose story was depicted in the 2010 Oscar-winning film, *The
King's Speech*, and whose name inspired that of the bakery), Matt refused to
let those odds win.

Backed by the loving support of his family, he attended the Southwest Autism Research and Resource Centre (SARRC) Vocational and Life Skills Academy Culinary Works programme. After graduating, he took three years' worth of one-on-one baking lessons from Heather Netzloff, the pastry chef and founder of Rumpelstiltskin Granola.

In 2012, Matt and his mother, Peggy, launched Stuttering King Bakery. Operating out of the Cottles' home kitchen, the company specialises in muffins, brownies, blondies, bars, cookies, and scones, specifically for event and business catering in the Phoenix metro valley. Matt handcrafts each pastry with high-quality, natural and locally sourced ingredients.

With King George VI's quote, 'The highest of distinctions is service to others,' ringing in his ears, Matt now plans to open his own brick-and-mortar bakery, where he will employ others with autism and teach them the art of baking.

MATT RESNIK, a young man with autism, founded the award-winning entrepreneurial bakery business, SMILE Biscotti, following his graduation from high school in 2013. SMILE stands for Supporting My Independent Living Enterprise. SMILE started as a community effort, thanks to the support of the Southwest Autism Research and Resource Centre (SARRC) and its Rising Entrepreneurs programme. The bakeries can now be found at various locations throughout Phoenix and Dallas and across the United States.

One of Matt's co-workers, Jon, says: 'I enjoy baking because I like the order a recipe provides and like taking steps one by one. I also like work that involves motion, like moving boxes, pushing heavy carts and delivering SMILE packages – all perfect for me!'[42]

One autistic worker, Slade, who joined SMILE as an intern in 2015, comments: 'I enjoy the quiet, predictable work atmosphere of biscotti labelling and packaging sessions. My role at SMILE has helped me to develop a structured schedule of community involvement as I transition to adult life.'[43]

JACOB WITTMAN, Shelly Henley's autistic son, inspired the creation of a bakery, No Label at the Table, in Indiana, devoted to hiring only workers with autism. Jacob develops many of the recipes himself. The bakery specialises in dairy-free, gluten-free food. Shelly chose the name of the company with her son to ensure that 'no label or diagnosis prevents my employees from living to their full potential, and no food label should limit any individual from having good food'.[44]

The story began after Jacob told her he wanted to be a chef when he was 18. 'To go to culinary school was out,' Shelly said, and because he can't meet the academic level of high school, he will not obtain a regular diploma. 'Nor would he ever make it through a job interview,' she added. 'He would've been relegated to a dishwasher position, and that's not where he wanted to be.'

Jacob is still taking high school classes through Hoosier Academies, a public online school, but focuses some of his studies on topics that support his bakery, such as business and chemistry. His hypersensitive sense of smell and precise palate allows him to develop inventive and balanced flavours, such as basil-strawberry muffins or lemon-almond cookies.

'Where it was once a battle to get him to do his literature courses, he's now constantly researching online for new recipes,' says his mother. 'He literally walks taller. He's a part of people's weddings. He's a part of people's birthday parties now. It has given him a purpose in life.'[45]

When the company started up, there were just three employees. Now there are 13. 'If we had our own storefront, we could eventually go to 25 employees, all on the spectrum,' says Shelly.[46] The paid positions range from four to 18 hours a week, but Shelly said they'd have some full-time employees when they established a permanent bakery. At the moment, it operates out of rented premises.

Notes

1   Luke Jackson (2016), *Sex, Drugs and Asperger's Syndrome – A User's Guide to Adulthood*. London: Jessica Kingsley, pp. 86–87.
2   *New Statesman*, 26 May 2017, p. 59.
3   See T. Grandin and D. Moore (2015), *The Loving Push: How Parents and Professionals Can Help Spectrum Kids Become Successful Adults*. Arlington, TX: Future Horizons, p. 36.
4   Dinah Murray in communication with the author, 9 April 2016.
5   Jon Adams, in conversation with the author, 6 July 2016.
6   See Cynthia Kim, 'Musings of an Aspie', https://musingsofanaspie.com/2013/08/09/the-challenges-of-being-a-self-employed-aspie/ (accessed 27 April 2018).
7   Ibid.
8   Ibid.
9   Ibid.
10   Ibid.
11   Ibid.
12   Ibid.
13   Laura James, in conversation with the author, 21 June 2017.
14   Ibid.
15   Ibid.
16   Laura James (2017), *Odd Girl Out*. London: Bluebird, pp. 111–112.
17   Ibid., pp. 112–113.
18   Laura James, in conversation with the author, 21 June 2017.
19   Jon McCulloch, in communication with the author, 22 August 2017.
20   Ibid.
21   Ibid.
22   See: www.alexlowery.co.uk/autism-and-employment-by-alex-lowery/ (accessed 9 February 2016).
23   Ibid.
24   Alex Lowery in conversation with the author, 20 May 2016.
25   Ibid.
26   Ibid.
27   *Reading Eagle*, 6 September 2017.
28   Ibid.
29   Ibid.

30   Ibid.
31   Ibid.
32   Ibid.
33   *Hastings Observer*, 4 August 2017.
34   *Eastern Daily Press*, 22 May 2012.
35   Ibid.
36   *Wall Street Journal*, 26 November 2017.
37   Ibid.
38   Ibid.
39   *Psychology Today*, 18 May 2016.
40   Ibid.
41   Ibid.
42   See: www.smilebiscotti.com/about-smile (accessed 27 April 2018).
43   Ibid.
44   *USA Today*, 1 September.
45   Ibid.
46   Ibid.

Chapter 6

Matching skills to jobs

Jobs for non-verbal individuals with autism

Lack of language should not – and must not – exclude people with ASD from the job market. Parents should bear in mind that there are a number of potential openings for this community: janitor, store re-stocker, library helper, factory assembly worker, warehouse helper, office helper, odd-job gardener.

Here is Temple Grandin's suggested list of possible jobs for people without language on the spectrum:

- Re-shelving library books
- Factory assembly work
- Copy shop
- Janitor jobs
- Re-stocking supermarket shelves
- Recycling plant
- Warehouse – loading trucks, stacking boxes
- Lawn and garden work
- Fast food restaurant – cleaning and cooking jobs with little demand on short-term memory
- Plant care[1]

Other examples of work being carried out by autistic workers without language include washing the dishes in a home for the elderly. One young man without language works in a paid job smashing bottles in a bottle bank – and enjoys every moment of it!

Interestingly, Temple Grandin believes that work-related social difficulties are often less severe for people on the autism spectrum who have more obvious disabilities, such as no speech: 'Once other employees understand autism, they are often very helpful. It is the people who are closer to being typical who have the worst problems with office politics and jealousy.'[2]

A 2015 study by Tiffany Johnson and Aparna Joshi endorses Grandin's view. They wrote:

> In some respects, these milder versions of mental disorders, such as high-functioning ASD, may be even more stigmatising than more severe forms of mental disorders. For instance, some individuals may trivialise these disorders ('everyone

has issues') and view the symptoms as controllable ('he's just throwing a fit to get what he wants'). Because individuals with milder mental disorders such as high-functioning autism may also come across as 'normal' in many situations, co-workers and supervisors may have higher expectations of them; so when they display symptoms of their disorder, their behaviour is viewed as highly socially disruptive.[3]

Thorkil Sonne, founder of Specialisterne, entirely agrees that the stereotypes – that everyone on the autism spectrum is good at IT and loves repetitive tasks – are well-meaning but misguided:

> In our case, it is a coincidence that software got such media attention. It's because that was my background. If I had been working at a hospital or a hotel that would have been my brand. Software testing is a good fit. People with autism often find things that deviate. But we do much more than that. At Microsoft, we brought in coders, analysts, designers. Our ambition is to have people fulfil themselves. We may go into the mining industry soon. We are also interested in agricultural industry – especially pig farming. For that, we need people who are good at working with animals. I claim that five per cent of all jobs should be a good fit for autistic workers.[4]

> From my time in the autism organisation in Denmark, I met people at all places on the spectrum. One of my biggest ambitions is to find a way to give people respect, self-confidence and quality of life and be rewarded by employers right across the spectrum for contributing to society. There is so much undiscovered talent among the non-verbal. I do not deal with them at the moment, I would love to start. It is a goldmine. You are treated as intelligent, but the problem may be elsewhere. We do not use the phone so much any more – we tend to use emails and texts, which is good news for autistic people. Non-verbal people with autism could also play a role in such an environment. Cooking is very scripted, for example. They could make wonderful cooks.[5]

❖ CASE STUDIES

- BRAD FREMMERLIND
- POETRY IN WOOD
- BRITTANY KARPIN

BRAD FREMMERLIND, a 25-year-old Canadian non-verbal autistic man in Edmonton, Alberta, has been making headlines with his furniture-assembly business, appropriately called Made by Brad.

Because he does not speak, Brad uses around 200 functional signs to communicate. Each day, he is driven from his group home to his day programme. There, he works with an iPad programme to improve his communication, attends various classes, like cooking and sign language, and goes on outings.

His mother, Deb, says that the idea behind his furniture business was to find a tool which would increase his social interaction with the community and to help with his life-long education. 'We want to develop Brad's social awareness and give back to the community by providing a service,' Deb told Autism After 16.

> Brad learned to build furniture from years of following diagrams, building plastic models and Legos. We'd buy Lego projects and send them to his day programme to give him something productive to do. Ever since he started at the programme, we wanted to figure out how to use his skills in building furniture ... My husband, Mark, loves classic cars and airplanes, so we'd buy plastic models. It was very deliberate; we chose them because they have wonderful picture diagrams. Then there was a lot of training, so [Brad] would learn to stay on task. We spent so much money on Lego projects, and that naturally flowed into furniture. Any furniture that comes in a box with a diagram, he can put it together. He's quite good at it, but it's a learned skill. We have engineers in the family ... but he's practised since he was three. We bought things for him to practise on ... but eventually, we just didn't need any more furniture![6]

Deb says the most difficult issue is Brad's ritualistic behaviour, but once he's in a new place, a new job, it broadens his social awareness. Brad does not like large crowds, so he goes into other people's homes and builds the furniture there.

At the moment, Made by Brad has not yet been established as a legal business. 'Financially, the business is so small it may never turn a profit,' says Deb.

> You can think of it like a kid with a grass-cutting or snow-shovelling business in their neighbourhood ...We're just being very cautious. We don't want Brad to be overwhelmed or overstimulated; we just want to enhance his social skills and give back to the community. If Brad gets too many demands, there can be behaviours such as noise, and sometimes – very rarely – aggressive behaviour, though he'll immediately apologise ... The clients are wonderful, but it has to be Brad-centred. If it isn't, it could be detrimental to him.[7]

Brad does three to four jobs a week and the price is determined by the size of the project and the proximity to his day programme. Brad travels to his jobs with his support worker, and each job usually takes two to three hours.

> We have to be careful not to set a pattern [with jobs] ... that's why it works to go into these different homes and build a variety of projects. We usually do jobs on a first-come, first-served basis, but sometimes that varies. We try to do jobs that are close to the day programme or to our house, and jobs that offer variety. For example, if we have too many desk orders coming in, then we say, OK, this doll's house project takes precedence. We've had amazing customers.

Brad's support worker is paid for by Alberta Province. Brad's own earnings go into his regular savings account. Deb says that the amounts are small, so they are not concerned about the possibility of Brad losing his benefits.

> Right now, [the business] is perfect for Brad. For his entire life, we've always tried to think outside the box, partly out of necessity. We just don't want him – or anyone! – to languish in a group home and do absolutely nothing,

says Deb. 'We don't know where this [business] is going to take Brad; it's solely determined by Brad's needs.'[8]

POETRY IN WOOD, a remarkable charity in Whitechapel, east London, employs people with learning disabilities, some of them non-verbal people (with autism), to make items out of wood that are then sold in local markets or by commission. The local authority, Tower Hamlets, pays towards supported employment in social enterprise. The rest is covered by their sales.

The Poetry in Wood Training Team runs a National Vocational Qualification (NVQ) course accredited by the Open College Network. The skills acquired include the use of woodworking tools, pyrography, machine-working and workshop safety. Each unit passed is awarded a certificate and towards the end of the course, the students are given work experience in Poetry in Wood's social enterprise – a supported employment scheme. The students pay £46 per session from their Personal Budgets for the training.

Figure 6.1 Thomas Robins, happily at work at Poetry in Wood

According to Poetry in Wood's manager, Jackie Remfry, around 75 per cent of the workers are on the autism spectrum and are aged between 19 and 74. Some initially arrive with support workers but this generally lasts no more than six months. For the non-verbal employees, the company has devised its own card system, rather than using PECS (Picture Exchange Communication System).

Because of the widespread problems with executive dysfunction, the five staff members ensure that the days are highly structured, Remfry told me.[9] The employees sell the products they make at markets and city farms and also design and create art installations for public and private companies. They are paid the London Living Wage of £9.70 per hour.

For the training course, students work on their own products. When they move to work experience in the social enterprise, they work as a group. 'Some of them do not like this way of working, because it entails group participation,' says Remfry.[10]

When I asked her what happened when the workers left, Remfry replied: 'They don't leave. Why should they move anywhere?'[11]

BRITTANY KARPIN, 21, has autism and is non-verbal, but happily volunteers two days a week as a cook at Our Kitchen Hand, launched in Sydney by the community organisation, Jewish Care, and the Australian Government. Sydney-born Brittany has been involved with the project since leaving school three years ago.

Her father, Rick, says:

> Brittany's always had a huge interest in the kitchen environment, and her skills are improving all the time ... even when she isn't participating productively in the preparation of food, she loves observing and feeling a part of the operation.[12]

Rick says that her work in the kitchen gives Brittany a sense of purpose and greater confidence: 'Everyone from the head chef down to the last member of staff all make her feel so welcome and a part of the team, and that gives Brittany a great deal of satisfaction.'[13]

Jobs for verbal learners – and those interested in words

- **Public speaking**
- **Acting**
- **The legal profession**

Many people with autism do not enjoy talking about their condition in public. However, some do and have even turned it into a profession. In fact, some professions which involve learning a 'script' are well-suited to people on the spectrum. Film stars like Sir Anthony Hopkins, Dan Aykroyd and Paddy Considine have been diagnosed with Asperger's syndrome (and claim their condition has been an asset – Aykroyd says that one of his symptoms was an obsession with ghosts and law enforcement: 'I carry around a police badge with me. I became obsessed by Hans Holzer, the greatest ghost hunter ever. That's when the idea of my film *Ghostbusters* was born.'[14]). But I am not referring exclusively to cinema or theatre acting here. In their 2015 study, Tiffany Johnson and Aparna Johnson, of Pennsylvania State University cited the case of an autistic tour guide who expressed enormous enjoyment

> just because you literally are reciting the script ... I got to do all this research and then incorporate it in and it was like putting on a little show. Then we get paid, but we'd also get tips from people instead. So that was a lot of fun and I actually got promoted to be assistant manager while I was working, which was awesome for me because I am just out of college.[15]

❖ CASE STUDIES

- ROS BLACKBURN
- DEAN BEADLE

ROS BLACKBURN is a remarkable example of a woman with autism who insists she is disabled – at 41, she is still in nappies, cannot be left unsupervised, cannot cross the road by herself, can't cook or care for herself at all and cannot read – and yet has carved out an international career as a highly articulate and illuminating, as well as entertaining, speaker. The actress, Sigourney Weaver, even based her depiction of an autistic woman in the 2006 film, *Snow Cake*, on Ros.

At 18 months old, Ros was diagnosed as severely autistic but with average intellectual ability. Today, she lectures all over the world about her condition. She told me that her parents never allowed her to 'get away' with being autistic:

> They had a problem in accepting the diagnosis. But they realised the real world was not going to accommodate me and my autism. It is not average to have autism, and I was the one who was going to have to fit in ... My parents set about teaching me – or in the end, training me, modifying me, programming me – to manage in the real world. It was the only way. Reality does not change because autism comes along.[16]

Ros says she feels totally disabled by her autism:

> I might as well be paralysed from the neck down, and have no one to push the wheelchair, because of my autism. I do not have the social ammunition, the flexible thinking, to be able to go out and handle things.[17]

She adds that she does not want friends:

> They talk about autistic people being 'trapped' in their own world. I'm not trapped at all – I choose to be in there … It's so safe, cushy, secure and gorgeous in there. Why leave the home when there's a hurricane blowing outside? The things that motivate me to leave the house are earning a living, so that I can pay for the house, and going trampolining and ice-skating.[18]

DEAN BEADLE was diagnosed with Asperger's syndrome at the age of nine. Having spoken at a few small local events about his experiences, at 16 he was asked to speak in a workshop at a National Autistic Society Conference in 2005, which was being headlined by Temple Grandin. That marked the beginnings of his highly successful career as a public speaker and since then, he has been presenting nationally for 10 years and around the world for three.

'Autism has made my job possible,' Dean told me.

> I have a fast processing speed. The only time I can focus on just one thing is when I am lecturing. When I see an audience, I draw a box around them and myself and I can control everything for an hour. I feel that the box around the audience is a vehicle that I am steering. I love the challenge and I love being in control.[19]

That hour is one of structured social contact – even in the question-and-answer session afterwards. He is obsessive about his delivery – especially comic timing.

> It's a science. I used to watch a lot of TV sit-coms and stand-up comedians in my childhood. I knew all about the pauses. And I have acquired an instinct for what will make audiences laugh. But at the same time, there will always be a serious point attached to a funny anecdote. All my talks include tons of teaching.[20]

Dean has also worked as a freelance journalist. He has written on music, physical fitness and done book reviews for his local newspaper, *Greenwich Times*. He also edited the NAS's e-journal, *Autism in Practice*, for 18 months. But he stopped working in journalism,

> because the next step would have been tabloid news journalism, and this was too high a price to pay. My idea of hell would be to work in a newsroom - that highly pressurised environment doesn't appeal. I've never regretted that decision. I also believe in right and wrong, which is not necessarily part of news ethics.

As for writing a book, 'I'm not very good at conforming to what other people think will sell.'[21]

Figure 6.2 Dean Beadle
Source: Oli Rudkin, Oli Rudkin Photography

Dean says that, although DSM-5 removed Asperger's syndrome as a separate category in 2013,

> I like my Asperger's label – it's my identity, it's how I have always identified myself. I have always used all of the terms, though: Asperger's, autistic, on the spectrum. And I will continue doing so, regardless of DSM-5 changes. I reserve the right to decide how I identify myself.

He often shares with audiences his personal experiences of anxiety:

> One of my anxieties was a fear I would bang my head and have a haemorrhage. Once a year, I have a cancer scare. Fear about ill-health has been a recurring theme in my anxiety, amongst many others. The older I get, the less social energy I have. I travel a lot, so I need more time on my own. I couldn't be around people all the time. I'm lucky to

work as a freelancer, which allows me to switch off. Being around people exhausts me.[22]

He adds:

Autistic people are changing the system from the inside by doing unexpected things. What we must avoid is offering them token jobs or quotas – because this is even more isolating. Not everyone with autism spectrum disorder likes data entry. Employing autistic people is not an act of charity. It benefits the company. I recently spoke to Sony film staff as part of Inclusion Week and urged them to engage with new types of brain. Different brains offer different ideas and different skills. It's time employers embraced that and realise they are missing a wealth of talent if they overlook autistic people. Autistic people don't succeed despite our autism; we succeed *because* of it.[23]

Anxiety is so prevalent in autism that some have come to consider it as a virtually automatic 'co-morbidity'. But how does it actually manifest itself? Here's how Dean poignantly described his feelings:

Anxiety isn't just pacing and sweating.
Sometimes it's an endless list of rituals which invade your day
Checking every plug socket is off once, twice, a hundred times.
A pervasive fear of unknown and uncertain threat
Anxiety isn't just pacing and sweating
Sometimes it's ignoring the phone and cutting yourself off from the world
Leaving groceries if the supermarket fridge door has been left ajar
Smothering yourself in anti-bacterial gel and hoping not to be touched
Anxiety isn't just pacing and sweating
Sometimes it's lying in the bath for ninety minutes because returning to the day is
    too much
Logistics seeming like mini-Everests between you and getting on
Putting off the smallest tasks until tomorrow
Anxiety isn't just pacing and sweating
Sometimes it's permanently being in the line of fire
A courtroom where you're the judge and jury and still get sentenced
Constant questions – did I say the right thing, do the right thing, was I wrong?
Anxiety isn't just pacing and sweating
It's that and so much more.[24]

Acting

The theatre is attracting increasing numbers of people on the autism spectrum. This may be because, to a certain extent, it is a 'rule-based' profession with a structure, often with a script and yet, in a strange sense it reflects the kind of peculiar challenges autistic individuals face in their day-to-day life. As one autistic actress, Stephanie Dawson, put it:

> It's trying to get out of your sense of something, and get into another person. It's hard to empathise with another character, and imagine how they're feeling, when you've got all these feelings trapped inside that you've got no way of expressing. But acting is a great way of expressing those feelings without having to talk to someone. And getting the feelings of another character is really hard, but because you're pretending to be someone else you can think: 'I don't have to be an autistic person. I can be anyone. I can step out of myself for a moment and be someone else.' And that's a great feeling![25]

Despite the two very uplifting case studies below, it should be emphasised that acting is by no means a problem-free occupation. Take the example of one woman with Asperger's syndrome, identified only as C., who was interviewed by Sarah Bargiela.[26] C. said:

> For quite a while, I really wanted to act. Since I act every day just to get by, it's one of the few things that felt really natural to me, and I even went as far as getting an agent briefly. But intense passion means that when you realise you're never going to be the best (I'm never going to be leading lady material – not tall/skinny/blonde enough for that), it hit me hard. Realising ... that the unpredictability of it as a career might not suit me was hard to swallow. Also, given most auditions are 'improv', which I suck at (I can run circles around a script, but without a script, I'm lost), it just seemed unfeasible ... When you love things so intensely, it can be hard to accept you'll never be world-class at them. It's expensive, too, because I don't learn well in groups, so I often have to book private lessons if I want to learn something, which is always at a premium.[27]

❖ CASE STUDIES

- JULIUS ROBERTSON
- CIAN BINCHY

JULIUS (JULES) ROBERTSON, the son of the Australian novelist, Kathy Lette, and the human rights barrister, Geoffrey Robertson, has Asperger's syndrome. At school, Jules had an encylopaedic knowledge of tennis, the Beatles and Shakespeare (he could quote most of *Hamlet* by heart). But he was bullied at school, which he called his 'Guantánamo Bay'. He was mugged at knifepoint at the age of 14. Yet he was brilliant. He would ask his mother inspired questions, such as: 'Why is there no other word for synonym?'

After he left school, Jules was rejected by one employer after another because he was 'different'. As Kathy herself says,

> these daily rejections are why it's vital to tell your special needs child that he really is special. There's no owner's manual for parents of autistic

Figure 6.3 Jules Robertson, star of the BBC medical drama, *Holby City*, pictured here with his proud mother, Kathy Lette
Source: Dave Poole

kids, but it's imperative to find what they're good at. It doesn't matter if it's moth wing fluctuations, igneous rock formations or Tibetan nose fluting – because you never know what their obsession could lead to. My own son wanted to study acting. I was dubious. How could anyone with autism empathise with a character's complex emotional nuances?[28]

Reluctantly, Kathy enrolled Jules in an acting course run by the remarkable London-based organisation, Access All Areas.

Amazingly, to my eyes, he excelled in class productions, but I suspected I was blinded by my Mum goggles. Yet soon afterwards, he was cast in two short films and won an acting award. He then went for an audition for a major BBC medical drama called *Holby City* – and secured the part. Jules has been a semi-regular since October .... He gets stopped for autographs and has a fan page. My main hope is that Jules' success will encourage other employers to think outside the neurotypical box and hire the 'differently abled'. We should stop forcing autistic people to act normal and help them to become their best autistic selves by focusing on what they can do, instead of what they can't.[29]

Kathy says she believes one of the reasons so few people with autism remain in full-time employment is their honesty. When she introduced Jules to the former British Prime Minister, Tony Blair, Jules declared: 'So *you're* the one my mother calls Tony Blah-Blah-Blah.'[30]

Jules told me that his first audition with Access All Areas was very daunting, although he passed with flying colours. His first role was as an extra on a Harry Potter film. He names the late Alan Rickman as an inspiration. Before his death in January 2016, Rickman emailed Jules to say 'Bravo'.[31]

'When I found out I'd got the part in *Holby City*, I had mixed emotions,' Jules recalls.

> I was excited but also nervous. I was walking into something completely new. But the cast were all so supportive and, as the months went by, I became comfortable. I think I've come a long way now, even though I have to leave home at 6.30 in the morning![32]

Jules adds the hopes he is seen as a role model. What frustrates Jules is the fact that more people with autism are not given acting roles in film, TV and theatre.

> I was watching all these films that had a character with autism and it was so often played by a neurotypical person. The directors can't be bothered to find the autistic talent. They're too dismissive. Why don't directors and producers do more research? There are people out there with the condition who can play these parts. Directors usually just get Dustin Hoffman to pretend to be the *Rain Man*.[33]

What does he consider his strengths in the workplace? 'I know what it's like to have autism from the inside. It comes automatically. People who are not on the spectrum have to guess.' And the challenges? 'I get anxious predicting the future. Even on the set, with a script. I like a fast director.'[34]

In the end, though, Jules is now happy in his own skin: 'I'm very proud to be Jules Robertson. I don't need to be anyone else.'[35]

CIAN BINCHY, now 25, told me that Access All Areas had 'saved my life' by finding him an outlet.

> If it wasn't for them, I wouldn't have much now. I'd still be in the benefits ghetto. They're a tiny little charity and they're paying me. They paid me

Figure 6.4 Cian Binchy, who was a consultant on the National Theatre's production of *The Curious Incident of the Dog in the Night-Time* and now stars in his one-man stage show, *The Misfit Analysis*
Source: Michael Wharley

before they had much money. They've gone out of their way to help people in my position.[36]

After working as an autism consultant on the National Theatre's *The Curious Incident of the Dog in the Night-Time*, Cian trained with Access All Areas, an award-winning theatre company that supports adults with learning disabilities to work in the arts, and runs the country's only professional training programme for the creative arts for people with learning disabilities.

Patrick Collier of Access All Areas said: 'It's not about helping someone with autism or Down's syndrome play Hamlet, although if they want to that's fantastic – it's about finding their own voice and to have that heard.'[37]

Like Jules Robertson, Cian was bullied at school – he was overweight and had a lisp. He stresses that Asperger's syndrome is by no means a mild form of autism: 'I get depressed. I can find change a bit daunting, although I don't need routine as much as I did.' At the same time, he adds, 'there is nothing wrong with being autistic as long as society shows us respect and knowledge. But even the experts can get carried away.'[38]

Cian graduated with a diploma in performance from the Royal Central School of Speech and Drama in London in 2014. The school, with the help of the Hackney-based Access All Areas, runs a course especially created for actors with disabilities. His one-man stage show, *The Misfit Analysis*, which he has put on around the UK, including at the Edinburgh Fringe, reflects his way of playing with my disability [and] also explaining how I feel about people and society getting the wrong end of the stick about autism and thinking they know it all when they don't. I want to emphasise the positives and also the multi-dimensional nature of autism. In fact, people should be talking about the 'autisms'.[39]

Cian says that employers in general are getting better about taking on people on the autism spectrum – 'slowly but not surely'. He entirely agrees with Jules Robertson that it would be far more authentic to have a person on the autism spectrum playing the part of an autistic individual:

I am somebody who knows how it feels to have autism. And when you see me performing, what you see is pretty much real and I am somebody who is actually going through a struggle, although I hate to call it that.

Though some celebrities, including actress Daryl Hannah, have spoken about their autism, the findings – published in the *Journal of Autism and Developmental Disorders* – should act as a wake-up call to the creative industries, said actor Cian Binchy, who performed his much-praised show *The Misfit Analysis* at the Edinburgh Festival in 2015.

There just aren't any people with learning disabilities – in this field I'm the only one. It's because people with learning disabilities may need a bit of extra support, and a lot of theatre companies and performers can't be bothered – it's too challenging for them.

It's time people with autism and other learning difficulties are seen as people first. I want to educate people without learning disabilities that I'm not all that different from them, and I want people who do have learning disabilities to feel better about themselves by showing my problems. They are not alone.[40]

The legal profession

The law appears to be an increasingly attractive profession for people on the autism spectrum. Partly, this is due to the fact that it is a rule-based occupation. It is also largely governed by logic, rather than emotions.

❖ CASE STUDY

- JONATHAN ANDREWS

JONATHAN ANDREWS was once advised to hide his autism from prospective employers. Instead, he is making his name by doing just the opposite. 'I saw it [being autistic] as an opportunity, not a weakness,' says Andrews, who was named campaigner of the year at the European Diversity Awards in 2016.[41] He started work as a trainee solicitor at one of Britain's leading law firms, Reed Smith, in August 2017:

> I wanted to work somewhere that wouldn't see the word 'autism' on an application and think: 'This is terrible.' The ones [prospective employers] that took it in their stride were the best workplace environments, rather than places that talk about it [autism] all the time, because they think you're this strange, exotic creature.[42]

Growing up, Andrews was an avid reader and writer but 'not interested in the same things as my peer group,' he recalls. His younger brother defended him from verbal abuse at school. 'It was words like "retard" ... I developed a thick skin, people used to tease but I felt it was best not to focus on them.'[43]

Andrews' anxiety made him a quiet teenager but 'just because you don't speak doesn't mean you don't have anything to say'. His bid to improve his confidence set him on the campaign path as he forced himself to speak up about autism.

> I wanted to achieve things like going to university and into law, and I knew someone wouldn't take you on just because you're nice – it's competitive – so I exposed myself to those [social] situations ... learning how people expect you to talk to them.[44]

Jonathan's first job was as a volunteer showing tourists round a Roman site in his home town at the age of 18. He did not mind working for free, at first, because it helped him to acquire skills. He was paid after the first year. He went on to study English at King's College, London. He says he has always enjoyed words. But he also found the law appealing: 'Lawyers interpret words,' Jonathan told me. 'A real focus on the precision of language is invaluable as a lawyer.'[45]

After securing four competitive vacation schemes (legal internships) in 2015, just after completing his English degree, Jonathan was offered a contract by Reed Smith as trainee solicitor. He then undertook a law degree (LLB) and MA at Brierley Price Prior (BPP), juggling the latter alongside an intense, bespoke year-long leadership course at the University of Cambridge as a Queen's Young Leader, joining the firm as a trainee solicitor in August 2017.

> I consider autism spectrum disorder an integral part of my identity and Reed Smith were the firm I felt best understood and respected this. I did not need physical adjustments throughout the process, but the freedom to discuss my work around autism and my personal perspective allowed me to shine at the interview.[46]

Once a month, Jonathan sits on the Westminster Commissions Board on Autism in the House of Commons in London, along with a cross-party group of MPs and authorities on autism. Andrews is a member of the first parliamentary commission on autism, and has advised the government on its green paper, covering work, health and employment, which proposes to help at least 1 million disabled people into work and to consult on overhauling the notorious work capability assessment. He is a board member at Ambitious about Autism, the national charity for children and young people with autism, as well as a board member of Stonewall, the largest LGBT equality organisation in Europe, and sits on the Law Society's Equality Board, where he is committed to ensuring autistic representation. And he has led the Commonwealth's 2016–2018 disability rights campaign, 'I Am Able', creating a toolkit which has been translated into several languages, as well as presenting to the Council of Europe and OECD on the importance of employing autistic people.

Andrews believes his autism means he possesses a number of personality characteristics law firms seek out in their trainees. These include honesty, punctuality, reliability, loyalty and attention to detail. He notes that several lawyers have also commented on his skills in marketing and PR – not something which is stereotypically associated with the spectrum but something he believes his autism has helped to hone, as it has given him the ability really to focus on what to say, and how to say it, in professional situations.[47] Moreover, he adds, Reed Smith 'is so open to people who are different'.[48]

He also finds time to indulge his love of words through his own poetry. In fact, he has also written verse, from a young boy, but when he left school he began to explore the possibilities of breaking and bending rules pertaining to metre and rhyme. He was taught poetry at King's College London by the celebrated poet, Ruth Padel. Today, his poems are published in King's College's *English Journal*. He is the Burgess Autistic Trust's resident poet and gives poetry workshops at special schools. In 2014, he won an international arts and poetry competition with a poem called 'Creativity' aimed at dispelling the common myth that people with autism are not creative, the misconception that everyone with autism is (in the words of the poem) a 'quaint, programmed husk who cannot think outside a rigid box … to form afresh new truths from old malignant lies'.[49]

Jobs for auditory learners

Auditory learners prefer to hear information. There are a considerable number of talented musicians on the autism spectrum. The well-known conductor, John Lubbock, of Music for Autism, has many accounts of unexpected positive relational and behavioural responses from children with autism when exposed to live music. (Lubbock's own son, Alexander, is autistic.) Professor Adam Ockelford, of Roehampton University in London, develops the gifts of exceptionally talented children with severe autism – including the extraordinary blind jazz pianist, Derek Paravicini, who has serious learning difficulties but is capable of enormously impressive improvisations at the keyboard – defying the long-held myth that autism and creativity cannot go hand-in-hand.

Not long ago, the Scottish singer, Susan Boyle, who was a runner-up in the 2009 television show, *Britain's Got Talent*, revealed she had Asperger's syndrome. Many people with autism have perfect pitch – and even more intriguingly, many people with perfect pitch have been found to have autistic traits. In some instances, music can be used to help young adults with autism on the difficult path of transition from school into the community.

Derek Paravicini's teacher, mentor and coach, Adam Ockelford, told me:

> In terms of employability, I think we need to distinguish between what can broadly be termed the 'Asperger's' group and the 'classic autism' group. Some members of the former have long found employment in the music profession. The latter (apart from Derek) have never done, as far as I'm aware. This is because the capacity to sing or play is only a part of the skill set required of a professional musician – not least the willingness to play whatever other people want, whenever they want it! A large part of my work with Derek was on these 'extra-musical' elements, which I realised early on would be needed for him to maximise his potential and be free to enjoy his abilities (and for others to enjoy them).[50]

Despite what Ockelford says, there seems to be no reason why even a severely autistic person cannot make a living as a musician. At birth, Tony DeBlois weighed less than two pounds, became blind within days and was later diagnosed as autistic, but he now plays 20 instruments and knows more than 8,000 songs. 'I feel special when I play this kind of music. I sort of blossom,' he said. Rabia Aytek, a Turkish girl with autism, not only sings but plays 20 instruments, including the piano, violin, cello, *kanun*, *baglama* and guitar. She was the first autistic child to be accepted into the Istanbul State Music Conservatory and the Department of Music at Mimar Sinan Fine Arts University with distinction. She has performed in numerous concerts and has taught music to students with disabilities, whom she affectionately refers to as her 'brothers and sisters' at the private Ayça Special Education School. Her dream is to open a music school: 'I want to give performances in different concerts. I will fight for other people with autism from now on; not for myself. I am their voice and I am proud of it. They should not fall into despair.'[51]

❖ CASE STUDIES

- SOPHIA GRECH
- LAUREN LOVEJOY
- DEAN RODNEY
- REX LEWIS-CLACK

SOPHIA GRECH, by her own account, spent her childhood staring into space. At her first school, in Portsmouth, she was badly bullied, spat at and punched. Her head teacher told her: 'I'm sorry but I can't expel everyone who bullies you. Perhaps you should move to a smaller school.' When the family moved to Weymouth in Dorset, her father did indeed put her in a private girls' school. Today, she is an acclaimed classical singer, much in demand all over the world.

> I started singing at 14. I was a great mimic and my parents paid me to have singing lessons. At 14, I was too young to be taken on by the Royal

Figure 6.5 Sophia Grech in full voice

College of Music [in London]. I was invited to sing at the Royal College of Music, where the head of singing, Margaret Cable, said to me: 'Would you like to be an opera singer? If so, I would like to start teaching you now.' I was too young to go there full time, so I went on Saturdays to have singing lessons with her. I couldn't even read music at the time. In fact, when I was asked what I knew about music, I said there was a man called Beethoven and piano keys are black and white.[52]

Music then became Sophia's life. There were many hurdles to overcome, however. When she turned 18, Margaret Cable told her: 'You'd be better off going to university than becoming a full-time student here. It's nothing to do with your singing. But the price is too high,' That comment hurt so much that Sophia went to bed for three days with depression. 'Cable was wrong, I didn't struggle at all at the RCM. She underestimated me. She didn't know I had autism.'[53]

Sophia graduated from the RCM in 1995 with the highest results in her year. She sometimes wondered whether she would have had such a successful career if she had been diagnosed with autism earlier.

> I have a pianist friend who was diagnosed at 17. He made allowances and other people did, too. He did not go to one of the royal colleges but to the Birmingham Conservatory. I'm glad I went to the Royal College of Music. It is so small – there were only 23 students in my year. All the students were talented and eccentric, so my autism got lost. Whereas the Birmingham Conservatory is larger and unusual behaviour gets noticed more easily.[54]

She was not diagnosed with Asperger's syndrome until the age of 45, in 2015. It came as a great relief, explaining why she felt so different. She is convinced that autism has played a positive role in her career:

> We become obsessed with things and this obsession helps us become brilliant at what we do. I would sit for hours with a pretend cello to make sure my voice sounded like an instrument. I see and feel things that other singers do not. I can hear when one of the instruments in the orchestra misses a note.[55]

Sophia said: 'I find most of the repertoire plain sailing. But opera productions can be difficult, because there are so many people involved and the stage directions can be confusing.' As a result, there are a couple of roles she tries to avoid these days.

> It's not musical. I find the instructions – stage left – difficult, and remembering what I need to be doing. I once played Mercedes in Bizet's *Carmen* and there is a card-playing scene near the beginning. The director was obsessed with my picking up the queen of hearts, even though the audience couldn't tell one card from another. She was a real bitch![56]

Sometimes, she covers her hotel walls with coloured paper to map out a particular scene. Of course, for many years, the conductor and her fellow musicians had no idea she had autism. When she finally did decide to disclose, 'some understand and others are confused. The younger generation seem to find it easier to grasp.'[57]

Sophia emphasised that her secure home life while growing up was a saviour: 'My two sisters are my best friends.' And today, her partner, Andy, is a police officer. 'He is very patient. I used to be in an abusive relationship, but I didn't understand this at the time. I'm much safer living with a policeman!'[58]

In 2016, she was invited to open the eleventh Autism Europe international conference in Edinburgh. She wants to encourage young people 'to follow your special interest and make it your goal in life – whatever that interest is'. Autism is not a negative, she says; it is people's lack of understanding and the general lack of support which makes its impact so potentially damaging.[59] As she told Autism Wessex:

> It is time we lessen the pressure on those with autism having to understand the world around them, because the world around them will finally take it upon itself to understand and accept autism. I am determined to be a part of that positive change for the next generation.[60]

LAUREN LOVEJOY, a singer and model with Asperger's syndrome, starred in the 2014 television talent show, *The X Factor*. Lauren, 24, faced daily taunts when she was a teenager that she was 'ugly and weird' – and was even pushed to suicidal thoughts – but beat the bullies by being crowned Miss Congeniality and Miss Not In Vain at the Miss Universe Great Britain Final in July 2014. She went on to become one of 38 women competing to become the Great Britain representative for the Miss Universe title.

Lauren says:

> I never thought I'd make it – there was a point when I believed every bad word the bullies threw at me. They broke my nose and shattered my confidence. In my lowest moments I thought I wanted to end my life. The new opportunities I was given through Miss Universe have opened my eyes – now I feel fantastic.[61]

She adds:

> When I'm on stage, it's like I take on a different role and I am this confident and sassy young woman. I love to joke and laugh and I wanted that side of me to show. So when I was selected, I really felt a sense of achievement that they picked me because they must have really liked me.[62]

Lauren says she is very sensitive to sound and some smells. 'I can take things that people say the wrong way, too, and that can make me very distressed.' But she finds the unstructured nature of modelling and singing a creative release from her symptoms of anxiety and stress.[63]

DEAN RODNEY is a 28-year-old man with autism. While still a teenager, he started coming to the remarkable east London organisation, Heart n Soul – which celebrated its thirtieth birthday in 2017. Dean founded the pop group, The Fish Police, in 2006. (Intriguingly, Dean claimed the name was his own invention: in fact, it comes from an old Hanna Barbera cartoon. So much for yet another fallacy associated with autism – that people on the spectrum are incapable of even a smidgen of deception!) According to Heart n Soul's co-founder, Mark Williams, Dean was into Daft Punk and also into Japanese culture – which made his first songs very different from other music at the time.[64]

In 2012, the London Olympics Committee commissioned Dean and Charles Stuart (Grace Jones' manager) to come up with 23 snippets of digital music which were shared across seven countries; Japan, China, Germany, Croatia, South Africa, Brazil and the United Kingdom. Dean travelled to all seven nations. 'Each track he came up with was a different part of Dean's universe,' said Williams.[65]

There was a time when REX LEWIS-CLACK could not even stand the sound of Christmas presents being unwrapped. One day, his father bought him a toy piano and Rex taught himself to play music. It turned out that, like many people on the autism spectrum, Rex had perfect pitch. Today, he tours the world playing piano and raising funds for charity.

Rex was born blind, with brain damage so severe it looked as though he would never walk, talk, or do much of anything. He was diagnosed with autism as a toddler, and then labelled a musical genius by the age of seven, when musicologists became astounded by Rex's ability to play back complex piano pieces he had heard only once, and then transpose them into other keys or improvise off themes with little effort. Considered a prodigious musical savant, Rex ranks as one of fewer than 50 people throughout history to combine blindness, intellectual disability and prodigious musical ability.

At seven, his abilities (coupled with disability) came to the attention of CBS's *60 Minutes*, who took the unprecedented decision to follow his life and development. *60 Minutes* aired Rex's first profile in 2003 called *Musically Speaking*, which was followed by two subsequent profiles, each entitled *Rex*, the first in 2005, and then a second in 2008 (winner of the 2008 Edward R. Murrow Award as Best Feature in a news magazine). In 2006, he was the winner of the 'Winspiration Award' in Germany. Rex was also featured alongside Derek Paravicini in the highly acclaimed 2006 British production, *The Musical Genius* (in conjunction with Discovery Health), for the series *Extraordinary People*.

In 2011, Rex was a scholarship recipient to attend two prestigious European piano academies, the International Piano Academy in Freiburg, Germany, and the Mozarteum in Salzburg, Austria, where he studied alongside gifted piano students from all over the world.

Jobs for visual learners

Visual learners prefer to see information presented in words, diagrams or pictures. Many activities in the workplace involve communication – but a surprising degree of communication is non-verbal. Some individuals with ASD have become successful and creative commercial artists, graphic designers, web designers (combining their visual talents with IT skills), cartoonists and photographers.

There are remarkable cases of hugely talented photographers with autism, like Luke Jackson; the TV wildlife presenter, Chris Packham, and Larry Arnold: their ability to focus on a small detail (the local processing bias which is known to be a feature of so many individuals with ASD) produces some of the most stunning pictures of the natural world. In April 2017, the Macrobert Arts Centre at the University of Stirling in Scotland staged an exhibition entitled 'Too Much Information: What autistic photographers want you to understand about autism.' The exhibition featured a series of 40 images created by a group of autistic individuals as they learned about photography. The budding photographers were mentored for six months by Graham Miller, an experienced documentary photographer and member of international photography. He said: 'Documentary photography is one of the most challenging of disciplines and our photographers have used it to communicate aspects of living with autism. The results are pure and beautiful. This important exhibition will challenge thinking.'[66]

One of the best-known examples is the remarkable British artist, Stephen Wiltshire. Much further afield, the Hollywood Foreign Press Association (HFPA) is providing funds for a new animation studio at Exceptional Minds, a working studio staffed by young visual artists on the autism spectrum.

The new studio, which opened in 2016, includes up to 16 work stations for producing professional animations for the entertainment industry. 'We are very fortunate to have the support of an amazing industry that has given these unique individuals the opportunity to become independent, productive adults' says Ernie Merlán, executive director of Exceptional Minds.[67]

❖ CASE STUDIES

- JON ADAMS
- STEPHEN WILTSHIRE
- NICOLA FRY
- LARRY ARNOLD
- SAMANTHA KASPAR

JON ADAMS, the artist, musician and writer with Asperger's syndrome, dyslexia and synaesthesia, says that, as a child, his interest in geology 'kept me going when I was being bullied. I could use my imagination. I was picking up fossils from the age of eight. Every stone has a personality: I can touch, hear and taste landscapes,' he told me.[68]

Jon was diagnosed with Asperger's 'late in life' – at the age of 52.

> Looking back, it's obvious, but I'm not surprised it was missed (alongside my dyslexia), as I'd finished school and was mostly through university when Lorna Wing first mentioned Asperger's syndrome [in 1981] ... I don't think there has been a day where creativity hasn't been the major part of my life. As a child, I was always assembling, collecting and drawing – never letting go of those desires or a pencil ever since. At six years old, when asked what I wanted, I said: 'to be an artist'. It seemed the most honest, logical and heartfelt answer I could give.[69]

He says he was hugely affected by an incident at primary school, when a teacher tore up his picture in front of the class just because he misspelt

Figure 6.6 Jon Adams
Source: Jason Baker

his name. But he found a passion – for geology. 'Stones have always been more alive to me than people,' he told me. 'Each stone has a personality. And because of my synaesthesia, I can touch, hear and taste landscapes.'[70]

Jon went on to study geology at King's College, London. 'I did not start writing creatively until the age of 39. Before and during my degree, I volunteered to work in a young people's camp in Devon.' After he graduated, he was offered a bizarre choice of work – either as a geologist on an oil rig in the North Sea or as a security guard at an art gallery. He chose the job at a major art gallery in London but lasted just a week. 'I asked to leave and move to another gallery, because I did not like the attendants: they were failed artists themselves. It was partly my fault, perhaps, because I was not very social.'[71]

Then he took a job working in security at another gallery. This time, after making friends, he lasted a year, always working day shifts: 'Sometimes, we didn't see sunlight all day. I didn't mind – I was self-contained.'[72]

He began drawing again at around 21 years of age. He showed his work to friends and colleagues and a couple of them bought paintings. His father ran a printing company and took him on, paying him to work in the dark room. Meanwhile, Jon began making prints and hand-colouring them.

> I sold a lot of prints in the 1980s and started getting commissions. Then Shell International offered me a job as an artist to do geological illustrations for promotional books. In the interview, they asked me to do a 3D seismic reflection. My dyslexia helped me in this. I had finally found a niche and I started working freelance for Shell International, doing things like drawing a huge aerial view of an oil refinery in Rotterdam, as detail was key.[73]

Jon says that social issues continued to be a problem.

> They got in the way. Most of life was a desert – the commissions were the oases. But I learned from experience to be friendly and affable, as well as punctual. We on the spectrum are more skilled in observing neurotypicals than the reverse. But although your skills in certain areas improve, your social skills never become innate.[74]

Jon's first marriage lasted about six years and he had three children.

> My son was diagnosed as dyslexic and I suspect that my first daughter may be Asperger's, too. That first marriage unfortunately broke up. I had to hold down a job while going to court with my ex-wife for custody of the children. I was being tested to illustrate a *Star Wars* book, but that opportunity fell by the wayside.[75]

He was delighted when he himself received a diagnosis of dyslexia in 1999

> because I could clear the label 'stupid' off my forehead. All my life, I'd been told I was hopeless. I started collaborating with the British Dyslexia Association and also writing poems (which was like drawing landscapes). One of the poems won a BDA competition.[76]

In 2001, the Japan Broadcasting Company (NHK) sponsored a major travelling international exhibition of the arts called 'One Heart, One World' – a compilation of 100 poems and 100 works of art by disabled artists in six countries. Jon contributed a poem rather than an artwork which was included. Britain's then Poet Laureate, Andrew Motion, who was one of the judges, told him: 'Never stop writing'.

At around the age of 40, Jon again became self-employed. 'The job centre wanted to send me on a traffic warden course. Idiots! I couldn't even read a number plate!'[77]

While he was doing a course on filmmaking for the unemployed, he was talent-spotted and hired to teach music, technology for a provider and memory techniques to people with dyslexia at The Foyer Centre in Portsmouth. 'People are always told what they can't do, not what they can. I helped everyone I worked with on their memory jobs, and became very popular.'[78]

It was at this point that people at The Foyer suggested Jon could be autistic, but although he agreed this might be possible, he did not seek a diagnosis at the time. Instead, in 2005, he took an unpaid residency opportunity with Artists Access to Art College. At around the same time, he met someone from the Arts Council 'who again recognised something in me that I didn't,' and was encouraged to apply for grant funding to Arts Council England. Two years later, in 2007, a major university appointed Jon as a 'research fellow' working alongside members of a project, working with autistic children. They provided him with an assistant who was also an artist.

> She tried to get my ideas down on paper but also acted as my 'social translator'. Unwittingly, my autism was creating barriers: I was very different. But paradoxically, I was also part of the mainstream. I called myself an outsider artist and had an exhibition of my work put on at the Pallant House Gallery in Chichester. I also applied for, and was given, a position on the Area Council of Arts Council South East, which raised my self-esteem, as we just like to feel useful.[79]

A major upheaval occurred in December 2011, when Jon suffered an allergic reaction to food. It was then that his post-traumatic stress disorder set in. By April 2012, he was becoming progressively unwell but he had lots of work. He was commissioned to produce artwork for the 2012 London Olympics, including a geological mapping project. 'I kept going but in May 2012, a GP officially diagnosed me with post-traumatic stress disorder.' In November 2012, Professor Simon Baron-Cohen in Cambridge suggested that Jon get a diagnosis of Asperger's syndrome in order to obtain a statement to gain further support and the following April, he was indeed diagnosed with Asperger's by a colleague of Baron-Cohen.

Fortunately, a collaboration with the celebrated theatre director, Peter Brook, on a production called *Valley of Astonishment* – a sensory meditation on synaesthesia – brought Jon some respite from other issues he could not control. 'Feeling useful and the sense that I belonged "kept me alive" and gave me hope.'[80]

More recently, the Speaker of the House of Commons, John Bercow (whose own son, Oliver, is autistic), commissioned Jon to lead a digital engagement project for Parliament, called Democracy Street, to celebrate the 800th anniversary of Magna Carta. As an autistic person, Jon prefers digital illustration and image manipulation, because these do not place limitations on his working activities, something which may happen as a consequence of his changing health situation.

'Sometimes, I'm not sure if I'm a scientist who can draw or an artist who likes science, a difference in mind-set only paper thin,' says Jon. Although he has worked as a solitary illustrator for the past 25 years,

> it's only recently I've felt I'm truly fulfilling that childhood wish, in parallel to accepting being with people. I've always been wary of people, their interactions often being confusing and hard to systemise, unlike the natural world processes around me. As an autistic person, I feel people can make or break you – those who 'understand' your different thinking being the most important in your life, providing opportunity and acceptance.

This is especially important in employment, he adds, where 'mistreatment', deliberate or not, adds mental health issues and post-traumatic stress disorder to 'the weight of the rucksack you carry already.'

> Without understanding on the employer's part, all this adds to low self-esteem and becomes a self-imposed barrier, stealing focus away

from what we can do and our talents. From recent experiences, I've unfortunately found that there are no grey areas – we are either enabled or 'left' to struggle. Autism awareness and listening to what we say we need is key.[81]

Jon noted:

In some employment situations, I feel the Autism Act is toothless. We, as autistic people, really need compulsory, statutory reasonable adjustments in the workplace. That is why I would like to see neurodiversity added as a separate category in the arts employment landscape.[82]

Probably the world's most successful artist with autism, STEPHEN WILTSHIRE, a 52-year-old Londoner who could not speak as a child, is now celebrated internationally for his ability to draw and paint detailed cityscapes, sometimes after looking at them only briefly. Stephen can look at a target once and then draw a very accurate and very detailed picture of it from memory. Since 2004, he has drawn London, Berlin, Tokyo, Hong Kong, Rome, Frankfurt and Mexico City on giant panoramic canvasses entirely from memory. His drawings – which also show New York, Paris, Venice, Edinburgh and Amsterdam – sell for thousands of pounds to clients all over the world.

Diagnosed with autism at the age of three, Stephen has a PhD in drawing and printmaking from the City & Guilds of London Art School and was awarded an MBE for his services to the art world in 2006. A year later, I spoke to him for my international autism magazine, *Looking Up*. Perhaps the most surprising thing he told me was that he actually enjoyed earthquakes – even though they destroyed the buildings he loved to draw – because they produced chaos, unusual shapes and formations.[83] (Yet another sign of the surprising creativity of the autistic mind.)

If you watch Stephen at work, he uses headphones while he draws, first in pencil and then going over the sketch in ink. His sister, Annette, says watching him work is like watching fine embroidery – each dart of the pen is a stitch in the intricate tapestry.[84]

At primary school, Stephen's teachers used his interest in drawing as a way of encouraging him to communicate. One teacher, in particular, took him out on drawing excursions and entered his work in competitions. He sold his first picture for £1,500 at the age of seven.

The late author and neurologist, Oliver Sacks, who met Stephen in New York, observed in the *New Yorker* magazine in 1995: 'His limitations, paradoxically, can serve as strengths, too. His vision is valuable, it seems to me, precisely because it conveys a wonderfully direct, un-conceptualised view of the world.'[85]

NICOLA FRY, a talented photographer, was diagnosed with Asperger's syndrome in 2013. She says the diagnosis came as a huge relief:

I had known there was something wrong for so long. I had learnt a little about autism, so I knew that this was what I had, and it was getting someone to listen and understand me. It's always been hard for me because people look at me and think: wow, you look and seem so normal you can't have anything wrong with you, but they really don't know and don't understand what it is like ... So getting my diagnosis made me feel better, because it put a name to my issues and helps me to learn new ways to cope.[86]

Nicola first became interested in photography at the age of around 11 or 12, after she was given a camera for Christmas.

I love to photograph animals and landscapes, which is great because you don't need to interact with other humans for this. [But] I also have a fascination with photographing people, which is weird, because communicating with people is never an easy thing for me. I am not really sure how to explain it, but I think it's because I find most people interesting, confusing and intriguing that I want to photograph them and capture their feeling and emotions because I find them hard to deal with. I think I like to look at the photos and see the feeling and emotions and learn from them. I also love photography because when I have to go to a social event and there is no way out of it, I can hide behind my camera and this acts as a barrier for me so I don't have to interact with people.

She says she especially likes to take pictures of other people on the autism spectrum because their faces

tell so many stories.... People with autism have that amazing expression on their faces and look so innocent ... I also want to raise awareness of autism though photography. They say that images speak louder than words. Just because we have autism does not mean that we are no good in this world.[87]

Nicola faced considerable challenges when she launched into photography as a business venture:

I feel like I can't really do it alone. What I was always looking for was not just help in business and work, but for in life in general, someone there just to give a helping hand when needed. I am sure a lot of other people with autism have an issue with asking for help and accepting it, too. I need a mentor or 'business befriender'. The main difficulty I have is believing in myself, believing that I am good enough to do it. Being a photographer means that you have to interact with the people you work with. I find it hard to say to people what I need them to do and it's hard to give them ideas to pose for a session. For example, if I am doing a session with a new-born baby, I find it hard to suggest ideas for the sitting. I just like to take the photos, I am no good at the rest.[88]

LARRY ARNOLD, a well-known British photographer diagnosed with Asperger's syndrome in 1999, says a lot of time was wasted at Hereward College – a further education college for young people with disabilities and additional needs –

> in something called job search. We were essentially left with a pile of newspapers to sort through and expected to apply for jobs, however unsuitable or unlikely we were to get them, in order to justify our continuing to receive benefits. In fact, I was under more pressure to apply for work than when I was signing on, in that at least I was exempt from applying for unsuitable work which I could not do.[89]

Larry adds:

> There was also the requirement to attend a job club, which was again a bit of a joke: none of the support in form filling, etc. which I would have needed was there in reality and I did no more than was necessary in registering with it but never attending.[90]

Eventually, as an IT expert as well as a passionate photographer, he obtained a work placement negotiated with a charity called Baby Lifeline. His job was to restore a corrupted and under-used donors' database to functioning order.

> I enjoyed this, as it gave me a real sense of doing something useful and this I believe to have been the turning point in the lifting of my depression. I suddenly began to realise I was not depressed and was content with my day. I looked forward to the work and felt satisfied when I had done it.[91]

He was already interested in photography by this time and simultaneously enrolled on a full-time course up at Hereward in TV and Video.

> There was one snag. The benefits system would not allow me to do it while I was still signing for work. This was a real anomaly, as this was a properly structured further education course in real practical skills taught by qualified people, not the ridiculous, put-together courses run by various training companies tendering to the employment department, which were just time fillers, as far as I was concerned. I had got advice that I would have to claim an incapacity benefit in order to continue and that I would need my doctor's support for this ... To my surprise, [the doctor] was sympathetic and signed me off without any trouble.[92]

As well as the TV and video course, Larry completed an A level in Psychology (before embarking on a year-long distance learning course at the University of Birmingham in autism spectrum disorders. He has also taken up painting and is pursuing studies in music technology to enhance his video skills.

When she was growing up, SAMANTHA KASPAR, now aged 20, spent most of her days painting and drawing. She expressed herself – and her autism – through her art, and continues to do so with her creative use of colour.

Samantha is one of five artists with autism commissioned in 2017 by Banana Peel, a slipper brand attached to the Unilab Foundation in the Philippines, to design flip-flops with the theme 'Explore in Colour'.

Michelle Kaspar, Samantha's mother, believes that this opportunity not only showcases her daughter's talent but sends out an important message: despite the challenges of being autistic, in one way or another, people with the condition can become assets to the community.[93]

Jobs for tactile and manual learners

Tactile learners are literally 'hands-on'. Although some people on the spectrum can be physically clumsy, others can show considerable dexterity. I know an electrician with Asperger's syndrome (and he clearly has excellent fine motor skills, otherwise he would be a danger to himself and others!). Creativity in the workplace can find inventive ways of tapping into these skills and enthusiasms. Eighty per cent of one car wash firm, Rising Tide Car Wash, are on the autism spectrum. Talking of cars, if you're American and your luxury vehicle hits mechanical trouble, look no further than John Elder Robison, who not only heads one of the leading car repair companies throughout the entire United States, but writes illuminating books about his own Asperger's syndrome. John puts as much love into fixing a luxury car as the musical instrument manufacturers we feature below show in their own handicraft. There are also many other potential job opportunities for people with autism involving manual work: walking dogs, for example, or gardening. Some people with autism may find the highly structured schedules involved in working in a factory conducive to their needs.

❖ CASE STUDIES

- JAMES MACAULAY
- MAYFIELD LYRES
- ERNIE STAVROSKY
- JAMES TREMBATH
- RISING TIDE
- JOHN ELDER ROBISON

At school, JAMES MACAULAY was locked in a cupboard, called cruel names and victimised by his classmates because of his 'weird' behaviour. Today, aged 19, he works as a Manufacturing Technician for Malvern Instruments in Worcestershire.

James's father, Simon, believes his son's success – which follows 'years of bullying and rejection' – shows that others like him can work. But they can do so only in the right job, and with the right support, he says. 'My son is not high-achieving – he is just in the middle – and he's had to cope with far more in terms of bullying and rejection in his short life than I have ever had to.'[94]

James did not learn to read until he was 12. He was asked to leave his first state primary school in reception because they said they could not cope with him. He also had issues at his second state primary school, so he had to settle on his own in the classroom before the bell rang for the other children. This made him feel so alienated that Simon and his wife, Kate, took him to an independent school. 'He got into a fight on the third afternoon but was given another trial. That changed his life.' Simon recalled.

At the age of 17, James started a college apprenticeship in September 2014. He had commenced day release at Malvern Instruments – a firm which manufactures and supplies laboratory analytical instruments – a year earlier. 'We took the brilliant advice of the woman who runs the special needs department at the school,' said Simon. She recognised that James was not academic and needed to prepare for leaving the protected and supportive school environment. 'It worked incredibly well with four days at school in the sixth form and two half-days at Malvern Instruments, where James was looked after with great kindness.'[95]

The company had a manufacturing system that suited the way James's brain works, including a Standard Operating Procedure document with 80 step-by-step images of the complex manufacturing process. This meant he could complete one stage, before moving on to the next – without having to retain any knowledge from the previous task or initiate steps himself.

Nevertheless, although James was always 'smiling' and '100 per cent focused on the job in hand', according to his father, his autism led to a number of other problems. He took too long on toilet breaks and, because his college's facilities 'languished behind' those at Malvern Instruments, he struggled with his course work. 'Malvern Instruments talked to me about the length of James's toilet breaks – I talked to him, and the issue was quickly resolved without drama,' said Simon.

> He was a 19-year-old boy who needed pulling back into line, that was all.
> The company accepts that he works slightly slower than his colleagues.
> He has other qualities that make him a satisfactory employee, like his
> reliability and his focus on the job.[96]

Malvern Instruments' Operations Manager, Chris Poole, worked closely with Simon and Kate throughout the 18-month course, offering them advice and support. Meanwhile, James's teacher brought an 'incredibly kind' retired engineer into the college as a volunteer so he could support the youngster through his mechanical module. On completion of his apprenticeship, he was given a pay rise by Malvern Instruments. He currently works 30 hours a week for the company as a technician.

Simon believes that if James had failed the course at the college, as easily could have happened, he may never have worked and would have been a huge drain on the state. 'I believe the reason this did not happen for James was down to the kindness and resourcefulness of the heroes of his story. But what happens when there are no heroes? What happens to autistic kids when they're adults?'

Simon urged companies to 'involve parents' and not give up on young autistic employees: 'All autistic children are different and their parents understand them the best,' he said. 'They are also the most motivated to find a solution – to help their child to lead a fulfilling life.'[97]

When asked if he enjoys working at Malvern Instruments, James replied:

> It works for me having a repetitive job because I work in sequences. The people are nice, I'm not big on sociability. If I ask for help, they give it to me without telling me off for not doing it on my own.[98]

He added that the best part of his job is getting lunch – and that he likes his colleagues. 'The closest I have come to being bullied was at the Christmas party when I mentioned about watching *Glee!* [the American musical comedy-drama TV set in a high school].'[99]

The Sheffield-based social enterprise, MAYFIELD LYRES, established by Autism Plus in 2013, employs people on the autism spectrum to manufacture precision-made bell lyres and glockenspiels which are of the highest standard of quality to be found in the UK and overseas. Each instrument is made to order and the company has clients across the globe.

At its base at the Exchange Brewery in Sheffield, a number of service users are currently being trained in aspects of production, marketing, sales and customer service support.

One satisfied customer wrote:

> The Mayfield Bell Lyre has added an entirely new dimension to our Marching Band. The sound it produces is fantastic – utterly crisp, sharp, and arresting, and the mere presence of such a high calibre instrument instantly elevates the status and professionalism of the band. It is something which we quite simply could no longer do without.[100]

ERNIE STAVROSKY works at the C.F. Martin guitar factory in Nazareth, Pennsylvania, in the US. 'I work on the bridge pins, inserting the pearl, sanding and polishing them to make them nice and beautiful. I cut fret wire, I match ribbons,' says Ernie.[101]

His parents are occasionally astonished that he can cope in a factory that can become very noisy at times, with the roar of saws and sanders. Ernie's state-funded job coach, Justin Tresolini, says that the young man's attention to detail has made him a stand-out employee.[102]

JAMES TREMBATH, a 17-year-old autistic man from Treorchy in South Wales, has found his niche: making windows.

James was initially referred to the European Social Fund-financed Real Opportunities project, which is jointly run by Remploy and the National Autistic Society. The project aims to motivate young people with autism and support them into work placements and work. 'James had been on work-based training and a work placement before he came to us,' said Alun Wilkins, a specialist Employment Advisor with Remploy. 'But unfortunately, the placement wasn't a success.'[103]

Wilkins worked with Sadie Middleton, from the NAS, to build James's self-esteem and prepare him for another try at work experience. 'Like many people with ASD, James had limited understanding of how his condition was affecting his life,' said Wilkins. 'One of the first things we did was to arrange development sessions that gave him – and his family – a better understanding of the condition.'[104]

A work placement at a local building products company, Vision Products, quickly followed – and this time it was an overwhelming success. 'Crucially, he continued to receive one-to-one support from Remploy and NAS in the workplace,' says Wilkins. 'He quickly struck up a friendship with his mentor and now he is even planning a night out with colleagues, which is a fantastic achievement for a person with ASD where social interaction is often a major issue.'[105]

James also proved an instant success in his job making windows. 'From day one, he achieved a 0 per cent error rate from quality control,' says Wilkins.

> His work rate increased dramatically and he is now able to produce the same number of windows as his colleagues, with minimal support. In fact, he has adapted so well that he has been offered a one-year paid apprenticeship. He has come on in leaps and bounds in the six months since he was referred to the scheme. It has been a joy working with him and he should be very proud of what he has achieved.[106]

Tom and John D'Eri, the founders of the RISING TIDE car wash company, have built a model in Parkland, South Florida, which relies on a rigid structure, broken down into dozens of discrete actions – 39 on the passenger's side and 46 on the driver's – including vacuuming the floor mats, wiping the door jambs and cleaning the insides of the windows. This carefully designed structure was appealing to the autistic workers and the firm has gone from strength to strength; within a year of opening, it was handling more than 10,000 cars a month.

The D'Eris ran into criticism – and even offensive insults – from those who claimed people with autism should not be segregated for work. But they recognise the diversity of the employment opportunities which match the heterogeneity of the autism spectrum: 'This is not a silver bullet. This style of employment could be a great solution for 30 to 50 per cent of people,' says Tom D'Eri.[107]

One man who works at Rising Tide, Matt Keller, had been bullied from childhood and could not even find a supermarket that would hire him as a bag boy after leaving college, 'When I got this job, I felt so happy. They tell me I'm very close to being a manager. I do so much stuff here. I don't think they would ever fire me. I am always here to help.'[108]

JOHN ELDER ROBISON today is, to a certain extent, to the US luxury car repair industry, what Temple Grandin is to the cattle ranch industry. However, he started his career managing rock bands like Kiss, but this barely brought in an income. By his own account, he would forage for leftovers at Bruno's Pizza in Amherst, Massachusetts.[109]

He began looking for jobs, searching the ads columns under 'Electrical Engineer'. One apparently genuine advertisement read: 'Money problems? Women trouble? Running from the law? You can find a home in the Foreign Legion.' Eventually, he applied to Milton Bradley, a firm of electrical engineers, designing sound effects. This seemed to be a good fit. 'My Aspergian ability to focus and learn fast saved me,' Robison says. 'Between Sunday, when I read the ad, and the interview eight days later, I became a passable expert in digital design.'[110]

At the interview itself, he made it sound as if he designed sound effects in a real lab, rather than on his kitchen table. He was offered the job, which made him feel both proud and scared: 'I had never worked in an organisation before, so I watched carefully to see how it worked and where I fit in.'[111]

The job entailed designing the first talking toys. Harking back wittily to his time on the road with a rock band, Robison said:

> I had been terribly afraid of what I'd find in a real job. But when I got there, it was easy. No one stood over me with a whip ... They seemed willing to pay me to think up new designs at my own speed, in my own space. It was unbelievable... No one carried a gun, at least not as far as I could see. There were no drunks passed out in our doorways, and our washroom sinks were never used as toilets. We didn't have any coke dealers or hookers in the parking lot, and it was always safe to walk to your car when work was done ... Within a year, I was responsible for projects on my own. I seemed to have made it into the normal world at last. If I was careful, I thought, no one would find out about my past.[112]

Robison's next job was at Simplex in Gardner. This was decidedly more 'posh'. He had an office, a secretary and, after a year, a staff of 20.

> But it proved to be a mistake. I wasn't happy. I felt I was surrounded by mediocrity, both in my own work and in my choice of employment. I had gone from designing toys (a fun thing) to overseeing the design of time clocks to keep track of America's factory workers (not a fun thing).[113]

He moved on to Isoreg, a small firm manufacturing power transformers, which required a 90-minute commute from his home. 'Life as an executive was not turning out the way they portrayed it.'[114]

Eventually, Robison realised he was not cut out to be a team player. In 1989, he started up a business, JE Robison Service, in Springfield, Massachusetts, repairing luxury cars such as Rolls Royces and Bentleys. The business combined his ability to design electrical circuits with his love of repairing cars:

> I had found a niche where many of my Aspergian traits actually benefited me. My compulsion to know everything about cars made me a great service person. My precise speech gave me the ability to explain complex problems in simple terms.[115]

In fact, Robison is sometimes reminded of Daniel Keyes' 1966 novel, *Flowers for Algernon*, in which scientists take a retarded janitor and turn him into a genius, although his brilliance then fades away.

> That's how I feel sometimes, looking back at the creative engineering I've done. Those designs were the fruit of a part of my mind that is no longer with me .... My story isn't sad, though, because my mind has the power it always did, but in a more broadly focused configuration.[116]

He says it has been 'a good trade. Creative genius never helped me make friends and it certainly didn't make me happy. My life today is immeasurably happier, richer and fuller as a result of my brain's continued development.'[117]

Today, Robison sits on the Interagency Autism Co-ordinating Committee, which advises the federal government in the US on autism-related research.

Notes

1 See: www.iidc.indiana.edu/pages/Choosing-the-Right-Job-for-People-with-Autism-or-Aspergers-Syndrome (accessed 27 April 2018).
2 See T. Grandin and D. Moore (2015), *The Loving Push: How Parents and Professionals Can Help Spectrum Kids Become Successful Adults*. Arlington, TX: Future Horizons.
3 See Tiffany D. Johnson and Aparna Joshi (2016), 'Dark clouds or silver linings? A stigma threat perspective on the implications of an autism diagnosis for workplace well-being', *Journal of Applied Psychology*, American Psychological Association, 101(3), 430–449.
4 Thorkil Sonne in conversation with the author, 6 March 2016.
5 Thorkil Sonne in conversation with the author, 6 March 2016.
6 See: www.autismafter16.com/article/03-07-2014/made-brad-thinking-outside-box (accessed 27 April 2018).
7 Ibid.
8 Ibid.
9 Jackie Remfry in conversation with the author, 29 June 2016.
10 Ibid.
11 Ibid.
12 See: http://lubavitch.com/news/article/2076503/Our-Kitchen-Hand.html (accessed 27 April 2018).
13 Ibid.
14 See: www.dailymail.co.uk/health/article-2521032/Dan-Aykroyd-I-Aspergers--symptoms-included-obsessed-ghosts.html (accessed 10 December 2013).

15 See Tiffany D. Johnson and Aparna Joshi (2016), 'Dark clouds or silver linings? A stigma threat perspective on the implications of an autism diagnosis for workplace well-being', *Journal of Applied Psychology*, American Psychological Association, 101(3), 430–449.

16 See Ros Blackburn's interview with the author, *Looking Up*, 2(1), 2000.

17 Ibid.

18 Ibid.

19 Dean Beadle in conversation with the author, 19 October 2017.

20 Ibid.

21 Ibid.

22 Ibid.

23 Ibid.

24 Dean Beadle, posting on Facebook on 24 August 2017. (Reproduced with Dean's permission.)

25 See: https://pardonmyfrenchtheatreblog.wordpress.com/2015/04/02/acting-and-autism-the-challenges-and-rewards/ (accessed 27 April 2018).

26 Bargiela, S., Steward, R. and Mandy, W. (2016), 'The experiences of late-diagnosed women with autism spectrum conditions: An investigation of the female autism phenotype', *Journal of Autism and Developmental Disorders*, October, 46(10), 3281–3294.

27 Ibid.

28 See: www.bbc.co.uk/programmes/articles/46HqQ1IFyX8mV0qTt8BKThm/a-new-beginning (accessed 27 April 2018).

29 Ibid.

30 See: www.thetimes.co.uk/article/relative-values-my-sons-aspergers-has-taught-me-so-much-vsxwvq0g5r5 (accessed 18 August 2013).

31 Jules Robertson in conversation with the author, 8 July 2016.

32 Ibid.

33 Ibid.

34 Ibid.

35 Ibid.

36 Cian Binchy in conversation with the author, 20 October 2016.

37 See *The Observer*, 22 August 2015.

38 Cian Binchy in conversation with the author, 20 October 2016.

39 Ibid.

40 Cian Binchy in conversation with the author, 20 October 2016.

41 Jonathan Andrews in conversation with the author, 8 June 2016.

42 *The Guardian*, 31 January 2017.

43 Ibid.

44 Ibid.

45 Jonathan Andrews in conversation with the author, 8 June 2016.

46 *The Guardian*, 31 January 2017.

47 Jonathan Andrews in conversation with the author, 8 June 2016.

48 *The Guardian*, 31 January 2017.

49 Ibid.

50 Adam Ockelford in communication with the author, 12 January 2017.

51 *Daily Sabah*, 4 January 2017.

52 Sophia Grech in conversation with the author, 21 June 2017.

53 Ibid.

54 Ibid.

55 Ibid.

56 Ibid.

57 Ibid.

58 Ibid.

59 Ibid.

60 Ibid.

61 *Mail Online*, 13 June 2014.

62 Ibid.

63   Ibid.
64   Mark Williams in conversation with the author, 12 June 2017.
65   Ibid.
66   See: www.autism.org.uk/get-involved/media-centre/news/2017-04-07-new-photography-exhibition.aspx (accessed 27 April 2018).
67   See: www.prweb.com/releases/2016/09/prweb13675167.htm (accessed 27 April 2018).
68   Jon Adams, in conversation with the author, 6 July 2016.
69   Ibid.
70   Ibid.
71   Ibid.
72   Ibid.
73   Ibid.
74   Ibid.
75   Ibid.
76   Ibid.
77   Ibid.
78   Ibid.
79   Ibid.
80   Ibid.
81   Ibid.
82   Ibid.
83   See the author's interview with Stephen Wiltshire in *Looking Up*, 4(7), 2007.
84   *The Guardian*, 4 May 2017.
85   Ibid.
86   See: https://livingautism.com/aspergers-syndrome-profession-living-autism-interview-photographer-nicky-fry/ (accessed 27 April 2018).
87   Ibid.
88   Ibid.
89   See: http://larry-arnold.net/Autobiog/2002.htm (accessed 27 April 2018).
90   Ibid.
91   Ibid.
92   http://larry-arnold.net/Autobiog/2002.htm (accessed 27 April 2018).
93   See: www.rappler.com/move-ph/188307-how-inclusion-empowers-artists-with-autism (accessed 19 November 2017).
94   *Daily Mirror*, 3 January 2017.
95   Ibid.
96   Ibid.
97   Ibid.
98   Ibid.
99   Ibid.
100   Information supplied by Autism Plus.
101   See: www.inc.com/magazine/201506/jeff-chu/making-it-work-the-spectrum-of-debate.html (accessed 27 April 2018).
102   Ibid.
103   Information supplied by Remploy.
104   Ibid.
105   Ibid.
106   Ibid.
107   See: www.inc.com/magazine/201506/jeff-chu/making-it-work-the-spectrum-of-debate.html (accessed 27 April 2018).
108   Ibid.
109   See John Elder Robison (2008), *Look Me in the Eye – My Life with Aspergers*. London: Ebury Press, p. 171.
110   Ibid., p. 177.

111 Ibid.
112 Ibid., pp. 179–180.
113 Ibid., p. 204.
114 Ibid., p. 205.
115 Ibid., p. 214.
116 Ibid., p. 209.
117 Ibid., p. 210.

Chapter 7

Public service jobs

Dean Worton, a man with Asperger's syndrome, stated:

> I would recommend any Aspie to look for work in the public sector. It is very difficult to lose your job in the public sector and, unlike in the private sector, you will probably have to do something illegal to be instantly dismissed.[1]

Many people on the autism spectrum *do* enjoy the feeling that they are contributing constructively to society through public service.

In 2017, the British government's Department of Personnel and Training (DoPT) wrote to all central government departments to ensure that 1 per cent of all posts be reserved for people with autism, intellectual disability, specific learning disability and mental illness. In the case of direct recruitment, 4 per cent of the total number of vacancies, up from the existing 3 per cent, shall be reserved for people with bench-mark disabilities, the order said. Benchmark disability means a person with not less than 40 per cent of a specified disability. This move to enhance reservation quotas for those with learning disability followed the passage of the Rights of Persons with Disabilities Act in 2016.

The National Police Autism Association is a 700-member, independent body supporting British police officers, staff and volunteers who are affected by autism, Asperger's syndrome, as well as other conditions such as dyslexia, dyspraxia, ADHD and depression – either personally or as carers for family members.

Not all the NPAA's members are on the spectrum but the association's vice-chair, Claire Masterton – who is autistic – says the reason many staff join the organisation is because they have dependants who have autism.

As for the military, the situation appears to be far more complex in the UK. According to the National Careers Service:

> a person with autism is unable to join the Army because the armed forces are not covered by the 2010 Equality Act, which prevents employers treating people with disabilities unfairly. Depending on where a person is on the autistic spectrum, they may be able to join the police force as an alternative career in a uniformed service.[2]

However, the facts do not bear out this advice. I have heard from a number of people with Asperger's syndrome who are serving in Britain's Territorial Army. One of them was advised, nevertheless, that he would need strong support from his doctor during the recruitment process to prove that he was capable of serving in the British Army.

The suitability, or otherwise, of a military career for individuals on the spectrum is certainly a matter for considerable debate. On the one hand, proponents have pointed out, the disciplined, rule-based lifestyle may appeal and some people with autism can remain calm and courageous under pressure. On the other hand, sceptics have noted that Army life thrives on group conformity and is scarcely known for its appreciation of differences – which is why bullying tends to be so prevalent in military life.

Some other countries seem to be taking a more flexible approach. In Israel, for example, military service is compulsory for all 18-year-olds following high school, but exemptions are issued on a number of grounds, including residence abroad, religious reasons or physical or mental disability. In 2008, the country ended the practice of issuing blanket exemption notices for autistic Israelis and instead began accepting them on a case-by-case basis, typically for secretarial roles or voluntary civil-service positions in hospitals and schools. And in 2017, the Israeli Army began recruiting young employees on the autism spectrum to scan high-resolution satellite images for suspicious objects or movements. The military benefits from their attention to detail. One such recruit, identified only as E., is a corporal in the Israel Defence Force's Visual Intelligence Division, otherwise known as Unit 9900, which counts dozens of Israelis with autism among its members.

❖ CASE STUDIES

- DAVID HARRIS
- ADAM O'LOUGHLIN
- TRANSPORT FOR LONDON
- PAUL SOUTHWARD
- NETWORK RAIL

DAVID HARRIS was diagnosed with Asperger's syndrome by Patricia Howlin in 1991. He began working at what was then British Railways in Slough in 1992. He moved to Paddington Station in London in 1997 and he has been in his current position there (in Customer Reception) since 2000.

By his own admission, David has had 'a tough background' – he was only seven when his mother died and his engineer father (who used to repair gearboxes at British Airways) committed suicide in 1995.

David has always been obsessed with planes and trains. He had always wanted to work for BA, but is now happily employed at the Great Western Railway information desk opposite Platform 1 on Paddington Station in London. David manages to remain admirably patient, even when customers become irate over train delays. He says having Asperger's gives him a number of advantages in this job: it gives him an excellent memory for train timetables and he can deal logically with complaints without panicking.

> It can be quite stressful sometimes, when there are cancellations or disruptions. The customers can be strict. I can sometimes be quite firm with them, but never rude. I don't swear. If they've lost their ticket, I tell them they must buy a new one.[3]

Figure 7.1 David Harris with his aunt, Carol, who took him to be diagnosed by Dr Patricia Howlin and Pam Yates at the Maudsley Hospital in London in 1991

As for travelling himself, he does two to three trips a year to Europe, as well as one long-haul journey. 'I've been round the world four times. And I get to around ten air shows a year.' Asked what he enjoys most about the job, he replies: 'We get free, unlimited travel on Great Western Railway trains! And as a safeguarded employee, I'm lucky enough to get free travel on other train companies' trains, too.'[4]

He says his Asperger's syndrome means he does not like change. 'About four years ago, my aunt thought my flat needed to be redecorated, I didn't enjoy the upheaval but I like it now – it's much posher!'[5]

Police Sergeant ADAM O'LOUGHLIN, who is based in Bath, was diagnosed with autism in 2016, at the age of 39. He says that getting diagnosed and going public about the fact he is on the autism spectrum has been a revelation. As well as now being able to factor autism into his reasoning as a policeman, he also feels less pressure to pretend to be like everybody else to try to fit in.

'Telling people I have autism was the best thing I ever did,' he said. 'Pretending to be like you guys is exhausting. You have to keep it up all the time or you're not going to get anywhere. Now I don't feel the need to pretend to be someone else.'[6]

Interestingly, Adam says that he has has to learn to curb his instinct to see the law as 'black and white' and to make sure it is obeyed to the very letter. Seventeen years of police service have taught him to take a broader view.

He has also recently been promoted to a position where he spends more time at his desk and less out on the beat. 'I've found myself in a job that very much fits with what I'm good at, based on my own peculiarities,' he says. 'I can concentrate for extended periods of time,' he says.

> And I can find intel on our computer system much quicker than anyone else can. My mind works in a way that helps me drag that information out. And we try to find where burglary hotspots are – I find that really easy as well.[7]

He is also happy to deal with the bureaucracy that eats up ever more police time, whereas it might drive others to distraction.

Sergeant O'Loughlin's superiors have been perfectly willing to make adjustments to accommodate his needs. And he is clearly enjoying life: 'Law enforcement attracts people who are on the spectrum,' he says. 'They like the uniform – you get to wear the same thing every day. And you get to enforce the rules.'

Adam adds:

> The police in Avon and Somerset have been trying to make sure we reflect the population in terms of visible minorities. In terms of things like ethnicity, we are struggling. But when it comes to autism, we're already there without even trying.[8]

TRANSPORT FOR LONDON (TfL) has a reasonable adjustments policy. This would then be applied for any person who joins the organisation and discloses his or her autism. According to Peter Fletcher (TfL's Communications and Engagement manager),

> there is no specific policy for autism, as the spectrum can be so wide. We will also be developing a neurodiversity policy. The policy will help staff better to understand our neurodiversity. It will also help managers in discussions with a member of staff to plan adjustments. We have a Staff Network Group for our disabled members of staff and there are members with autism.[9]

David McNeill, TfL's Director of Public Affairs and Stakeholder Engagement, told me:

> Basically, we operate two strands of activity. Jobs matching is important. For people on the autistic spectrum, there will be certain roles that will play to strengths. For example, we have a lot of very technical jobs that require meticulous focus and analytical skills, such as coding, data analytics, traffic modelling and the like. Where we have an applicant who is recognised as being on the autism spectrum, we will ensure we reduce barriers for applicants with autism, by adapting our assessments and interview process.
>
> The reasonable adjustment policy was required of us by legislation, but it has also been informed by real-world observable experience. A good example of real-world observations is that we realised that the people who were best at understanding the complex interdependencies and peculiar butterfly effects of managing London's 3,000 traffic lights, for example, might be on the autism spectrum/have Asperger's syndrome.
>
> TfL is generally a very supportive environment and supportive colleagues ensure that reasonable adjustments take place in different teams and that these are then fed into recruitment practice. The policy itself seems to have been the result of frustrations by the recruiting officers, who were feeling that the requirement for 'soft' skills was getting in the way of recruiting people with the right technical skills. These technical skills are highly valued. For example, the phasing of one set of traffic lights at Trafalgar Square at different points in the day and during moments of disruption is absolutely critical to the flow of traffic in Central London. If the phasing is wrong, then the West End goes into gridlock within 15 minutes, which then spreads to the city in 30 minutes – and will take up to three hours to clear. The second area is in a specific programme for people with learning difficulties/disabilities. This is much more of a supported and managed employability programme.[10]

PAUL SOUTHWARD, who works for Transport for London, says his experience of having Asperger's syndrome is marked by difficulty with social situations:

> I cannot maintain eye contact for more than a few seconds and find remembering names and faces extremely difficult. Small talk and understanding social norms is also a challenge. Physically, however, I'm fine – which is why I have walked six long-distance footpaths and have served as a soldier in the Territorial Army for over eight years.[11]

Paul began to struggle after he left university and his life had less of a structure.

> When I entered the world of work, I encountered real problems. I started work at a transport planning consultancy and began getting stress headaches. After the consultancy, I worked in a control room for Network

Rail. For me, things were great when they went wrong because I was very busy and there was a problem to solve. But when I didn't have a problem to work on, things got worse because the monotony of the work bored me; there was no end in sight. I found myself becoming increasingly anxious. The only way I could cope with the headaches was by drinking heavily.

After joining TfL, I recognised my drinking was a problem and in October 2007 I approached Occupational Health for help. They referred me to the drug and alcohol advisory service where I could talk about my concerns confidentially. They in turn sent me to a psychologist who diagnosed Asperger's syndrome. I was stunned to find out the cause of my problem but it proved to be a turning point. I started reading about Asperger's on the Internet and it was staggering, it was like reading my life story online.[12]

Paul urges people not to make assumptions:

People with Asperger's learn how to deal with it. Many people with the condition think very logically and are very focused on a subject and this is an ability I have, so Asperger's is a different set of abilities, not a disability. When I discovered I had Asperger's, I had already been serving in the TA for four years. I approached my chain of command and told them the problem. They said it wasn't an issue, as I did what I was told. Also, they had dealt with the issue in their own workplaces. It was eventually decided we tell the rest of my squadron. We did this and nobody had a problem with it. Actually, they had already guessed I was a bit different – you can't hide things when you work that closely with people – and now they know it wasn't an issue.[13]

Paul says that, since his diagnosis, he has changed his working habits in order to cope with his condition, including getting into work early when fewer people are around, thus avoiding the social anxiety he experiences when walking into a room full of people.

People with Asperger's like to focus in on specific problems and then solve them using their analytical skills, so the project-based work I do at TfL suits the way my brain works.

That said, work is still difficult and TfL could do a lot more. For example, in my old team, at the start of every row we had a list of the people who sat there. Also included was a picture of them, job title and where they sat. It was easy – if I had to find someone I simply walked down the rows looking at the names until I found the person I wanted. Even better, I gradually learnt who people were, their names, faces and what they did. Now, with hot-desking, all the names and pictures have gone and I don't know most of my team, where they sit or what they do. I can only hope that eventually we move back to everyone having their own desk and we can have some sort of order back in our office.[14]

NETWORK RAIL, the UK's national rail network, is taking a particular interest in neurodiversity among its staff, according to Ian Iceton, its group transformation and efficiency director. Iceton told me at Network Rail's headquarters in Euston, London, that the company was much better educated about autism than it used to be, and employees on the spectrum receive a great deal of moral support. 'We use mentors, although not specifically for autism.'[15]

On the issue of introducing reasonable adjustments in the workplace, Iceton says: 'The concept of helping people in this way is absolutely right, but navigating towards what is reasonable is tricky. We need to recruit without making assumptions.'[16]

IT, computing and website design

This book has been at pains to dispute the well-meaning but over-simplistic stereotypes about autistic individuals in the workplace, including the notion that all people with Asperger's syndrome are supremely proficient at IT. (I have met many who are not.) But the fact remains that many do have a particular gift in using computers creatively – and have proven superb assets for the company where they work.

❖ CASE STUDY

• JAMIE KNIGHT

JAMIE KNIGHT, 28, is a top website developer for the BBC who lives in London. Jamie has been building websites since 1999, when he was only nine. He grew up in foster care and became homeless at 16. He did a couple of A-Levels and then a foundation degree in business and management, all the while running his own business building accessible websites. He was offered a job with Apple but ended up at the BBC instead. It was initially supposed to be for a few months to try his hand at a nine-to-five job before heading to Apple. But he liked it so much that he stayed. He started in the Radio Development team, where he led on the front-end build of BBC iPlayer Radio. He then moved to the Platforms team, where he worked on various backend tools and code, which runs on most BBC pages.

Jamie is well-known for his attachment to Lion, a 4ft-long soft toy – sometimes known as a *plushie* – which never leaves his side. Jamie's coping strategies include eating the same meal every night – filled pasta with sauce – and having Lion beside him, no matter where he goes.

What does he believe are the specific strengths he brings to the job?

We don't treat autism as a 'force' that acts on me. We don't attribute positive or negative things to 'autism'. It's just part of how I am. I'm autistic. I'm also male and gay. They all contribute to my identity and needs,

Jamie told me.

When my needs are met and the environment stops disabling me, I can be very productive and autonomous. If my needs are not met, the environment disables me and life becomes very difficult. We follow a social model, rather than the medical model approach.[17]

He added:

I'm not sure I personally have an advantage in the workplace. However, an advantage to all workplaces is to have people with a wide range of experiences and perspectives. More perspectives tease out better solutions. I experience the world differently and that can lead to neat solutions and ideas. One of those experiences is that I have an intense focus for things which interest me, such as software development. At its heart, software development is the act of explaining to a computer what you would like it to do. Explaining things turned out to be a transferable skill. A well-structured presentation and a well-structured piece of code isn't all that different, really. I bring a different perspective from most other people and I enjoy explaining things. That's a useful combination. It's also true for many other minority groups.[18]

What about the challenges?

The areas which challenge me most are environmental. I am sensitive to noise, light and motion, so large open-plan offices distract me and prevent me from working well. I work from home most of the time. It's just simpler! My team and the people I work with are spread around the country anyway, so there's no big benefit to travelling to an office every day. Travelling is a challenge. It's not an efficient way for me to use energy. If I need to travel somewhere (like Sweden or Manchester), I access support to help me. There's no point travelling if I get to the other end too tired to do anything or too spaced out to communicate effectively. It's better to accept some help and let someone else who finds it's much easier lead the way.[19]

The third environmental challenge in Jamie's life is communication:

My speech is unreliable so we build other forms of communication into my environment. For example, when working with my team, we mostly use Slack, which is text-based. I find politics and guessing at other people's intentions difficult, so I collaborate with my team when I get stuck, just as we would for anything else. It took me five years of work before I realised that trying to 'mask' and 'be more normal' wasn't a sustainable or useful approach. It just drained energy I could better use for work.[20]

When I asked Jamie how Lion helped him to 'cope' with his work, he replied:

The direct answer is that I don't 'cope' with my work. Coping implies finding ways to put up with something which isn't working. We just fix things if they don't work. Coping doesn't scale and quickly become unsustainable. Lion doesn't help me cope, he is just part of how I thrive. Lion just makes me happier and more comfortable with the world. He's always around and consistent. He can also sometimes act a bit like a white cane. He makes an invisible difference visible and normal, that's a positive thing to do.[21]

Jamie's autism means that at times he is non-verbal – unable to talk – although he can communicate using messaging services and apps.

There are, in fact, others on the autism spectrum who rely on a toy animal to negotiate everyday life. Tilley Milburn is a comedian and actress with Asperger's syndrome who works with the remarkable east London charity, Heart n Soul (see Chapter 26). She spotted the patchwork pig she calls Del in a shop. It would become her best friend and collaborator, a character with its own voice who even pipes up in business meetings.

Today, Jamie says he is 'autistically happy with my work. Many things we do are unusual, but it works well and I am productive so it doesn't really matter how "normal" it is.' He adds that the BBC has been very understanding:

My digestive issues have always been frustrating and the BBC understand that I have a long-term illness. I can't wait for a cure for my tummy issues. But the BBC doesn't need to be 'understanding' about autism. Like any other member of staff, I have things to offer and it benefits the BBC to remove barriers which get in the way of my work. I am fortunate to have a team who collaborate well and understand how to help each other. At a wider scale, the BBC have a good grasp on diversity. There's a focus on making buildings, culture and process friendlier and easier to use for everyone. Neurological diversity is part of that.[22]

Notes

1   See Genevieve Edmonds and Luke Beardon (eds) (2008), *Asperger Syndrome and Employment.* London: Jessica Kingsley, p. 72.
2   See: www.q2a.co.uk/armyentryaf0710.htm.
3   David Harris in conversation with the author, 24 June 2016.
4   Ibid.
5   Ibid.
6   See: www.bbc.co.uk/news/disability-43584212.

7   Ibid.
8   Ibid.
9   Peter Fletcher, in communication with the author, 16 June 2016.
10 David McNeill in communication with the author, 4 May 2016.
11 Information provided by Transport for London.
12 Ibid.
13 Ibid.
14 Ibid.
15 Ian Iceton, in conversation with the author, 10 July 2017.
16 Ibid.
17 Jamie Knight in conversation with the author, 17 December 2017.
18 Ibid.
19 Ibid.
20 Ibid.
21 Ibid.
22 Ibid.

Chapter 8

Other job openings

The media

Counter-intuitive though it may initially appear, journalism – with its emphasis on inter-action with the world and other human beings – can prove a fruitful area to explore for people on the spectrum, especially if it taps into a specific area of interest. Dean Beadle, the speaker with Asperger's syndrome previously mentioned, used to write a regular column on music in his local paper. We featured the prominent print journalist, Laura James, in our section on self-employment and there are also a number of cases of people with autism forging successful careers in broadcasting through their unusual – and appealingly quirky – way of seeing the world and presenting their particular passion.

❖ CASE STUDY

• CHRIS PACKHAM

One of British television's best-known faces, the BBC presenter and wildlife photographer, CHRIS PACKHAM feels the United Kingdom has fallen far behind other developed countries in using the skills of adults on the autism spectrum.

Packham, 56, who is the co-host of BBC Two's *Springwatch* and *Autumnwatch* programmes, was inundated with public support after he revealed he had Asperger's syndrome in 2016 – and after the publication of his fine autobiography, *Fingers in the Sparkle Jar*, which revealed his lonely, animal-loving childhood in Southampton, marked by merciless bullying and his thoughts of suicide both by the death of a pet kestrel at the age of 15 and, in adulthood, of two pet dogs. After the second dog died in 2003, Packham found himself counting out pills and considering an overdose; he stopped only because he did not think the 39 tablets in his possession were sufficient.

He says he was virtually unemployable after leaving university (where he studied zoology). But his sister, Jenny, suggested that he go on television and talk about animals – instead of constantly boring the family by doing so! He is convinced his Asperger's syndrome gave him a distinct advantage because of his focus and encyclopaedic knowledge. Indeed, on the BBC Television documentary, *Asperger's and Me*, he declared:

> There is no way I could do my job without Asperger's ... Being able to see things with greater clarity, to see the world in a very different, visual way ... That difference is an enormous asset and has to be seen as a gift, not what you can't do but what you can do ... I am very fortunate to be able to reap the benefits, but not all autistic people are so lucky.[1]

Packham was actually diagnosed with Asperger's in 2005 at the age of 44. He has recently spoken about the challenges the condition poses for him, both professionally and personally. On *Springwatch*, the filming crew know that they must not alter the layout of his location caravan in any way. His girlfriend, Charlotte Corney, owner of Isle of Wight Zoo, makes a note every time he says something entirely inappropriate.[2] His other immediate family consists of his sister, the fashion designer Jenny Peckham, and his stepdaughter Megan, the daughter of a former girlfriend, of whom he is extremely proud.

Packham says:

> I think that there are many in the UK who still suffer because of their autistic diagnosis or autistic traits. The more that we can bring this into the open and have discussions about it, the better people who aren't autistic can understand the condition and how they might better facilitate an environment where autistic people don't have to suffer ... It's worth getting to grips with people like myself because we do have something to offer and also it's a great shame if people who are Asperger's don't have the opportunity to have a fulfilled life and actually put something back into other people's lives.[3]

He says that he meets many people with Asperger's syndrome in his walk of life: 'It's a mode of mind that suits an interest in wildlife and science. I think if you can overcome what some people call handicaps – I call them tasks – you can get on and achieve great things.'[4]

> The more that we can bring this into the open and have discussions about it, the better people who aren't autistic can understand the condition and how they might better facilitate an environment where autistic people don't have to suffer.

Speaking on *BBC Breakfast*, Packham said that his career stemmed from his passion for the natural world, admitting that he had often felt a 'closer bond' with animals than with some people.

> I grappled early on, as many people of my age would have done with Asperger's, because it wasn't recognised at school or at home ... it

wasn't in the public consciousness and even throughout the 1980s and 1990s people were grappling with what it was and trying to classify it and understand it ... For years, I thought something was wrong with me, but actually there is nothing wrong with us at all, we are just different and difference is not a crime.[5]

In *Asperger's and Me* – the candid new documentary broadcast in 2017 – Packham allowed BBC camera crews to film his daily struggle with autism for the first time, and travelled to the US to visit clinics and educational programmes which claim to be able treat the condition. Packham said he was disturbed that the positive aspects of autism were often ignored in the desire of 'charlatans and sharks' to 'stamp out' the condition by 'throwing random science at it and then peddling it like snake oil over the fence'.[6]

Packham said his own Asperger's syndrome had allowed him to acquire an encyclopaedic knowledge of the natural world by honing his focus on plants and animals, to the exclusion of everything else. However, he had been forced to develop a range of coping mechanisms to allow him to work as a television presenter, including learning to look people in the eye and suppressing urges to make inappropriate or unprofessional comments:

> I've spent 30 years on the telly trying my best to act normal, when really I am anything but ... But I realise now there is no way I could do my job without Asperger's. What I do in terms of making programmes is afforded to me because of my neurological differences. Being able to see things with perhaps a greater clarity, being able to see the world in a very visual way.[7]

Interestingly, in view of the common perception that people on the autism spectrum find non-literal language difficult to use or understand, Packham and his co-host Michaela Strachan, have been known to drop a few double-entendres into the wildlife show to attract a broader audience. So they have been known to admire a pair of 'great tits', to giggle about 'cock in the flesh' or quiz one another about 'deep shags'.[8]

Banking and accountancy

In 2016, Ben Affleck starred in Gavin O'Connor's movie, *The Accountant*, about an autistic man who combines mathematical savant skills with ruthless, unblinking killing instincts. It is fair to say that film was not universally admired. Some critics felt it gave the impression that the character's autism inclines him towards carnage. 'Any opportunity to shine a light on this world is important,' says Ernie Merlán, executive director of Exceptional Minds, a non-profit vocational centre for young adults on the autism spectrum in Sherman Oaks, California. 'My only concern is that this is a Hollywood shoot-'em-up like we're used to, but this time it's a protagonist who has autism, with guns.'[9] Autism has been inaccurately implicated in the media as a cause of extreme violence, says Laurie Stephens, director of clinical services for Education Spectrum, a therapeutic centre for autism based in Altadena, California. 'There's absolutely no relationship between violence like this and having an autism spectrum disorder or Asperger's.'[10] Jonathan Victory, a writer and filmmaker with Asperger's syndrome living in Dublin, wrote:

> I am rubbish at maths. But if you were going by popular culture, you'd think autism is a superpower that makes you a mathematical genius ... Ben Affleck is good-looking, so they got that part right! I also liked how medically accurate a clinician's explanation of autism was ... [But] without portraying diversity in how the condition affects people, a passive viewer could develop misconceptions about autistic people from the movie where they're mastermind criminal killers; harmful misconceptions that can further stigmatise an already-misrepresented group.[11]

On the other hand, Tom Iland, a certified public accountant on the autism spectrum, wrote:

> I could relate to not only some of the talents of Christian Wolff (Ben Affleck), but also a lot of the personal and professional struggles he had. I spent six years in college pursuing an accounting degree and one more year studying for and taking the CPA Examination, one of the most difficult exams there is. I worked for seven years in accounting, tax and other financial positions, which helped me relate to Christian's professional journey and his talent for numbers. However, I never had Christian's extreme experiences of working for criminals and mob bosses and having to protect himself with guns and other weapons! ... Christian had his accounting system in place and when it was disrupted, he would become upset. I had my own frustrations working as a temporary employee or 'temp' after I got my CPA licence, whether it was about the accounting work itself or the expectations in the office setting. Those who know autism and the social awkwardness associated with it will really appreciate certain scenes in this movie ... especially those where Christian interacts with women. Whether it is Christian receiving the missing piece to a puzzle from a young girl, to responding apathetically when a client asked him if he liked her necklace, to self-disclosing that he has a high-functioning form of autism to his female accounting colleague, the difficulties are clear.
>
> I encourage [employers] to be part of the solution of this problem. Invest time, money and resources in hiring and understanding people with autism. Rather than seeing the person as a PR, HR or legal nightmare, see the potential. This person might be the one who improves systems currently in place, betters workplace rapport or strengthens customer loyalty. The possibilities are endless! Speaking from personal experience, when someone took the time to really listen to my situation and offer a helping hand, I was happier at work, which resulted in me working harder and doing a better job. Imagine what positive things you can unleash by being there for someone with autism in the workplace! People with autism are willing and able to work. Will you be the one that puts them to work?[12]

In the end, Iland – who is a board member of The Art of Autism non-profit-making organisation – realised that accounting was not the right occupation for him.

> I decided to walk away from my full-time job, with excellent pay and benefits, to dedicate myself to helping others affected by ASD. I am very pleased to say that I made the right decision because my new career as a writer, speaker, consultant and trainer makes me happier and helps me help others.[13]

Some people on the autism spectrum make very good accountants – without going on violent rampages! One such case is Oliver Leonard.

❖ CASE STUDY

• OLIVER LEONARD

OLIVER LEONARD is one of the great successes of Little Gate Farm in Sussex, southern England. Oliver is a talented young man with a gift for numbers and organising. He also has autism. With the support of the farm and the supported employment team, Oliver was hired as an accountancy clerk at Ashdown Hurrey in Hastings. Oliver has flourished in his new role: he is professional, hard-working and liked by all the staff who work with him.

'My life has changed since working at Ashdown Hurrey,' says Oliver. 'It has given me purpose. I enjoy the work, it is not difficult for me. The staff are nice and friendly and it's good to get paid at the end of the month.'[14]

Claire Cordell, the chief executive officer at Little Gate Farm, said:

> Oliver has worked hard to prepare himself for the workplace and is a great role model to other young people going through our work training programme into paid employment. The training programme at Little Gate Farm focuses on preparing young people like Oliver for paid work by supporting them with confidence, independence and communication, Oliver did really well during this preparation phase, and was really motivated to find a paid job in an area in which he could excel. With the right support, young people like Oliver can thrive in the workplace.[15]

Librarianship

There are many people on the autism spectrum who enjoy cataloguing and organising files and systems. This can make them very valuable staff in libraries, for example. The problem, as James Christie points out below, is that libraries are an increasingly fragile species in the UK.

❖ CASE STUDY

- JAMES CHRISTIE

JAMES CHRISTIE was diagnosed with Asperger's syndrome at the age of 37 in 2002 and is the author of two books, *Dear Miss Landau* and *The Legend of John Macnab*. He has been working in the library trade for nearly 25 years – but despairs for its future.

> [People with] Asperger's can be natural cataloguers but … between 2010–2016 the number of UK libraries declined from 4,290 to 3,765, and 7,933 paid staff were 'slaughtered' while volunteers doubled from 15,861 to 31,403 … Given my long experience of a library 'profession' brimful of jargon, bereft of leadership and bare of jobs, I do not believe the Chartered Institute of Library and Information Professionals (CILIP) is able 'to encourage and develop the library workforce and especially new recruits and graduates'.[16]

James is quick to emphasise that his career as a librarian did not begin badly at all:

> My library course was mumbo jumbo, but my first job was the extraordinary experience of manually cataloguing antiquarian monographs worth millions of pounds in a stately home. [People with] Asperger's have a firewall between their everyday personalities and the manic nutter sub-routine needed effectively to catalogue. If I joke that 'cataloguers make accountants look like hippies,' I'm not actually joking. I spent three years living, breathing and stacking books in a library like a time capsule from Victorian days.[17]

In a valuable corrective to the stereotypical (and vastly over-simplistic) connection between individuals with Asperger's syndrome and IT, James adds:

> Cataloguing, cleaning, handling and researching rare and mystical books with my own hands was a wondrous experience. To arrange them in plumb lines on shelves in a library which had fallen into decay before Victoria took the throne was to see the past restored vibrantly to life, once again able to talk to the present and future. Computers do not hold the same fascination for me. In the end, they are only tools and, compared to what I saw in that private library, they mean nothing.[18]

However, when he tried to find another job, 'it was a torrid tale of frustration and fading hopes, my skills withering on the vine, my interest in rare books dying for lack of development and my patience shortening like a lit and burning fuse'.[19]

In 2006, he wrote an article

> intending to crucify myself, commit professional suicide and probably get myself beaten up by a rampaging mob of respectable librarians into

the bargain, but I'm now so disillusioned with the profession that I would rather fall on my sword than stagger through interviews mumbling tripe I don't believe about metadata, revalidation, ICT, twelve-digit Dewey numbers and all the other pseudo-professional jargon we have invented. ... Senior library managers should be shot out of the *USS Enterprise*'s shuttle bay doors in their underpants.[20]

An email similarly criticising librarians' jargon actually won Letter of the Month in the library journal, *Update*, in 2008. But James believed his career had come to a juddering halt in 2011 when the National Health Service did not give him the library assistant's post which he says they had already offered him in writing.

I was reduced to a nervous wreck and left hanging in redeployment hell for years by one of the cruellest employers I'd ever known. It was the NHS – the so-called 'caring' profession. They had offered me a permanent part-time library assistant's post *in writing*,

says Christie.

Make no mistake, for a middle-aged autist, this was manna from heaven: security, a structured work environment and a chance to save for a better pension. This was a golden opportunity. I had to do a 12-week trial at the library, and boy did I work at it. I turned up half-an-hour early every morning, I crossed the Ts and dotted the Is. For the record, I was supervised by NAS Scotland, JobCentre Plus and Access to Work. I passed with flying colours, but by the last week I heard the dread rumour that 'a library manager would be attending' the meeting where I'd be offered the job. Oh, she attended all right. She swept in, baldly announced 'there wasn't any work' (a fact the NHS had known all along) and dashed my hopes more thoroughly than you can ever imagine. The NHS blamed the library people, the library people blamed the NHS, I blamed both of them; and though there are scarcely words to describe how far my opinion of librarians and employers dived, I will try to find them: After that truly pathetic débacle, I considered them tenth-grade paperweights, men and women of straw. I literally no longer even felt that 'quantum of solace' for them. I did not care whether they lived or died.[21]
In addition to gaining a degree and postgraduate qualification in librarianship, plus membership of librarianship's professional body, I had the unique experience of three years cataloguing rare books in the private library of a stately home (sister house to Abbotsford). That experience was priceless, I can literally claim to be a walking piece of Scottish library history, but I still couldn't get a job out of it.[22]

Nevertheless, in 2015, James joined Culter Library in South Lanarkshire, Scotland – a roomful of rare books near Leadhills Miners Library – the oldest subscription library in the British Isles.

Despite all that (and goodbye to all that!), I succeeded. But I sometimes think that, rather than claw and scrape for mindless jobs all that time, I might as well have stayed at home writing about vampire flatmates and Scottish history! I think I'll just say it crudely, inelegantly and honestly: most employers I've met didn't have a clue how to deal with autism. They didn't listen, didn't want to learn and did me nothing but damage. In crude and simple terms, I spent about 27 years writing in my own time and 27 years grinding away in low-level jobs which completely failed to make any use of my abilities (now proven), and in fact nearly pulped my talent into little pieces,

says James.[23]

Gardening and agriculture

Many people with autism have a love of the open air – my own son, Johnny, included. Indeed, it can be hard to coax Johnny back indoors, even when it is growing dark and cold outside. This can lead to problems which are hilarious, in hindsight, but much more troublesome at the time. Once, when he was much younger, I took him to the playground in the park at the end of the road and, as dusk began to fall and it started to rain, that was the point that Johnny decided, for sensory reasons, that his clothes were irritating him and he started to remove them all. I began chasing him around the playground to persuade him both to put his clothes on again and to come back home. At that moment, of all moments, a police car pulled up outside the playground. I suddenly realised, to my horror, what it must look like to the policeman emerging from his car to see a grown man chasing a giggling, half-naked boy around a swing. Fortunately, I managed to convince the cop that I was indeed Johnny's Dad and that his state of undress was due to the sensory discomfort associated with his autism!

Such mishaps aside, a love of horticulture or bird life is fairly common in autism. We have already seen the case of the successful nature-loving TV presenter, Chris Packham. Here are some further uplifting examples.

❖ CASE STUDIES

- ALAN GARDNER
- LITTLE GATE FARM
- GREEN BRIDGE GROWERS

Birmingham-born ALAN GARDNER, 57, is one of British television's best-known gardeners. In his TV series, Alan redesigns gardens for neurotypical clients with his five-strong team of trainees, all of whom are amateur gardening enthusiasts and all on the autistic spectrum. His opening line sets the show's upbeat tone: 'I am A. Gardner – I literally am, it's my name: Alan Gardner.' (His choice of career would appear to support nominative determinism – the notion that names can influence choice of professions. This hypothesis stemmed from a genuine paper on urinary tract infection by Splatt and Wheedon.[24])

In fact, it was not until the age of 15 that Gardner became interested in gardening. He says his passion began after he bought a cactus from a local florist which he nurtured on his bedroom window sill and then flicked through a seed catalogue. 'When I looked at that catalogue and saw all the things that you could grow, the family garden quickly became a menagerie,' he recalled. 'To be honest, it was a welcome relief to my parents, as neither of them were gardeners.'[25]

Gardner went on to work for the Birmingham Parks Department before setting up on his own as a garden designer in 1986. He has earned a huge reputation for his original approach to landscapes and, over the years, he has created 40 Royal Horticultural Society gardens and won numerous awards at Chelsea, Hampton Court and Tatton Park flower shows and he now charges £100,000 for commissions. But today, most people recognise him from his trademark pink hair on Channel 4's hit show, *The Autistic Gardener*.

> I wasn't sure about going for a diagnosis for autism,' says Gardner, 'but Channel 4 didn't want to put that name [The Autistic Gardner] to the show for fear people would say I wasn't autistic, that I only thought I was. I'd been with my son Reiss, who was 18, at college for his parents' evening. He was going to have a dyslexia test and I ended up sitting in, and the guy said: 'I see you both have ASD – autism spectrum disorder.' I knew I saw the world in a different way but I had no clue why.[26]

Gardner believes that being on the autism spectrum gives him – and others – a special gift when it comes to creating stunning spaces: 'Many autistic people are drawn to spinning as a visual stimulation. It's the predictability of the repetition that gets us.'[27]

His straight-talking presentation style subverts the formulaic script usually associated with TV makeover shows. His voice-over is refreshingly original, as in the following example: 'The executive producer wants there to be some form of pressure. I've got Asperger's. I don't do pressure.'[28]

Alan says his goal is 'to prove that people with autism are not broken computers – we are different operating systems'. He added:

> I also believe that gardening has the potential to empower those with autism – to build confidence that will flow into other areas of their lives, no matter where they lie on the spectrum. So often a diagnosis brings with it a negative perception which can be disheartening; all the more reason why building ability – and therefore greater resilience – is key.[29]

For Gardner, his Asperger's gives him a unique eye for design and sequential detail, along with a fantastic drive to be the best that has helped him become the highly successful, award-winning garden designer he is today. As he says: 'gardening isn't a lesser career, it's an amazing thing to do.'[30]

Gardner lives in Sutton Coldfield with his wife Mandy, a pre-school classroom assistant, and their children Haydn, 24, Reiss, now 22 and Deanna, 16. He has since discovered that all three children are on the autistic spectrum. 'The diagnosis helped me and when my children were diagnosed it helped them too. But more importantly, *The Autistic Gardener* put autism on the map. Social media went ballistic with 900 positive tweets from the first episode.'[31]

LITTLE GATE FARM near Rye has a horticulture project which teaches people how to grow vegetables, which they sell at a farmers' market every week, providing the workers with the opportunity to practise customer service and cash-handling skills. In the Charcoal project – which is now entirely Ranger-led – adults with autism and learning disabilities make and sell charcoal using wood from their woodland. This ethical and sustainable charcoal is sold to local businesses such as farm shops and teaches the workers how to plan to synchronise supply and demand, manage orders and build relationships with business customers.

> The increased focus on employment skills has led to a decision to reduce the number of animals that we care for at the farm, because we recognised that the work generated by animal care was unlikely to lead to useful skill acquisition,

says Little Gate's chief executive officer, Claire Cordell. 'Meat production is not an area where many of our Rangers are likely to find employment and it has a shorter shelf life than charcoal!'[32]

Cordell says that, among the many lessons they have learned are: always to put the learning-disabled adult at the centre of everything they do; to set achievable personal goals; to recognise the need to support families; to work closely and continuously with employers and work colleagues to maintain support at work; to match the training on the farm closely with the skills required in the workplace; and finally, that many skills, such as communication and working in a team, are transferable across a wide range of tasks.[33]

GREEN BRIDGE GROWERS, in Mishawaka, Indiana, in the US, is a social enterprise empowering employment for highly capable young adults with autism through an urban aquaponics farm. The venture provides jobs while also producing an abundance of fresh, local produce for the local community.

A startling 90 per cent of all food consumed in Indiana is trucked in from out-of-state. Farming in the Midwest has also become heavily dependent on corn, compounding the situation, and traditional farming methods are extremely wasteful of water, a resource becoming ever-more scarce. Green Bridge's aquaponics is a highly sustainable, innovative growing method where fish and plants grow in harmony. Fish effluent is converted into the nutrients that the plants require for growth, and the plants, in turn, clean the water which is circulated back to the fish. This closed-loop system has many benefits, including four-season growth, reduced harvest time and the consumption of 90 per cent less water than traditional farming. Green Bridge also grows herbs, lettuces and specialty greens, which are sold to high-end restaurants, local grocers and at the farmers' market.

The co-founder of Green Bridge Growers, Jan Pilarski, has an autistic son, Chris. 'He'd pursued his love for French and chemistry at college, and his experience was overwhelmingly positive. Best of all, we were proud that he had connected to a terrific circle of friends and mentors,' says Pilarski.

> Work was another story, and much harder. Chris was hired as an environmental researcher the summer after graduation. But the social challenges he faced because of his autism proved too great for him. Within three months of starting that job, he was fired … We realised that outside-the-box thinking was needed to jumpstart Chris into the workforce. The more we thought about it, the more it seemed that an entrepreneurial approach was needed to address the huge problem of joblessness experienced by Chris and his peers. To us, such a huge problem required a very different solution. Where traditional employers merely saw the deficits of autism, we saw opportunity to use the strengths of autism as a new way to do business.
>
> What Chris was passionate about was organic farming. He related his love of chemistry to a desire to grow food healthfully and organically. While in college, he had even had several internships in the field. Why not be entrepreneurial and structure a business around that passion for farming and the demand for local, fresh food? … About two years' worth of research, training, and planning went into our venture before launching. We sought partnerships, involved stakeholders, and visited existing entrepreneurial models like Asperitech and learned a lot. We're filling a niche in our community by growing produce year-round, primarily using a method called aquaponics where fish and vegetables grow in harmony. Our core workforce is people on the spectrum, and the scheduling, precision, and monitoring needed in aquaponics is a terrific match for their skills.[34]

Cooking and catering

❖ CASE STUDIES

- LIAM POPE
- PADDOCK SCHOOL CAFÉ
- LATIMER'S SEAFOOD DELI
- DIRT COFFEE

LIAM POPE, 21, spent four years from 2010 at LVS Hassocks School for children with autism in Sussex, southern England, learning to cook and gaining qualifications. Now he has secured a position as Chef de Partie at Wycombe Abbey girls' school, one of the top girls' boarding schools in the United Kingdom. He started work there in September 2017.

At the time Liam was at LVS Hassocks, he was able to make no more than a pot noodle and had absolutely no thoughts of a future career. However, an encounter with the celebrity chef, Paul Rankin, at the school's official opening in 2011 ignited his interest, before LVS Hassocks capitalised on it to develop Liam's prospects of leading an independent life beyond the school.

By the time he left the school at 17, Liam had a planned career path thanks to hands-on work experience with the Yummy Pub Co, an NVQ Level 1 qualification in Food Preparation and Cooking and academic qualifications. He also enjoyed an apprenticeship, funded by members of the Association of Licensed Multiple Retailers (ALMR), to run alongside an NVQ Level 2 in Food Production and Cooking. An apprenticeship working for Sodexo in Ascot led to a permanent position, during which time he became national Young Chef of the Year at the Sodexo Salon Culinaire.

Liam says:

> LVS Hassocks' giving me the opportunity to cook for myself, as a way of becoming independent, triggered my interest in it as a career. As I became more and more interested, they also allowed me to cook in the school kitchen with the catering team there to get used to the equipment and what to expect, and also set up valuable work experience for me with the Yummy Pub Co at The Wiremill in Surrey. It all combined to make a huge difference to me and help me develop a career.[35]

His career progression continued and in July 2017, Liam said goodbye to his friends and colleagues in Ascot ready to take on his new challenge with greater responsibility as chef at Wycombe Abbey.

Sarah Sherwood, LVS Hassocks' director of special educational needs, said:

> Liam is now an independent and ambitious young man enjoying life and his career. This is a great example to all the learners that we are currently developing through work experience, a range of qualifications and the building of their independence and social skills.[36]

The PADDOCK SCHOOL CAFÉ opened in south-west London in 2013. The school itself is spread over three sites and caters for pupils aged between four and 19 with severe learning difficulties. A number of pupils with autism work in the Café, which is in Wandsworth. They include Ramandeep Singh, who enjoys working on the till.

The café is open to the public every Wednesday from 10.00am to midday and every Thursday from 10.00am to 2.00pm. It has two professed aims: to provide work experience for the school students and to showcase the abilities of young people with learning disabilities. The students are taught the many skills of working in a café: to carry a tray, to read a menu, work the till, clear tables, deliver orders to customers, and to wash up, among others. And the students cook tasty home-made cakes, sandwiches, soup or shepherd's pie.

Emily Hayward, the head of the secondary school, told me:

The in-house work experience is so successful due to being highly structured. Pupils know what is expected of them and are given visual support to complete tasks. Ensuring the right systems are put in place to enable pupils to complete tasks independently is so important.[37]

LATIMER'S SEAFOOD DELI in Whitburn, near Sunderland, has taken on its first autistic employee – and she is thriving. Sophie has skills in both social media and design and the Latimer family encouraged her to use these abilities in the workplace within the business. She began to design platters for customers, using her artistic flair, as well as taking photographs of products and updating the company's social media accounts.

Latimer's came up with a new way to update the business: a mascot – a crab named Claude. Aware that Sophie was a polymer clay artist, they invited her to a meeting to discuss what she created in her spare time and to see some of her work. The company were impressed and explained they wanted to introduce a clay mascot which could be hidden on beaches in the north-east of England to be found and returned for a reward. They asked Sophie to provide a sample and an invoice for work. This, in itself, taught her new business skills. Latimer's were delighted with Sophie's prototype and placed a large order of 50 crabs.

The impact on Sophie has been remarkable. A year ago, she was suicidal. Unable to accept her diagnosis of Asperger's syndrome, she felt broken and useless. Today, she is happy and confident. Her delighted parents are enormously appreciative of Latimer's approach: namely, encouraging the things she is good at rather than focusing on the challenges. She has stopped self-harming and finally feels valued. Moreover, whereas before, she would rarely venture out socially, she now mixes more with her work and college friends.[38]

Daniel Boone is an outgoing young man and, like his namesake – the pioneering eighteenth-century American frontiersman – he is a trailblazer. For three years, he has been working for DIRT COFFEE, a new non-profit-making company in downtown Denver, Colorado, in the US, with a mission to train and employ adults with autism.

Daniel throws himself into his work every day: 'Beautiful day out in the city today, huh?' he says as he leans out of a truck window to hand over a cup of fresh brewed coffee. 'I'm having a fantastic morning. Thank you! Have a magical day, Sir.'

He told CBS: 'I've been working my caboose off for a couple of years now.'[39] Daniel is a train-lover and when he became Dirt's Employee of the Year in 2016, he was given a conductor's hat rather than a certificate.

Lauren Burgess, who started up Dirt in 2013, explains its name: 'We are all about building a foundation, planting seeds that inspire and cultivate growth.'[40]

Dirt Coffee falls under the broader auspices of Teaching the Autism Community Trades (TACT), which was founded by Danny Combs (who has a son with autism). 'We're giving our community something they can do for employment and fulfilment and be happy,' said Combs. 'It's wonderful.'[41]

Cleaning jobs

Obsession with hygiene and cleanliness can be common in some (but by no means all!) people on the autism spectrum. For these individuals, a cleaning job may represent a good match.

❖ CASE STUDY

- CHRIS LYNCH

CHRIS LYNCH, a 28-year-old man with Asperger's syndrome from Ashington, was recently appointed a professional cleaner by City Facilities Management, the team that handles the Asda superstore cleaning. An added bonus is he finds himself working alongside his father, who is the store's handyman.

Chris had found it impossible to find a job when he and his family moved to the north-east of England six years ago. After staff at Ashington's Jobcentre Plus suggested that Chris visit Remploy's new specialist services recruitment branch in Newcastle, he enrolled on a two-week course with Remploy, designed to enhance his employability skills. He regained his self-esteem, and learned effective interview techniques and how to write a CV that would attract the attention of employers.

Within a day of starting his four-week work trial with City Facilities Management at Asda, Chris had convinced his new boss that he would be a real asset to the team and he was appointed on the spot.

'My role is to help keep the store's bakery in tip-top condition, but I also help out in other areas too,' said Chris.

> It's brilliant to be back in work after years of trying to convince other employers that I could do a good job – I was beginning to think it would never happen. I have been, and still am, a volunteer with Groundwork North East, an environmental charity. But it's nice to work and earn a wage at the same time.[42]

Dance

Although some young adults on the autism spectrum may be physically clumsy, parents should not assume that this is the case for their child. He or she can demonstrate surprising skills in creative arts which require physical movement, such as ballet.

❖ CASE STUDY

- JAMES HOBLEY

In 2015, JAMES HOBLEY, a 15-year-old autistic boy from Redcar, was offered a place at the English National Ballet School. (His twin brother also has autism, as does his elder brother.)

Their mother, Sheila, initially decided to home-school the children. 'I worked at home with them and tried to find ways to engage them in an activity. A leaflet came through my door advertising dance lessons for freestyle disco dancing and that is where James's story started,' Sheila recalled.[43] That was 11 years ago, when James was eight. At that time, just getting to the lesson was not easy for him.

As James himself explains:

> Autistic people find it hard to go out the house, especially to go out to the town and order fish and chips or pizza or anything... it's very hard. I was in my own little world I guess... I didn't understand what was really going on out of that world. Interacting with people was very hard, because everybody else was making normal conversation. Making friends is that 'warmth of normal' that I get attracted to every time, but I've never really experienced it.
>
> My earliest memories are at around four years old. I was always quiet and hardly spoke. There was no need to speak, my twin brother did all the talking for the two of us. I followed in his shadow. I wasn't really interested in the world outside my house. It scared me. I was happiest lying on the floor with my cat, staring into his eyes and examining his fur in minute detail.
>
> I didn't have any friends ... to be honest I didn't know what a friend was. I attended a special needs school where many of the other children had learning difficulties and autism. Not many of them interacted with one another so I didn't have to deal with friendships. I just followed my twin brother, George, around as he attended the same special needs school. I remember not liking school and I really hated having to play any games or hold hands with any teachers or children. I liked to have my own space and not have to touch others. I hated them touching me or getting too close. Making friends can be difficult for someone with autism but I have had plenty of practice at my current school and I have even become a prefect!
>
> I didn't like looking at people's faces much and detested giving eye contact. I used to look at the floor in front of me all the time when I danced. My eye level was always low. I have had to work really hard, and still do, to raise my eye level and look at people and project my emotions out to an audience.[44]

Sheila says she has always encouraged her children to follow their dreams 'no matter how out of reach they seemed'. With her help, James managed to overcome those first hurdles and started dance lessons. It didn't just help him mentally but physically in a dramatic way.

> Before I started dancing, I had orthopaedic boots and splints on the back of my legs because I used to walk on my tiptoes a lot. I hated them. I couldn't run or do anything whilst wearing them. Walking was painful and I spent a lot of time in a large pushchair on shopping trips because my legs ached so much when I walked. The only time I got to take the braces and boots off was during sports at school, which I always enjoyed. I loved running and swimming.

Soon after starting his disco class, things began to change dramatically. Within six months, James didn't need the splints any longer and he found that he was naturally flexible and after three months he was doing the splits. The most difficult thing for James was performing in front of people. His autism meant he didn't like to give eye contact. He became totally engrossed in his own world when he danced and his teacher had to remind him constantly to look at the judges at competitions and to smile.

James enjoyed disco dancing, and won many competitions, but when he was ten he discovered a whole new world of classical ballet. He went to see his first ballet as part of a BBC documentary filmed about his life, *Autism, Disco and Me*. It was the Moscow Ballet's *Nutcracker*. 'I will never forget the first time I saw a ballet on stage,' says James.

> I was ten years old. It was something very new to me and I didn't quite understand everything, but I was hooked! I loved the way the dancers moved and the musicality. I just had to find out more. I knew on that first night that I wanted to be a ballet dancer, even though I wasn't sure what it entailed and didn't realise the years of hard work and dedication that lay ahead of me. I didn't really know what dancing was. When I saw the other kids doing walkovers, splits, and high kicks I was in awe. They sometimes brought in the trophies they had won at competitions and I knew I wanted to win competitions too! I felt like I was a part of something ... something exciting and big.[45]

A year later, James won a scholarship to attend the Hammond School in Chester, where he now boards. The school is a specialist musical theatre and dance school and claims to be the leading provider of Performing Arts education in north-west England.

In 2010, Sheila spotted an advertisement for people to audition for the TV show, *Britain's Got Talent*. James got through to the 2011 final. Four years later, he won his ENB School scholarship. During that time, he has certainly come a long way. He has performed at the O2 Arena in London and in Times Square, New York, carried the Olympic flame and opened an international autism conference in Spain. And in 2017, he performed in the English National Ballet's *My First Ballet: Cinderella*.

'Dancing, for me, was like turning on a switch,' James says.

> I don't have many memories before I started dancing and my family think this is because I didn't always communicate with other people very much. Autism can make it hard to communicate the emotions you are feeling, but I think dancing and performing has allowed me to find a way to express myself.[46]

He says that he is excited to be appearing in his first ballet: 'I've enjoyed learning the different roles and thinking about each of the characters and their personalities and how you portray that on stage. I'm also really looking forward to the experience of being on tour with my friends.'

James is also a patron for Anna Kennedy's charity, Autism Got Talent. He says this is amazing, 'because I get to help other people on the autistic spectrum and inspire others to achieve great things'.[47]

Modelling

In 2017, the BBC's African Service featured the story of three autistic teenage girls in Ghana – Yacoba Tete-Marmon, Nana Ohenewaa Kuffour and Maame Bema Baffour Awuah – who had become successful models. They have won awards and been made brand ambassadors for a water company in Ghana.[48]

Far better-known is the case of Heather Kuzmich, a fashion model with Asperger's syndrome who leapt to international attention when she became fourth runner-up on Season 9 of *America's Next Top Model* in 2008. She is currently signed up with Elite Model Management, and is living in her home town, Chicago, where she is studying video game design and continuing to model.

Heather was diagnosed with Asperger's and ADHD at the age of 15. She was initially reluctant to audition for *America's Next Top Model* but caved in to pressure from friends and family. As it turned out, her portfolio was one of the strongest on the show: she won nine Cover Girl of the Week awards and she was chosen by Enrique Iglesias to star in a music video. She did run into difficulty, however, relating to the other girls on the show and during challenges where she was required to speak in front of an audience or deliver lines.

Sports

The sporting arena has provided fruitful opportunities for a number of individuals on the autism spectrum. Although some autistic people have poor gross motor skills, others have gone on to achieve considerable sporting success. (There are unsubstantiated claims that Lionel Messi, the Barcelona and Argentina footballing superstar, might have been diagnosed with Asperger's syndrome as a young boy.)

Kevin Pelphrey, director of George Washington University's Autism and Neurodevelopmental Disorders Institute, is in the process of publishing a study on 'affinity therapy' with 24 seven- to 13-year-olds. Affinity treatment was popularised in the book by the journalist, Ron Suskind, *Life Animated*, in which his autistic son, Owen, uses his love of Disney to connect with the world (later turned into a movie). Pelphrey and his team see a chance to use a patient's passion for sports as a framework for their treatment. 'When sports are going well, it's the best of social interaction,' he says.

It's a great opportunity to teach these skills. When therapists have wanted to extinguish interests that seem over-the-top, it's been virtually impossible, so why not see them as something you can utilise? It's about taking what you've got to work with and making the most of it.[49]

❖ CASE STUDY

- JESSICA-JANE APPLEGATE

JESSICA-JANE APPLEGATE, a 15-year-old schoolgirl with Asperger's syndrome from Great Yarmouth, became the first British athlete in the controversial 'intellectually disabled' classification to win a gold medal at the 2012 Paralympic Games in London. She won the 200 metres freestyle swimming final. (Intellectually disabled athletes had been welcomed back into the Paralympic fold only recently following the controversy of the Spanish basketball gold medal-winning team at Sydney in 2000 which contained no players with intellectual impairment and one who was a professional.)

Few would begrudge Jessica, who is an aspiring underwater photographer, her moment of glory – especially as she had to undergo a toe operation shortly before the London Games. Since then, she has gone on to achieve even greater success, despite serious health issues. In Rio de Janeiro in 2016, she won three more Paralympic medals just nine weeks after a career-saving throat operation.

In November 2016, she hinted that she might have to give up the sport after her funding was cut. But financial support from her local community in Norfolk has enabled her to persevere with her career.

'Swimming has made a huge difference to my life,' Jessica told her local newspaper. 'I dread to think where I could have ended up without it, as I was on a very slippery slope. It has given me a purpose, a routine, discipline, confidence and social skills. Everyone should try it.'[50]

The medical profession

Many readers will, I suspect, have watched the ABC television series, *The Good Doctor*, which aired on Sky Living in November 2017 in which Freddie Highmore plays a brilliant autistic surgeon, Dr Shaun Murphy. The programme has been well-received, not least by viewers on the spectrum. But can people with autism genuinely make it in the health service?

Britain's General Medical Council recommendations stipulate that doctors are expected to have good relationships with their patients and colleagues and to communicate well: to have respect for their colleagues and to be able to consult them and to take advice. While none of this is incompatible with autism, it is easy to see why – in the words of Dr Tom Berney, of Newcastle University – 'someone might be particularly prone to difficulty in this area'.[51]

Berney said professional problems frequently arose in three areas:

- Problems with colleagues: Alienation of those with whom they work, a one-sided approach to issues which presents as vigorous persuasion rather than discussion or negotiation, and inaccessibility to monitoring/supervision.
- Problems with patients: Inadvertently giving offence by an unthinking comment, a failure to appreciate the patient's perspective and needs so that, for example, the patient may call for unnecessary appointments or be dumped, without explanation, at the end of their programme of treatment or assessment.
- Idiosyncratic practice: The single-minded pursuit of a topic which, no matter how unproductive, may turn into a feud or quest, an inflexible adherence to rules/guidelines that takes insufficient account of individual circumstances or, more broadly, a rigid and over-methodical approach no matter how inefficient or inappropriate, and a difficulty in organising themselves efficiently, often in the management of their time or priorities.[52]

Nevertheless, Berney emphasised:

I have known a number of psychiatrists whose skills in managing patients, families and staff were in sharp contrast with the awkward aloofness of their domestic lives. New situations can be coped with, provided the individual is in the right frame of mind (neither unduly relaxed nor emotionally aroused) and has time to think.[53]

❖ CASE STUDY

- VAUGHAN BOWEN

Surrey-born VAUGHAN BOWEN, a successful surgeon with Asperger's syndrome, said that, as a child, he was particularly interested in geography and the flute.

I excelled at schoolwork but was too uncoordinated for sport. I could run but I did not understand the complexities of team games. I have some 'invisible' difficulties that make it difficult to interact socially and to sometimes appear 'odd', says Bowen.

> I have remarkable ability when it comes to non-verbal reasoning, abstract problem-solving, special reasoning and visual/motor capabilities. I am well adapted. My special abilities make me ideally suited to orthopaedic surgery.[54]

He says he has lived a double life:

> Outside observers have seen a great success story. I obtained a medical degree from a good university. I can fly an aircraft ... Fixing broken people is easy for me. I have had a very successful career. Other aspects of life, however, have been a mystery: unpredictable and difficult to interpret. I had severe depression in my 20s. My wife, an operating room nurse, has looked after me well and been a great mother for our two adopted children. We have moved from one university job to another, apparently climbing the academic ladder but, more likely, attempting to pacify my social anxiety.

This anxiety, he says, has been 'my perpetual life partner'. He recognises that he has strange responses to textures, sounds and other sensory stimulation.

Bowen adds: 'People like me and do not realise I am uncomfortable socially. I live in Canada. I find life less complex there and my apparent eccentricities are tolerated and attributed to me being "British".'[55]

The caring professions

Despite the supposed lack of empathy in autism – as we have seen, the situation is not what it seems – quite a few people with Asperger's have been shown to want jobs which help or benefit others. Indeed, as Anne Cockayne has noted, the ability to remain detached yet interested can constitute a strength. On the other hand, Cockayne quotes one manager as having to explain to an employee with Asperger's syndrome working on a mental health ward why she needed to be empathetic to a self-harm patient – something he would not have expected to do for others working in similar roles. Later that day, the same employee dealt with this same patient, this time in a distressing situation (somebody had cut their arms) from which others shied away, leading her manager to conceptualise that this level of emotional detachment could indeed also be an advantage. 'That's a strength in dealing with an emergency. Sometimes you need those people to have those skills to just get on with it.'[56]

❖ CASE STUDIES

- HOLLY TADMAN
- RYAN TEBBIT

HOLLY TADMAN is a young woman with autism and pronounced dysarthria, who came to Little Gate Farm after leaving college. Her time at college hadn't been easy and Holly had often felt excluded by her peers and isolated. When she came to the farm, her confidence was low. Very quickly, Holly found her way on the farm and proved herself to be a very able, committed, hard-working young lady, mature beyond her years.

Holly had just won a gold medal at the world special Olympics in Los Angeles in Judo, and had previously won gold at the European championships. When she joined Little Gate, she worked hard to overcome her social anxiety and embraced opportunities to attend public speaking events with the team at the farm. Holly started working as a lunch-time assistant in a large care home in Bexhill. She enjoyed the work and especially the residents, and she really enjoyed the feeling of having a job.

After a year, Holly informed the farm that she had an aspiration to be a carer, and the home were so impressed that they offered her a trial. Holly and her job coach worked hard to learn the systems of caring and do every activity to a high standard. She was offered a permanent role at the home, and now, because she has learnt to perform each task to the highest standard, she is often asked to support agency staff. Holly says her job means more to her than all her sporting medals.[57]

RYAN TEBBIT, a therapist working for Elaine Nicholson's charity Action for Asperger's, has found his vocation as a counsellor after years of unhappy employment and workplace bullying. 'I've had many years of therapy as a client and after some time, I decided to train as a counsellor myself,' he says.

> The final bit of therapy I had where I was a client, pre-diagnosis but post-awareness of my autism, was particularly fruitful for me and really opened

Figure 8.1 Ryan Tebbit

my eyes to the power of therapy. Progressing my career from a support worker to a counsellor seemed to me like a very obvious and appealing next step. Once I began the training, I became aware that my autism may pose some challenges and at times I felt that I should quit. However, because of this autistic bullishness that I seem to have, I persevered as I became extremely focused, nearly to the point of obsession as well as a sense of defiance and a strong sense of self-belief.[58]

Ryan says that, through his work as a counsellor, he has often experienced empathy with his clients. He quotes Olga Bogdashina, who wrote: 'If many autistic individuals are emotionally hypersensitive, how can we explain their (alleged) lack of empathy?'[59]

In Ryan's own words:

> If I am particularly tuned in to one of my clients and they begin to cry, quite often I cry too. In this way, I can feel what someone else is feeling but at the same time, I never lose the 'as if' element: I am always myself, feeling as if I am sharing an emotional space with them. For me, the idea of empathy is about seeing pictures of someone situated in their life and watching their movie play out, with curiosity. For me, it just does not follow that the lack of, or delay in, theory of mind equals a lack of empathy; they are distinct things and can be worked with different techniques in the counselling room. Being autistic doesn't give me a special ability with my autistic clients, but it does provide me with an insider's view that few therapists at the moment have.[60]

Ryan points out that, from a conventional point of view, autism and the caring professions would appear to be a poor match. Simon Baron-Cohen's extreme male brain theory of autism would seem to imply that people with a 'female brain' are likely to make better counsellors, nurses, carers, therapists, social workers, whereas those with the male brain make fine scientists, engineers, mechanics, technicians, musicians, architects, electricians, plumbers, taxonomists, cataloguists, bankers, toolmakers, programmers or even lawyers. 'In some ways, I can relate to Baron-Cohen's idea,' says Ryan, 'but I have felt differently in that I have always had a strong interest in other people, and working with them and helping them. This does not fit with Baron-Cohen's categorisations,' writes Ryan.[61]

Historically, his interest in counselling started when he was 'sent' to counselling at the age of 16.

> My mother had wrongly suspected I was using illegal drugs and sent me to a local drug user support centre for counselling. It didn't work and it was in some ways quite damaging, but the idea of talking as helpful became illuminated for me ... [However], it wasn't until my thirties, whilst engaged in Cognitive Analytic Therapy (CAT), that the penny started to drop about how therapy was going to be helpful for me ... and it was a shock which hurt. I suddenly realised that I didn't like myself, or more accurately, I actively hated myself ... At this time I was in a fairly

dysfunctional co-habiting relationship. One day, my girlfriend expressed a vague interest in doing some counselling training. On hearing this, my emotions took over me and I felt immediately compelled to go into competition with her ...

After completing my introductory courses and PG Certificate years, I was ready to apply for the PG Diploma year which is a full-time year-long course at the end of which I could call myself a qualified counsellor. The term 'full-time' doesn't really do it justice, because it was more like a year-long whirlwind of lectures, assignments, placements, skills practice and long hours of group time. Just surviving it felt like a huge achievement.[62]

Ryan adds:

I have spent my life misunderstanding others and being misunderstood by others. Communication is a very, very difficult thing for me to do. It all feels overwhelming and confusing; it is a big problem in my life ... From what I have read about Wittgenstein, communication was clearly a problem for him and so he tried to solve the problem using logic. I have a suspicion that these links between communication and philosophy taking me on a path towards fulfilment are very central to why I decided to become a counsellor. Through this, I could find answers. Relationships and communication have been at the heart of my problems during life so far. So why wouldn't I train as a therapist? A profession where creating meaningful, functional and deep (working) relationships is the purpose. Problem solved! ...

I believe the key factor is the relationship you create with your therapist, not the theoretical approach. Once you have built up trust and shown your client you are not going to judge them in any way, eventually you can reach a real depth in this trust. As a therapist with autism, I am very much tuned into my client's words and their literal meaning for me. Up until now, this is the only way I can see of learning how to be empathic. Understanding the client's words was simply a starting point for me and gradually I have learnt to use all my senses to simply reflect my client's process back to them.

My counselling training changed my life but never in the way that I would expect. I would describe it as watching a profound action movie of the universe. I left the cinema dazed and deeply affected and that's when my learning really began and continues. It showed me a new way to 'be' (my way) and now I want to devote my life to practising and honing this new way. The awareness that I continue to develop within me has opened the door to a whole universe of learning and now I'm working on my own, in my way, I can really entertain the possibility.[63]

Non-traditional employment opportunities

As previously noted, Luke Jackson, the talented British photographer with Asperger's syndrome, has emphasised the importance of thinking laterally and fearlessly seeking out non-traditional routes of employment, if this is appropriate, because 'if you're good at something, more often than not, work will find you.'[64]

❖ CASE STUDIES

- GUS SNOWDON
- CHARLES BURNS

Doorways open up in unexpected ways and places. Indeed, one young man with autism has actually found his niche as a doorman. GUS SNOWDEN is still only 16 but he works on the front desk of his family's apartment block in New York City. According to his mother, Judith Newman, Gus knows the names of all the building's residents, their dogs, their apartment numbers. Despite Judith's constant reminders that it's rude to ask people where they are going or what they are doing that night or who the 'new person' they've come in with is, Gus keeps asking.

Judith says that if Gus saw someone come into the building with a gun, he'd probably ask the guy what kind of gun it was and what street he bought it on. 'Gus can do every part of a doorman's job except the part that involves keeping people out,' she adds.[65]

In 1985, CHARLES BURNS, a man with Asperger's syndrome, began to make ends meet by working as a street artist in London's Covent Garden, drawing pencil portraits of tourists and other passers-by. He charged £5 per portrait and did this for ten years – during which time, he got married, had two children and bought a house.

By 1995, he was charging £15 a portrait. But as a sideline, he began cutting silhouette profiles. To his enormous surprise, he started to receive bookings as an 'artist-entertainer', cutting silhouettes of guests at parties and corporate events.

'As a young man, I had always hated parties and would have run a mile to avoid such employment,' he says.

> Today, I work full-time in the events and entertainment industry, and spend my life travelling the country (and occasionally abroad) from one event to another cutting silhouettes with scissors. This obscure eighteenth-century art has become my livelihood. I have been booked for some extraordinary events and met – and cut portraits of – many famous people. I have written a book about silhouettes and even made a documentary film.[66]

Notes

1   *Asperger's and Me*, first broadcast on 17 October 2017.
2   *Daily Telegraph*, 3 April 2017.
3   Ibid.
4   *Mail Online*, 21 October 2016.
5   Ibid.
6   *Daily Telegraph*, 9 October 2017.

7   Ibid.
8   *Mail Online*, 21 October 2016.
9   *USA Today*, 12 October 2016.
10 Ibid.
11 See: www.headstuff.org/film/film-review-the-accountant/ (accessed 27 April 2018).
12 See: http://thomasiland.com/review-accountant-cpa-autism/ (accessed 27 April 2018).
13 Ibid.
14 Information supplied by Little Gate Farm.
15 Ibid.
16 *Huffington Post*, 28 July 2016.
17 Ibid.
18 Ibid.
19 Ibid.
20 Ibid.
21 James Christie in communication with the author, 18 August 2017.
22 Ibid.
23 Ibid.
24 See A. J. Splatt and D. Weedon (1981), 'The urethral syndrome: Morphological studies', *British Journal of Urology*, June, 53(3), 263–265.
25 See: https://theautisticgardener.wordpress.com/about-alan/ (accessed 27 April 2018).
26 *Mail Online*, 16 June 2017.
27 Ibid.
28 Ibid.
29 See: www.telegraph.co.uk/science/2017/10/09/chris-packham-living-aspergers-spent-30-years-telly-trying-best/ (accessed 9 October 2017).
30 See: www.theguardian.com/global/2015/sep/11/chris-packham-interview-countryside-alliance-bbc-foxhunting (accessed 11 September 2015).
31 www.telegraph.co.uk/science/2017/10/09/chris-packham-living-aspergers-spent-30-years-telly-trying-best/ (accessed 9 October 2017).
32 Information supplied by Little Gate Farm.
33 Ibid.
34 See: www.autismspeaks.org/wordpress-tags/green-bridge-growers (accessed 27 April 2018).
35 *Mid Sussex Times*, 14 August 2017.
36 Ibid.
37 Emily Hayward in conversation with the author, 4 September 2017.
38 Ibid.
39 See: http://denver.cbslocal.com/2017/12/17/autism-dirt-coffee/ (accessed 17 December 2017).
40 Ibid.
41 Ibid.
42 Information supplied by Remploy.
43 See: www.gramilano.com/2015/04/autistic-ballet-dancer-james-hobley-wins-place-at-english-national-ballet-school/ (accessed 27 April 2018).
44 Ibid.
45 Ibid.
46 See: www.ballet.org.uk/blog-detail/james-hobley-dancing-my-first-ballet-cinderella/ (accessed 27 April 2018).
47 Ibid.
48 See: www.bbc.co.uk/news/av/world-africa-42919873/ghana-s-autistic-models-turn-heads-and-win-awards (accessed 27 April 2018).
49 See Jon Wertheim and Stephanie Apstein, 'Defying expectations, people with autism are participating and excelling in sports', www.si.com/sports-illustrated/2016/11/01/people-with-autism-spectrum-disorder-embrace-sports-athletics (accessed 1 November 2016).
50 See: www.edp24.co.uk/news/how-swimming-changed-my-life-british-paralympian-and-gorleston-girl-jessica-jane-applegate-shares-her-tale-1-5083621 (accessed 30 June 2017).

51   See: www.rcpsych.ac.uk/pdf/Tom%20Berney.pdf (accessed 27 April 2018).

52   Ibid.

53   Ibid.

54   See: www.getsurrey.co.uk/incoming/fixing-people-easy-life-mystery-6910686 (accessed 3 April 2014).

55   Ibid.

56   Ibid.

57   Information supplied by Little Gate.

58   See Ryan Tebbit (undated), *An Autoethnographic Inquiry Into My Experiences and Journey of Autism and Becoming a Counsellor*.

59   See Olga Bogdashina (2013), *Autism and Spirituality: Psyche, Self and Spirit in People on the Autism Spectrum*. London: Jessica Kingsley, p. 68.

60   Ryan Tebbit, op. cit.

61   Ibid.

62   Ibid.

63   Ibid.

64   Luke Jackson (2016), *Sex, Drugs and Asperger's Syndrome – A User's Guide to Adulthood*. London: Jessica Kingsley, pp. 86–87.

65   See: www.rd.com/advice/parenting/autism-son-job/ (accessed 27 April 2018).

66   See Caroline Hearst (ed.) (2015), *Being Autistic: Nine Adults Share Their Journey from Discovery to Acceptance*. Reading: Autangel, p. 3.

Part III

Applying for a job

Chapter 9

Before the interview

Mark Haggarty, a man with Asperger's syndrome who describes his obsessions as France and grabatology (collecting ties), has some sage advice for those responding to a job advertisement:

> Find out as much as you can about the organisation to which you will be applying. Begin with simple things, such as when the company was established, how many people they employ and exactly what type of business they are involved in. Knowing this information should make the process that is to follow less daunting and it will give you an idea as to whether the organisation will make a suitable workplace for you. As well as that, it will also mean that you can show a certain degree of knowledge about the company should you go for an interview. It is never a good idea to go for a job interview without any knowledge of the company you could potentially be going to work for![1]

The CV

A number of common issues arise when it comes to a prospective job candidate preparing his or her curriculum vitae. Jo Loudon, a human resources adviser at the University of Strathclyde, in Scotland, has some useful pointers in this regard. First of all, she notes, the information on the CV tends to be too unfocused. It is often a standard CV and is not tailored to the specific job for which the person is applying. It is also a good idea for someone to proofread the CV before it is submitted and provide feedback.[2]

There are plenty of free CV templates on the Internet which give you useful ideas on how to structure your CV. As Sarah Hendrickx, of the Brighton organisation ASPire, rightly counsels, do not be afraid to 'blow your own trumpet' (sing your own praises), because all the other candidates will be doing so.[3]

But do not lie. Michael John Carley usefully compares this part of the process to television advertising:

> Most of us know that a TV commercial stretches the truth – the product that's being sold might be liked by some people, but it certainly isn't as universally *loved* as they depict in the commercial. So too do we need to advertise ourselves sometimes.[4]

Making contacts

Temple Grandin talks about the importance of 'finding the backdoor'. A chance meeting with the right person helped her get into a well-known meat plant in Arizona at the start of her career.

> At an Arizona cattle meeting, I met the wife of the plant's insurance agent. She was impressed with my hand-embroidered western shirt. I was wearing my 'portfolio' but I did not realise it at the time. People respect talent and she saw my abilities in my shirt. Back doors are everywhere. You just have to be creative and find them. Of course, it could be argued that this was an instance where luck played an important role – and so it did. But you have to lay yourselves open to these chance encounters and channels.[5]

Temple Grandin says she 'had to sell my work, and not myself. I sell clients my livestock equipment designs, I made portfolios of photos and drawings. They thought I was weird, but they respected me when they saw my work.'[6]

Indeed, Grandin's portfolio actually saved her from being sacked from her first job, writing articles for the magazine *Arizona Farmer Ranchman*. At one point, the magazine was sold and the new owner thought she was very peculiar. Fortunately, an astute colleague working on the page layouts advised Grandin to make a portfolio of all her articles and when the new boss saw this, he was not only impressed but increased her salary.

Grandin says a portfolio should contain no more than five or ten pages. Only the best work should be included in the portfolio and it must be appropriate for the employer to whom it is being sent. 'Elaborate science fiction art is not going to impress an advertising agency that does ads for banks.'[7]

You also have to make it easy got a busy employer to contact you in response to the portfolio. 'I am appalled at the amount of emails and letters I get that do not contain complete contact information,' says Grandin.[8]

Notes

1 See Genevieve Edmonds and Luke Beardon (eds) (2008), *Asperger Syndrome and Employment*. London: Jessica Kingsley, p. 100.
2 See: www.autismnetworkscotland.org.uk/files/2015/10/2-Jo-Loudon.pdf (accessed 27 April 2018).
3 See Sarah Hendrickx (2009), *Asperger Syndrome and Employment – What People with Asperger Syndrome Really Really Want*. London: Jessica Kingsley, p. 103.
4 See Michael John Carley (2016), *Unemployed on the Autism Spectrum*. London: Jessica Kingsley, p. 68.
5 See Josie Santomauro (ed.) (2011), *Autism All-Stars: How We Use Our Autism and Asperger Traits to Shine in Life*. London: Jessica Kingsley, p. 41.
6 Ibid., p. 40.
7 Ibid.
8 Ibid.

Chapter 10

To disclose or not to disclose?

The pros and cons

A crucial issue throughout the application process is whether to disclose your condition to the employer in advance. Autism is a 'hidden' disability, with no external physical signs (unless there is a medical comorbity such as cerebral palsy), and it encompasses a huge range of people, behaviours, abilities and challenges which, for many non-autistic people, takes time to appreciate and understand. The decision about whether to reveal your autism spectrum condition is a personal decision and must be considered with great care. Companies will benefit from the specific skills associated with autism – ability to focus, punctuality, honesty, etc. But bosses and colleagues might not even know someone is autistic, just that he or she is struggling to fit in. Disclosure in advance allows enlightened employers to tailor the working environment and the specific tasks to ensure that both employer and employee produce the optimal result.

The situation is far from simple, however. Thorkil Sonne, founder of Specialisterne, told me:

> It would be wonderful to be able to discuss the challenges openly. But I've also met many people who say that when they disclosed, they were dismissed shortly afterwards. What I'm trying to promote is openness and understanding. Employers are interested in your talent. We want the employers to be a trusted partner. Our role is to match talents with companies. Recruiters tend to be risk-averse. When something deviates from the pattern, they go to the next case to see whether that fits, rather than looking for talent. The recruiters are very important stakeholders. My hope is that all recruitment or human resources departments will have an autistic employee. How about an autistic recruiter in the HR department? I met a person with autism in Google HR and I was really inspired. I would encourage every HR department to hire someone with autism. They can understand the strengths of workers on the spectrum.[1]

Sharon Didrichsen, the chief executive of Specialisterne Northern Ireland, adds:

> We do not always recommend disclosure. Autistic people tell us that sometimes this helps and at other times disclosing did not seem to help at all. When perception of autism is sufficiently nuanced, disclosure seems to be easier, as it allows autistic people to be themselves rather than fitting into yet another stereotype. We need to add colour to the black and white.[2]

Dinah Murray has written: 'Disclosure of an autism spectrum diagnosis means disclosure of the fundamentally flawed personhood implied by the diagnostic criteria. It is likely to precipitate a negative judgement of capacity involving permanent loss of credibility.'[3]

One man with Asperger's syndrome, Ian Wombell, starkly articulated the dilemma of disclosure in the British daily, *The Guardian*, in 2001:

> If I put on a job application that I am suffering from Asperger's syndrome, I don't get an interview. If I don't tell people about my disability when I go for the interview, they cannot understand what is wrong with me.[4]

Jamie Knight, one of the BBC's leading website developers, told me:

> I would say people should disclose that they are autistic if they apply to work for the BBC. Because if you treat being autistic as a secret, you force yourself into a closet. Masking who you are is a waste of energy and ultimately the BBC hire you for your talents, insights and perspectives. Why waste some of that on masking? All of you is valuable. An autistic perspective is an asset to be valued, not something to be hidden.[5]

Sarah Hendrickx cites the example of one young man who went to work at a shop selling hot snacks without disclosing that he had Asperger's syndrome. Soon he found himself unable to sustain a full day's work and his behaviour became increasingly bizarre and difficult to handle. When a volunteer mentor at Hendrickx's Brighton-based organisation, ASpire, informed his boss that the young man had Asperger's, the employer expressed relief and willingness to try and work things out. More significantly, he said he wished he had known about the young man's condition from the outset, because he might well have offered him a part-time position.[6]

Non-disclosure can lead to misunderstandings: one woman on the spectrum was constantly running her fingers along her files, perching on the edge of her seat, twirling her hair, standing up and sitting back down repeatedly in order to focus, but her work colleagues misconstrued this behaviour as inattention or distractibility. Another autistic woman was anxiously snapping her fingers as a self-soothing 'stim' (auto-stimulation) only to be chided by a co-worker for being impatient.

For his part, Jesse Saperstein's advice is as follows: 'If something ain't broke, then don't fix it. But if you have a history of never making it past the interview, then you probably have little to lose with the revelation.'[7]

Jesse himself decided that it was unnecessary to disclose his Asperger's syndrome when he went for an interview for a manufacturing job at a computer plant: 'People skills are not necessary to assemble parts and many of the employees seemed nuttier than a holiday fruitcake. But I have always disclosed in environments that involve working with children or similarly sensitive settings.'[8]

Roger Meyer, an authority on employment and autism, has written: 'Autism is not something that most people understand. Telling everyone about your Asperger's syndrome will leave a lot of folks confused, often wondering why you bothered to tell them in the first place.'[9] Meyer goes on to advise most people to keep quiet about their autism and to attempt to solve workplace problems 'on a need-by-need basis'.[10]

Jane Meyerding, a woman diagnosed with autism in 1996 at the age of 46, disagrees:

> Staying in the closet will be easiest for those with good communication skills who also get on well with the supervisor or co-workers with whom one must negotiate changes in the workplace. Unfortunately, those characteristics are far from universal among autistics.[11]

Stephen Shore acknowledges the dilemma of disclosure:

> In a workplace situation, disclosure is especially important, as employers are often reluctant to retain employees who they feel will require extra attention, inconvenience and additional costs in making accommodations. However, many accommodations can be effected with little or no additional expenditure of resources.[12]

Dennis Debbaudt, who trains the emergency services to recognise and handle autism across the United States, recommends 'soft' disclosure of autism in the workplace. (By this, he means revealing certain difficulties, rather than a specific diagnosis, allowing employers to introduce adjustments or accommodations while avoiding the stigmatising disability label). Debbaudt told me:

> Disclosure is always going to be up to either the independent autistic person or, if dependent on others for care and safety, their carer. The soft disclosure allows for accommodation in the workplace or in public places that may not necessarily require a policy decision. In most cases, the accommodation would come firstly, because it's easy and secondly, it's simple common courtesy. If the accommodation requires a change in policy, a hard disclosure such as 'I have a diagnosis of ...' may become necessary. Both of the above can work as good options. Disability as a stigma is solely in the eyes of the beholder. Neither I nor my [autistic] son believe that ASD or any other disability is bad, wrong or stigmatising. I feel bad for, and pity, those who do believe that.[13]

Mark Haggarty believes it is distinctly unwise to disclose autism in your CV, because this could risk putting off 'ill-informed' employers at the very initial stage of the application process.[14]

> If you *do* choose to raise the subject in interview, do make sure you convey some of the positive attributes associated with the condition which would be desirable to your prospective employer ... [For example] showing attention to detail, not getting easily distracted from the task in hand, being punctual, proactive, perfectionist, careful, accurate, having a dislike of breaking rules.[15]

Nevertheless, Haggarty adds, if there is no aspect of your Asperger's that causes any significant impediment in the workplace or you do not exhibit behaviours that suggest that you are not 'neurotypical', you might prefer not to mention it. On the whole, Haggarty believes that it is beneficial to let colleagues know:

It just means that if you happen to display apparently eccentric behaviour, your colleagues will understand why ... Telling your employer will also allow you to address any issues that you may have with your working environment from a sensory perspective ... The benefits of revealing your Asperger's syndrome (at least to immediate colleagues) outweigh any ramifications.[16]

Tiffany Johnson and Aparna Joshi, of Pennsylvania State University, dedicated an entire paper in 2015 to the potential 'stigma' which may arise from disclosure of autism in the workplace. Drawing on in-depth interviews with individuals on the autism spectrum who had held full-time or multiple part-time positions in various organisations – including education, information technology, management, customer service and administrative support – the authors found that, compared with individuals diagnosed later in life, individuals who were diagnosed at an earlier age experienced greater organisation-based self-esteem and lower perceived discrimination when they disclosed their disability, worked in jobs that placed lower social demands on them, or were employed in organisations that offered policies to support workers with ASD. The authors point out that, unlike race, gender, sexual orientation or a physical disfigurement, developmental disabilities are directly linked to task (and social) performance at work. 'Rather than benefiting from directly or indirectly expressing information regarding their stigma, under some circumstances individuals with developmental disabilities may experience further ostracism, discrimination, marginalisation and isolation ....'[17]

One of those interviewed by Johnson and Joshi commented:

I don't wish to disclose my autism in my job. I don't really feel I need to, to be honest ... Unless something comes up in which I really need to, I'd rather not. I don't want people treating me any differently.

Another said:

They knew about my diagnosis but didn't know how to deal with it. I mean, I didn't mention it until they thought that I could do the job without any special help because they encouraged all of us through our training to watch their sessions ... to come and sit in the sessions and the more you observe, the more you practise, the better you'll get.

Some respondents said it would feel 'weird' to mention one's Asperger's syndrome for fear of being judged or evaluated. (This also led to some employees on the spectrum not asking for help, when it was needed.) Overwhelmingly, respondents tried to pursue non-disclosure. One noted that she avoided disclosure because of all the misleading (and 'stigmatising') stereotypes about autism. Instead, she preferred to be labelled an introvert. Another respondent shared his concern that disclosure not only violated privacy and opened the door for others to monitor his behaviour at work, but also granted them power to monitor all of his life decisions and behaviours: 'You know, I get the feeling that they are going to be making decisions about where I live, what I do, how I work, what I spend, which bills I pay first.' In general, the tendency was to disclose intentionally only to individuals whom they perceived as supportive.[18]

Johnson and Joshi concluded:

Drawing on our interview data, these privacy concerns and feelings of over-exposure may be particularly salient among those who are diagnosed later in life. As individuals age, they may experience greater threat as a result of disclosure because they have – or perceive that they have – fewer opportunities to learn new skills or to seek alternative employment. They may also be more sensitive to the possibility that others see them through a stigmatised lens following their disclosure. Among those diagnosed earlier, our interview data showed that greater support and career guidance received prior to entering the workplace may make disclosure seem more beneficial because they have been made aware of how and when to disclose.[19]

They added:

We found that disclosure is a significant decision. Specifically, we found that disclosing to others at work was not beneficial for our respondents diagnosed at later ages (in terms of higher perceptions of discrimination) and for our respondents diagnosed at earlier ages (in terms of anxiety). Based on these findings, we suggest that employees on the autism spectrum avail themselves of additional extra-organisational support to identify appropriate targets of disclosure at work. For example, getting help from employment counsellors or job coaches to identify who is a trustworthy workplace ally should be beneficial to the disclosure decision-making process. We also propose that greater awareness of developmental disabilities be integrated into diversity training programmes, so that managers and employees who could become targets of disclosure are able to process and respond favourably to stigma-related information from the focal employee, whether this information is provided intentionally or unintentionally. Such awareness should focus on stereotype-disconfirming information ... Training that facilitates awareness about autism-related stereotypes can aid co-workers and managers to understand individual differences among employees with ASD, so that jobs can be tailored/assigned to better accommodate their specific challenges.[20]

Why disclose?

Disclosure will allow employers to make reasonable adjustments to the workplace and be more prepared for any problems which may arise there. Disclosure does not prevent judgement from co-workers but it can explain certain behaviours. As Luke Jackson says:

Disclosure in the workplace is hugely important – it's so easy to just assume everything will be OK, especially when everything seems fine at the start. You've just started a new job, you feel great, empowered even. The kicker is that when something goes wrong, you're 'up shit creek without a paddle', as the old saying goes. If you seek support in the workplace, it doesn't make you in any way different, and it doesn't make you weak. Disclosure is an issue I've struggled with all through life, and it's stretched to employment, too – I never wanted to be construed as weak-willed in any way. The point is, however, that disclosing an ASD to an employer at your workplace doesn't change anything, and it's important to remember this. If you have an ASD, it doesn't matter whether you tell someone or not, you still have it, but if you let a prospective employer know, you have a safety net. If you have problems in the workplace attributed to being on the autism spectrum, then you can get the help you need before things spiral out of control.[21]

When to disclose?

Some employees choose to disclose before the interview. This is obviously helpful for someone who needs support during the interview itself. It would, for example, give potential employers a chance to offer the interview questions in advance and also permit extra time for verbal responses or to complete written tests. Other employees prefer to disclose after being hired. This is considered a way of avoiding the possible 'stigma' misguidedly associated with autism. Sometimes, employees never officially disclose their condition to their employers at all but explain it informally to their colleagues.

How to disclose?

The crucial point here is to ensure that the applicant's disclosure reaches the people who will be conducting the interview (assuming you want to disclose in advance). If you prefer to disclose during the interview itself, it is important to wait for an appropriate time in the conversation to raise the issue. Often, this could be at the end of the interview, when the interviewee can ask: 'What kind of support would be available to me as someone who has autism?' Again, here it is important to be positive and emphasise your strengths over and above any adjustments that might need making.

Jesse Saperstein insists that, if you disclose that you are on the autism spectrum, this disclosure must be 'augmented by your presentation of the abilities you will bring to the workplace and the desire to improve with consistent feedback'.[22] It is pointless, he says, to inform your employer about how difficult your life has been: the specific challenges, the bullying. 'The employer wants to know what you can offer the company and whether you will be an asset or a liability.' Always keep in mind that you are disclosing your autism spectrum condition 'not to excuse yourself from taking responsibility but to strengthen your chances of being successful at the position, if you are hired'.[23]

Stephen Shore has some useful examples of *how* to disclose. In order to advocate for a change from fluorescent lighting, an employee could ask: 'Have I been clear in explaining how the type of lighting has a significant impact on the quality of my work?' Or when explaining linguistic problems, Stephen proposes that an employee declares: 'I work best if people are very direct with me instead of trying to mince words on a subject they might think would be upsetting to me.'[24]

Finally, if you choose to disclose after being hired, the most confidential approach is to do so by speaking with someone from the human resources department.

❖ **CASE STUDIES**

- GEORGE HARVEY
- DAMI BENBOW

GEORGE HARVEY, a checkout operator with autism, feels it is important for managers to be aware of their employees' condition.

> The misconception is that, because someone with autism may have learning difficulties, they won't be able to handle the pressures or requirements of a certain job. But if this were true, why would they apply for the job to begin with? If anything, they have better knowledge of their autism and what their limitations are.

George does add, however, that managers should not tell other employees about certain colleagues having autism. 'This should be left up to the people themselves, so they won't feel like they're being singled out.'[25]

There are, of course, horror stories following disclosure. DAMI BENBOW, the participation co-ordinator of the charity Ambitious about Autism, revealed his autism to colleagues before one internship. In response, they bullied him and told him: 'Autism is a made-up diagnosis so that people can get away with whatever they want.' Dami has now found a happy niche at Ambitious about Autism, helping young people with autism to become active citizens in their communities through his myVoice project. 'Having this job has let me rebuild my shattered confidence and self-esteem,' he says.[26]

Notes

1 Thorkil Sonne in conversation with the author, 6 March 2016.
2 Sharon Didrichsen in conversation with the author, 4 August 2017.
3 See Dinah Murray (ed.) (2006), *Coming Out Asperger: Diagnosis, Disclosure and Self-Confidence.* London: Jessica Kingsley, p. 13.
4 Quoted in the *Guardian*, 13 May 2001.
5 Jamie Knight in conversation with the author, 17 December 2017.
6 See Sarah Hendrickx (2009), *Asperger Syndrome and Employment – What People with Asperger Syndrome Really Really Want.* London: Jessica Kingsley, p. 54.
7 Jesse A. Saperstein (2014), *Getting a Life with Asperger's. Lessons Learned on the Bumpy Road to Adulthood.* New York: Perigree, p. 138.
8 Ibid.
9 See Dinah Murray (ed.) (2006), *Coming Out Asperger: Diagnosis, Disclosure and Self-Confidence.* London: Jessica Kingsley, p. 45.
10 Ibid.
11 Ibid,. p. 248.
12 See Dinah Murray (ed.) (2006), *Coming Out Asperger: Diagnosis, Disclosure and Self-Confidence.* London: Jessica Kingsley, p. 182.
13 Dennis Debbaudt, in communication with the author, 1 August 2017.

14   See Genevieve Edmonds and Luke Beardon (eds), (2008), *Asperger Syndrome and Employment*. London: Jessica Kingsley, p. 103.

15   Ibid., p. 104.

16   Ibid., p. 105.

17   See T. Johnson and A. Joshi (2016), 'Dark clouds or silver linings? A stigma threat perspective on the implications of an autism diagnosis for workplace well-being', *Journal of Applied Psychology*, American Psychological Association, 101(3), 430–449.

18   Ibid.

19   Ibid.

20   Ibid.

21   Luke Jackson (2016), *Sex, Drugs and Asperger's Syndrome – A User's Guide to Adulthood*. London: Jessica Kingsley, p. 82.

22   Saperstein, op. cit.

23   Ibid.

24   See Dinah Murray (ed.) (2006), *Coming Out Asperger: Diagnosis, Disclosure and Self-Confidence*. London: Jessica Kingsley, pp. 182–183.

25   See Jonathan Andrews (ed.) (2016), *Autism in the Workplace – Untold Stories, Untapped Talent*, Ambitious about Autism.

26   Ibid.

Chapter 11

The interview

The process of undergoing an interview can prove nightmarish for many people with autism. Jesse Saperstein, the man with Asperger's syndrome quoted earlier, has pointed out that the first part of Stephen King's novel, *The Shining*, is entitled 'Job Interview', as is the beginning of Stanley Kubrick's 1980 cinematic adaptation of the book. 'It is an appropriate start to one of the most terrifying works of literature and film ever created.'[1]

The interview is, indeed, one of the most challenging stages in the application process for people on the autism spectrum. A Canadian study in 2015 indicated that adults with autism fared poorly in job interviews and that impaired communication skills may be apparent even in those considered 'high-functioning'. The study was led by Wendy Mitchell of the University of Alberta in Edmonton and was presented to the International Meeting for Autism Research in Salt Lake City in 2015. Based on an audio-analysis, it demonstrated that listeners who had no experience of autism clearly picked up on communication impairment during job interviews and that this had a negative impact on the results. Specifically, the autism group did notably less well than the non-autistic sample in terms of their use of grammar, vocabulary, speech speed, use of pauses, and patterns of stress and intonation. They also displayed a greater tendency to use overly formal language, to shift or repeat topics abruptly or inappropriately, and to inject irrelevant details, the findings showed. Significantly, listeners said they would offer only 30 per cent of the autism group a second interview, compared with 75 per cent of the non-autism group.

Eye contact, social interaction, the use of metaphorical and open-ended questions (such as 'Where do you see yourself in five years' time?' – which one French-Canadian woman with Asperger's syndrome interpreted as 'Where will you be living in five years' time?') may all constitute tremendous problems.

There are three main types of interviews:

- **Traditional one-on-one job interview:** When you arrive on the day, you'll meet one representative of the company, usually the manager of the position you applied for. They will be working with you directly if you get the job so they will want to get to know you better in the interview stage.
- **Telephone interview:** You will usually be invited to a phone interview before a face-to-face interview and once confirmed, you can write down some notes to keep you focused. However, some organisations like to see your face beforehand and may request a Skype interview.
- **Group interview:** Depending on the role, you might be invited to a group interview. This means other candidates who are applying for the same role as you

will be there on the day. If you want more details on this, do not hesitate to call the company and confirm how many people will be attending and what the topics will be to help you prepare.

Preparing for the interview

The thing to remember is that the interview is an artificial situation, As such, you must sometimes resort to artifice. It is important to prepare a 'script' in order to handle the most frequently asked interview questions. The first step in preparing for an interview is to research the company to which you are applying thoroughly on their website. This will allow the candidate to reply to a very common interview question: 'What interests you about this job?' The answer should definitely *not* focus on salary or benefits.

The applicant should come prepared to sell his or her skills. This self-advocacy is something many people on the autism spectrum find difficult. Arrive promptly, well-groomed and above all try and look confident. In response to the frequent question: 'Why should we hire you over other candidates?' answer in a calm but enthusiastic voice, naming your positive attributes which relate directly to the position for which you are applying.

Jo Loudon, of the University of Strathclyde, suggests carefully reviewing both the job advertisement and the application before the interview and remembering that the panel is not trying to catch you out – even though it may sometimes seem that way at the time! Loudon also recommends doing a 'dry run' to the venue where the interview is going to be held.[2]

Loudon says that common issues during the interview itself include: not knowing how much, or what, to say; failure to ask the panel to repeat or clarify a question if its meaning is not easy to grasp; failure to observe non-verbal signals from the panel if you have been speaking for a long time.[3]

During the interview

Jesse Saperstein has some valuable advice on how to conduct yourself during the interview.

- Arrive early.
- Be properly groomed and hygienic.
- Be confident but not arrogant.
- Use a strong opening line.
- Do not make money the focus of the interview.
- Use humour sparingly and with extreme caution. In fact, you have to be as surgical with humour as a sushi chef cutting up a puffer fish to avoid the poisonous sections.
- Above all, KIP – Keep It Positive. For example, do not say 'I have poor eye contact' but rather 'I have always had trouble looking people in the eye, but this has improved'. Do not say 'Certain loud noises make me flap my hands' but rather 'I am sometimes startled by loud noises and may overreact by jumping two feet in

the air. But unless you plan to have fire drills almost every day, I am going to be fine 95 per cent of the time. If there are any problems, then I'll deal with them and not let them interfere with my job performance.'[4]

Mark Haggarty, the tie-loving man with Asperger's syndrome cited earlier in Chapter 9, has his own very useful tips for how to behave during interviews.

> You must do everything you possibly can to give you the best chance of securing that job when you go into that interview room. If necessary, that means *not* being yourself and putting on rather more of an act. I am not suggesting for one second that you should go in there and feed your interviewers with falsehoods about yourself and your abilities. That is an absolute no no! Rather, you have to say what they want to hear. Whilst remaining truthful, act in a manner that they want to see and also present yourself as having an agreeable personality.[5]

Haggarty recommends being careful with body language: keep still but relaxed, and avoid waving your arms around, because this could make you look uncomfortable.[6] Barbara Bissonnette agrees. She points out that most communication is non-verbal: you won't look too enthusiastic at the interview if you sit with your arms folded tightly across your chest, or slumped in your chair, or staring at the floor or the ceiling, or fidgeting with any object to hand, or stalwartly avoiding smiling.[7]

Haggarty adds that, if you are one of those people on the autism spectrum who finds it hard to be a self-advocate, it is important to train yourself to 'act vociferously and talk about your strengths with confidence (but without seeming cocky)'.[8]

He has brilliant suggestions for how to present something actually considered a strength as a weakness – and with a dash of positive humour thrown into the mix. You might, for example, tell the interview panel that you tend to become excessively absorbed in a task, which means that you occasionally lose track of the time. Or you could inform the panel that you were liable to drag yourself into work even when feeling ill, whereas you really should have stayed in bed.[9]

❖ CASE STUDY

• THOMAS MADAR

THOMAS MADAR has sometimes struggled in interviews where, by his own admission, he would not sell himself as someone who was likeable and who fitted into teams. He says his social skills have improved over the years. Asked about his strengths in the workplace, he replies: 'I'm thorough, intelligent, creative, objective, with good research skills and an ability to pick up on small discrepancies.' As for the continuing challenges: 'I still have difficulties attracting conversation from other people. I don't like noisy environments. I may have difficulties with time and task management and avoid multi-tasking if at all possible.'[10]

Notes

1 Jesse A. Saperstein (2014), *Getting a Life with Asperger's. Lessons Learned on the Bumpy Road to Adulthood*. New York: Perigree, p. 131.

2 See: www.autismnetworkscotland.org.uk/files/2015/10/2-Jo-Loudon.pdf (accessed 27 April 2018).

3 Ibid.

4 Jesse A. Saperstein (2014), *Getting a Life with Asperger's. Lessons Learned on the Bumpy Road to Adulthood*. New York: Perigree, p. 139.

5 See Genevieve Edmonds and Luke Beardon (eds) (2008), *Asperger Syndrome and Employment*. London: Jessica Kingsley, p. 101.

6 Ibid.

7 See Barbara Bissonnette (2013), *Asperger's Syndrome Workplace Survival Guide*. London: Jessica Kingsley, p. 26.

8 Ibid.

9 Ibid., p. 102.

10 Thomas Madar in conversation with the author, 14 July 2016.

Chapter 12

Advice to employers

Interviews can involve a number of features that some people with autism may find more stressful than neurotypical people. Among the specific points, employers should be aware that a job interview is often the very worst method of determining whether an autistic applicant is qualified for a given position: the entire point of an interview is social communication, eye contact and fluency of speech, all of which are clearly problems for a candidate with ASD. But where interviews are essential, employers should ask closed and specific questions, if possible – for example: 'Describe your work history for the past five years' rather than the vaguer 'Tell me about yourself' – or even worse, 'Where do you see yourself in ten years' time?' Hypothetical ('What if?') questions should be avoided.

Communication during an interview can create a disadvantage for an applicant with autism. Some people with autism may give monosyllabic answers to questions or not realise when they are being asked to talk about something in detail. Employers need to ask specific and direct questions in a logical order. For example, candidates are unlikely to show themselves in a good light if they are given an open-ended question like 'Tell us what you did in your last job?' A likely response is one that is memorable to the candidate, which may also be negative, like 'I made this mistake…' A request like 'Tell me about yourself' is simply too broad – it could invite virtually any form of response.

Jargon and metaphorical language should be avoided. Competency-based questions should be concrete rather than abstract. For example, if someone with autism was asked what they would do in a difficult hypothetical situation, he or she may not be able to answer the question. If they were instead asked what they did when a difficult situation arose in the past, they may have a basis for answering the question. A candidate with autism may also require more time to process information than other people.

If possible, it would be an advantage for a candidate with autism to be permitted to see the questions in advance, reducing stress levels. Allow candidates with autism to be accompanied by someone who can repeat questions asked during the interview. And again, if possible, permit these applicants extra time to complete written tests.

Adapting how the interview process is structured was a key action taken by advisory company and insurance broker Willis Towers Watson in its bid to attract colleagues on the autism spectrum. As the standard interview can seem intimidating for a candidate with autism spectrum disorder (ASD), a work trial or test can often be a better way to assess skills, explains WTW's global employer brand manager, Andrew Farmer.[1]

Reviewing the types of questions to ask and how they are phrased is another idea. So for instance, it's about removing abstract language or hypothetical questions, which might be too distracting. Through our project, we found that stigma, and the perception of stigma, can be a significant challenge for people. Also [we suggest] the removal of open-ended questions that could be quite problematic, because they might not be able to sell themselves in the right way or elaborate on further points. Another good idea is providing extra time to complete written tests,

Farmer adds.[2]

Because we are becoming increasingly aware of the heterogeneity of the autism spectrum, job opportunities should accordingly become more diverse. As Professor Simon Baron-Cohen, director of the Autism Research Centre at Cambridge University, puts it:

Employers need to make reasonable adjustments to enable people with ASD to enjoy the same benefits that employment brings as other people do. And once employers have opened their eyes to how to make it easier for such people to make their contribution in the workplace, they may even discover how the person with the diagnosis is actually better than other employees in certain invaluable ways.

For the person with a diagnosis of autism, Baron-Cohen adds, employment – with the right support – may be a powerful way to change that individual's life immeasurably for the better and prevent the negative impact on mental health, such as depression, that is associated with unemployment.[3]

Over recent years, employers have become more confident in making adjustments for people with non-visible disabilities. In its 2014 report, 'Think Autism', the British government set out an update on the strategy for adults with autism that followed the Autism Act (2009) and the Autism Strategy (2010). The update outlined 15 priority challenges for action that government departments should take to improve the lives of people with autism. One of these priority challenges was: 'I want support to get a job and support from my employer to help me keep it.' The strategy identified many subsequent steps to achieving this priority challenge, including the Disability Confident campaign and a Disability and Health Employment strategy to provide tailored employment support to disabled people.

Employers also appear to have an increasing interest in hiring people with autism. For example, Microsoft launched a programme to hire people with autism in 2015. The programme featured a non-traditional interview process designed to help those on the spectrum to highlight their talents and overcome barriers to employment. Microsoft's Corporate Vice President of Worldwide Operations, Mary Ellen Smith, herself the mother of an autistic daughter, said: 'Microsoft is stronger when we expand opportunity and we have a diverse workforce that represents our customers. People with autism bring strengths that we need.'[4] She added that the reason Microsoft was recruiting workers on the autism spectrum was not in order to fulfil the obligatory quotas, but rather because these workers 'represent a reservoir of talent and strengths which can be used as a competitive advantage'. The German software giant, SAP, has declared that it intends to gain 'a competitive advantage' over its rivals by actively employing people with autism spectrum disorder.

Nevertheless, job descriptions and advertisements frequently include irrelevant language or information, such as the person needing to be 'a good communicator,' when that is often not a core element of the role. The difficulty is that people with autism can take what they read in a job description very literally and because of this, they will not apply for positions. This unnecessarily reduces the talent pool for recruiters.

Many talented people on the autism spectrum may not have qualifications but they could be very capable in a role. This may be due to barriers experienced in education or in previous roles. Recruiters should consider aptitude. Specialists have recommended placing greater weight on what could be achieved by the person rather than irrelevant qualifications.

Dean Beadle, the prominent autistic British public speaker, who met staff at Sony Films in London in 2016, made the following useful suggestions to recruiters looking to employ people on the autism spectrum:

- Remove phrases such as 'must have good social and interpersonal skills' from job advertisements. This adds huge pressure for some autistic people and is verging on discrimination. Instead, list the job-related skills that are required.
- Advertise in logical places: that is, publications centred on common autistic special interests (such as IT journals, science fiction magazines, trainspotting magazines, etc.), as well as autism magazines and websites. Perhaps circulate the advertisement to support groups and autistic-led organisations. Directly market to autistic people.
- Change the way you conduct job interviews – instead, invite prospective workers into the office to do work trials. Showing your skills can be easier than being forced to articulate them in a socially pressurised environment (the interview).[5]

Work trials

It is widely acknowledged that work trials are essential to successfully recruiting people with autism. These do not necessarily need to be paid trials but an opportunity for the person to show his or her ability. They also help the employer to understand the person as an individual.

The following qualities are strengths which have been noted in employees with autism:

- Accuracy and ability to focus on detail
- Reliability
- Excellent memory for facts and figures
- Able to thrive in a structured, well-organised work environment
- Enjoy consistency
- Persistent
- Logical and systematic

The dangers of stereotypes – and 'cream-skimming'

Employers must avoid falling into the trap of embracing well-meaning, but over-simplistic stereotypes, however. While it is certainly encouraging that more private companies, such as Microsoft, SAP and Ernst & Young, are deliberately recruiting people on the autism spectrum (because many of them have mathematical and technical abilities, are able to focus on detail and show considerable skills at pattern recognition) this tells only part of the story. As illustrated in previous sections, by no means do all individuals with autism have these skills – although they may well have other, different ones. Like all stereotypes, this one is misguided.

An American specialist in autism employment, Dr Paul Shattuck, director of the life course outcomes programme at the A.J. Drexel Autism Institute in Philadelphia, is concerned that companies are engaging in 'cream-skimming' by focusing their initiatives on high-functioning autism, not all disabilities. He understands the reasoning: businesses want to hire people who qualify for initiatives aimed at people with disabilities but who also help contribute to the bottom line. 'It's a tricky situation,' he says. A company like Ernst & Young (EY) has very few lower-skilled jobs. Because EY rents its office space, at least in the US, and thus does not hire its own cafeteria and maintenance staff, the vast majority of positions require specialised education and skills.[6]

Employers must also consider the clarity of their message when it comes to recruiting people with autism, advises Emma Jones, employment training manager for Britain's National Autistic Society.

> At the recruitment stage, ambiguity is the biggest challenge for them. Employers need to ensure their recruitment process is as accessible as possible. It's also about making sure that the hiring manager can recognise the characteristics of autism, as it's a spectrum of conditions.[7]

Some firms have overhauled their interview process to accommodate candidates with high-functioning autism. That's the approach EY took in the US when it embarked on a pilot programme to recruit individuals with Asperger's for its accounting support associate function. EY worked with training provider Specialisterne to hold an initial one-day assessment and asked selected candidates to build robots from Lego.

Things like competency-based frameworks can have built-in discrimination to someone on the spectrum, Emma Jones explains.

> For example, they can have a typical grading structure with an emphasis on team working. There is an ingrained assumption that people need good leadership and people management skills, and these are areas some autistic people would struggle with more than a neurotypical person.[8]

Employers are beginning to become aware of the very real stress – and distress – that the interviewing process can represent for people on the autism spectrum. Some have agreed to provide questions beforehand to allow a support worker to accompany the candidate to the interview to repeat questions, allowing the applicant more time to process the meaning and consider a suitable response. But this is still not the norm.

Specialisterne creates 'hangouts' – comfortable gatherings, usually lasting half a day, in which neurodiverse job candidates can demonstrate their abilities in casual interactions with company managers. At the end of a hangout, some candidates are selected for two to six weeks of further assessment and training (the duration varies by company). During this time, they use Lego Mindstorms robotic construction and programming kits to work on assigned projects – first individually and then in groups, with the projects becoming more like actual work as the process continues. Some companies have additional sessions. SAP, for example, established a 'soft skills' module to help candidates who have never worked in a professional environment become familiar with the norms of such a setting. These efforts are typically funded by the government or non-profit-making organisations. Trainees are usually paid.

Specialisterne's founder, Thorkil Sonne, told me:

> If we have ten jobs, we try to see thirty potential candidates. We have a basic questionnaire. Then we have a short talk with the individuals. After that, we host a workshop for four or five hours and they are each given a box of Lego robots and asked to do simple programming. By observing how they interact (up to eight in a group), we learn not only about their professional skills but also who would benefit from a four- to five-week assessment programme. We also have verbal one-on-one discussions with them while they are working with the Lego. We try to find out about the person, their career ambitions, etc.[9]

(For more on Neurodiversity in the workplace, see Part V.)

Cultural aspects of the interview process

A little-mentioned – but very important – aspect of the interview process is the cultural influences at play. Employers may look disapprovingly at lack of eye contact on a candidate's part. But this might not be related to autism at all. As Jonathan Andrews has pointed out,[10] Asians often have additional difficulties with social interaction, due to a greater chance of facing language or cultural barriers. Many Asian cultures see direct eye contact as rude. In Japan, eye contact is seen as aggressive and is discouraged – so avoiding it is not necessarily a sign of autism. In addition, many of the guidelines for spotting autism are Eurocentric (they make sense only within mainstream Western culture) so are less useful for diagnosing autism in 'ethnic minority' communities in the UK.

> Recruiters should be aware of how different cultures/ethnicities experience autism differently. However, a lot of these differences boil down to individual differences and can be solved by asking an employee/applicant for more clarity on how autism affects them individually,

says Andrews.

> Recruiters should, though, be aware that it's more likely for a black and minority ethnic (BME) employee to have undiagnosed autism than a white employee, due to the difficulty many BME families face in obtaining an official diagnosis. It might be

a good idea for BME at firms to be more closely linked to autism/disability events – so that BME people can learn more about autism and how to spot it, whether in themselves or in others.[11]

New and assistive technology

Fears have long been expressed that robots may take over many jobs that were previously in the hands of human employees. Little attention has been drawn, in contrast, to the potential benefits that new technology – including robotics – can play in smoothing the path into and during employment for people on the autism spectrum.

There have been some interesting recent attempts to use new technology to assist autistic applicants through the interview process – most notably, a 'virtual' interviewer to permit the candidate to rehearse beforehand. A number of studies have demonstrated that a virtual interviewer can prove helpful. In a system called the Virtual Interactive Training Agent, a hidden human operator controls the virtual experience, moving the avatar to new questions as a student gives answers. Instructors score recordings of the virtual interviews and discuss them in class. Six avatars, men and women of different ethnicities, appear in various moods and settings to give the students experience with the many types of interviewers they might encounter. The programme designers insist that using avatars is more efficient and consistent than role-playing with people, and that it is also less stressful for students with autism, who may feel uncomfortable in social situations. In a pilot study, it was found that four sessions with an avatar improved students' interview scores by 80 per cent.[12]

At Northwestern University in Chicago, Matthew Smith uses a similar system with war veterans and those with severe mental illness, among others. Smith's programme, which uses videos of actors, was not designed for people with autism. But in 2014, Smith and his colleagues published a trial of 26 young adults with autism. They found that 8 of the 15 people who received the virtual training found a job or volunteer position within six months, compared with 2 of the 8 who were not trained. (The difference was significant only after the researchers controlled for prior employment and post-training self-confidence.) Smith, a social worker and assistant professor of psychiatry and behavioural sciences, has applied for funding to adapt his virtual reality programme for people with autism.[13]

Another new system being trialled in the United States is a wearable augmented-reality glass platform called LittleHelper to provide customised supports for individuals with ASD in enhancing social communication during a job interview. Using the built-in camera and microphone, LittleHelper can detect the position of the interviewer relative to the centre of the camera view, and measure the sound level of the user. Based on these inputs, appropriate visual feedbacks are provided back to the user through the optical head-mounted display.[14]

Robots may also help once an autistic employee has made it safely into the workplace. Researchers at Heriot-Watt University (HWU) in Edinburgh say their new robot, Alyx, helps workers on the autism spectrum negotiate their way through the social minefield. 'The main issue is not that they can't do the work,' says Dr Thusha Rajendran, associate professor of psychology at HWU and one of Alyx's creators. 'It's the workplace politics, especially being able to understand what people really mean, rather than simply what they say. And part of that is understanding emotional expression.'[15]

Figure 12.1 Alyx, the robot designed to help negotiate the social minefield in the workplace

Alyx's face is simple, with very few features: humanoid, Dr Rajendran explains, but not human-like. This is entirely deliberate: human faces generate many small, extraneous signals which people with autism can find difficult to decode. By contrast, Alyx's basic, easily controllable robotic face makes it an ideal teacher of social cues. In a training session with Alyx, a user performs a clerical task, like filing paper, and Alyx responds with a sign of approval or disapproval. Alyx's creators argue that this is the principal obstacle that autistic adults need to overcome in the workplace: namely, knowing whether or not they are doing a good job. A camera mounted in Alyx's head will also provide additional feedback to therapists.

'You can actually infer quite a lot from people's body position and their posture,' says Dr Peter McKenna, research associate at HWU.

> We can use that information to help the robot understand what kind of emotional state the person is currently in, as well as taking in information from the face. So you get quite a rich picture of the user. And then by developing the robot's architecture, not only does that information feed in, but the robot can then respond in a socially appropriate way.[16]

Dr McKenna adds:

> This helps adults with autism deal with social signals in workplace situations, improving employment opportunities. This information is vital for developing a socially competent companion for our future work with autistic adults. At present, impaired social communication and interaction hold back the working potential

of those with autism. However, robots like Alyx can help change this outcome by offering additional assistance and knowledge of social skills, thereby creating more opportunities for everyone, regardless of diagnosis.[17]

Initial work with Alyx has used the robot's head, but the Scottish researchers are currently working on a full-bodied, autonomous version which in the future will teach further social skills. The HWU team plans to turn the Alyx prototype into a full-bodied, autonomous version, operating in a mock workplace, with clinical trials planned thereafter.

As Dr Rajendran has written:

When dealing with the otherness of disability, the Victorians in their shame built huge out-of-sight asylums, and their legacy of 'them' and 'us' continues to this day. Two hundred years later, technologies offer us an alternative view. The digital age is shattering barriers, and what used to be the norm is now being challenged. What if we could change the environment, rather than the person? What if a virtual assistant could help a visually impaired person with their online shopping? And what if a robot 'buddy' could help a person with autism navigate the nuances of workplace politics? These are just some of the questions that are being asked and which need answers as the digital age challenges our perceptions of normality ...

Today, we face similar challenges about differences versus abnormalities. Arguably, current diagnostic systems do not help, because they diagnose the person and not 'the system'. So, a child has challenging behaviour, rather than being in distress; the person with autism has a communication disorder, rather than simply not being understood. In contrast, the digital world is all about systems. The field of human-computer interaction is about how things work between humans and computers or robots ... An autism-friendly environment is not just the physical and sensory environment (many cinemas now offer autism-friendly screenings), but about the social environment. Reading emotions and understanding people's underlying mental states and desires is one of the major challenges that people with autism face. Our robot buddy allows us to isolate the features of the face, to make them more discernible to people with autism, so they might better recognise the key features of when, say, someone is annoyed with them.[18]

Notes

1   *Marketing Week*, 30 May 2017.
2   Ibid.
3   *Daily Telegraph*, 23 June 2015.
4   See: http://uk.businessinsider.com/microsoft-hiring-people-with-autism-2015-4 (accessed 27 April 2018).
5   Dean Beadle in conversation with the author, 19 October 2017.
6   *Fortune*, 26 October 2016.
7   See: www.hrmagazine.co.uk/article-details/why-firms-are-embracing-neurodiversity (accessed 27 April 2018).
8   Ibid.
9   Thorkil Sonne in conversation with the author, 6 March 2016.

10 See Jonathan Andrews (undated), *Autism and the Workplace: Common Myths and Untapped Talent.*

11 Ibid.

12 See: http://ict.usc.edu/prototypes/vita/ (accessed 27 April 2018).

13 See: https://news.northwestern.edu/stories/2014/05/adults-with-autism-virtually-learn-how-to-get-the-job/ (accessed 27 April 2018).

14 See Q. Xu, S. Samson Cheung and N. Soares (2015), 'LittleHelper: An augmented reality glass application to assist individuals with autism in job interview', *Proceedings of the Asia-Pacific Signal and Information Processing Association Annual Summit and Conference (APSIPA)*, 1276–1279.

15 See: https://qz.com/1176130/a-new-robot-is-teaching-people-with-autism-to-navigate-office-politics/ (accessed 12 January 2018).

16 *Reuters*, 28 December 2017.

17 See: www.hw.ac.uk/about/news/cutting-edge-robot-could-reduce-autistic.htm (accessed 16 October 2017).

18 See: https://theconversation.com/how-robots-can-help-us-embrace-a-more-human-view-of-disability-76815 (accessed 4 May 2017).

Part IV

Holding down a job

Chapter 13

Research findings

Retaining a job remains a serious problem for people on the autism spectrum. In recent decades, workplace environments have increasingly become open-plan offices, with more distractions and a greater demand for emotional intelligence, flexibility and adaptability. New demands for flexibility have also affected employers, with a shift from prescriptive legislation to framework regulations and guidance. This brings specific challenges for people with autism, including distractions, unpredictability and uncertainty.

Other requirements may prove more problematic for some people on the spectrum: arriving appropriately dressed, following instructions, handling disagreements in an unemotional fashion or relating in a friendly manner to work colleagues. Supported employment schemes should prepare and 'train' future employees with autism in these areas. Engaging in eye contact and a reasonable amount of small talk is a valuable 'ice-breaker'.

On the other hand, employment-based studies have highlighted average or above-average job performance in people with Asperger's syndrome (Hagner and Cooney, 2005; Hillier et al., 2007).[1] A number of common themes emerged from these studies: many of these individuals demonstrated considerable skills in good tasks involving data and some, but by no means all, enjoyed tasks disliked by others because of their repetitive nature or social isolation. However, as Anne Cockayne, senior lecturer in Human Resource Management at Nottingham Trent University, has pointed out, at the same time as creating strengths, these characteristics also place Asperger's syndrome as a disability protected under Britain's Equality Act (2010) on account of the very real impairments that individuals with AS experience: for example, being frequently troubled by loud noises and by feelings of being different from their peers.[2]

Cockayne, together with Lara Warburton, of Rolls Royce, conducted an 'exploratory study' in 2016 which found that managers with employees with Asperger's syndrome conceptualised high work ethic and IQ as strengths but, interestingly, attention to detail, honesty and directness, flexibility and social interaction were conceptualised variously as strengths or weaknesses, depending on the specific job role, working environment and the norms governing HR processes and ways of working.[3] The researchers conducted in-depth interviews with line managers of Asperger's employees and human resources specialists and employees at six organisations, including Rolls Royce, Center Parcs and HMRC. The responses indicated that many managers were unaware of the prevalence of Asperger's – which can present as frequently as one in 200 of their employed workforce, possibly with greater occurrence in particular skill areas.

All the managers interviewed by Cockayne pointed to the reliability, trustworthiness and professionalism of their employees with Asperger's syndrome. 'In the workplace, ableist norms predominate in relation to productivity and this may be one reason that disabled employees may choose to work harder than their colleagues,' wrote Cockayne, citing Jammaers et al. (2016).[4] 'It is likely that the hidden nature of AS predisposes this "working hard" reaction from individuals, more so than someone with a visible disability.'[5]

The majority of managers questioned in the Cockayne study rated employees as being more intelligent than others in similar roles but despite this, most of these employees worked in semi-skilled roles involving routine and repetitious tasks.

> A troubling reality therefore may be that individuals are working in roles beneath their intellectual capability ... Given that some AS people will know that some aspects of their role or workplaces can impede their performance, their decision to choose to work at skill levels lower than their qualifications and intellect would predict is entirely logical and is supported by findings that show many AS employees have made deliberate decisions to accept part-time and casual work in the face of concerns about their own capacities to meet expected productivity levels. However, it may be that these decisions are not simply a matter of choice and can be viewed more critically in terms of exclusionary outcomes, where demanding ways of working ... create disparities between AS people and their non-AS counterparts of similar IQ or qualifications, earning less and in lower-status roles.[6]

Every manager interviewed by Cockayne noted that their AS employees had some difficulties with interactions at work, whether with customers or colleagues. However, one manager acknowledged the beneficial effects of having people in a team who did not engage in gossip, relating these to savings in time.[7]

Attention to detail was construed as an asset where the work involved checking fine detail, or a constraint where someone working through the detail takes a long time to complete a task. Similarly, using a blunt and direct communication style was also construed as a strength, because people were willing to highlight problems with 'refreshing' honesty but, Cockayne added,

> it is not hard to see how the same directness can also create problems for managers. It may also impact AS employees as they negotiate progression pathways that typically demand a degree of political and tactful consideration, which may be more difficult to navigate than for neurotypicals.[8]

The managers in the 2016 study cited lack of flexibility as a major issue for almost all of their employees with Asperger's syndrome. This inflexibility manifested itself as experiencing more difficulty than others in adapting to changing roles and working environments. In her important conclusions, Cockayne stated that employers

> need to understand how social demands and constraints of the physical working environment can create problematic and disabling workplace experiences so they become better equipped to identify which roles ought to be avoided in recruitment, progression and redeployment scenarios. Employers should question if positive valuations of these 'softer' skills are always appropriate or if they are based upon

subjective and arbitrary notions, as well as more precisely specify the attributes or skills that are actually required, for example: what attributes or ways of working count as teamworking? Is being empathetic and a 'good' communicator always necessary? When and where might different decision-making styles be best deployed, considering also if everyone needs to attend all team meetings for all of the time. Other areas for review are those workplace activities with high 'social' content – Christmas parties, celebratory occasions and team away days, which demand particular social interaction that does not easily 'fit' with many AS employees.[9]

Line managers of employees with the condition spoke about the strengths of having a high work ethic and a higher than average IQ. At the same time, Cockayne observed:

> While having an employee who is willing to do important but repetitive or menial tasks is of obvious benefit to an organisation, it does raise the question of whether allocating someone a disproportionate amount of routine work is the 'right' or the 'wrong' thing to do. Employers need to be more aware of the great potential for those with Asperger's in roles which require high IQ levels, the ability to handle complex data and systems, and the ability to systemise, all of which are associated with the 'hard' skills needed in the various engineering and STEM [science, technology, engineering and mathematics] disciplines.

Some of the common Asperger's traits raised by line managers in Cockayne's 2016 study were described as both strengths and weaknesses, such as attention to detail, social interaction and working with others, and honesty and directness. Two were thought to be more frequently problematic: being inflexible and being hypersensitive to lights and noise which led to stress and anxiety. Attention to detail was considered a positive aspect in the accuracy and quality of work, but could often affect the speed at which Asperger's employees complete their tasks. Managers also reported exemplary timekeeping as a positive, but inflexibility and a dislike of change presented challenges.

The majority of managers cited the tendency to be honest, direct and 'speak their mind' as a positive aspect of employing the individual. While criticism is unlikely to be universally welcomed, line managers appreciated having a team member who was willing to criticise or point out problems with a particular decision or process, or ask questions and articulate complaints that others might be afraid or embarrassed to raise. The Cockayne study also suggested that line managers faced a challenging role in ensuring that the working environment was not too noisy or bright, as this could have disproportionately adverse effects on someone with sensory differences and make working closely with other people difficult.

Cockayne's study challenged stereotyped views that people with Asperger's do not enjoy talking to others and instead supported clinical studies which considered the negative effects of particular environments. Cockayne concluded:

> The majority of current employment processes do not suit those with Asperger's because they often lack the 'soft' skills needed to be successful in an interview and the skills required in competency frameworks, such as flexibility. They do, however, bring many other skills and employers need to be mindful of this when recruiting.

Many individuals with the condition who are already in employment choose not to disclose it for a number of reasons, one of which is the attitude and awareness of their line manager – trust is key. It is therefore recommended that all line managers receive training on the condition and how it can be supported in the workplace.[10]

Interestingly, the important, previously cited 2015 study by Tiffany Johnson and Aparna Joshi, of Pennsylvania State University, found that people diagnosed with autism at an early age tended to be more vocal about their distaste for jobs with high social demands. One of these respondents worked in a library and became anxious when she had to have social interactions with customers (they would unexpectedly ask her for directions around the library). She expressed the fear that her social discomfort would get in the way of her ability to help them adequately.

If respondents diagnosed earlier did enjoy jobs that involved social interactions, these kinds of social jobs involved adhering to more scripted behaviours ... Social demands associated with a job were not necessarily viewed as detrimental for those diagnosed at later ages; instead, the type of interactions was more salient to individuals,

the authors wrote. They cited, as examples, various comments from people diagnosed with autism later in life: 'I want to be social but I don't want to get overwhelmed with crowds';

I applied to a messenger company and they hired me. It was kind of fun ... the job was demanding but I do well with the work because it's not face-to-face and because... I'm on the phone, I'm in control of the situation.[11]

Notes

1   D. Hagner and B. F. Cooney (2005), '"I do that for everybody": Supervising employees with autism', *Focus on Autism and Other Developmental Disabilities*, May, 20(2), 91–97; A. Hillier et al. (2007), 'Two-year evaluation of a vocational support programme for adults on the autism spectrum', *Career Development and Transition for Exceptional Individuals*, May, 30(1), 35–47.
2   See: www.cipd.co.uk/Images/an-investigation-of-asperger-syndrome-in-the-employment-context_2016_tcm18-20003.pdf (accessed 27 April 2018).
3   Ibid.
4   E. Jammaers, et al. (2016), 'Constructing positive identities in ableist workplaces: Disabled employees' discursive practices engaging with the discourse of lower productivity', *Human Relations*, June, 69(6), 1365–1386.
5   Ibid.
6   Ibid.
7   Ibid.
8   Ibid.
9   Ibid.
10 Ibid.
11 See T. Johnson and A. Josh (2016), 'Dark clouds or silver linings? A stigma threat perspective on the implications of an autism diagnosis for workplace well-being', *Journal of Applied Psychology*, American Psychological Association, 101(3), 430–449.

Chapter 14

The 'hidden curriculum' of the workplace

> Going to work isn't just about work. It's about what you wear, what you eat, what your environment looks like, what it feels like, how your boss behaves and how your co-workers treat you. There's so much more to a job than what the tasks are.[1]

So says the American author with Asperger's syndrome, Rudy Simone.

Daniel Lightwing, the mathematician whose story was depicted in the film *X+Y* and who had problems with the social issue when working at Google, says that his Asperger's syndrome is not a disability but rather

> an extremely different kind of personality ... When you have Asperger's, you are putting on a mask and trying to pretend you are normal, but what you are thinking is not normal. People with autism have polarised emotions. If it gets too much, you withdraw from everything.[2]

Being social

Once you have successfully negotiated the interview and find yourself in the new workplace, there come the difficulties related to what Brenda Smith Myles has called 'the hidden curriculum'[3]: the obligation to engage in 'small talk', to understand rules in context and avoid taking them too literally. Barbara Bissonnette cites the instructive case of a woman with Asperger's syndrome who was first reprimanded by her boss because she texted her boyfriend in office hours (she protested that the rules stipulated no personal 'calls') and was then dismissed from her job because she took a toilet roll back home because she realised she did not have time to pass by the shop (again, she complained, in vain, that the regulations prohibited no removal of office materials and that the toilet was not the office).[4]

The 'water-cooler' or 'coffee machine' conversations can spell trouble. 'A person with Asperger's will go to work to work. They are not there to win a popularity contest,' writes Rudy Simone. 'Unfortunately, they find that reality is different — that they are expected not just to perform the job but also to succeed socially.'[5]

Many of the people Simone questioned said their job failures had been due to their failure to socialise, rather than anything to do with the actual job performance. She quotes a self-employed watchmaker, Walter, as saying: 'I am completely unable to navigate small talk. I am great at introductions, public speaking, etc. I just can't seem to have a conversation that works. Worse, I am often totally misunderstood.'[6]

Luke Beardon, of Sheffield Hallam University, observes:

> It is true that the workplace is often one in which friendships and relationships develop. However, I have yet to meet anyone who puts on their application form, or states at interview, that the social opportunities within a post are what drive them to apply. Similarly, if I was interviewing for a post and a candidate told me they were applying for the job to socialise and make friends, I would instantly be on my guard.[7]

Tom Brundage, former director at Specialisterne UK (which later became SpecialistsUK), agrees: 'Virtually every job description will include as a requirement: must have strong communication skills, must have good personal skills, must be able to work in a team environment',[8] and yet many of the roles his company recruits into rely on an ability to analyse data and complete tasks efficiently, not how you get on with colleagues.

Problems with social interaction can create tremendous obstacles. One woman with Asperger's syndrome, identified only as D., told Sarah Bargiela, of University College London:

> There are a hundred other interactions going on throughout those days so you get more and more anxious in general, you find it more difficult to process the other interactions that are happening. So I've got a list at the moment of people who're possibly angry with me because of the way I've interacted with them, because I've been thinking about the interaction I've had with this person instead of the interaction I'm having then, so it just goes on and on.[9]

John Elder Robison, one of the most successful luxury car repair entrepreneurs in the United States, still hates small talk. If he meets a friend he has not seen for a while, and the friend looks bigger, Robinson will say to him: 'You seem fatter than the last time I saw you.'[10]

He points out that, if you do not reveal that you are on the autism spectrum (see Chapter 10 for much more on whether or not to disclose),

> there is no external sign that I am conversationally handicapped, so folks hear some conversational misstep and say: 'What an arrogant jerk!' I look forward to the day when my handicap will afford me the same respect accorded to a guy in a wheelchair. And if the respect comes with a preferred parking space, I won't turn it down.[11]

Luke Jackson, the photographer with Asperger's syndrome cited in earlier sections of this book, says it is important to distinguish between friendship and professional relationships in the workplace, because the differences are crucial:

> Keeping neutrality in the workplace means keeping conversation light and knowing when certain conversational topics are 'out of bounds'. Humanity is a mixing pot of differing opinions and this is a great thing. However, if you have very strong opinions on a topic, there's a pretty good chance that topic is not for use in conversation with customers or colleagues.[12]

Political leanings, as Jackson points out, are not a good topic for the workplace because they prompt people to judge you, and should therefore be avoided at work. So should medical issues (apart from disclosing autism itself), religion, sex life, finances and any kind of gossip.

Jesse Saperstein agrees. 'Avoid workplace gossip like the plague ... [it] is the black magic of the workplace. There is the temptation to dabble in it but nothing good ever came out of discussing personal business.'[13]

Interestingly, Jesse adds that this is where having Asperger's syndrome may prove to be an advantage,

> because our inner thoughts may be dancing with science fiction paraphernalia, clay animation movies, nuggets of Thomas the Tank Engine nostalgia, or whatever special interests float your particular boat. The bulk of our cerebral energy, however, should be absorbed with what we need to do in order to make an outstanding contribution as an employee, not whether Christina in Human Resources snuck into the broom closet with Justin from Data Processing two months ago for a 9pm liaison.[14]

Temple Grandin has written: 'Before you go to work, learn the social rules of the work world well by practising them at home with your family. This is very important, for the workplace is a social institution.'

Grandin has pinpointed three useful elements in autistic people who have managed to hold down a job:

- Someone helped to develop their talents
- Good mentors helped them to develop social skills
- They took medication or special diets, where necessary, to help manage their sensory issues, depression or anxiety. (Temple has often told me that she found sensory impairments a debilitating factor).[15]

As Grandin adds:

> Talent earns respect ... If you are talented, you can often get away with being eccentric at work, but you usually can't get away with poor grooming – a very important part of social skills. To be out among others, you have to fit in as much as possible, and that includes the way you groom yourself. You don't have to look like everyone else, but you must not be a slob.[16]

(Grandin is speaking from personal experience here – at one of her first jobs, her manager advised her to use deodorant!).

The social expectations

One of the sad truths for many people with autism is that the higher up the employment scale one climbs, the more social one is generally expected to be. John Elder Robison, the US car repair executive, puts it this way: 'The higher I advanced in the corporate world, the more I had to rely on my people skills and the less my technical skills and creativity mattered. For someone like me, that was a formula for disaster.'[17]

❖ **CASE STUDY**

• JOHN WILTON

JOHN WILTON, 55, was diagnosed with autism at 50. He worked as a solicitor for 30 years. 'I have had a successful career,' he says.

> But the legal profession is very 'pally' – you need to be 'one of the lads'. I was very good at my job, but as you get older, the job slowly changes and becomes more people-oriented as you advance up the ladder. That is the part which did not work for me – which is why I decided to leave the profession.

Excessive honesty

Grandin also learned that too much honesty could get you into trouble, when she criticised shoddy workmanship. There are ways of criticising tactfully, she notes. 'I learned about diplomacy by reading about international negotiations and using them as models.'[18]

Anne Cockayne cites several instances in which the excessive honesty typical of autistic people raised hackles in the workplace. In one such incident, a programme employee told a colleague 'You stink at your job'. As Cockayne notes, coaching by managers and mentors can help address such situations.[19]

EY, the consulting company formerly known as Ernst & Young, values the (sometimes blunt) honesty of its autistic employees. According to the firm's director in the United States, Hiren Shukla, he and his colleagues did not believe it when a newly hired employee on the spectrum immediately criticised the instructions for setting up their voicemail. But the autistic employee was correct. It turned out that thousands of other, non-autistic employees, feeling hesitant to say anything, had been wasting their time puzzling over the wrong instructions.[20]

The hierarchy of the workplace

Damian Milton, who works part-time for the National Autistic Society and for London's South Bank University, researching mentoring with autistic adults as well as lecturing at the Tizard Centre, University of Kent, is someone who has experienced particular difficulties with the hierarchical structure of the workplace.

A hierarchical structure can suit some people but hamper others, because of the spiky profile of individuals on the autism spectrum. I do not like hierarchy. I see people as equal, and tend not to see status as such. I do not consider my boss superior,

Damian told me.

I understand the different status on a sociological level. But the idea that you want to be boss or be bossed around is anathema to me. I consider PDA [Pathological Demand Avoidance] to be rational demand avoidance. I do not like power or manipulation. I am not aggressive – in fact, I am generally passive and agreeable – but I can also sometimes be stubborn. I'm also honest, which gets me into trouble with managers.[21]

Before he was diagnosed with Asperger's syndrome at the age of 36 in 2009, Milton was made redundant from his position as further education lecturer in Kent. 'I fell out with my manager, who ganged up with her team against me. The principal supported the manager, but the head of personnel managed to get me a good redundancy package.'[22]

Milton says that there has been a 'slight improvement' among employers in appreciating honesty more. 'But some managers have a terrible empathy problem. And an autistic person can have difficulty knowing what a manager wants. Rapport and trust are crucial: between the manager and worker, or between the mentor and student.'[23]

The empathy issue

Jonathan Andrews, the lawyer and prominent advocate for autism employment, believes that the so-called 'empathy deficiency' in autism urgently needs revisiting and nuancing. For Andrews, individuals on the autism spectrum experience difficulties with cognitive empathy – the ability to understand someone else – whereas, in stark contrast, some studies indicate that autistic people may experience more 'affective' empathy than non-autistic people, causing them to realise they have offended somebody once the person bluntly informs them of this fact, but may not understand why. 'Since they don't want to repeat the experience, they then withdraw from the relationship. They are then characterised as "cold and aloof," ' writes Andrews. 'This can cause problems in the workplace.'[24]

He adds:

While everyone will be different, some autistic people may find it easier than most to learn cognitive empathy, as long as a system for developing this is presented. And it should not be assumed that actions which offend are taken out of malice – this rarely happens. Rather, they more likely simply haven't considered whether their remark will cause offence. Once they learn, the vast majority will stop (though it may take time for them to learn).[25]

Notes

1   Rudy Simone (2010), *Asperger's on the Job*. Arlington, TX: Future Horizons, p. xv.
2   *London Evening Standard*, 19 March 2015.

3   See Brenda Smith Myles (2004), *The Hidden Curriculum: Practical Solutions for Understanding Unstated Rules in Social Situations*. Shawnee, KS: Autism Asperger Publishing Company.

4   See Barbara Bissonnette (2013), *Asperger's Syndrome Workplace Survival Guide*. London: Jessica Kingsley.

5   Op. cit., p. 12.

6   Op. cit., p. 13.

7   See Genevieve Edmonds and Luke Beardon (eds) (2008), *Asperger Syndrome and Employment*. London: Jessica Kingsley, p. 12.

8   See: www2.cipd.co.uk/pm/peoplemanagement/b/weblog/archive/2014/11/20/business-is-still-scared-of-autism.aspx (accessed 27 April 2018).

9   See S. Bargiela, R. Steward and M. Williams (2016), 'The experiences of late-diagnosed women with autism spectrum conditions: An investigation of the female autism phenotype', *Journal of Autism and Developmental Disorders*, 46(10), 3281–3294.

10 See John Elder Robison (2008), *Look Me in the Eye – My Life with Asperger's*. London: Ebury Press, p. 194.

11 Ibid.

12 See Luke Jackson (2016), *Sex, Drugs and Asperger's Syndrome – A User's Guide to Adulthood*. London: Jessica Kingsley.

13 Jesse A. Saperstein (2014), *Getting a Life with Asperger's. Lessons Learned on the Bumpy Road to Adulthood*. New York: Perigree, p. 156.

14 Ibid., pp. 155–156.

15 See Josie Santomauro (ed.) (2011), *Autism All-Stars: How We Use Our Autism and Asperger Traits to Shine in Life*. London: Jessica Kingsley, p. 38.

16 Ibid., p. 28.

17 See John Elder Robison (2008), *Look Me in the Eye – My Life with Asperger's*. London: Ebury Press, p. 204.

18 See Josie Santomauro (ed.) (2011), *Autism All-Stars: How We Use Our Autism and Asperger Traits to Shine in Life*. London: Jessica Kingsley, p. 30.

19 See: www.trainingzone.co.uk/develop/talent/going-beyond-the-stereotypes-managing-employees-with-aspergers (accessed 27 April 2018).

20 *The Atlantic*, 28 June 2017.

21 Damian Milton in conversation with the author, 15 July 2016.

22 Ibid.

23 Ibid.

24 See Jonathan Andrews (undated), *Autism and the Workplace: Common Myths and Untapped Talent*.

25 Jonathan Andrews in conversation with the author, 8 June 2016.

Chapter 15

Sensory issues

Many, if not most, individuals with autism experience sensory processing abnormalities in the workplace as intensely as anywhere else, if not more so: they may feel as though they are being bombarded with unpleasant sights (for example, fluorescent lighting), smells (certain perfumes), tactile sensations (uncomfortable formal clothing) or noises (even the low hum of a laptop fan). DSM-5, published in 2013, finally included sensory differences in its definition of autism spectrum conditions. (For many decades, Temple Grandin has been insisting – to the author of this book, among many others – that her sensory issues have been the most debilitating problem of living with autism.) The 'sensory landscape' in the workplace can constitute a metaphorical minefield. Significantly, a study by Mostafa in 2007 indicated that acoustics were ranked as the most influential architectural factor when it came to autism, and recommended that efforts should be made to minimise acoustic disruption.[1]

It is not difficult for employers to adjust the working environment to address these issues. (Clearly, this is a two-way process: an individual with ASD who is hypersensitive to smells should not apply for work at a petrol garage or a printing plant.) As Sarah Hendrickx puts it: 'For an employer, it's important to understand that the provision of a desk lamp, or allowing the wearing of headphones in a noisy office, can make the difference between employment and unemployment for someone with Asperger's syndrome.'[2]

Natural lighting is not only much more suitable than fluorescent lights but it is a natural anti-depressant, helping to improve mood and enhance energy; if natural lighting is impossible, then at least employees should install full-spectrum fluorescent lighting which includes blue.[3]

As Beatriz López and Liz Keenan, of the University of Portsmouth, put it in their important 2014 paper:

> While sound proofing of a workplace can be too costly, background noises – such as electrical noise or conversational noise – can be controlled or removed quite cheaply. A careful assessment of the individual needs of the person with ASD needs to be made, as although it has been proposed that it may be beneficial to have private, quiet areas where the person with autism can go when feeling overwhelmed, assigning people with autism to separate rooms can lead to their feeling different from the majority.[4]

It is best to avoid fluorescent lighting, as it cycles on and off 60 times per second, and this can feel more like a strobe light to someone with hypersensitivity to stimulation.

The use of lights and lamps which reflect upwards, rather than downwards, has been recommended. Even better is the use of natural lighting, since this will not only make the room brighter but ease transition between workspaces. Yet even here, the heterogeneity of autism throws up exceptions. James Hoodless, a young man with Asperger's syndrome who works as a presenter for Autism Oxford, told me that sunlight was the problem for him and that he actually coped more easily with fluorescent lighting.[5]

It is also important to note that some sensory experiences can be extremely pleasurable for individuals on the spectrum. As Ann Memmott, another autistic speaker working for Autism Oxford, put it: 'There can be sensory delights, and some of these can be useful.'[6]

❖ CASE STUDY

- GEORGIA GRANGER

GEORGIA GRANGER, an autistic disability advocate in Northern Ireland, experiences considerable difficulties with sensory issues:

> The offices I've worked in were open-plan, where even if I wasn't required to do phone work, there would be phones ringing and people speaking on them all day – my brain can't tune out other noises around me, it always focuses on them and it means I can't really do anything else but listen to them. In one office, I was told that I couldn't put earbuds in, even without music playing, because it didn't look like I was working, even though I was still doing the task I had been assigned of writing content for a website.
>
> Office lights quite often make me feel anxious (a sign for me that I'm getting close to sensory overload), because I'm hypersensitive to light levels and they are usually a bright blue-white light, whereas I work best in dim lighting or with warm-coloured lights. Natural light is also quite difficult for me because of it changing throughout the day, so I can't work next to windows. Most office chairs make me fidgety ... I'm much more able to focus if I have a laptop on my knee, or at least a keyboard, because then it feels like I have a tactile connection to what I'm meant to be doing.[7]

A woman with Asperger's syndrome, interviewed by Sarah Bargiela and identified only as C., provides a good illustration of just how wide-ranging sensory issues can be:

> The biggest is sound, but I also have significant issues with touch and smell, and reasonable difficulty with sight and taste. Sound-wise, I have no filter. It's good in that I can hear things other people can't (like being able to hear someone at the door before they knock/ring the bell) but mostly it's just traumatic. I can't tune out of noise, so I have never found a place peaceful and quiet. ... After all, in places like Guantánamo Bay,

constant intrusive noise is used as a form of torture. So is lack of sleep. I have both, all day, every day. With touch, hard touch is usually OK, but soft touch (like someone brushing past you in town) is hugely aversive for me. The area that has been touched will tingle, burn or hurt for hours afterwards ... Smells are straightforward – certain smells make me gag. My parents have had to stop eating certain foods, or eat them in a different room to avoid distress. It causes huge problems when I can't use loos or go near certain areas because of smells.

Taste is similar to smell – one of the biggest for both is bananas. I can't stand the taste or smell, and have almost learnt not to like the feel of them because of it. Fruit is a key here – I like almost no fruit. I like lemon cake. I like orange sweets. But I basically don't eat fruit at all, and I recently figured out why. I think it's because individual fruit can be so different. In one bunch of grapes, some will be sweet, some tart, some firm, some squishy. The lack of predictability has made me too anxious to try anything.

Sight is an interesting one, because I didn't think I had anything sight-based, but the more I thought about it, the more I realised I did. I don't deal well with very bright light (I would be squinting on overcast days because it was too bright). Electric light is very tiring. I think it's because I can see the flickering, and it does my head in. Bright colours are incredibly over-stimulating for me ... Busy patterns are massively confusing and disorienting for me. Reading is a huge one – my Mum could never understand why I hated reading, since most bright kids love it. My new understanding is that I struggle to decipher the patterns. I know how to read, and I read well, but if the text is small, or I have to face large chunks of text, I kind of lose the ability to read. It's exhausting trying to focus on the one word you're trying to read when my visual field is so distracted by all the patterns around it.[8]

Employers should adopt a sophisticated approach to the heterogeneity of autism and try to meet each individual's particular needs (assuming that the individual has disclosed his or her condition, of course). Many people on the autism spectrum have great difficulties sifting out background noise – even at very low levels. However, here again, the profiles can be startlingly variable. I was once speaking to Cos Michael, an autism consultant and trainer specialising in adulthood and ageing, diagnosed with Asperger's syndrome at the age of 50. We were sitting in a hotel in east London, next to a noisy children's play area, and Cos (understandably) found the loud and generally joyous children screaming difficult to handle. But she was also disturbed by the piped music in the hotel, which I had not even noticed. On the other hand, when I took Temple Grandin to dinner in a restaurant in Cardiff, she appeared to have no problem tuning into our conversation despite the loud voices from neighbouring tables. (She was also much better at using chopsticks than me, but that's another story!)

Hypersensitivity to touch can be an issue, especially when it comes to clothing. Anyone who has met Stephen Shore (the author of *Autism for*

Dummies – I consider him a good friend) will know that he always wears sandals and hates wearing ties, which he finds too constricting, even at formal gatherings.

Rudy Simone points out that, apart from the sensory issue of direct contact with certain materials, the problems can also be caused by having to make a concrete decision on which particular outfit to wear.[9] (Temple Grandin resolves this problem by consistently sporting her 'cowboy' apparel.)

Incidentally, instances of tactile *hypo*-sensitivity can also be striking. My own autistic son, Johnny, used to prefer holding an ice lolly by the freezing lolly end, rather than the stick!

An important point to note here is the differences between the diagnostic criteria in DSM and ICD. The American Psychiatric Association's DSM-5, published in 2013, takes sensory issues into account, whereas the World Health Organisation's ICD-10 published in 1992 – ICD-11 is due out shortly) does not.

One of the world's leading authorities on sensory differences in autism, Dr Olga Bogdashina, has written that many autistic individuals may become sensorially overloaded in situations that would not bother other people.

> Learning to recognise sensory overload is very important. It is better to prevent it than to 'deal with the consequences'. As soon as you notice early signs of coming sensory overload (which are different for different individuals), stop activity and provide time and space to recover, e.g. invite the person to get into a quiet place or outside. It is useful to teach the individual how to recognise the internal signs of the overload, and ask for help or use different strategies (e.g. relaxation) to prevent the problem.

> The sensory environment is very important for autistic people. They lack the ability to adjust to sensory assaults other people accept as normal. If we accommodate it and try to 'keep it clean' in order to meet their very special needs, the world could become more comfortable for them … Many behaviours that interfere with learning and social interaction are, in fact, protective or sensory defensive responses of the person to 'sensory pollution' in the environment … Structure and routines make the environment predictable and easier to control. Routine and rituals help to facilitate understanding of what is going on and what is going to happen next. Introduce any change slowly and always explain beforehand what is going differently and why …

> A person with mono-processing may have problems with multiple stimuli. Find out which channel 'is open' at the moment and reduce all irrelevant stimuli. Always present information in the person's preferred modality. If you are not sure what it is or which channel 'is on' at the moment (in the case of fluctuation), use multi-sensory presentation and watch which modality 'works'. Remember, though, that they could switch channels.

Direct perception in autism is often hyper. Some autistic individuals actually hear (understand) you better when they are not looking at you. Some autistic people seem to be hypersensitive when they are approached directly by other people. For some, if they are looked at directly, they may feel it as 'a touch' – sort of 'distant touching' with actual experience. ... Never force eye contact ... Let them use their ways to explore the world. In many ways, 'autistic perception' is superior to that of non-autistics. Autistic individuals with their heightened senses often can appreciate colours, sounds, textures, smells, tastes to a much higher degree than people around them. Their gifts and talents should be nurtured and not ridiculed, as it is often the case. ... Give them time to take in your question/instruction and to work out their response. Be aware that autistic individuals often require more time than others to shift their attention between stimuli of different modalities and they find it extremely difficult to follow rapidly changing social instructions.[10]

Notes

1 M. Mostafa (2007), 'An architecture for autism: Concepts of design intervention for the autistic user', International Journal of Architectural Research, 2(1), 189–211.
2 See Sarah Hendrickx (2009), Asperger Syndrome and Employment – What People with Asperger Syndrome Really Really Want. London: Jessica Kingsley, p. 45.
3 See Rudy Simone, op. cit., p. 50.
4 B. López and L. Keenan (2014), 'Barriers to employment in autism: Future challenges to implementing the Adult Autism Strategy', Autism Research Network.
5 James Hoodless in conversation with the author, 13 September 2017.
6 Ann Memmott addressing Autism Oxford conference, Royal College of Psychiatrists, London, 13 September 2016.
7 See: www.ambitiousaboutautism.org.uk/georgia-granger (accessed 27 April 2018).
8 See S. Bargiela, R. Steward and W. Mandy (2016), The experiences of late-diagnosed women with autism spectrum conditions: An investigation of the female autism phenotype, Journal of Autism and Developmental Disorders, October, 46(10), 3281–3294.
9 Simone, op. cit., p. 61.
10 See: http://network.autism.org.uk/knowledge/insight-opinion/top-5-tips-autism-professionals-dr-olga-bogdashina-sensory-difficulties (accessed 27 April 2018).

Chapter 16

Executive dysfunction

'Executive function' is a broad term that refers to the cognitive processes which help us regulate, control and manage our thoughts and actions. It includes planning, working memory, attention, problem-solving, verbal reasoning, inhibition, cognitive flexibility, initiation of actions and monitoring of actions.

As Elisabeth Hill, of Goldsmiths, University of London, a world authority on executive function, has written:

> The theory of executive dysfunction in autism makes an explicit link to frontal lobe failure in this disorder in analogy with neuropsychological patients who have suffered damage in the frontal lobes and have impaired executive functions. Executive dysfunction can be seen to underlie many of the key characteristics of autism, both in the social and non-social domains. The behaviour problems addressed by this theory are rigidity and perseveration, being explained by a poverty in the initiation of new non-routine actions and the tendency to be stuck in a given task set. At the same time, the ability to carry out routine actions can be excellent and is manifested in a strong liking for repetitive behaviour and sometimes elaborate rituals.[1]

Most people on the autism spectrum have some degree of impaired executive function. One person actually wrote online: 'For me, executive dysfunction is one of the most disabling parts of being autistic.'[2] This frequently creates problems in understanding how long a task will, or should, take. Georgia Granger, the autistic disability advocate in Northern Ireland, expresses this well:

> I constantly have to balance how much effort and energy I put into something with whether I'll have the time to recover from it ... It's really difficult for me to start and stop something I'm working on while that focused.[3]

Here again, individuals with ASD vary in their profile of executive function strengths and deficits. One recommendation, by Barbara Bissonnette, is to draw up a daily activity log. Here, the SMART goals template may be useful. **SMART** is an acronym representing the five important steps: Making the goal **S**pecific; Making success **M**easurable; Selecting a goal that can be **A**chieved; Checking that the goal is **R**easonable and Making that goal **T**ime-limited.[4]

As Janine Booth has pointed out, employers prefer to see work done promptly, rather than accurately.[5] Without an intact executive function, it may prove very difficult to concentrate, to respond spontaneously or to cope with changes to routine or structure. Such changes are a frequent occurrence in the workplace: colleagues may change due to illness or there may be last-minute alterations in schedules or requirements. Some occurrences may feel trivial to many non-autistic employees but can prove anxiety-causing or even distressing for people on the spectrum: the canteen may be closed for renovation, the drinks machine may run out of coffee.

A change of boss can certainly spell trouble. When Temple Grandin was working for *Arizona Farmer Ranchman* magazine, her manager was replaced and this unsettled Grandin considerably.

Cynthia Kim, the writer with Asperger's syndrome, has written on her blog:

> If you have poor EF, people might mistake you for being disorganised, lazy, incompetent, sloppy or just plain not very bright. Why? Because executive function encompasses so many essential areas of daily living. Nearly everything we do calls on areas of executive function. Cooking. Cleaning. Parenting. Work. School. Self-care.[6]

Workplaces are notoriously full of distractions. As Kim has pointed out: 'People who have difficulty filtering out environmental stimuli (selective attention) tend to have poor working memory. And who has more difficulty filtering out environmental stimuli than people on the spectrum?'[7]

The attention component of executive function is closely tied to working memory. For Kim, attention functions along two axes: top-down control of attention by our executive function system (via our brain's prefrontal cortex) and bottom-up control of attention by sensory inputs.

> Poor working memory makes it harder to filter out sensory input, allowing the bottom-up system to dominate. When the bottom-up system dominates, working memory suffers, creating a vicious cycle. This is why having a quiet, distraction-free environment seems to work miracles when it comes to productivity and focus. Purposely reducing sensory distractions quiets the bottom-up attention system, making it easier for the top-down system to actively direct attention to the task at hand.[8]

People with poor executive functions also have difficulty with time management and with monitoring and regulating their behaviours. These difficulties can include monitoring and changing behaviour as needed, planning future behaviour when faced with new tasks and situations, and anticipating outcomes and adapting to changing situations.

The Job Accommodation Network has some useful tips for both employers and workers to ease the problems associated with executive dysfunction in the workplace:

Time management

- Divide large assignments into several small tasks or chunks
- Set a timer to sound an alarm after assigning ample time to complete a task

- Provide a checklist of assignments
- Use a wall calendar to emphasise due dates
- Develop a colour-coded system (with each colour representing a task, event, or level of importance)

Memory issues

- Provide written instructions and checklists
- Allow additional training time for new tasks
- Provide minutes of meetings and trainings
- Use a flow-chart to indicate steps in a task
- Provide verbal or pictorial cues
- Use a colour-coding scheme to prioritise tasks
- Use sticky notes as reminders of important dates or tasks

Concentration issues

- Provide a noise-cancelling headset
- Relocate employee's office space away from audible distractions
- Install space enclosures (cubicle walls)
- Reduce clutter in the employee's work environment
- Take breaks for mental fatigue, including short walks, getting up for a drink of water, and rotating through varied tasks.[9]

Notes

1 See E. L. Hill (2004), Evaluating the theory of executive dysfunction in autism, *Developmental Review*, 24, 189–233.
2 See Cynthia Kim, 'Musings of an Aspie', https://musingsofanaspie.com/2013/08/09/the-challenges-of-being-a-self-employed-aspie/ (accessed 27 April 2018).
3 See: www.ambitiousaboutautism.org.uk/georgia-granger (accessed 27 April 2018).
4 See Barbara Bissonnette (2013), *Asperger's Syndrome Workplace Survival Guide*. London: Jessica Kingsley, p. 107.
5 See Janine Booth (2016), *Autism Equality in the Workplace: Removing Barriers and Challenging Discrimination*. London: Jessica Kingsley, p. 45.
6 See Cynthia Kim, 'Musings of an Aspie', https://musingsofanaspie.com/2013/08/09/the-challenges-of-being-a-self-employed-aspie/ (accessed 27 April 2018).
7 Ibid.
8 Ibid.
9 See: https://askjan.org/media/execfunc.html (accessed 27 April 2018).

Chapter 17

The importance (and dangers) of literal language in the workplace

Skilled and talented workers on the autism spectrum can come unstuck if employers use too much jargon and metaphorical, non-literal language or expect the employee to understand implied meanings. This is another argument in favour of disclosing autism before entering the workplace: it allows the employer to adjust communication accordingly.

Here are some examples of figurative phrases frequently heard in the workplace which, as Marcia Scheiner and Joan Bogden point out, will leave many people on the autism spectrum confused:

- The ball is in your court
- We need to be on the same wavelength
- Pick his brain about the merger
- Bring me up to speed on the project.[1]

The other side of the coin is the fact that many people on the autism spectrum are liable to use language too literally (or directly) themselves. Rudy Simone quotes the example of a worker with Asperger's syndrome, Mia, who burst into a quiet office and shouted out to a male colleague: 'I would love to eat your nuts.' (She was actually referring to the bowl of nuts on his desk!)[2] A man with Asperger's syndrome working in the finance department at King's College, London, when asked by a colleague 'How are you doing?' replied: 'I'm doing the best I can.'

The perfectionism which is such a strength of people on the autism spectrum can sometimes also prove a hazard. If a piece of work is less than ideal (even the boss's!), an autistic employee may well say so.

Rudy Simone has some sensible advice: 'Curb your urge to inform unless you are being asked for advice or information. No one likes a know-it-all.'[3] She also suggests 'gift-wrapping' words with tact, rather than shooting them like an arrow.[4] Employees, for their part, should listen to *what* their staff members say, not *how* they say it, and should not allow a person's (perceived or actual) unpopularity to prompt an instant dismissal of their good ideas.[5]

Jesse Saperstein has variously worked as a care professional at a group home for people with severe disabilities, a night shift worker at an IBM plant, an assistant director at a funeral home, a motivational speaker and a creative writing teacher. In many ways, his most successful position was at the funeral home, because it taught him to restrain what he calls his 'loose mouth'. It is the kind of mouth which led him to enrage a customer at his family's clothing store by commenting: 'Did you say your son's name is Damien? Isn't that also the name of the Anti-Christ in those *Omen* movies?'[6]

Jane Meyerding writes that people on the autism spectrum are more likely to converse only (or primarily) about substance, not recognising that their manner of conversing is perceived by the non-autistic person as forming part of a personal social relationship.

> What I say is much less likely to be determined by my relationship with the other person, and more likely to be determined by the subject matter and my relationship with the subject matter. Part of what that means is that I am less likely to (think to) tailor what I say to suit/match the person to whom I am talking. As a result, I may be seen as pedantic, condescending (if I am going into too much detail, given the other person's background) or overly esoteric, when in fact, what I am doing is processing/ organising the subject in my own mind, talking to myself, as much as to anyone else.[7]

It is true that many people with Asperger's syndrome tend to talk *at* their interlocutors, rather than *to* them. John Biddulph, a teacher with degrees in both music and art history, recalled that, as an assistant teacher at one school, he began speaking to a visitor about the composer, Frederick Delius – and continued to do so for about two hours before the visitor eventually burst into tears. 'There is nothing about the information concerning the life and music of Frederick Delius that could cause offence or extreme sadness, so I can only assume that the duration and intensity of the discourse were responsible.'[8]

Often, it is the sheer weight and confusion of *incoming* – not outgoing – information which can represent the crucial problem. Alex Brown, a librarian with Asperger's syndrome, says:

> I don't know when I am being told something for my information, or whether I am supposed to act on it in some way ... we are given such a lot of information. It would be helpful to know which is the really important and relevant bit, or to be told that they want me to do certain things.[9]

In 2014, the neuroscientist Daniel Levitin argued 'Information overload keeps us mired in noise ... This saps us of not only willpower (of which we have a limited store) but creativity as well.'[10] In a paper published in *Psychological Science*, Bar and Baror described how 'conditions of high load' fostered unoriginal thinking. Centuries earlier, Samuel Johnson wrote: 'Imagination, a licentious and vagrant faculty, unsusceptible of limitations and impatient of restraint, has always endeavoured to baffle the logician, to perplex the confines of distinction, and burst the enclosures of regularity.'[11]

One of the great paradoxes, of course, is how to communicate that you have a communication problem when you have a communication problem. When Neil Shepherd began work in an IT department, he told everyone there about his Asperger's syndrome. He reassured them that it was not contagious, that he was not deranged, that when he did not look them in the eye, he was not being rude.

> To a certain degree, I did become 'contagious', as what little interaction I'd had before totally disappeared. I was isolated and exiled by most of the department. Second, the head of department, who was smart enough to know I wasn't

contagious, then tried to downplay my 'traits': 'Oh, everyone gets anxious,' 'We're all bad at talking to people,' etc. You can see what he was trying to do, but it was actually the polar opposite of what was needed. If you look at Asperger's syndrome from a totally logical point of view, a lot of the 'problems' are merely the same as those experienced by 'norms' ... But with AS, they're intensified to such a degree that they cause a level of anxiety that is well beyond 'normal' or acceptable.[12]

Rachel ('Chase') Patterson, a woman with Asperger's syndrome, says:

I also have a lot of 'autopilot'. phrases or behaviours that are socially acceptable and that I default to under stress or when I can't figure a situation out. The worst part is, I don't have any control over it ... We put an awful lot of time and effort into processing our own behaviour, and that of the people we're interacting with. Imagine you're having a very important meeting with a person you've never met before. It turns out they speak a different language – one you've never learned a word of. And then they give you a translation dictionary/phrase book and expect you to translate in real time. Now, imagine you actually have to deal with the subject of the very important meeting *on top of* the real-time translation. That's exactly what it's like for us. Every interaction we have is littered with things we have to consciously register, interpret and respond to. Every time someone squints slightly or wrinkles their nose, I need to figure out why it happened, what it could mean, what it's most likely to mean, which responses might be appropriate, which response is most appropriate based on what the most likely meaning is ... At the same time, I'm going through an identical process with speech – what did they say, what are all the possible meanings, what's the most likely meaning, what are all the possible responses, what's the most appropriate response based on the most likely meaning, how do I say it (what tone, inflection etc.), how do I tell if I've got it right or not ...

All of this is being done at the same time as trying to actually cover the subject of whatever meeting/conversation/interaction etc. The problem is – especially for girls – if we've gotten good at it, most people can't tell that that's what's going on in our head. Because that's a ridiculous amount of data to try and process at any given time. Most people never even think about it – they just *know*. And they have no clue what it's like not to know. But again, it takes a *huge* toll on the energy of the person trying to do it. The longer they're required to do it, the more tired they get. The more tired, the more likely you are to get it wrong. You start slipping up and picking the wrong meaning, and responding to it incorrectly or in an unsociable or odd way... It's part of the reason why things like email are so much better for us – everything above is cut down to 'what do the words mean'. Nothing else. It's so much easier to process.[13]

From the employer's point of view, it is important to ensure that workplace communication is clear. As Janine Booth correctly points out:

There are so many stories of autistic workers getting into trouble because they have been given a sloppy request or instruction and have carried it out literally. Workplaces often have their own dialect or jargon, but although workers are taught the technical jargon of the work process, we are not usually taught the social jargon. Don't have unwritten rules. If there are rules, write them. Better still, negotiate them among the workforce, so that not only does everyone know them, but they also had a role in deciding them. Facilitate each worker to use his/her preferred form of communication; some prefer to exchange information in writing rather than in meetings; some hate the telephone; some want to use diagrams; others may benefit from assistance from a support worker or intermediary. Break down the culture of management pressure, of favouritism ('blue-eyed-boy-and-girl syndrome'), and the drive to competitiveness that pits workers against one another. Practices such as performance-related pay, hand-picked promotions, judging workers based on their socialising, and ever-harsher performance management regimes make workplaces into distressing and discriminatory environments where communication clashes abound.[14]

Employers should be fully aware that imprecise directions – such as 'Go over these figures later' – can be bewildering to someone on the autism spectrum. What does 'later' mean? In an a hour, a day, a week? As Scheiner and Bogden note, most non-autistic people would be able to interpret the request on the basis of past experience or the context of the situation in which the remark was uttered. 'An individual with autism, however, needs to be told exactly when, how and how much he needs to do, so he can focus on the task rather than the interpretation.'[15]

The benefits can be broader. Interestingly, one executive told that efforts to make corporate communications more direct, in order to account for the difficulties autistic employees had with nuance, irony and other fine points of language, had improved workplace communication overall.[16]

❖ CASE STUDY

- RICHARD MAGUIRE

RICHARD MAGUIRE, the public speaker and mentor with Asperger's syndrome introduced in Chapter 2, worked in a cycle shop at 15, but lasted only eight weeks.

> I had not developed enough social skills to get along in a daily work environment. I remember being in charge of fixing punctures. The shop owner said she thought it would be better to replace an inner tube than to repair one. Up until then, the practice was to make a repair. I thought she was voicing her thoughts and did not realise she was giving an instruction.
>
> It was implied meaning that caught me out. Being autistic, I do not comprehend implied meanings. I hear words and process them literally. Later in life, I grew aware of looking out for these indirect communication traits to try and guess someone's alternative meaning. I frequently do not get it right (ask my incredibly patient wife). If my boss at the bicycle shop had said 'change inner tubes from now on', I would have done just that. So I was told to leave because she thought I did not follow orders.[17]

Notes

1 See Marcia Scheiner and Joan Bogden (2017), *An Employer's Guide to Managing Professionals on the Autism Spectrum*. London: Jessica Kingsley, p. 94.

2 Rudy Simone, op. cit., p. 26.

3 Ibid., p. 21.

4 Ibid.

5 Ibid., p. 23.

6 Jesse A. Saperstein (2014), *Getting a Life with Asperger's. Lessons Learned on the Bumpy Road to Adulthood*. New York: Perigree, p. 154.

7 See Dinah Murray (ed.) (2006), *Coming Out Asperger: Diagnosis, Disclosure and Self-Confidence*. London: Jessica Kingsley, p. 248.

8 See Genevieve Edmonds and Luke Beardon (eds) (2008), *Asperger Syndrome and Employment*. London: Jessica Kingsley, p. 85.

9 Ibid., p. 49.

10 Ibid.

11 Ibid.

12 Ibid., p. 60.

13 Rachel Patterson, in communication with the author, 28 August 2017.

14 Janine Booth, interviewed by Damian Milton on the JKP Blog, 15 July 2016 (www.jkp.com/jkpblog/2016/04/autism-equality-workplace-interview-janine-booth/ (accessed 27 April 2018).

15 Scheiner and Bogden, op. cit., p. 94.

16 See R. D. Austin and G. P. Pisano (2017), 'Neurodiversity as a competitive advantage', *Harvard Business Review*, May–June, 96–103.

17 See Richard Maguire (2014), *I Dream in Autism*. CreateSpace Independent Publishing Platform.

Chapter 18

Bullying, harassment and discrimination in the workplace

Bullying

Much has been written on the important issue of bullying of ASD pupils in schools. The problem of bullying in the *workplace* has been seriously neglected, in comparison. A 2012 survey by the UK's National Autistic Society found that a third of adults with autism had been bullied or discriminated against at work.

As Janine Booth has pointed out, trouble can arise from direct bullying but also from excessive scrutiny, as well as being treated as a problem rather than someone with strengths and positive assets.[1]

❖ CASE STUDY

THOMAS MADAR

Although he enjoyed his first job in software development when he left university in the late 1970s, THOMAS MADAR, from Nottingham, now 60, found difficulty in fitting in. Like many people on the autistic spectrum, he experienced problems in the workplace and was dismissed as a poor communicator. Thomas told me: 'Employers *do* want people with creativity but they also demand excellent verbal communication.'[2]

Thomas's part-Jewish father, a Hungarian doctor, was interned during the Second World War and fled during the 1956 uprising. Thomas was diagnosed with autism at the age of three in Glasgow in 1960. The family moved around a great deal: London, Birmingham, Margate, Bournemouth, before finally settling in Folkestone. Thomas was clearly extremely intelligent, but he was bullied at school and suffered severe mood swings.

He studied botany and zoology at the University of Wales in Aberystwyth. While there, his careers adviser told him that if he didn't 'come out of his shell', he would be unemployable, because employers placed a premium on people who

Figure 18.1 Thomas Madar, pictured at Bosworth Battlefield in Leicestershire

were socially 'involved'. 'I was advised to go into the IT industry, because there was a great demand for workers. I *did* like computer programming.'[3]

In 1978, Thomas found a job as a software engineer at Plessey and Co in Poole, Dorset, designing software for traffic control systems in Norwich and São Paulo. After a while, due to his difficulty in making friends, he suffered social rejection and bullying and was eventually dismissed by Plessey. The inability to find another post, combined with the bullying, led to serious depression. 'I still feel socially inferior to this day,' he says. Life improved dramatically in the early 1980s, when Thomas's parents persuaded him to return to Aberystwyth to take a postgraduate diploma in computer studies. He thoroughly enjoyed this course. 'It was as though I had stepped out of my autism. I found it much easier to make friends. There was a different environment, which placed greater weight on things I was good at.'

After an enjoyable cycling trip around Europe (it was a 'healing experience, except for a near head-on collision with a car at Roussec – I had to learn the French for a back wheel – and being falsely accused of stealing cash and a camera in Alicante'), Thomas found a new job at Marconi Radar in Chelmsford. 'The company knew I had autism, but I was still bullied and misunderstood.'[4]

On his return from another foreign trip, this time to Morocco, he had a terrible time finding work 'because I couldn't sell myself at interviews.' Finally, in the 1990s, he was offered a position as a software engineer at Lucas Aerospace at Whitney in Oxfordshire. For a year, he thrived and was popular with colleagues. 'My social skills improved. I became an accepted member of the team.' However, as the work became more routine and allowed less and less scope for creativity, he grew bored. Moreover, although he did his work thoroughly, he also did it slowly. 'Employers prefer speed to accuracy,' he told me. 'Time management is a big problem for me.'[5]

Thomas completed a Masters in Information Systems from the University of Leeds and, in the mid-1990s, he also began giving public presentations on his experiences in the workplace. That was when he came to the notice of the National Autistic Society's employment scheme, Prospects, which initially found him a job as a data administrator at the Nottingham headquarters of Boots the Chemists. This database administrator role did not work out, as it involved a great deal of interaction with customers, the requirement to cope with scant instructions and some time pressure.

> I was moved to a software development role, which I found much more suitable. In 2002, my role was outsourced to a consultancy known as Xansa in order to save money and in 2006, my job was outsourced to India where the cost of software development was much lower. I still worked for Xansa, but in software development roles around the UK. I was obliged to travel a lot and stay in hotels (all paid for), as these roles were well outside of daily commuting distance. In 2008, even these roles dried up, and I was made redundant.

He sought the advice of a careers coach who recommended that he seek a career in website design and development. He spent an 'adrenaline-charged' year studying for a Master's in web development at Edge Hill University in Ormskirk, Lancashire, from which he emerged with a distinction in 2011.

Nevertheless, despite two more postgraduate qualifications, substantial exposure to many computer programming languages and over a decade of commercial software development experience, Thomas still found it difficult to find work. Why? 'Employers reject me on the ground of not having absolute expertise or years of commercial experience in a specific set of skills,' he said back in 2014.

I feel most upset at being wasted like this ... Is there any employer who will see sense? Despite being in my fifties, I have much to offer in terms of good character, high intelligence and original thinking. And yet I get treated like a bum and thrown on the scrapheap ... Short-sightedness, together with a cult of personality, abounds. Employers demand that applicants meet numerous criteria which they themselves can scarcely match. They aim to hire an employee who is not only a mighty likeable fellow but who is fully productive the moment that he or she first crosses the office threshold. Do these make the best employees? Whatever happened to the pursuit of character? Whatever happened to patience and far-sightedness? I am made to feel more like an object than a person. To most employers, I am no more than one of a number of apples being sold in a crate displayed on a market stall, or one of a number of garments to be found in a bargain basket positioned near a supermarket checkout.[6]

Fortunately, just weeks after making those remarks, Thomas came to the attention of Specialisterne, Thorkil Sonne's organisation specialising in employment of people on the autism spectrum, and through them obtained work as a software tester at Ernst & Young in 2014, where he was successfully employed for two years, when compulsory redundancy struck again. On this occasion, he discovered Auticon, an IT consultancy specialising in employing people on the autism spectrum on account of their distinctive abilities, and was offered employment at this consultancy. An extremely successful contract followed with Experian in Nottingham.

Thomas says that his strengths in the workplace are that he is thorough, intelligent with an ability to pick up small discrepancies, 'I would also say I have creativity, objectivity, good research skills, tenacity and strong problem-solving abilities,' Nevertheless, he concedes that he may have difficulties with time and task management and still dislikes noisy environments.[7] But Thomas Madar is a success story – he has overcome many hurdles.

Harassment

There have been distressing instances of employees on the spectrum falling prey to sexual predators. Many people with autism tend to be more vulnerable to – and less aware of – other people's intentions.

❖ CASE STUDIES

- RYAN TEBBIT
- GOLDEN CORRAL RESTAURANT

RYAN TEBBIT is a therapist today working for Elaine Nicholson's Action for Asperger's (see Chapter 26 for more details of this charity). After a year of failing at his engineering course, Tebbit left college and started to look for a job.

I eventually got one working as a sound engineer for a local recording studio. I didn't have any particular skills for this job and so I was given a few weeks of shadowing the other sound engineers. I was not a natural and it took me a long time to understand what I was supposed to be doing. All the electronic equipment was so complicated and confusing and I couldn't picture the processes of recording and mixing in my head ... it was all very abstract. Eventually, I was given the night shift, which meant starting at 10pm and programming musical backing tracks into sequencer software until 8am the next morning. I was all at sea. I tried so hard to re-create the songs I was given but they ended up sounding amateurish, at best. After a year of trying and failing to become a good engineer, I was moved into the office of the studio to assist the boss, who had taken a shine to me and complimented me at every opportunity. I naively thought that this meant I was good at my job and my confidence grew. But growing confidence for a 19-year-old boy meant that I lurched from feeling totally inadequate and needing constant reassurance to becoming arrogant and believing I knew it all. I was given the task of managing the office and office staff, but I had no comprehension about how to interact with my staff and I treated them in a patronising way. I couldn't understand why my staff seemed to hate me so much. I thought I was executing my duties with efficiency and passion.[8]

Ryan continues:

Meanwhile, my boss continued to pay me a lot of attention and took me out for meals. At the time, I was totally oblivious that this attention could mean anything else except niceness. I was in for a shock when he physically came on to me and tried to kiss me one day when we were out in his car. It's so difficult to look back on this event now, as I cannot believe I thought that his trying to kiss me was him just being 'nice' to me ... but I really did. I do remember pushing him away and him being very offended and cross with me. I did categorically say that I wasn't gay but this didn't seem to put him off. Over the next few very uncomfortable weeks, I continued to state that I didn't like being hugged or kissed by him and he got more and more angry with me. It all ended abruptly when I pushed him away one morning and he exploded and physically threw me and my belongings out of the front door. I was overwhelmed, crushed, humiliated and discombobulated. I went back to my parents' house and lay crying in my bed for what seemed like days. I simply couldn't see why this had happened. I had been clear and direct with him at all times. Why did I feel like the loser? The whole incident had left me feeling broken and it took a monumental effort to start again and find a new job.[9]

Luckily, Ryan did find new work, this time at a map and travel bookshop in London's West End – appropriate, given his childhood obsession with maps:

It was like a dream come true for me. I was encouraged to familiarise myself with the stock of each department and I dived in. Having all these wonderful maps and charts around me, I started to spend 'too much' time poring over them and not enough time selling them. I naively thought that I was doing a good job by building up an encyclopaedic knowledge of all the different series of maps, but my managers were not happy. I was accused of 'playing' at work, which I didn't understand … Once again, this job ended with bad feeling on both sides and I left to get another job at the British Library. I thought the national library would be a peaceful and quiet workplace but it was anything but. After three years of running the photocopying desk in the main reading room, I was signed off work with stress and depression. There were so many restrictions on what you could photocopy from the library's collections that I had frequent arguments with readers who wanted entire books copied and I was the one that had to uphold the library's preservation rules. I was so glad when my doctor agreed to sign me off from this crazy and overwhelming role.[10]

Ryan spent the following year smoking cannabis and playing endless video games whilst living on unemployment benefit.

I rarely left my flat and slowly sank into a deep pit of depression and fear about the world outside. I started to resent people and eventually became suspicious of others and started to withdraw almost completely … convinced that there was a worldwide plot to humiliate me. I started to find solace in listening to the radio, and in particular talk radio, late at night. It took me away from my fears and paranoia and tuning in for every news and sport broadcast became more important than living my life. It gave me a sense of confidence that I knew everything about every news story that was broadcast and was able to relate them in great detail to other people. The upshot of all this immersion in the 'media' spelled paranoia, fear and psychosis for me and before too long, I was sectioned under the Mental Health Act.[11]

Eventually, Ryan found fulfilling employment as a counsellor (see Chapter 3).

An unidentified autistic man who washed dishes during the night shift at the GOLDEN CORRAL RESTAURANT in Matthews, North Carolina, in the US, was targeted with sexualised verbal harassment by his boss before being sexually assaulted on the job, according to a lawsuit by the federal government.

The workplace abuse went on for more than a year at the restaurant on East Independence Boulevard before the employee told his mother what he had been enduring, the Equal Employment Opportunity Commission said. The federal agency, which handles complaints of workplace harassment, says a male assistant manager verbally harangued the employee with lewd and insulting comments, ranging from soliciting sex acts to insulting the worker's intelligence, before sexually groping him in 2016.

'All employees, men and women alike, are entitled to a workplace free from sexual harassment,' said Lynette Barnes, regional attorney for the Charlotte

District of the EEOC, in a statement after the filing of the complaint. 'Likewise, all employees have the right to work without being harassed due to their disabilities. It is particularly alarming when harassment is perpetrated by a supervisor.'[12]

The Golden Corral franchise in Matthews is owned by Jax LLC of Charlotte. Golden Corral's attorney, Keith Weddington of Charlotte, said Jax denied the allegations.

The complaint says the harassment began shortly after the dish washer was hired in late February 2014. In the lawsuit, Yolanda Brock, a local EEOC trial attorney, said the employee had 'high-functioning autism', which was known to his employer. The employee did his job well. Yet, according to the complaint, the assistant manager, often the only one on duty during the night shift, regularly referred to him as 'retard' and 'stupid'. The sexual harassment also began at around the same time, the suit said. At least once a week, according to the complaint, the manager confronted his employee with graphic terms soliciting sodomy and oral sex while also regularly asking: 'Do you wanna get fired?' Despite the employee's complaints, the manager also used a litany of profane, sexual and racial slurs around him, the lawsuit says. In several instances, according to the suit, the boss pinched the employee's rear.

On the night of 9 January 2016, the assistant manager sexually assaulted the employee, later telling him: 'Don't bother coming in tomorrow', the complaint alleged. After the assault, the employee asked to be moved to the day shift so he could avoid his boss. On 16 January, his first day back at Golden Corral, the assistant manager also worked the day shift. According to the complaint, when the employee went outside to empty some garbage, the assistant manager followed him. There, according to the complaint, the boss crudely solicited oral sex.

The employee left work after making up an excuse that he was about to get sick to his stomach. Later that day, he finally let his mother know about what had been happening at work, the complaint said. Afterwards, the parents brought their son back to Golden Corral to file a complaint with the manager and district manager of the company. The family then filed a police report, the complaint said. It was unclear whether charges were filed. The son never returned to Golden Corral.[13]

Discrimination

Although employers are prohibited by law from discriminating against workers because of their disability, in practice it can be very difficult to prove that this was the motive for discrimination (or in some cases even dismissal). However, parents should not be put off from pursuing a law suit if they are convinced that there is persuasive supporting evidence. There have been a number of encouraging recent instances of employees with autism winning their cases for unfair dismissal.

Under the Equality Act 2010, the following actions by an employer are considered unlawful:

- Direct discrimination: treating a disabled person less favourably than other employees.
- Indirect discrimination: applying a provision, criterion or practice that is discriminatory in relation to an employee's autism – i.e. a provision which does not apply to non-autistic employees, or which puts autistic employees at a particular disadvantage, and is not a proportionate means of achieving a legitimate aim.
- Discrimination arising from disability: treating an autistic employee unfavourably because of something arising as a consequence of that employee's autism, and being unable to show that the treatment was a proportionate means of achieving a legitimate aim.
- Harassment: engaging in unwanted conduct related to the worker's autism which had the effect of violating that person's dignity, or creating an intimidating, hostile, degrading, humiliating or offensive environment for the autistic worker.[14]

After the passage of the Rights of Persons with Disabilities Act in 2016, all British government organisations have been asked to appoint 'grievance redressal officers' to look into complaints. A Department of Personnel and Training (DoPT) order released to all central government departments in 2017 declared: 'Any person aggrieved with any matter relating to discrimination in employment against any person with disability may file a complaint with the grievance redressal officer of the respective government establishment.' Every complaint shall be investigated within two months of its registration and outcome thereof or action taken thereon shall be communicated to the complainant or person with benchmark disability, the DoPT said. (It will be recalled, from Chapter 7, that benchmark disability means a person with not less than 40 per cent of a specified disability.)

Despite increasing legal protection from work discrimination, many lesbian, gay, bisexual, and transgender (LGBT) people across the world still suffer from discrimination and harassment in the workplace. They may be denied employment, fired, passed over for promotion, or given less desirable assignments or compensations because of their sexual orientation or gender identity. While these 'formal' discriminations may or may not be protected by governmental or organisational policies, LGBT persons also encounter 'informal' discriminatory actions, such as being isolated by co-workers, vandalism, 'heterosexist' remarks or jokes, or even physical assault. Furthermore, discriminatory acts have become more subtle recently, causing self-doubts on the part of LGBT individuals.

In the UK, while protection and equality for LGBT individuals have improved significantly due to the Employment Equality (Sexual Orientation) Regulations (2003), this does not necessarily translate into improved experiences. As The Psychologist pointed out, interviews with 50 lesbian and bisexual women in 2008 revealed instances of heterosexism and sexism, and most of them had not revealed their sexual orientation to clients or customers.[15]

We have already discussed, in depth, the issue of whether, when and how a heterosexual autistic person should disclose his or her condition (see Chapter 10). Clearly, for LGBT employees with autism, there is an additional, and equally important, area of disclosure in the workplace, namely their sexuality. The Psychologist observed that possible benefits of disclosure could include 'relief and the freedom to be oneself; increased self-esteem and affirmation; closer interpersonal relationships; opportunities for resources, support, and mentoring; and being part of organisational and social change'. On the other hand, the costs could be 'loss of employment, discrimination, harassment, social isolation and physical assault'. Environmental support for identity disclosure

> includes successful role models who have come out at work, presence of heterosexual alias, and institutional support and protection. The interactions among these multiple factors could make disclosure decisions complicated and difficult for LGB persons.[16]

It is also important to consider cultural differences. Whereas LGBT identities are socially constructed, endorsement and disclosure of such identities may not fit people from cultures without that kind of identity construction.

> Some LGBT people of colour may endorse a Western-dominated LGBT identity, but decide to use different identity management strategies when dealing with their own cultural community, as well as across family, friends and work relationships. These persons may achieve harmony and satisfaction even though they do not fit the Western ideation of fully integrated and disclosed LGBT identity.[17]

There has been a perceived overlap of the issues faced by autistic and LGBT individuals. Indeed, inspired by LGBT Pride events, the first Autistic Pride Day was celebrated in 2005 by the online community, Aspies for Freedom. It is now marked worldwide. In 2017, Dan Barrett, a young British autistic man who faced discrimination for being LGBT, made a short documentary about his experience after coming out as gay five months earlier. 'We should all be treated the same,' he said, 'and that's how I felt when I came out as gay … If you're in a wheelchair or not, you're still a human being, if you're lesbian, gay, transgender or not, you're still a human being.'

Jonathan Andrews, the successful lawyer and poet with Asperger's syndrome featured elsewhere in this book, co-founded the London Bisexual Network in 2016. He says:

Figure 18.2 Jonathan Andrews
Source: Disability Confident

Talented people come from all groups, and those from diverse groups often have special talents – such as coping strategies honed young when managing a disability – which employers should seek out. If an organisation has a culture where everyone, whatever their background, can feel supported and welcome, talented people from diverse groups will naturally be more keen to apply to it ... I think it's important for employers to understand how these issues intersect, rather than splitting them out into 'women', 'ethnic minorities', etc. There are many similarities between groups – for example, I'm bisexual as well as autistic, and both are invisible differences, whereas gender and race are often (though not always) visible – and I think employers should think about holding more events focused on this.[18]

Andrews added:

I also think discussion around diversity can too often be reduced to labels – it's important to remember the individuals behind the labels too, and events which aren't rigid for one group or another help this. I'm a big believer in promotion of diversity of thought, too – there's little point increasing representation of one group if everyone you hire thinks the same, and a lot of the business case for diversity comes from people with different opinions challenging established practice and 'groupthink'.[19]

Despite being British, many minority ethnic individuals with learning disabilities – including autism – continue to face prejudice and discrimination. According to Parmi Dheensa, the mother of a severely learning-disabled son, now 20, this does not constitute blatant discrimination but instead reflects the insidious 'bias culture' facing black, Asian and minority ethnic (BAME) people with learning disabilities and their families. For Deensa, they face double discrimination – the disadvantages experienced by all learning-disabled people (including health inequalities or austerity), plus a lack of cultural awareness and language barriers. There is often stigma about learning disability in their own communities, too.[20]

Dheensa founded a BAME support charity, Include Me Too, in 2002 after working for the voluntary sector and council in Wolverhampton in various BAME and disability support roles. Include Me Too works with 1,500 families a year, and has launched a campaign for the British government to review its equality duties in relation to special needs education and support for BAME communities. Recent research from the Equalities National Council and Scope suggests the number of disabled (but not specifically learning disabled) BAME people totals one million in the UK.

BAME families also experience a lack of awareness within their communities. Dheensa, who was once told by a member of her community that her son's learning disability might have something to do with 'karma', noted: 'We don't even have the language for disabilities. When we're trying to explain to families certain conditions in many of our Asian community languages, we haven't got the words that describe cerebral palsy, autism or epilepsy, for example.'[21]

Aniisa Farah, originally from Somalia, a single parent with an autistic daughter, launched a group, Somali Autism Awareness, in the UK after noticing a gap in support. She said: 'I didn't know about autism before my daughter was diagnosed aged six; there's no word for autism in Somali. Some people – including family and friends in the community – would call her "crazy girl".'[22]

There are a number of promising initiatives to address this issue of cultural and linguistic misunderstanding of autism. The National Autistic Society's Tower Hamlets Autism Support in east London has specialist interpreters. However, very little is being done to tackle the specific issue of discrimination against people from ethnic minorities in the workplace.

Jane Hatton, who founded Evenbreak, an award-winning, not-for-profit British social enterprise run for and by disabled people, told me:

> Many studies show that on average, disabled employees are just as productive as their non-disabled colleagues (sometimes more so), have less time off sick, fewer workplace accidents and stay with their employers longer, increasing retention and saving money on recruiting and training new staff. Showing a positive approach towards disability also tends to foster good relations with other staff and generally enhances your reputation as an employer of choice.[23]

Hatton added: 'Employers are becoming more interested. They are starting to see autism as an advantage, rather than a disability, and to consider employing them as a commercially sensible thing to do, rather than a charitable act.' Nevertheless, she says, plenty of 'ridiculous' barriers remain to employment,

> I do not think that the UK laws [the Autism Act and the Equality Act] stipulating the need for reasonable adjustments in the workplace have many teeth. After all, these adjustments are not so difficult. They are not rocket science and they don't cost a fortune. But employers still do not tend to realise this.[24]

Susan Scott-Parker, founder and chief executive of the Business Disability Forum, says many employers could be discriminating against people who do not fare well in social situations:

> It is interesting that we still place such a reliance on interviews, when everybody knows they are terrible predictors of performance. Just because someone is good with data doesn't mean they want to sit on their own in a darkened room. You need to make adjustments to enable them to contribute, but you make adjustments for everybody... You allow somebody to come in at 10am because they have to do the school run, so why not allow someone with Asperger's to put a note on his desk that says 'Don't move my stuff'? It's not special treatment, because you should be doing it for everybody.[25]

One man with autism wrote the following heartfelt plea in response to an online article on discrimination:

> Autistic people do not need tokenism. We do not need labels or discrimination (either positive or negative). We just need to be judged as individuals, on our personal strengths and weaknesses, and given a fair crack of the whip, the same as everyone else. Quite rightly these days, no employer would dare assume that a woman could not do any given job well, just because she is a woman. Why is it OK to assume someone with autism (or any other supposed disability) cannot do a given job well, without evidence specific to that person?[26]

❖ CASE STUDIES

- ANDREW EVERITT
- TERRI BROOKES
- CHESTER ZOO
- MO

ANDREW EVERITT, 25, was awarded £15,484 by a British employment tribunal in December 2016 after it ruled he had suffered discrimination because of his autism. The judgment said Andrew had arrived at work at the Subway takeaway in Bury St Edmunds on the morning of 19 October 2015, to find out-of-date and defrosted food left out by the previous shift. Since he had to open the shop, he decided to deal with the matter later, but at 9am a Subway inspector arrived and the store failed its inspection. According to the judgment, Andrew told the owners he would not do things their way. The tribunal accepted that this referred to re-labelling out-of-date food (which he claimed the Bury branch did). He received a dismissal letter, while the employee who had left the food out received only a warning. Andrew appealed and was offered the job back, but felt too 'bullied' to accept.

Andrew was supported by the anti-discrimination charity, Ipswich and Suffolk Council for Racial Equality, whose discrimination advisor, Sallie Davies, declared:

> This victory is a testament to his strength of character. It was a blatant case of disability discrimination to dismiss someone with autism while someone without autism only gets a verbal warning. It should encourage others living with autism not to accept the lazy prejudice of employers who will not recruit or employ those with disabilities and who, when faced with a disabled employee, fail to put in place adjustments which allow that employee to continue working.[27]

A UK tribunal in 2017 found that TERRI BROOKES, a woman with Asperger's syndrome, had been discriminated against during the recruitment process for the Government Legal Service (GLS).

Terri – who represented herself at the hearing – had been asked to take a situational judgement test as part of the initial stage of her application. Brookes asked to be allowed to submit short written answers to the questions, as she claimed the multiple-choice format of the test placed her at a disadvantage. While the GLS made time allowances for Brookes, she was not provided with an alternative test format: the GLS argued that the testing was a proportionate method for determining the best candidates for the position.

Terri subsequently took the multiple-choice test in July 2015 but scored 12 out of a possible 22, two points lower than the required pass mark of 14, and her application failed. Evidence provided to the tribunal showed that, of the small number of applicants to have declared themselves as having Asperger's and taken the test, just one had passed.

An employment tribunal ruled in 2016 that there was no other identifiable reason to explain why Brookes had failed the test, other than her disability, and by being asked to take the test as it stood, the GLS had indirectly discriminated against her. The GLS subsequently appealed the ruling but the Employment Appeal Tribunal upheld the original ruling and refused permission to appeal the case any further.

Commenting on the case, an employment law consultant, Emma O'Leary, from the business support firm, ELAS Group, warned that an array of candidates could be disadvantaged by multiple-choice tests, such as those with dyslexia, as well as those with Asperger's.

> It highlights the importance of considering reasonable adjustments for disabled candidates, and if your recruitment process includes testing such as this, or any other method that could be considered a PCP [Provision, Criterion or Practice], it is imperative that you can demonstrate that the PCP is a proportionate means of achieving a legitimate aim if it's capable of putting a particular group at a disadvantage. This case would not have failed if the GLS had allowed the claimant to answer the questions in a different format from the multiple choice they insisted upon.[28]

Dr Sybille Steiner, a partner solicitor at the UK law firm, Irwin Mitchell, told *Recruiter* that the case also highlighted the risks for recruiters conducting such tests on behalf of clients.

> Recruiters need to ensure that in addition to simply allowing extra time, they should consider with the client whether they can make adjustments to the chosen method of testing in cases where a disabled applicant asserts that the method of testing puts them at a disadvantage. In the case, the medical evidence was inconclusive yet the GLS were still held liable, so it is best to err on the side of caution.[29]

In terms of how to get hiring processes right, Sue Warman, HR director (Northern Europe & Russia) at the analytics firm, SAS UK & Ireland, told *Recruiter* that flexibility was crucial. In 2015, the company launched a disability internship programme from SAS's UK headquarters in Marlow, offering work experience to interns on the autism spectrum.

> It would be extremely unfortunate for both the employer and the candidate if great potential was missed because of an unwillingness to change process. Statistics, computing and problem-solving are areas that autistic people can excel in, but their abilities are frequently overlooked because they fail to impress at interview,

said Warman.

> Mathematical competence, attention to detail, problem-solving and the ability to look at challenges from different angles mean people on the

spectrum fit perfectly for many emerging roles. The nature of modern work, especially in data science, means that teams of employees need a range of different and complementary skills to perform optimally. Not every team member needs to be a talented communicator who can directly manage clients, and there is a shameful waste of potential where this attitude exists. There is plenty of room for both the confident speaker and the tenacious problem-solver in today's workplace.[30]

Explaining the difficulties people with autism can have when coming up against multiple-choice testing, Mike Adams, founder at Purple, an organisation with a recruitment agency component helping disabled people into work, told *Recruiter*:

> With autism, there are issues around understanding human contact, understanding interpretation – whether that's written, description or body language. So if you're asking an individual to read something and interpret what is required, and that is your key competence, then I think people with autism – and I don't want to make sweeping statements – might struggle.

> If you were to say, what we want you to do is tell us the answer to this very specific question and tell us what the patterns are and tell us what it means, then you're into a different ball game. Very much it's the case that people with autism are very good at the black and white and struggle with the grey – that's how I would describe it.[31]

CHESTER ZOO, which has signed up as an autism champion, told a young employee with the condition to 'make better eye contact' with customers. Difficulty holding eye contact is a common feature of autism. Within weeks of his review, the worker was told to attend a group interview if he wanted to work the following season. But the boy, who had worked at the zoo since his teens, said he felt unable to stay.

'They knew when they employed him that my son had autism, so to make that comment is shocking,' said the mother of the boy, who has not been named. She said the comments by the zoo bosses had left her son 'humiliated', adding:

> If they knew the first thing about the condition they'd have thought before saying that about him. He's devastated. It's the only job he's ever had and he loved it. If customers had a problem with him not always looking at them, the zoo should have been big enough to stand up for him. He's not been able to work since and it has severely affected his confidence.[32]

The mother's comments were backed by Professor Simon Baron-Cohen, director of Cambridge University's Autism Research Centre.

The telling case of MO, who works in a ticket office for a railway company and has a young daughter who has autism, was highlighted by Janine Booth, the trade unionist with Asperger's syndrome, in her TUC report, *Autism in the*

Workplace. Mo's daughter needs a very stable and predictable home routine, but Mo's roster meant that one week, he was doing early shifts, the next week late shifts, etc. His daughter was very distressed. He applied for 'flexible working' to have regular hours, but his manager was hostile. She grudgingly agreed to a short period of fixed hours, but undermined it from the start. A trade union representative accompanied him to all meetings and challenged the manager's attempts to put him back on the round-the-clock roster.

Union members organised a petition of his workmates supporting Mo's fixed-hours arrangement, which made the manager look rather silly when she claimed that his workmates had complained about it! The case was reported to the union branch, and members would have been willing to take industrial action in support of Mo. When the manager failed to follow the policy and tried to cancel the fixed-hours arrangement, the union appealed to a higher-level manager, and got Mo's hours restored to what he needed.[33]

Notes

1   See Trades Union Congress (2014), *Autism in the Workplace*, report by Janine Booth.
2   Thomas Madar in conversation with the author, 14 July 2016.
3   Ibid.
4   Ibid.
5   Ibid.
6   *Nottingham Post*, 10 June 2014.
7   Ibid.
8   See Ryan Tebbit, *An Autoethnographic Inquiry Into My Experiences and Journey of Autism and Becoming a Counsellor*.
9   Ibid.
10   Ibid.
11   Ibid.
12   See report in *Charlotte Observer*, 11 September 2017.
13   Ibid.
14   See Trades Union Congress (2014), *Autism in the Workplace*, report by Janine Booth.
15   See: https://thepsychologist.bps.org.uk/volume-28/march-2015/managing-and-coping-sexual-identity-work (accessed 27 April 2018).
16   Ibid.
17   Ibid.
18   See: www.inclusivenetworks.co.uk/jonathan-andrews-talks-network-groups/ (accessed 5 October 2016).
19   Ibid.
20   See: www.theguardian.com/society/2017/aug/08/midlands-mother-autistic-son-ingrained-minority-ethnic-prejudice (accessed 8 August 2017).
21   Ibid.
22   Ibid.
23   Jane Hatton in conversation with the author, 18 August 2017.
24   Ibid.
25   See: www2.cipd.co.uk/pm/peoplemanagement/b/weblog/archive/2014/11/20/business-is-still-scared-of-autism.aspx (accessed 27 April 2018).
26   See: www2.cipd.co.uk/pm/peoplemanagement/b/weblog/archive/2014/11/20/business-is-still-scared-of-autism.aspx (accessed 27 April 2018).
27   *Bury Free Press*, 26 December 2016.

28 See: www.recruiter.co.uk/news/2017/05/asperger%E2%80%99s-employment-case-highlights-caution-multiple-choice-testing (accessed 27 April 2018).
29 Ibid.
30 Ibid.
31 Ibid.
32 *Chester Chronicle*, 31 July 2016.
33 See Trades Union Congress (2014), *Autism in the Workplace*, report by Janine Booth.

Chapter 19

What employers should know – reasonable adjustments in the workplace

Britain's Equality Act (2010) defines a disabled person as someone who has a physical or mental impairment which exerts a *substantial* and long-term adverse effect on his or her ability to carry out normal day-to-day activities. 'Substantial' means a person has to complete a day-to-day task differently or requires help to complete this task. 'Long-term' means 12 months or likely to last 12 months or more. A 'reasonable adjustment' – as stipulated in the Equality Act – is an adjustment made by an employer to individual circumstances to enable a disabled person to enter into employment or an existing employee to fulfil his or her role.

Employers should realise that autism involves a different cognitive style, one which may confer advantages in certain contexts. The significant 2015 study from the University of Stirling in Scotland cited earlier in this book demonstrated that people with autism display higher levels of creativity. This link between autistic traits and unusual and original ideas should be widely welcomed and applauded by employers.

Above all, employers should concentrate on what adults with autism *can* do, their strengths, not their deficits, and the specific talents which come with their differences. A sound business case should be made for employing workers on the spectrum. At the same time, the very real challenges must not be ignored.

The following are workplace difficulties described by adults with autism:

- They may be reluctant to discuss their problems and articulate the impact these may have on their performance.
- They may lack confidence in asking questions or requesting help.
- They may frequently experience difficulties with social understanding and communication, and these may lead to their behaviour being misinterpreted by others.
- They may appear very able yet face genuine problems getting to appointments on their own, coping with changes or routine or performing well in interviews.
- They may have difficulties in dressing or presenting themselves appropriately for the work setting.
- They may find it hard to remain calm if they feel irritated or frustrated by other people or by the environment.
- They may become confrontational if they are uncertain about what is required of them.
- They may experience some form of sensory sensitivity

Britain's 2009 Autism Act and the 2010 Equality Act specify that employers should endeavour to introduce 'reasonable adjustments' to help disabled employees function well in the workplace.

These 'reasonable adjustments' may include:

- Providing one-to-one training, rather than in a group, if required.
- Keeping to routines, as far as possible.
- Explaining in advance to allow the employee time to understand when changes to their routine are likely to occur.
- Avoiding offering too many options or choices.
- Avoiding using abstract or hypothetical language or jargon.
- Avoiding jokes or statements not to be taken literally.
- Avoiding distracting or disturbing sensory stimuli (for example, fluorescent lighting).

Janine Booth correctly points out that the obligation on employers to make reasonable adjustments echoes the *social* model's positive aim of removing barriers to employment, but employees must still prove they are 'disabled' – and to demonstrate this, they must first prove what they *cannot* do. This is the *medical* model's approach (since the reasonable accommodations are measures introduced because of the employee's deficits).[1] Perhaps if employees could be persuaded that they were introducing the adjustments in order to adjust to differences, rather than disabilities, this might not amount to reverting to the social model, after all?

Gareth Headley, director of the diversity consultancy Clear Company, who works with a number of employers who are recruiting people with autism, has noted that many of the challenges which exist in the workplace for people with autism often require only simple, low-cost solutions:

> These adjustments are often easily identifiable and enable the individual to perform better. It's so important for HR that they get those adjustments in place. Where they do this, it can show a direct business benefit where employers keep people for longer and get the most out of them in training.[2]

Allowing an autistic employee to wear sunglasses indoors (because of sensitivity to flickering light), or ensuring they have a quiet space to work, are modifications that cost little. But it is as much about preparing the existing team with an 'office awareness orientation,' says Tom Brundage, 'as it is about making reasonable adjustments.'[3]

Janine Booth sees the legal right to reasonable adjustments as a step forward.

> However, it is also a sign of failure. How so? Because an accessible, autism-friendly workplace would not need adjusting. Imagine a wheelchair user having to ask for a ramp to be installed as a reasonable adjustment. Yes, it's a positive thing that the ramp is then installed. But it is surely a problem that he or she had to ask in the first place, as the work space was not already accessible. Similarly, an autistic worker can ask for controllable light at his or her desk, but wouldn't it be better if all workers could control their lighting levels through the provision of controllable lighting as standard?'[4]

Damian Milton also says there is a problem with the concept of reasonable adjustments. 'It's better than nothing. But what do you mean by "reasonable"?' he told me. 'The adjustments often tend to be adjustments from the narrow norm, rather than making proper adaptations.'[5]

Workplace example

Samir has excellent IT skills and began work at a retail store helping to repair computers. However, he found problems relating to customers and was told that he could be rather abrupt at times. Moreover, there were sensory issues: he initially found the noise in the open-plan setting distressingly loud and he also found that he was distracted by other colleagues walking straight past him.

Solution: His location was altered so that he was facing a wall and away from the main flow of traffic from passing colleagues. He also began wearing headphones while working on a computer in order to reduce the background noise. He received specific guidance in how to talk to customers.

Result: Samir is on time for work, has never taken a day off sick in five years and fulfils all his duties efficiently and accurately.

Lucy Kenyon, a specialist consultant in health and expatriate well-being services at Delaroche Solutions, argues that incorporating arrangements for people with autism reduces the impact of stress at work and subsequent performance and absence problems. A range of services is available, the most common being occupational health (OH), case management (CM) and vocational rehabilitation (VR).

Britain's National Institute for Health and Care Excellence (NICE) offers recommendations on therapies that should be prescribed for certain health conditions, but provision of NHS counselling services remains inconsistent.

OH nurses and case managers 'collaborate with clients by assessing, facilitating, planning and advocating for health and social needs on an individual basis,' according to Case Management Society UK. The objective of a professional case manager is to maximise a productive life for clients, while identifying disability support that represents value for money. Effective CM should improve the 'social, ethical and financial health' of a business (Case Management Society, 2015).[6] VR emphasises individualised employment arrangements for those with severe disabilities. However, businesses with comprehensive and effective reasonable adjustment policies are usually well equipped to participate in the support process.[7]

❖ CASE STUDY

- ALANA

Lucy Kenyon cites the case of ALANA, a graduate trainee working as a data analyst for a large financial organisation. She was referred to OH as part of the disciplinary procedure, following an incident at work when she had shouted at a colleague. She had been diagnosed with autism at university and reported her autism condition when she applied for the post. The British government's Access to Work scheme, which helps disabled people into employment, had supported her during this process, and she could not understand why she had been referred. In her view, she did not have a problem at work and wanted to be left alone to do her job.

'To establish communication and trust, I used her job description to structure my assessment model,' writes Kenyon.

> I requested a copy of her performance review, which showed that she excelled at analytical skills and the ability to deal with large volumes of numerical data. She had good organisational skills but had disagreed with her manager on workload priorities and struggled when making strategic recommendations and presenting findings. She was subject to a disciplinary procedure for taking what she had considered to be the 'calculated risks' required by her job description.[8]

Key misunderstandings had stemmed from the description of the required behaviours: 'start with the customer and work backwards'; 'collaborate effectively at all levels across organisation' and 'take calculated risks'. Interventions included providing a work buddy for day-to-day debriefing and support and mediated meetings to redefine and re-establish relationships. Reasonable recommended adjustments included: rewriting Alana's job description in unambiguous and direct terms with examples, and providing resources to assist and coach her in the areas she found difficult, such as making strategic recommendations. The analyst positions were therefore restructured into specialist analyst and business support roles. This enabled all the individuals within the organisation to work to their strengths.[9]

The Job Accommodation Network recommends the following ideas for employers to assist with some of the social skills difficulties associated with their workers on the spectrum:

- Provide a job coach to help understand different social cues
- Use training videos to demonstrate appropriate behaviour in the workplace
- Encourage employees to minimise personal conversation, or move personal conversation away from work areas
- Provide sensitivity training (disability awareness) to all employees
- Adjust the method of communication to best suit the employee's needs
- Where possible, allow the employee to work from home.[10]

The following general approaches and their implications may also help employers of people with autism:

- using specialist employment agencies to assist employers and applicants;
- having clear unambiguous codes of conduct, job descriptions and competency frameworks;

- using direct and unambiguous communications; and
- creating documents including agendas containing standard and specific points for discussion timescales.[11]

Adjustments or adaptations that could be made for an employee with an ASD include:

- a consistent schedule/shift/manager(s);
- a defined set of job responsibilities;
- use of organisers to structure jobs;
- a reduction of idle or unstructured time;
- clear reminders;
- feedback and reassurances;
- assistance from a CM/VR specialist where appropriate;
- working arrangements and responsibilities of OH, line managers, HR; and
- positive behaviour support.[12]

Employers should consider any request on its individual case merits rather than worrying about setting a precedent.
An assessment should explore:

- social interaction deficits;
- cognitive inflexibility; and
- sensory abnormalities.

Adjustments should support individual needs and include the provision of:

- equipment;
- training;
- mentorship;
- supervision;
- time off or flexi-time to attend a health improvement programme to improve performance or attendance, for example cognitive behavioural therapy; and
- temporary redeployment or alternative work activities to support VR or promote skills or rehabilitation after an acute episode.[13]

As Lucy Kenyon correctly notes, employers who embrace the principles of VR and build these into health management policies 'may have a similarly positive impact for neurotypical workers, and this will help promote them as employers of choice and support staff retention'.[14]
For Janine Booth, if workplaces become autism-friendly, this will also take the pressure off individuals to 'come out' as autistic in order to obtain tolerable working conditions, and it will make the workplace better for everyone, autistic or not.

Support at work

Adjusting the job description and responsibilities according to the abilities and strengths of the employee with autism, or by reassigning tasks between employees, can be a useful way of ensuring that an autistic worker can function as well as possible. Employers often re-assign tasks, so this is nothing unusual.

People with autism may find full-time work too overwhelming at the beginning of their employment. Commencing employment on a part-time basis and gradually increasing hours of work could provide helpful assistance.

Identifying additional support people – colleagues, supervisors, employment specialists, family members or friends – can ease tensions at work by providing consistent but flexible support. Stress can also be relieved by allowing the employee regular breaks or providing a designated area to go to, to reduce anxiety.

Dealing with change

Barbara Bissonnette correctly advises employees on the autism spectrum not to panic if a change is announced in the workplace. Instead, 'take constructive action to adapt'. Look for similarities between your work situation before and now. What skills can you carry over to your new situation – or perhaps to a new employer. But definitely avoid comparing one unfavourably with the other – however justified the comparison may be![15]

Here are some useful pointers for employers:

- Many people with autism find it difficult to regulate their own arousal levels. Levels of arousal can have a significant impact on successful transitions between tasks.
- Just because an individual on the autism spectrum has good verbal communication skills, this does not mean that he or she does not need visual timetables to indicate the structure of the day ahead and make it more predictable and, therefore, more manageable.
- Even subtle changes can have a major impact: for example, a different perfume, a slight drop or raise in room temperature. What may appear outwardly to be unusual behaviour may be related to this small change. Allow the employee time to process this unexpected change.

In their important 2015 study, Tiffany Johnson and Aparna Joshi found that people diagnosed with autism earlier in life were more able to ask for workplace support because they were aware of the specific challenges to performing the job successfully. One the other hand, some respondents rejected the notion of formal support, suggesting that this was unnecessary or that it would serve as too much of a 'crutch'. One even commented:

> I do try my best to just go with the flow and try to deal in the real world. Because I do think that's the problem with a lot of this generation ... getting diagnosed so early ... they're getting accommodations so early. In the real world, people aren't as nice.

Some respondents even feared negative stigma-related career consequences of accepting support.[16]

Line Managers

Line managers are a key component in ensuring a smooth transition for autistic employees into the workplace, according to Daniel Wiles, disability consultant for the Business Disability Forum.

> It's vital that line managers are trained to identify barriers for the autistic employee and make adjustments in the workplace. It's important that HR ensures line managers are trained to do this. For example, what changes do you need to make in the working environment? Is it better to communicate in an alternative format?[17]

Wiles recommends that employers give work trials to candidates with autism as an alternative to the traditional interview process.

> It's a different format from an interview. Autistic candidates get used to the workplace and they can be assessed on their ability to do the job rather than how well they can tell someone how they can do the job.[18]

Good line managers will know how to make adjustments, be flexible, tolerant and understanding. A good line manager will understand that the employee can learn strategies to manage in the workplace but that there may always be underlying problems understanding different perspectives. Working will improve a person's confidence and self-esteem, whereas anxiety can lead to other behaviours or challenges.

A good line manager will also be aware that sensory stimulation differs from one autistic individual to another and, with sufficient flexibility, will be willing to make the necessary adjustments. Adjustments can be steps as simple as removing distressing fluorescent lighting or allowing an employee with autism to wear headphones to counteract excess external noise. But there are often many other adjustments to be made apart from these alterations to the sensory environment. Changes may be made to the way people socialise and communicate. Employers should avoid using metaphoric language but instead provide clear and simple instructions. Where possible, they should allow autistic workers more time to complete tasks, because their attention to detail – and executive dysfunction – may make them slower but more accurate than non-autistic colleagues.

Anne Cockayne, of Nottingham Trent University, has written:

> People with Asperger's syndrome find it very hard to concentrate in environments which are excessively noisy or brightly lit. They often find team meetings unnecessary and a distraction from the task in hand. Instead, employers could question the value of having all of the team present at all meetings, all of the time. Having a different way of processing information and experiencing the world around you is for the most part a very private matter. A person with Asperger's syndrome doesn't wear a badge telling colleagues to watch out for particular characteristics. Differences in outward behaviours may be highly visible, yet the disability itself remains unseen, making it hard for line managers and HR teams to understand completely why employees find such constraints disabling. So while it's obvious to a company that a wheelchair user needs a ramp or a visually impaired person needs better lighting, someone who thinks differently, is hypersensitive to noise or

other stimuli, finds team meetings a strain often doesn't receive the same support. If line managers have a healthy curiosity and are able to find out what works for the individual, it is often the case that minor changes can make a major difference.[19]

Above all, enlightened employers will realise that – as Luke Beardon has pointed out – workers with autism will have good days and bad days, but in this they are no different from non-autistic employees. On the other hand, it did not particularly help when one employer – clearly trying to show empathy – declared: 'Everyone gets anxious' and 'Lots of us are bad at small talk'.[20] People with Asperger's syndrome tend to get extra-anxious. 'Employees must understand the extreme nature of the problem, not play it down.'[21]

Some private sector companies now reward their managers for retaining a diverse workforce that includes specific targets around the employment of people with autism. Other line managers in the same sector are appraised based on the integration of employees with autism in their teams.

The 'work buddy'

Barbara Bissonnette emphasises the importance of the 'work buddy' – someone in your department other than a supervisor or a human resources representative. He or she may be a designated mentor but it can also be a colleague whom you like and trust. Bissonnette advises extreme caution when choosing your work buddy. It should be someone who is patient, ready with important and helpful information and someone who will act as a 'social lubricant', facilitating your invitation to office lunches or to social events outside the workplace.[22]

Help from the trade unions

Janine Booth is a firm advocate of every employee joining a trade union and speaking to the union representative if problems arise in the workplace:

> Every worker is entitled to join a union, whether or not there is already one in your workplace. The Trade Union Congress can put you in touch with a union that is appropriate for the sort of job you have. Some managers can make life very difficult for autistic workers, and even well-meaning ones may be doing so unintentionally. Trouble can come from direct bullying, but also from excessive scrutiny, and from treating you as a problem rather than as someone with strengths and positives. If you arm yourself with knowledge of your rights and with a union membership card, then you can do something about it. You don't have to put up with bullying or overbearing management.[23]

Notes

1   See Janine Booth (2016), *Autism Equality in the Workplace: Removing Barriers and Challenging Discrimination*. London: Jessica Kingsley, p. 27.
2   See: www.hrmagazine.co.uk/article-details/why-firms-are-embracing-neurodiversity (accessed 27 April 2018).

3   See: www2.cipd.co.uk/pm/peoplemanagement/b/weblog/archive/2014/11/20/business-is-still-scared-of-autism.aspx (accessed 27 April 2018).

4   Janine Booth, interviewed by Damian Milton on the JKP Blog, 15 July 2016 (www.jkp.com/jkpblog/2016/04/autism-equality-workplace-interview-janine-booth/ (accessed 27 April 2018).

5   Damian Milton in conversation with the author, 15 July 2016.

6   Case Management Society UK (2015), Working together to promote excellence in case management.

7   See Lucy Kenyon (2015), 'How to manage autism in the workplace', Personnel Today, 21 August 2015.

8   Ibid.

9   Ibid.

10 See: https://askjan.org/media/execfunc.html (accessed 27 April 2018).

11 See D. Hagner and B. Cooney (2003), 'Building employer capacity to support employees with severe disabilities in the workplace', Journal of Prevention, Assessment and Rehabilitation, 21(1), IOS Press.

12 See C. M. Schall (2010), 'Positive behaviour support: Supporting adults with autism spectrum disorders in the workplace', Journal of Vocational Rehabilitation, 32(2), 109–111.

13 See Lucy Kenyon, op. cit.

14 Ibid.

15 See Barbara Bissonnette (2013), Asperger's Syndrome Workplace Survival Guide. London: Jessica Kingsley, p. 71.

16 See T. Johnson and A. Joshi (2016), 'Dark clouds or silver linings? A stigma threat perspective on the implications of an autism diagnosis for workplace well-being', Journal of Applied Psychology, American Psychological Association, 101(3), 430–449.

17 See: www.hrmagazine.co.uk/article-details/why-firms-are-embracing-neurodiversity (accessed 27 April 2018).

18 Ibid.

19 See: www.cipd.co.uk/Images/an-investigation-of-asperger-syndrome-in-the-employment-context_2016_tcm18-20003.pdf (accessed 27 April 2018).

20 See Genevieve Edmonds and Luke Beardon (eds) (2008), Asperger Syndrome and Employment. London: Jessica Kingsley, p. 60.

21 Ibid.

22 See Barbara Bissonnette (2013), Asperger's Syndrome Workplace Survival Guide. London: Jessica Kingsley, p. 41.

23 Janine Booth, interviewed by Damian Milton on the JKP Blog, 15 July 2016. www.jkp.com/jkpblog/2016/04/autism-equality-workplace-interview-janine-booth/ (accessed 27 April 2018).

Chapter 20

Examples of good practice by employers

Anne Cockayne, of Nottingham Trent University, found that companies with neurodiverse programmes design and maintain simple support systems for their new employees. The German company, SAP, defines two 'support circles' – one for the workplace, the other for an employee's personal life. The workplace support circle includes a team manager, a team buddy, a job and life skills coach, a work mentor, and an 'HR business partner', who oversees a group of programme participants. Buddies are staff members on the same team who provide assistance with daily tasks, workload management, and prioritisation. Job and life skills coaches are usually from social partner organisations. Other social partner roles include vocational rehab counsellor and personal counsellor. Usually, families of employees also provide support 'pods' of about 15 people, where they work alongside neurotypical colleagues in a roughly 4:1 ratio while two managers and a consultant are responsible for addressing neurodiversity-related issues.[1]

Employers (as illustrated in the two cases below) should realise that autism involves a different cognitive style, one which may confer advantages in certain contexts. However, they should also be aware of the specific hurdles that face individuals applying for a job.

The point is to shape the job to the employee, rather than the employee to the job: in other words, to match a particular task to the strengths of the member of staff, instead of forcing the employee into a pre-established job description. Enlightened employees should realise that they are hiring someone *because* of his or her differences, not in spite of them.

There is a telling paradox here: some of the most important companies employing staff on the spectrum adapt the structure to fit in with the presence for 'rigidity' or 'sameness' in ASD – but this understanding of the autistic need for predictability requires flexible thinking on the part of the employers.

Georgia Granger, the autistic disability advocate in Northern Ireland cited in previous chapters, puts it brilliantly: 'Choosing to hire me based on my autistic accomplishments, and then expecting me to work in a non-autistic way, doesn't really make much sense.'[2]

Mike Jennings, who runs the Grenache restaurant in Walkden, Manchester, was horrified when customers requested not to be served by an autistic waiter. The waiter, Andy Foster, 45, had joined the restaurant three weeks earlier. He is also carer for his mother, who is battling Alzheimer's. Jennings said:

> The customers seemed to have a problem with him, even though his service was
> good. I explained that he suffered from autism and their response was that they

didn't want to be served by him. They asked me why I would give him a job in a restaurant like ours. I couldn't believe it.[3]

Jennings was so shocked by the incident that he took to the restaurant's Facebook account to ask anyone with a similar attitude NOT to book a table there. The post was liked and shared by hundreds of people who support the restaurant's decision to back Andy. Jennings said:

The incident really knocked his confidence and we had to take him to one side and let him know that we certainly didn't feel that way. All we care about is someone having enthusiasm and passion. The rest we can teach.[4]

Chris Poole, Operations Manager of Malvern Instruments in Worcestershire, who worked closely with James Macaulay's family to ensure that he could fulfil his potential at his factory, said:

James is a valued member of the manufacturing team here at Malvern and has developed well into his role of Manufacturing Technician. When initially asked about James applying for a work experience placement at Malvern, we knew very little about autism or how autistic people would perform in a manufacturing environment, but as a company, we like to give people opportunities where possible so endeavoured to find out more. Initial discussions with James's parents – who have been fantastic throughout this process – highlighted where we thought James would be best suited within the company.[5]

There were a few minor issues to deal with at work, but working with James's father Simon, these were quickly resolved. Once James had completed his apprenticeship and, again, after discussion with his parents, we were pleased to offer the permanent role.[6]

Poole added:

My advice to other employers would be to give autistic people a chance in the workplace. Like any employee, they will have skill sets more suited to some job roles than others and working with people who understand autism (in our case, James's parents) you can find how to best align these skills to the business needs.[7]

Notes

1   See Anne Cockayne and Lara Warburton (2016), 'An investigation of Asperger Syndrome in the employment context', Conference paper, CIPD Applied Research Conference on The shifting landscape of work and working lives (Conference paper number: CIPD/ARC/2016/5).
2   See: www.ambitiousaboutautism.org.uk/georgia-granger (accessed 27 April 2018).
3   *Manchester Evening News*, 4 March 2016.
4   Ibid.
5   *Daily Mirror*, 3 January 2017.
6   Ibid.
7   Ibid.

Part V

Neurodiversity in the workplace

Chapter 21

Embracing difference

'Neurodiversity is the idea that neurological differences like autism and ADHD are the result of normal, natural variation in the human genome,' says John Elder Robison, who as well as being the chief executive of a successful luxury car repair company and having Asperger's syndrome is co-chairman of the Neurodiversity Working Group at the College of William & Mary in Williamsburg, Virginia. 'Indeed, many individuals who embrace the concept of neurodiversity believe that people with differences do not need to be cured; they need help and accommodation instead.'[1]

Robison emphasises the advantages of employing people on the autism spectrum: 'In many business situations, logic rules the day, and autistic people are kings of logic and reasoning.'[2]

Neurodiverse conditions encompass dyslexia, dyscalculia, dyspraxia, attention-deficit hyperactivity disorders (ADHD) and autism, including Asperger's syndrome (even though Asperger's was officially removed as a separate category from DSM-5 in 2013). This means that neurodiversity is by no means a rarity. Bringing neurodiverse talent into a business often means changing the hiring process in recognition of the fact that different people express themselves in different ways. Employees in neurodiversity programmes need to be allowed to deviate from established practices. As Robert Austin and Gary Pisano have pointed out, this approach shifts a manager's orientation from assuring compliance through standardisation to adjusting individual work contexts.

> Most workplace adjustments (or accommodations, as they are known in the United States), such as installing different lighting and providing noise-cancelling headphones, are not very expensive. But they do require managers to tailor individual work settings more than they otherwise might.[3]

Austin and Pisano observe that the case for the hiring of neurodiverse staff is especially compelling, given the skills shortages that increasingly afflict technology and other industries. The European Union faces a shortage of 800,000 IT workers by 2020, according to a European Commission study. The biggest deficits are expected to be in strategically important and rapidly expanding areas such as data analytics and IT services implementation, whose tasks are a good match with the abilities of some neurodiverse people.[4]

The same authors found that some companies had entered into relationships with 'social partners' – government or non-profit-making organisations committed to helping people with disabilities obtain jobs. SAP has worked with California's

Department of Rehabilitation, Pennsylvania's Office of Vocational Rehabilitation, the US non-profits EXPANDability and the Arc, and overseas agencies such as EnAble India, while HPE has worked with Autism SA (South Australia).

> Such groups help companies to navigate local employment regulations that apply to people with disabilities, suggest candidates from lists of neurodiverse people seeking employment, assist in pre-screening, help arrange public funding for training, sometimes administer training, and provide the mentorship and ongoing support (especially outside work hours) needed to ensure that neurodiverse employees will succeed.[5]

Neurodiversity programmes can produce a broad range of benefits. Firms have become more successful at finding and hiring good and even great talent in tough-to-fill skills categories. Products, services, and bottom lines have profited from lower defect rates and higher productivity. Both SAP and Hewlett Packard Enterprise (HPE) have cited examples of neurodiverse employees participating on teams who generated significant innovations (one, at SAP, helped develop a technical fix worth an estimated $40 million in savings).

Nevertheless, the neurodiverse population remains a largely untapped talent pool. Programme participants repeatedly told Austin and Pisano that, despite their solid credentials, they had previously been obliged to settle for the kinds of jobs many other people left behind in high school. Moreover, the researchers point out, there is a conflict between scalability and the goal of acquiring neurodiverse talent.[6] Furthermore, although there are plenty of potential candidates, many are hard to identify, because universities – sensitive to issues of discrimination – do not classify students in neurodiversity terms, and potential candidates do not necessarily self-identify. In response to this problem, HPE is helping colleges and high schools set up non-traditional 'work experience' programmes for neurodiverse populations. These involve video gaming, robotic programming and other activities. Microsoft, too, is working with universities to improve methods of identifying and accessing neurodiverse talent.

The general consensus is that an employer's awareness of autism should be based on understanding and removing barriers in the workplace. Findings from various research studies suggest that it is crucial that line managers, and those responsible for making adjustments, are trained in autism awareness based on removing barriers.

As noted in the Business Disability Forum's report, *Square Holes for Square Pegs*, it is not essential for employers or line managers to have a medical understanding of autism. The condition is complex and heterogeneous and, as such, the effects vary from person to person. Nevertheless, it remains the case that some autistic employees could face unconscious bias in the workplace, as autism is a non-visible disability and it must be preferable if generally neurotypical people understand the day-to-day difficulties encountered by people with autism.[7]

Above all, employers should understand the challenges facing workers with autism spectrum disorder and seek to remove these barriers by making 'reasonable adjustments', as stipulated in both the 2009 Autism Act and the 2010 Equality Act in the UK. As we have seen, common obstacles confronted by people with autism arise from the way neurotypical individuals socialise and communicate. Other disadvantages may be caused by sensory overload, problems in time planning and changes in routines or structures. Employers who are willing to make adjustments are more likely to succeed in retaining and gaining the most from employees with autism. Moreover, it is generally agreed that a workplace which is made suitable for employees with autism is likely to be more appropriate for the workforce as a whole.

Employers should also be made aware that employing workers with autism makes good business sense – and should by no means be considered an act of charity. Companies can save money by employing highly skilled people, to keep up with their competitors, and to recognise the advantage in, and push for, a neurodiverse workforce. As emphasised in previous chapters, many people with autism are exceptional at process-driven tasks and possess excellent attention to detail, making them more productive than neurotypical people in roles that rely on these specific skills.

Ray Coyle, chief executive of Auticon UK, notes that a lack of diversity in firms leads to a lack of diversity in thought, which is not the best way to solve problems or increase profit: 'What you need is variety and diversity in a workforce, not for philanthropic reasons, but because it is good business.' Coyle added:

> We don't necessarily regard people with autism to be disabled and many people with autism do not regard themselves as being disabled, but the legal status is that autism is regarded as a disability, and we are therefore allowed to do this.[8]

Despite increasing awareness of autism among employers, the findings of a 2014 study by Beatriz López et al. at the University of Portsmouth, suggested that more needed to be done in terms of addressing employers and staff awareness training. Specifically, the findings indicated a need to increase awareness across all sectors, and not just public services. This same study found that employers failed to make reasonable adjustments in the workplace and that this was a major barrier to successful employment. 'The unique ways in which each individual both interacts and processes information about their environments are particularly complex and not readily understood by their neurotypical employers, colleagues and supporters,' the study authors wrote.[9]

They also cited a 2005 study by Helen Tager-Flusberg of Boston University in the United States (one of the world's leading authorities on language issues in autism): 'Many difficulties will present in subtle ways which are neither easy to detect by others nor to communicate to others by the person with ASD, given their communication difficulties.' López noted that, in the absence of appropriate and reasonable adjustments, 'this may have a major impact on performance and behaviour in the workplace and a negative impact on the employee's experience, leading to potentially harmful effects of work-related stress'.[10]

Steve Silberman's 2015 book, NeuroTribes, popularised the idea of neurodiversity (he points out that the incidence of autism is particularly high in places like Silicon Valley and he and others have hypothesised that many of the industry's 'oddballs' and 'nerds' might well be on the autism spectrum). Temple Grandin has frequently expressed her conviction, in conversations with me, that the majority of people working at Google headquarters are autistic. With this in mind, hiring for neurodiversity could be considered an extension of the tendencies of a culture that recognises the value of 'oddballs'. The tech industry does have a tradition of employing such staff. To cite just one example among many I have come across (this one emerged from the audience after I had given a presentation on autism and neurodiversity in the workplace together with Professor Simon Baron-Cohen at the Latitude Festival in 2017): John Sisk & Sons, Ireland's largest construction and property company, employed a young British man with Asperger's syndrome, Oliver Wiltshire, and gave, as one of the reasons for his successful application, the fact that his friends described his sense of humour as 'weird'.[11]

There has certainly been a regular stream of articles and essays about neurodiversity in recent years. David Platzer, a doctoral student in medical anthropology at Johns Hopkins University in Baltimore, whose autistic brother is in his early thirties and who has been unemployed for most of his adult life, has travelled throughout the United States, in addition to spending time in Bangalore, India. He has spoken to people on the spectrum, as well as employers, job counsellors and representatives of most of the major neurodiversity employment initiatives and prominent advocacy organisations.

Platzer is convinced that the concept of neurodiversity employment is slowly entering mainstream work culture. Nevertheless, his message is a nuanced one:

> As Americans, work isn't something we do just to bring in a pay cheque or to put food on the table, the way it is for many other cultures. For Americans, work is the primary avenue of our adult social lives. Most of our friends as adults are work buddies and so much of our identity is based on what we do for a living. While these corporate hiring programmes are rightfully celebrated, we also need to move beyond finding work for only those who present immediately competitive skills. Yes, there is a business case for hiring some autistic employees, but those aren't the only ones who deserve a job.[12]

Platzer says his autistic brother is currently looking for work as a life guard.

> He has an incredible way of looking at the world and a lot to offer everyone he meets. But he also has problems with attention, anxiety and other things that make productivity hard for him. He struggles with social cues and, like [Temple] Grandin, describes human behaviour as a little bit mysterious. To be blunt, people sometimes find him odd. And so most jobs he has had have not lasted for more than a few months at most. He is also isolated socially, though he would very much like a less lonely existence. He may not bring a competitive advantage as the term is commonly used, but it's hard not to see some role in the job market as good for him, and good for the broader society.[13]

Platzer adds:

> While diversity hiring initiatives were once considered largely a form of corporate social responsibility and resourced accordingly, more recent diversity recruitment initiatives have emphasised the corporate economic value of employee diversity and the value of diversity to the bottom line.[14]

What about the argument, raised in some quarters, that companies are actually demonstrating positive discrimination by actively seeking employees who are on the autism spectrum, and that such practices even risk producing a segregated, almost 'ghetto-like' environment for autistic workers? I put this point to Thorkil Sonne, founder of Specialisterne.'I do not see ourselves as segregated at all,' Sonne told me.

> The latest development of us being trusted partners of companies shows that our task is to make employers aware and give them access to people. Many employers do not want to give support to people with autism. We are very aware of this. I dreamed twelve years ago in Denmark that people with autism *would* have too many favours. We want to support them but not to create a special environment. The positive benefit of bringing people into the workplace is that a place where autistic people thrive will probably be better for everyone. But the critics are right to say that we have a select target group – autistic people. Until they have the same opportunities in the workspace, we will keep on working with this population.[15]

Jon Adams, the artist with Asperger's syndrome and synaesthesia cited in previous chapters, is convinced that it is

> the creatively divergent way of thinking that's enabling as an autistic artist, but this can't usefully exist in isolation. It needs an opportunity to be revealed and nurtured, and an understanding of neurodiversity is vital. We can see and reveal patterns, thoughts and ideas very differently, and when 'compelled to make' can do so with great concentration and detail.[16]

He added:

> Autism creativity can be a double-edged sword. We can be haphazard with finance because that's not our primary motive, and obsession with detail leads to levels beyond what is expected. This may be time-consuming, but I couldn't have it any other way. I'm confident with my neuro-difference. I wouldn't change anything, other than maybe people's attitudes and their understanding – but that's something hopefully I can help to achieve with the work I make and show.

> Some people think of us as 'with autism', as if it's something optional or accumulative, as if we're broken or just plain failed neurotypical people. Language engenders attitudes – if you always look at a tree as being an evolutionary failed cat, you can never focus on the tree's beauty, perfect in its rightful niche in biodiversity. The same goes for neurodivergent people: we're just one part of innate human neurodiversity.[17]

Notes

1   See John Elder Robison (2013),'What is neurodiversity?' *Psychology Today*, 7 October.
2   *Worcester Business Journal*, 15 May 2017.
3   See Robert Austin and Gary Pisano (2017),'Neurodiversity as a competitive advantage', *Harvard Business Review*, May–June.
4   Ibid.
5   See Robert D. Austin and Gary P. Pisano (2017),'Neurodiversity as a competitive advantage', *Harvard Business Review*, May–June, pp. 96–103.
6   Ibid.

7 https://members.businessdisabilityforum.org.uk/media_manager/public/86/Resources/ Square%20Pegs_Final_GF.PDF (accessed 27 April 2018).

8 *Computer Weekly*, 22 December 2016.

9 B. López and L. Keenan (2014), 'Barriers to employment in autism: Future challenges to implementing the Adult Autism Strategy', Autism Research Network.

10 Ibid.

11 Oliver Wiltshire, in communication with the author, 27 August 2017.

12 David Platzer, as quoted in Michael Bernick's article, 'Increasing autism employment: An anthropologist's perspective', *Forbes* magazine, 9 May 2017.

13 Ibid.

14 Ibid.

15 Thorkil Sonne in conversation with the author, 6 March 2016.

16 Ibid.

17 Ibid.

Chapter 22

Examples of good practice

In April 2017, 50 companies – including JP Morgan, Ford and EY (formerly Ernst & Young) – came together for a summit on how to bring more autistic adults into the workforce. It was hosted at the German company SAP's Silicon Valley campus. José Velasco, the head of SAP's Autism at Work programme, told CBS News: 'I have been in this industry for close to 30 years, and I can tell you it's probably the single most rewarding programme that I have been involved with.'[1]

The biggest surprise for Velasco has been the variety of candidates applying. 'Very quickly, we started getting résumés from people who had degrees in history, and literature in graphic design, attorneys … the whole gamut of jobs … They are good at just about every role.'[2]

In recent years, a few pioneering companies have formalised and professionalised a greater understanding of creative differences in the workplace. They include SAP, Hewlett Packard Enterprise, EY, JP Morgan and Freddie Mac. Although their programmes vary, they have elements in common, not least because they all draw on the body of knowledge developed at Specialisterne, the company founded by Thorkil Sonne in 2004, after his third child, Lars, was diagnosed with autism. Specialisterne, which hopes to find jobs for a million people on the autism spectrum by 2026, has since developed and refined non-interview methods for assessing, training and managing neurodiverse talent and has demonstrated the viability of its model by running a successful profit-making company focused on software testing.

In 2012, the German software maker SAP launched the pilot version of its Autism at Work Initiative in India and later expanded it to Ireland. In India, according to Specialisterne, six people with autism have been hired as software testers. SAP offices in the US, Canada and Germany are now using the programme, too. In 2013, SAP announced that it wanted people with autism to make up 1 per cent of its workforce – a proportion chosen because it roughly corresponds to the percentage of autistic people in the general population. Microsoft, HPE and others are also working to enlarge their programmes, although they have declined to set numerical targets. In April 2015, Microsoft announced a pilot programme to hire people with autism at its headquarters in Redmond, Washington. In 2017, it expanded those efforts to the UK.

SAP boasts a retention rate of about 90 per cent for their autistic employees. Part of that may be due to the fact that they are assigned a mentor from within the company so they do not feel they are coping alone. SAP, Microsoft and Freddie Mac assign employees who do not have ASD to help workers with autism in their new roles. At Freddie Mac, these mentors are typically parents of children who are on the spectrum.

The success of neurodiversity programmes has prompted some companies to think about how ordinary HR processes may be excluding high-quality talent. SAP is conducting a review to determine how recruiting, hiring, and development could take a broader view. Its stated goal is to make its mainstream talent processes so 'neurodiversity-friendly' that it can ultimately close its neurodiversity programme. Microsoft has similar ambitions.

Despite the undoubted improvement in the overall picture – with the increasing willingness of enlightened employers not only to consider employing people on the autism spectrum but actively to recruit them – there have been claims that some tech companies are 'falling over themselves' to recruit white, middle-class autistic men (but not women) with technical and coding experience. The companies themselves deny these claims.

David Perkins, of AS Mentoring, told me:

Exceptionally bright autistic techies (men and – yes, to a lesser extent – women) will always be recruited, provided they're the right kind of autistic. By which I mean they don't make the neurotypical employees who tend to predominate in these companies too uncomfortable. So yes, white, middle-class, behaviour-eccentric but not too challenging. But then these are not too far from the hurdles that Black and Minority Ethnic (BME) and/or female and/or working-class NTs face, I don't think they're particular to autism.[3]

❖ CASE STUDIES

- SPECIALISTERNE
- SAP
- EY
- MICROSOFT
- WILLIS TOWERS WATSON
- HEWLETT PACKARD ENTERPRISE
- BBC – PROJECT CAPE
- FREDDIE MAC
- JP MORGAN CHASE
- WALGREENS

SPECIALISTERNE

Dissatisfied with the rate at which his own company could create jobs, Thorkil Sonne established the Specialist People Foundation (subsequently renamed the SPECIALISTERNE Foundation) in Aarhus, Denmark, in 2004 to spread his company's know-how to others and persuade multinationals to start neurodiversity programmes. Most companies that have done so have worked with the foundation to deploy some version of the Specialisterne approach. and Specialisterne (whose headquarters are in Wilmington, Delaware) now operates in more than 14 countries across the globe, assessing, training and employing people with autism and helping to place them as consultants and employees at around 100 companies worldwide.

Sonne's son, Lars, was born in 1996. 'He was caring, smart and trustworthy. But then, at kindergarten, outside his comfort zone, they saw a different child,' Sonne told me.

> We didn't expect the diagnosis of autism at all. It was a difficult time. What got us used to the idea was that Lars was the same boy. We parents were confused and stumbling but he was the same. We had to learn to support him. I became the chairman of the local branch of Autism Denmark. I was technical director in an IT company so I could relate to the skill sets I saw in my son: pattern recognition, attention to detail. I was able to use these for software control and data analysis. I met so many autistic adolescents with similar skills to Lars' but none of them had a job that used their skills. I learned a lot about the Danish welfare system which I am proud of. But it is aimed at physical disability. So I thought it was *society* that should change. That's why I founded Specialisterne in Aarhus in 2004.[4]

Although the neurodiversity movement frequently refers to autism as a difference, rather than a disability, Sonne is adamant that autism is indeed a disability.

> Actually, I think that often, the higher the IQ, the more severe the challenges. If you have a high IQ but you never succeed in finding a job, this can be more difficult than when you are elsewhere on the autism spectrum and it is more obvious what help you need. Highly intelligent people outside their comfort zone can be very challenged. In their comfort zone, they can be extremely able.[5]

He adds:

> It is a paradox, because you have to recognise the disability before you recognise the strengths. Some governments set disability quotas. I would love to live in a world where we do not have to talk about disability and quotas, but that is an ideal world, not the real world. They will get competitive jobs. They'll go from unemployment to earning six figures. One of the calls we got was from a mother who said: 'I'm really glad you got my son a job, but how do I tell my husband our disabled son now earns more than he does?'[6]

Specialisterne uses non-traditional, non-interview-based assessment and training processes. It has created 'hangouts' – comfortable gatherings, usually lasting half a day, in which neurodiverse job candidates can demonstrate their abilities in casual interactions with company managers. At the end of a hangout, some candidates are selected for two to six weeks of further assessment and training (the duration varies by company). During this time, they use Lego Mindstorms robotic construction and programming kits to work on assigned projects – first individually and then in groups, with the projects becoming more like actual work as the process continues.

'People with autism bring directness, honesty, loyalty,' Sonne told me.

> Our biggest contribution is to expand the pipeline of talent. They can innovate. They come up with alternative ways of doing things. In a global market economy, you need to be able to manage innovative people. Most innovation will come from the different 'outliers'. There are short-term benefits (filling posts) – and long-term benefits (increasing capacity for innovation).[7]

There is a great deal of creativity on all sides. Tom Brundage, former director at Specialisterne UK (which later became SpecialistsUK), says:

> We are talking to a number of banks to encourage them to use people on the autistic spectrum in their fraud detection units, or to prevent money laundering. The idea, as always, is to match autistic candidates with employers looking for specialist technical skills.[8]

Brundage adds:

> The poor communication skills of some autistic candidates can be off-putting to employers who increasingly value teamwork and emotional intelligence. But it doesn't have to be that way: plenty of people on the spectrum are leaders in their fields, including actuaries, software testers and proof-readers.[9]

SAP

The Autism at Work summit hosted by the Walldorf-based software company, SAP, and Microsoft in April 2017 attracted more companies, advocates and parents than in any previous year. Major firms, such as Airbnb, Salesforce, LinkedIn and Facebook, are adding neurodiversity employment to their other diversity and inclusion efforts.

SAP, with nearly 80,000 workers worldwide, began its Autism at Work programme in 2013. Participants complete a 30-day screening and interview process in which their skills are assessed. Anka Wittenberg, SAP's chief diversity and inclusion officer, says all the research shows that a more sustainable business case and superior performance are promoted if your company is diverse:

> There's always a very clear correlation between diversity and inclusion and employee engagement, customer orientation and innovation. Now, we have rolled out the programme in nine locations in five countries and we have onboarded over 100 people with autism.[10]

When SAP began its Autism at Work programme, applicants included people with Master's degrees in electrical engineering, biostatistics, economic statistics, and anthropology and bachelor's degrees in computer science, applied and computational mathematics, electrical engineering and engineering physics. Some had dual degrees. Many had earned very high grades and graduated with honours or other distinctions.

The Autism at Work programme, the largest of the autism employment initiatives with over 120 participants, has launched a research effort, seeking to quantify results, develop a neurodiversity employment cost–benefit justification and even a science of autism advantage in the workplace. A recent Harvard Business School case study lauded the SAP programme for its ability to demonstrate the competitive advantage of an autism hiring programme, in turn encouraging greater support from senior management. The Autism at Work programme includes, as one of its guiding principles, that people with autism are considered for various different types of jobs. They employ graphic designers and IT project managers on the spectrum. In May 2013, SAP announced its aspiration to have 1 per cent of its 65,000 workforce represented by people on the autism spectrum. To date, the company has hired 120 employees on the autism spectrum for 22 roles in nine countries and across 17 locations. Approximately 80 per cent are full-time employees, while the other 20 per cent are interns or contractors.

'I had conversations with some of our peer companies, like Microsoft, who shared a concern that very valuable candidates were not able to make it into the company because the processes in place did not really accommodate their differences,' says José Velasco, SAP's vice-president of products and innovation, and co-leader of the Autism at Work programme.

> If we were to use the standard procedures of hiring individuals, we would not have hired a large degree of the 120 employees that we have and as a result, we would have missed out on things like an intern, who after being with us for eight months, filed two patents.[11]

As a result, SAP implemented the SAP Enterprise Readiness Programme, a six-week pre-employment training programme teaching potential candidates about collaboration, corporate etiquette and communications, as well as building their awareness of SAP products.

'People on the autism spectrum are sensitive to change and, by being here at the company for six weeks, they start getting immersed little by little and feeling more comfortable with the company,' Velasco explains.

> As a result, by the time they finish their training they feel much more comfortable and confident. They apply for a job with an understanding of our company that is significantly deeper than they would have had coming to the interview for the first time.[12]

Velasco stressed that SAP remained committed to the programme's continued rollout to the Czech Republic, Brazil and elsewhere 'because of the business value and innovation promise it delivers ... This is not about social responsibility or philanthropy. SAP values the unique skills and abilities that people with autism bring to the workplace.'[13]

SAP now has an intake of autistic individuals from eight US universities, as well as bringing people on board through its links with the government and specialist training organisations.

Perhaps the most surprising benefit is that managers have begun thinking more deeply about channelling the talents of all employees through greater sensitivity to individual needs. SAP's programme 'forces you to get to know the person better, so you know how to manage them,' says Silvio Bessa, the senior vice-president of digital business services. 'It's made me a better manager, without a doubt.'[14]

SAP uses a metaphor to communicate this idea across the organisation: People are like puzzle pieces, irregularly shaped. Historically, companies have asked employees to trim away their irregularities, because it's easier to fit people together if they are all perfect rectangles. But that requires employees to leave their differences at home, differences which firms need in order to innovate. 'The corporate world has mostly missed out on this [benefit],' says Anka Wittenberg. This suggests that companies must embrace an alternative philosophy, one that calls on managers to do the hard work of fitting irregular puzzle pieces together – to treat people not as containers of fungible human resources but as unique individual assets. The work for managers will be harder. But the payoff for companies will be considerable: access to more of their employees' talents along with diverse perspectives that may help them compete more effectively. 'Innovation,' Wittenberg adds, 'is most likely to come from parts of us that we don't all share.'[15]

SAP now operates worldwide. As an example, Horacio Joffre Galibert, the founder of the pioneering Argentinian organisation, APAdEA (Association of Parents of Children on the Autism Spectrum), told me that he had signed a partnership agreement with SAP in 2015 and, since then, ten autistic employees had found work as data installers with companies in Buenos Aires. The firms in question pay APAdEA to send highly trained mentors to accompany the employees in order to smooth their passage into the workplace and resolve any issues which may arise.[16]

In the US, Mike Seborowski was hired three years ago and works in cybersecurity at SAP's office outside Philadelphia. In 2018, he was due to leave for a long stint at SAP's world headquarters in Germany.

'If you'd told me six years ago that we would have an employee who was openly autistic in the company, going on a business trip to Germany for a month, I would have not believed you,' said Velasco.[17]

Another autistic employee at SAP's Philadelphia office is Gloria Mendoza, 26. Even though she had two degrees from Gettysburg College in Pennsylvania – one in music (she has a beautiful singing voice), and another in computer science – she was unable to find a job until being taken on by SAP. 'Probably the best part about working here is that I can use the skills which I have studied whilst being among people that understand who I am and how I'm different from everybody else,' Gloria told CBS News.[18]

She works at Digital Business Services, where she deals directly with customers. Asked what dream she really wanted to come true, Gloria replied: 'Probably, that I can be really up there in my department, earning a lot of money, and still keeping the friends that I have.'[19] (Most of her new friends are co-workers in SAPs autism programme.)

EY

EY, the consulting firm formerly known as Ernst & Young, launched its neurodiversity programme in 2016. Instead of checking for a firm handshake and a can-do smile during an hour-long meeting, EY takes job candidates on the autism spectrum through a two-week process that combines virtual interaction and an in-house 'super-week' of team building and skills assessment. During that week, EY tries to acclimatise the individuals to the office environment. Those who 'pass' get job offers. Some of the employees have trouble sitting still, so they have permission to take breaks to roam around during long meetings.

EY works with university offices of disability and vocational rehab agencies to recruit potential new employees. People with autism are often unemployed or under-employed, even in their 20s. Those who do have jobs might be stuck in roles like stocking shelves or filing, which spare them human interaction but also do not use their intellect.

Corporate programmes such as EY's are one sign of a shift in thinking when it comes to finding people 'meaningful work in the community,' according to Dr Paul Shattuck, director of the life course outcomes programme at the A.J. Drexel Autism Institute in Philadelphia.[20] This more integrated employment approach represents a stark contrast with the sheltered workshop model which for decades employed disabled people in isolated settings.

Shattuck appreciates that profit-making businesses are keen to hire people who qualify for initiatives aimed at people with disabilities but who also help contribute to the bottom line, but, as mentioned earlier, he is concerned that companies are engaging in 'cream-skimming' – focusing their initiatives on high-functioning autism, not individuals right across the spectrum.[21]

Lori Golden, who oversees EY's accessibility programmes, acknowledges that 'organisations like ours have very few lower-skilled jobs'. Because EY rents its office space, and thus does not hire its own cafeteria and maintenance staff, the vast majority of positions require specialised education and skills.[22]

• SAM BRIEFER

When SAM BRIEFER, 23, graduated from West Chester University of Pennsylvania in 2016, he began hunting for jobs. At first it was slow going. He secured a few interviews, but was never called back. Then, in March 2017, EY offered him a full-time position on its accounting team.

Sam was excited to find that EY treated his autism as a competitive advantage and tailored the workplace to fit his needs. On-the-job instructions were stripped of expressions or common conversation shortcuts, which can be hard for autistic people to understand. He also received a few hours per week of additional coaching on workplace interactions through the Arc of Philadelphia, a service provider for people with disabilities.

Six months after joining EY, Sam was already feeling much more comfortable in social settings. 'It's definitely pushing me to communicate with my team a lot, and breaking me out of my nervous social-anxiety shell,' he said.[23] EY's approach to his autism reflects his own. In previous job interviews, he could tell that the employers viewed his condition as 'an obstacle for me to get over.' But he considers it differently: 'Once I put my mind to something, lots of ideas start shooting out of my head, and I'm able to come up with a creative idea. So I see it as a gift, too.'[24]

MICROSOFT

In 2015, MICROSOFT – the tech giant based in Redmond, Washington – announced it was launching a small pilot programme where it would hire people with autism for full-time positions in collaboration with Specialisterne.

'Microsoft is stronger when we expand opportunity and we have a diverse workforce that represents our customers,' said Mary Ellen Smith, the company's corporate vice-president of worldwide operations, who is herself the mother of a 19-year-old son with autism. 'We believe there is a lot of untapped potential in the marketplace and we are encouraged by the strong level of readiness from the vendors who cater to this segment.'[25]

Christopher Pauley, 27, an autistic graduate from California Polytechnic State University – where he earned a degree in computer science – was profoundly disappointed not to be offered a job anywhere. 'In fact, there were days where I would either hardly fill out any applications at all, or just simply not apply on anything,' he told CBS News.[26]

After being taken on by Microsoft, Christopher was offered a mentor: Melanie Carmosino, who herself has a son with autism. She said Microsoft's autism programme 'gives hope to parents like me, and it gives hope to people like my son that a company can, and will, look past their differences and see their gifts and let them contribute to society just like everybody else'.[27]

Christopher is now independent, living on his own in a high-rise apartment, something he's always wanted. He says he could never imagine he would be earning the salary he is today: 'Honestly, I would have been perfectly happy with, like, half the money I'm making now.'

His positive message is: 'Don't give up, and make sure to always aim high. Don't aim in the middle. You know, shoot for the stars every time, because you never know what might happen.'[28]

WILLIS TOWERS WATSON

WILLIS TOWERS WATSON is planning to hire people with autism in the UK as part of its efforts to push diversity and inclusion in the insurance industry. The company is extending the employment programme in the UK after it was piloted in its New Jersey and Philadelphia offices, where five people with ASD have been given permanent job contracts. 'This programme delivers many benefits. It allows us to hire talented individuals with unique strengths and capabilities,' says Nicolas Aubert, head of Willis Towers Watson in the UK. 'Diversity is strength and bringing varied abilities from people who experience autism is integral to our commitment to our firm's diversity.'[29]

In 2015, Willis Towers Watson's global CEO John Haley committed to hiring people on the autism spectrum, partnering with not-for-profit organisations and charities to reach this untapped talent pool. Since then, the US arm of the company has recruited 18 people to work as data analysts, inspiring the UK to take part in the programme.

While still in the early stages, Willis Towers Watson's UK ASD programme is focusing on the data solutions area of the business, working with external organisations and charities to make adjustments to the recruitment, onboarding and training processes. The company was hoping to recruit six to eight colleagues by the end of August 2018.

HEWLETT PACKARD ENTERPRISE (HPE)

HEWLETT PACKARD ENTERPRISE, the tech company based in Palo Alto, California, has operated one of the leading autism employment initiatives since 2014, the Dandelion Program, increasing to 58 employees as of early 2017. The workers are employed as analysts and software testers in IT operations and cybersecurity. HPE has sought to capture and quantify the benefits of hiring neurodiverse employees using economic and statistical metrics through partnerships with academic researchers at the Institute on Employment and Disability at Cornell University in New York and La Trobe University in Melbourne, Australia. HPE's Dandelion Program employees work in three fields: software testing, data analytics and cybersecurity. The largest number, 37, are in software-testing 'pods' – teams working collaboratively and contracted out to the Australian government's Department of Human Services (DHS).

According to Michael Fieldhouse, HPE's director of emerging businesses and federal government at the technology company, the pods of neurodiverse workers are achieving a higher quality of testing than any software testers in the organisation. They are demonstrating greater thoroughness and focus, especially on repetitive tasks that many neurotypical people consider monotonous and often cannot do with accuracy or efficiency. The Dandelion Program has also proven a major psychological benefit for the workers involved, who now have new social networks at their disposal.[30]

Over the past two years, HPE's programme has placed more than 30 participants in software-testing roles at Australia's Department of Human Services (DHS). Preliminary results suggest that the organisation's neurodiverse testing teams are 30 per cent more productive than the other, 'neurotypical' teams.

HPE, which employs more than 10,000 people, also uses autism consultants – 'team leaders' who have completed autism awareness and management training. They 'help with onboarding and work with the individuals on their development plans,' says Fieldhouse. To smooth the way, HPE has a buddy programme to acclimatise the employees to their roles at the company. It holds autism awareness sessions for managers and team members, and it strives to promote job and career movement, says Fieldhouse, who is based in Australia. Individual development plans are focused on life and executive function skills. 'This helps build resilience and retention,' he says.[31]

Despite the social difficulties experienced by many neurodiverse people, candidates often display complex collaborative and support behaviours during the project-based assessment period. At HPE, groups were asked to devise a reliable robotic pill-dispensing system. During the presentation of solutions, one candidate froze. 'I'm sorry, I can't do it,' he said. 'The words are all jumbled up in my head.' His neurodiverse teammates rushed to his rescue, surrounding and reassuring him, and he was able to finish.[32]

Inspired by the successes at DHS, the Australian Defence Department is now working with HPE to develop a neurodiversity programme in cybersecurity. Participants will apply their superior pattern-detection abilities to tasks such as examining logs and other sources of messy data for signs of intrusion or attack. Using assessment methods borrowed from the Israeli Defence Forces (IDF), it has found candidates whose relevant abilities are 'off the charts'. (The IDF's Special Intelligence Unit 9900, which is responsible for analysing aerial and satellite imagery, has a group staffed primarily with people on the autism spectrum. It has proved that they can spot patterns others do not see.)

BBC (PROJECT CAPE)

Now in its third year, the BBC's PROJECT CAPE (Creating a Positive Environment) initiative uses the power of cognitive design to develop accessible user experiences for people with neurodiverse conditions.

Funded until 2019, the project is led by the head of cognitive design, Sean Gilroy, and the senior designer, Leena Haque, both based in the BBC's user experience and design department. 'Sean was my line manager and I explained some of the challenges and issues faced in gaining employment [for people with neurodiverse conditions] after finding accessible and supportive colleges or universities,' says Haque.[33] Gilroy agreed that the topic was being overlooked and it was important for the BBC to improve the support available, as well as highlight the talents of people with neurological differences. 'Through our project, we found that stigma, and the perception of stigma, can be a significant challenge for people,' Gilroy says.

> They can be worried that disclosing their condition will affect their careers, as well as how managers and colleagues perceive and interact with them. We also know equally that in workplaces, not everyone understands conditions such as autism or how to ask for or find help.[34]

The declared aim of Project CAPE is to promote the idea that differences in brain functioning, such as autism and dyslexia, are not disabilities but natural variations and that differently wired brains can help devise new design processes, drive innovation and find fresh perspectives. In collaboration with the BBC, Academy Project CAPE has produced two films, the first using a video game scenario to highlight a day in the life of a neurodiverse individual in the workplace. The second, a 360-degree VR film using visual effects and motion graphics, recreates the sensations and experiences associated with neurodiverse conditions.

The BBC, which became the first broadcaster to gain a National Autistic Society Accessibility Award in March 2016, is using the project to bring in new creative talent, as well as to produce innovative and accessible content for its audiences.

FREDDIE MAC

FREDDIE MAC, the federal home loan mortgage corporation based in McLean, Virginia, in the US, has been hiring recent college graduates with autism as paid interns through a partnership with the Autistic Self Advocacy Network (ASAN) since 2011. The graduates come from fields including computer science, mathematics or finance. ASAN helps the company train managers who help the interns acclimatise to corporate life and also assists with crafting job descriptions for the company.

In a 2014 interview with the *Wall Street Journal*, Aaron Cohen, the firm's first full-time employee hired as a result of the partnership, said: '[I]t's a good fit for me. I like number crunching; that's always something I've liked doing.'[35] Cohen, a data analyst in the firm's information-technology department, has Asperger's syndrome.

Stephanie Roemer, Freddie Mac's diversity manager, said the programme had been a success. 'Historically, there seemed to be a certain perception of this population as being incapable of performing corporate level work,' Roemer said. 'In reality, people on the spectrum offer so much to an organisation … They are willing to think outside of the box and we view this cadre of talent as a "value add".'[36]

Freddie Mac also trains interviewers and hiring managers on how to interact with candidates. 'The limp handshake, the lack of eye contact, the soft-spoken voice – those aren't things that determine your ability to do the job or not. They shouldn't be taken into consideration or used as early red flags,' says Roemer. 'We're coaching all of our managers to suspend judgement for as long as possible in assessing for the skills that the individual has.'[37]

Roemer adds that this has been one of the biggest benefits for the corporation: an increased awareness about the value of those who are different. Others at the organisation are 'not judging [workers with autism] on that difference but assessing them on the ability to do the job'.[38]

Four years ago, working with the Autistic Self Advocacy Network, a Washington, DC-based disability rights group focusing on autism, Freddie Mac introduced an internship programme that identifies candidates with autism and trains hiring managers and co-workers to support their success. The effort has become so successful, Roemer says, that the corporation has turned to other organisations, such as Computer Aid Inc., the George Washington University Disabilities Programme and Autism Speaks, to find additional talent.

- BERTRAM NICHOLLS

Each weekday, 24-year-old BERTRAM NICHOLLS – a Marymount University graduate who holds a Bachelor of Arts degree in liberal studies – leaves the three-storey home he shares with his mother in Washington, DC, and heads off for the offices of Freddie Mac, where he has been working for the past year in software testing and data entry as an intern in support of the company's business and technology projects.

'I've definitely come to enjoy being at the computer and doing the various types of work,' says Bertram.

> Doing something repetitively has always been kind of rhythmic to me. A lot of the things I do … require you to pay very close attention to what you're going through. You have to make sure you're catching every detail. Because of my autism, I kind of have an advantage in that.[39]

JP MORGAN CHASE

James Mahoney, executive director and head of Autism at Work for JPMORGAN CHASE, says:

The embracement of this untapped workforce allows our company to benefit from the unique blend of talents provided by these detail-oriented, rule-bound, logical and independent-thinking individuals. And it is paying off: Many studies show that the performance of autistic individuals in certain functions exceeds their peers without autism.[40]

The pilot programme introducing employees on the autism spectrum into the workplace was launched in 2015. According to the programme, after three to six months working in the Mortgage Banking Technology division, autistic workers were doing the work of people who took three years to reach the same level – and some were even 50 per cent more productive.

Jim Sinocchi, head of JP Morgan Chase's Office of Disability Inclusion, remarked that, just 20 years ago, companies tended to hire people at lower pay rates because hiring them at all was seen as an act of charity. 'This is a new era,' he said.

People with disabilities are coming into firms with the right qualifications and competing for jobs that able-bodied people are doing. And they are not here to replace able-bodied people, by no means – they want to be part of a workforce because they have the skills.[41]

WALGREENS

WALGREENS, the second largest pharmacy store chain in the United States, based in the Chicago suburb of Deerfield, employs a high number of individuals with autism and other disabilities at a distribution centre in Anderson, South Carolina, which it opened in 2007. The pilot programme in Anderson had such strong results – the facility turned out to be the company's most productive, and more than 200 other companies have trialled it – that Walgreens expanded the model to other distribution centres. In addition, Walgreens has built a mock store in Evanston, Illinois, as part of a workplace training programme for individuals on the spectrum and with other disabilities. It established the programme in partnership with the Have Dreams Academy.

The programme was spearheaded by Randy Lewis, formerly senior vice-president of Walgreens. Lewis' own son, Austin, has autism. As stated in the Introduction, Lewis told me:

Although progress is slow, I continue to see signs that employers are opening up to the idea of employing people like our children who are on the spectrum. But it is not fast enough and people like you and me need to keep pushing.[42]

Notes

1   See: www.cbsnews.com/news/the-growing-acceptance-of-autism-in-the-workplace/ (accessed 11 February 2018).
2   Ibid.
3   David Perkins, in communication with the author, 21 May 2018.
4   Thorkil Sonne in conversation with the author, 6 March 2016.
5   Ibid.
6   See: www.shrm.org/hr-today/news/hr-magazine/1016/pages/companies-see-high-return-on-workers-with-autism.aspx (accessed 27 April 2018).
7   Thorkil Sonne in conversation with the author, 6 March 2016.
8   See: www2.cipd.co.uk/pm/peoplemanagement/b/weblog/archive/2014/11/20/business-is-still-scared-of-autism.aspx (accessed 27 April 2018).
9   Ibid.
10 Ibid.
11 *Marketing Week*, 30 May 2017.
12 Ibid.
13 See: www.huffingtonpost.co.uk/entry/autism-employment_n_7216310 (accessed 27 April 2018).
14 See Robert Austin and Gary Pisano (2017), 'Neurodiversity as a competitive advantage', *Harvard Business Review*, May–June.
15 Ibid.
16 Horacio Joffre Galibert, in conversation with the author, 14 November 2017.
17 See: www.cbsnews.com/news/the-growing-acceptance-of-autism-in-the-workplace/ (accessed 11 February 2018).
18 Ibid.
19 Ibid.
20 See: http://fortune.com/2016/10/26/autism-jobs-employment-ey/ (accessed 27 April 2018).
21 Ibid.
22 Ibid.
23 *The Atlantic*, 28 June 2017.
24 Ibid.
25 See: https://blogs.microsoft.com/on-the-issues/2015/04/03/microsoft-announces-pilot-program-to-hire-people-with-autism/ (accessed 27 April 2018).
26 See: www.cbsnews.com/news/the-growing-acceptance-of-autism-in-the-workplace/ (accessed 11 February 2018).
27 Ibid.
28 Ibid.
29 See: www.insurancetimes.co.uk/willis-extends-autism-employment-programme-to-uk/1419846.article (accessed 27 April 2018).
30 See Michael Bernick's article, 'Increasing autism employment: An anthropologist's perspective', *Forbes* magazine, 9 May 2017.
31 Ibid.
32 Ibid.
33 *Marketing Week*, 30 May 2017.
34 Ibid.
35 See: www.reuters.com/article/health-autism-recruitment/thinking-differently-autism-finds-space-in-the-workplace-idUSL5N0EF30520130604 (accessed 27 April 2018).
36 Ibid.
37 See: www.shrm.org/hr-today/news/hr-magazine/1016/pages/companies-see-high-return-on-workers-with-autism.aspx (accessed 27 April 2018).
38 Ibid.
39 See: www.shrm.org/hr-today/news/hr-magazine/1016/pages/companies-see-high-return-on-workers-with-autism.aspx (accessed 27 April 2018).

40 See: www.jpmorganchase.com/corporate/news/insights/jmahoney-autism-at-work-program.htm (accessed 27 April 2018).
41 See: www.jpmorganchase.com/corporate/news/stories/disability-as-an-asset-in-the-workplace.htm (accessed 27 April 2018).
42 Randy Lewis in communication with the author, 30 June 2016.

Part VI

Gender in the workplace – the costs of camouflage

Chapter 23

What the research tells us

The Hollywood actress, Daryl Hannah, made headlines in 2013 for opening up publicly about being autistic, a diagnosis which she received as a child. Hannah is 52 and a woman, which makes her what some people still erroneously consider to be a rare creature in the autistic population: female and middle-aged. Hannah said that her autism left her with debilitating shyness and a need to rock for self-soothing and made public events a terror for her. At the time she was diagnosed, Hannah's medical professionals recommended that she be medicated and institutionalised. Years later, the cost of 'camouflaging' her differences proved so exhausting that she walked away from Hollywood altogether to find some peace with her boyfriend and a rescue pig named Molly.

Autism continues to be described as a condition that affects three or four times as many boys as girls. But some experts insist that females often go undetected, not standing out as much from their peers as autistic boys across the spectrum often do. 'There are definitely more women seeking a diagnosis now, because there was a myth that autism was only a male condition ... women are recognising the signs much more,' says Professor Simon Baron-Cohen in Cambridge. 'I think a lot of females who might have autism were being overlooked, possibly because women on the spectrum tend to be less socially impaired.'[1]

Hollywood has not exactly helped. As a film critic myself, I believe I have probably watched nearly every movie ever made featuring autism. As far as I know, very few 'mainstream' feature films have included a female character with autism – and most of these have been profoundly disappointing. For example, in the 1969 Elvis Presley vehicle, *Change of Habit*, Presley insists that Amanda can be 'cured' of her autism by being hugged tightly and told repeatedly that she is loved. Then, in 1999, Elisabeth Shue reinforces myriad stereotypes about autism in her portrayal of a young woman on the spectrum in *Molly*. (There have been honourable exceptions, such as *Mozart and the Whale*, *Snow Cake* and *Temple Grandin*, and in 2017, the American children's TV show, *Sesame Street*, introduced a female autistic puppet called Julia.)

Dr Judith Gould, director of the NAS Lorna Wing Centre for Autism – who, with Wing, introduced the concept of the autism 'spectrum' and the Triad of Impairments in 1979 – points out that girls with autism tend to have better imagination and more pretend play, can have a rich and elaborate fantasy world with imaginary friends but experience difficulty in separating fantasy from reality and tend to collect information on people, rather than things (in fact, the interests of girls on the spectrum are similar to those of other girls – animals, soap operas, celebrities, fashion).[2]

Dr Meng-Chuan Lai, Director of Gender Research in Autism at the University of Toronto, believes that autism, as defined and diagnosed today, is skewed towards identifying males because they have been the predominant clinical research population for autism since Hans Asperger and Leo Kanner first described the condition. Indeed, the absence of girls and women from autism research has led one investigator to call them 'research orphans'.[3]

There seems to be an overall consensus among scientists that, at the more severe end of the spectrum – characterised by low intelligence quotient (IQ) and repetitive behaviours – there is little outward difference between girls and boys with autism. It is at the other end of the spectrum that the science is fuzzier. Given the small numbers of women with autism in the studies, there are few definitive answers.

In early childhood, boys and girls with autism are about the same. If anything, girls appear to be more social – whether because they actually are or are just perceived to be. As they edge closer to adolescence, however, girls with autism may lose this early social advantage, becoming less and less likely to have friends and more likely to be isolated. 'It can be very, very tough for them,' says Dr Kevin Pelphrey, director of the Autism and Neurodevelopmental Disorders Institute at George Washington University in Washington DC and himself the father of two autistic children. He is leading a study on girls with autism, funded by the National Institutes of Health, focusing on genes, brain function and behaviour through childhood and adolescence. Preliminary findings suggest that there are differences in the brains of girls and boys with autism. Brain imaging shows that girls with autism seem to have less of a disruption in the area of the brain which processes social information. Girls may be more likely to understand – indeed, may be acutely aware of – social expectations, even if they cannot fully meet them.

The pressure to conform is so strong that it can often end up influencing behaviour, as illustrated by the case of Gunilla Gerland, a celebrated autistic writer from Sweden. As a girl, she did not want to wear rings or bracelets because she hated the way metal felt on her skin. Observing that adults could not fathom that a little girl might not like these things, she resigned herself to getting gifts of jewellery, and even learned to thank the giver, before stashing the object away in a box at the earliest opportunity.

Girls with autism tend to be quiet and 'behave more appropriately', says Marisela Huerta, a psychologist with the Weill Cornell Medical College in New York. She co-authored a survey of clinicians who specialise in autism. The clinicians were asked to compare the severity of symptoms in females, compared to males. Seventy per cent of them reported clear gender differences in autism symptoms, with boys more likely to exhibit repetitive behaviours, fixated interests and being less likely to engage in social interactions. Girls tended to be more verbal and socially interactive, at least at younger ages.[4]

Another characteristic of autism is a tendency towards compulsive behaviour. And here again, girls and boys can differ considerably, according to Dr Louis Kraus, a psychiatrist at the Rush University Medical Centre in Chicago. Boys, he says, can become obsessed with objects like rocks, for example, to the point that they carry pounds and pounds of them around in a backpack and talk about them endlessly. 'This fixation can drive them away from socialising, whereas girls' obsessions don't seem to ostracise them from social development,' Kraus maintains. 'They may get fixated on collecting shells, for example, but this behaviour seems endearing and culturally acceptable.'[5]

What are the implications for employment? How do the research findings relate to practical issues in the workplace? Kevin Pelphrey told me:

The systems dealing with stress are constantly being taxed. Women with autism have two jobs – to pass as neurotypical and to do the job itself. They are not given as wide a latitude for being different. Exceptions are made for boys: if boys are a little bit unsocial, that is not usually deemed as being mean or cold.[6]

Adolescent boys tend to socialise in loosely organised groups focused on sports or video games, allowing a boy with minimal social skills to slide by, says Kathy Koenig, associate research scientist at the Yale Child Study Centre. 'For girls, socialisation is all about communication, all about social-emotional relationships – discussions about friendship, who likes who and who doesn't like whom and who is feuding with whom,' Koenig says. 'Girls on the spectrum don't "get it".'[7]

Pelphrey told me that many women on the autism spectrum reported finding it more comfortable working with men: 'Other women with autism would be their favourite colleagues, but men are more accepting and women do not have to try so hard to relate.'[8]

Approximately one-third of Specialisterne Northern Ireland's applicants are female. Its chief executive, Sharon Didrichsen, acknowledges that work can hold specific challenges for autistic females. 'At times, females may have perceptual challenges to overcome by dint of being female, in addition to perceptual challenges related to being autistic and being female'[9]

Jonathan Andrews, the lawyer and autism employment advocate cited extensively in previous chapters, writes:

> Plenty of evidence suggests that there are likely to be more women with HFA [high-functioning autism] in society, but since women are better able to mask their traits, they evade formal diagnosis. Women with Asperger's or HFA report feeling like a 'chameleon' – they're able effectively to disguise their 'true selves' and be whoever the situation wants them to be. Ironically, then, women with HFA might be perfectly suited to tasks requiring diplomacy, since they're less likely to let their true feelings show in professional settings, like negotiations.[10]

The unpublished observation that in girls with autism, the social brain seems to communicate with the prefrontal cortex – a brain region that normally engages in reason and planning and is known to burn through energy – is particularly intriguing. It may be that women with autism keep their social brain engaged, but mediate it through the prefrontal cortex – in a sense, intellectualising social interactions that would be intuitive for other women.

Learning the rules of social interactions, however, can be stressful. 'It's exhausting, because it's like you're doing maths all day,' says Pelphrey.[11]

'Without their self-report telling you how stressful it is to maintain appearances, you wouldn't really know,' observes Professor Francesca Happé, Director of the MRC Social, Genetic and Developmental Psychiatry Centre at the Institute of Psychiatry, Psychology and Neuroscience in London. 'They have good imitation, good intonation in their language, body language. Surface behaviour isn't very useful for a diagnosis, at least for a certain set of women on the spectrum.'[12]

Overall, the concept of compensation in women with autism has not been well studied, Happé says. Compensation could be cognitive – learning the rules intellectually rather than instinctively, as Pelphrey describes it – or social, such as learning to mimic others. There are also societal factors at play. 'Are we more tolerant, at least in some Western societies, of a girl who is very, very quiet and socially aloof, compared to a boy? I don't know; I suppose you could say we have higher expectations of women,' says Happé. 'All of these are hypotheses and they're only interesting if they're testable.'[13]

'Part of me thinks that it could be quite self-serving,' says Emma Jones, employment training manager at Britain's National Autistic Society. 'We often find that females are misdiagnosed. But the issue is being recognised more widely now with the "women with autism" advocacy push, Autism in Pink.'[14] (The Autism in Pink project is an innovative partnership, funded by the European Union, between four European autism organisations which has been set up to carry out research into autism in women – see Chapter 24.)

Meng-Chuan Lai points out that girls are generally diagnosed later in life and that unless an autistic girl has accompanying intellectual disability or other issues, she is less likely than a boy with the same traits to receive an autism diagnosis. And because autism is considered a 'male' condition, autistic girls and women can find themselves instead misdiagnosed with a variety of disorders. Obviously, this misdiagnosis carries repercussions that can include misapplied interventions, wrong assumptions and lack of much-needed understanding and support.

One key gender difference seems to be that autistic girls tend to be better at copying what they see others doing socially. When they are younger, their autism-related behaviours tend to help them because they can come across as less disruptive, being absorbed in their own interests. They fly under the radar until they reach an age where they are expected to be socially able with other girls, and then the differences can become stark. 'Defined our way, it's not a female-specific phenotype,' says Lai. 'It's actually in everyone who is on the spectrum.'[15]

Before now, autism camouflaging had not been studied in a systematic and standardised manner. The 2016 open-access study by Lai and his colleagues, published in the journal *Autism*, was the first to offer systematic, methodologically sound evidence in support of higher camouflaging in women than men with autism. They defined camouflaging as the discrepancy between internal and external states in social-interpersonal contexts. For instance, if an autistic person maintains eye contact during a conversation because he or she has learnt that this is socially appropriate, even though this clashes with how they really want to behave, this would be an example of camouflaging. Lai and his colleagues used clinical instruments that are well established in autism research to measure the contrast between internal and external signs of autism among 30 women and 30 men with a confirmed diagnosis of autism. Both gender groups were matched on age (average age: males 27.2 years and females 27.8 years) and intelligence and were free from intellectual disability. The researchers employed the Autism Diagnostic Observation Schedule (ADOS), which includes several tasks requiring social interaction with an experimenter, to measure overt behaviour (external state). And they used the Autism Spectrum Quotient (ASQ; a questionnaire assessing autistic traits) and the 'Reading the Mind in the Eyes' test (a computerised task that measures social cognitive ability, for example, inferring how people feel based on their facial expression) to provide information about internal states. Relatively low scores on the ADOS (that is, few signs of autism), combined with poor performance on the ASQ and the Reading the Mind in the Eyes, were considered to be a sign of camouflaging.[16]

Because camouflaging probably comes at considerable cognitive and emotional costs, Lai and his team also studied their participants' levels of anxiety and depression, as well as their executive function. Finally, they also used magnetic resonance imaging to scan the structure of their participants' brains. As the researchers expected, women with autism had significantly higher camouflaging scores than their male counterparts, although there was considerable variability in both groups. Across the whole sample, higher camouflaging scores were associated with higher levels of depression, but not anxiety. When investigating gender differences, the association between camouflaging and depression remained significant only in the men (so it could be speculated that men are more susceptible to the negative consequences of camouflaging). Conversely, verbal intelligence was not associated with camouflaging in either the whole sample or genders separately. Interestingly, camouflaging correlated with executive function in females, but not males. This indicated that women who camouflaged more tended to have better executive function. The extent to which individuals with autism engaged in camouflaging was not related to their age. This indicates that camouflaging may not necessarily increase with greater learning experience, as might be expected with older age. Neuroanatomical findings differed between sexes, with links between brain structure and camouflaging generally more pronounced in the women. For instance, higher camouflaging was associated with smaller volume in temporal, cerebellar and occipital brain regions in women, but not in men. While there is no easy explanation for this sex difference, it could be speculated that the brain areas involved have a different function in camouflaging for women compared with men. These brain regions are associated with emotional processing, so perhaps they are involved in an emotional component of camouflaging that is more relevant to women. However, this needs to be rigorously examined in future studies.[17]

Since the Lai study found evidence of men who engaged in camouflaging and women who did not, camouflaging is unlikely to constitute a uniquely female presentation of autism. To help to clarify the picture, three researchers from University College London – William Mandy, senior lecturer in clinical psychology; Robyn Steward, (a woman with Asperger's syndrome and visiting research associate at UCL) and Sarah Bargiela – conducted a pioneering study, also in 2016, using an unconventional approach which involved paying careful attention to the experiences of women with autism. They interviewed 14 women with autism about their lives, focusing on women diagnosed with autism in adulthood. Many participants felt that clinicians brushed off or ignored their concerns. One participant's special education teacher told her she was 'too poor at maths' to have autism. Other women believed they were misunderstood because teachers and clinicians did not know anything about female-typical features of autism. Most said their lives would have been easier if their autism had been noticed earlier.[18]

> Our findings suggest that teachers and clinicians need more information about how autism manifests in girls and women. They should know that even girls who have a close female friend or an interest in making friends could still have autism. And they should know that high levels of anxiety, along with social difficulties in a girl, are a potential sign of autism. All too often, these professionals instead misinterpret the considerable difficulties of these girls as simply 'shyness',

the researchers said.[19]

Most of the participants were experts at pretending not to have autism – or 'camouflaging'. They said they wore a 'mask' or adopted a persona which was carefully constructed from copying the behaviour of popular peers or fictional characters, or by studying psychology books. The majority of the women said they found the effort of passing as neurotypical to be exhausting and disorienting, and many thought it contributed to their delayed diagnosis. There are no tests for camouflaging, and this is a major barrier to clinicians and researchers understanding and helping women on the spectrum.[20]

Sarah Bargiela, co-author of the ground-breaking 2016 study, told me:

> The women I interviewed were both fragile and resilient. On some levels, there is so much sensory overload. But the strategies they found to cope with their social and sensory problems were astonishingly courageous and admirable. I felt humbled and inspired.[21]

The women Bargiela interviewed included one who worked in the emergency services. She loved the job but found it difficult when a procedure was interrupted halfway through – not to mention the sound of the siren and the flashing blue light on the ambulance itself. Another of the females Bargiela interviewed was severely bullied but then found working with animals allowed her to cope. 'The crux is to channel the person's interests – this is the key to success,' said Bargiela.[22]

Most of the young women interviewed by Bargiela were diagnosed between the ages of 20 and 30, and many shared how they thought a delayed diagnosis had been detrimental to their well-being and education. One declared:

> I think women tend to be diagnosed later in life when they actually push for it themselves ... when you're a child, you don't realise that you're anxious and depressed ... [that] your education is going to suffer because of that and I think that if I had known, and if people had helped me from earlier on, then life would've been a whole lot easier.

Some of the women expressed regret and anger at having 'tried to be good') for so long, and as a result, had been missed. One young woman felt that knowing about her diagnosis could have protected her in risky social situations: 'Had I known about Asperger's, I think I'd have known that I'm more suggestible ... and I might not have ended up in the situations that I did.'[23]

One of the women with Asperger's syndrome, identified only as S., told Sarah Bargiela:

> Perhaps males, particularly adolescent males, are more likely to be more physical in expressing their emotions ... whereas perhaps [it's different in] girls ... because I think there's huge expectations on girls to bottle things up and be a perfect hostess, even when there's no party around ... to hurt yourself inwardly as long as all the china is there in place ... Girls are better containers. And the cost is to be more inwardly damaged and no one would ever know.[24]

Another of the women interviewed by Sarah Bargiela, identified as R. said:

When I lost my job, I wasn't really that surprised because I had had a lot of time off with depression … So I was going to be the one who went, but they didn't go about it in a very good way and there was a part-time position that, if … you offer it to the person who's been there the longest, it should have gone to me but they offered it to some fella who had been there five minutes but he was normal, which I was not.

A third female, C., told Bargiela:

I could do a bit of small talk with colleagues but didn't really make friends. I had two jobs – one in Woolworths and the other in facilities at a local council. The second one was the one where I was bullied, and a lot of it was my boss being very unclear – giving me conflicting instructions, telling me off for things that happened before I worked there … Not coping with the first job made me get the second. Not coping with the second got me signed off. There was a day near the end of my second job where it was snowing really heavily and my Dad was driving us to work (he worked in a different department at the council) and I was sure we couldn't get there. Anyway, we got so far and he said we'd make it, and I just burst into tears because I couldn't face it. My Dad pulled into a services on the motorway and said he wasn't prepared to watch me go through it, so we got there, turned round and said we couldn't make it through the snow. I think the thing is, I didn't cope. I'd just about hold it together at work (sometimes going to the loo or whatever to cry a bit) but at home I wasn't sleeping, I was crying every night.[25]

C. has found a meaning in life through her love for animals:

[They] are my biggest therapy. The dogs, in particular, have helped me talk to people. They calm me down and give me structure and a reason to go out. They got me an award which helped with the confidence (and looks good on a CV if I ever go back to work). But mostly, animals just make life that little bit bearable. I don't think I could live without animals in my life. I find interacting with them so much easier than with people, and I have really deep connections to animals I barely know, whereas I have little to no connection to humans I've known my whole life … Animals are often soft, which is massively calming to me on the touch front. They also don't involve intellectual understanding – I don't have to read anything to know about them, I just have to watch them or interact with them. They also often make noises I find calming.[26]

Female participants in the UCL study spoke of making a deliberate effort to learn and use 'neurotypical' social skills. The researchers wrote that their findings suggested

that the development of such neurotypical personas may rely on concerted and prolonged auto-didacticism based on, for example, careful observation of peers, reading novels and psychology books, imitating fictional characters, and trial and error learning in social situations. In addition, we also identified unconscious elements to camouflaging that warrant further investigation, whereby women reported their social behaviour being copied from others around them without even realising they were mimicking in this way.[27]

The UCL researchers also reported that camouflaging appeared to be associated with various disadvantages. These included a sense of exhaustion and confusion about the individual's true identity. Moreover, some women believed that a tendency to mimic others and prioritise fitting in above their own needs had led them to be manipulated and abused by others, and had caused others not to notice their needs for help. Some women in the sample reported a conflict between their desire to accept their autistic selves, and perceived pressures to fulfil traditional gender roles. Some participants described feeling pressure to play certain traditional feminine roles (the wife, the mother, the girlfriend), and finding this incompatible with how they wanted to live as a person with autism. The study found an increased risk of sexual abuse or exploitation among women on the autism spectrum.

The UCL researchers concluded that research to define the female autism phenotype 'must include the development of measures of camouflaging, so that this phenomenon can be studied quantitatively, increasing understanding of its prevalence and effects on diagnosis and well-being'.[28]

David Skuse and William Mandy at UCL have devised a new checklist for detecting sex differences in behaviours shown during an ADOS assessment. The checklist, called the Gendered Autism Behaviour Scale (GABS), consists of 18 behaviours that the researchers expect to be part of female-specific presentations of autism. These behaviours fall into four broad categories: masking autism features by, say, imitating typical peers, making an effort to establish friendships, having anxiety or depression, and being fixated on relationships with others, whether real, imaginary or even non-human. The researchers obtained video recordings of ADOS assessments for 22 boys and 22 girls with autism, all between 9 and 15 years of age. These children all had average or above-average intelligence and verbal ability. After reviewing each video for signs of the 18 behaviours on the GABS checklist, Skuse and Mandy found that girls with autism reported being more affected by social acceptance and rejection than did boys with the condition. The girls also suffered from greater levels of anxiety and depression than the boys did and were more likely to talk about restricted interests in relationships, particularly with animals. By contrast, boys with autism tended to talk about non-social interests such as puzzles or computer games.[29]

'[Girls] do have restricted interests, but their restricted interests are more socially appropriate,' said Skuse. For example, a 10-year-old girl with autism might bombard a listener with facts about her favourite pop star, whereas a boy might rattle off train timetables, and an autistic teenaged girl might obsessively collect make-up rather than old coins. Clinicians may be more alert to certain stereotypical restricted interests, such as trains, than they are to female topics. 'The problem is that the way we have defined autism, conventionally, is a male stereotype,' Skuse added.[30]

Simon Baron-Cohen's group at Cambridge University is also developing what he calls a 'faux pas test'. If a woman is coping by learning social rules one rule at a time, she is bound to make a lot of mistakes, says Baron-Cohen, because she is likely to encounter a situation for which she has not yet learned the rules. Francesca Happé, for her part, is creating tests based on real-life scenarios in which her team asks women not only why somebody said something, but also what they themselves would say next. 'That really trips people up. It would require them to, on the spot, get it,' she says.[31] (Nevertheless, Baron-Cohen, Happé and others emphasise that women may have learned to cope sufficiently well that they do not actually need a diagnosis. 'If they're coping, do they want to think of themselves or for others to think about them in that way?' asks Happé. 'Then it becomes a big ethical issue, doesn't it?')[32]

Other studies are also attempting to adapt diagnostic tools for use with female subjects. A team made up of Australian scientists Sarah Ormond, Charlotte Brownlow, Michelle Garnett and Tony Attwood, and the Polish scientist, Agnieszka Rynkiewicz, is currently elaborating a specific questionnaire for young girls, the Q-ASC ('Girls' Questionnaire for Autism Spectrum Conditions'). They presented their work at IMFAR in San Francisco in May 2017. At the beginning of that year, volunteers were recruited for a study on 'autism in women' conducted by Professor Laurent Mottron, of the department of psychiatry at the University of Montreal, and Pauline Duret, a doctoral student in neuroscience, in collaboration with Fabienne Cazalis, a researcher at the Ecole des Hautes Etudes en Sciences Sociales (EHESS) in Paris, and Adeline Lacroix, a woman diagnosed with autism who is studying for a Master's in psychology at the EHESS. Since September 2016, the Francophone Association of Autistic Women (Association francophone des femmes autistes, or AFFA) has been fighting for recognition of the specific ways autism manifests in women.

Many of the new studies underline the importance of not relying solely on the ADOS when diagnosing autism. They also highlight the need to modify diagnostic tests to detect the condition better in girls. The findings are consistent with previous studies showing that females diagnosed with autism tend to be more severely affected than males. They are also in line with the hypothesis that more genetic mutations are required to produce autism in females. A new study found that women with autism tended to have more large disruptions in their genomes than did autistic men.[33] 'This strongly argues that females are protected from autism and developmental delay and require more mutational load, or more mutational hits that are severe, in order to push them over the threshold,' says the study's lead researcher, Evan Eichler, professor of genome sciences at the University of Washington in Seattle. 'Males, on the other hand are kind of the canary in the mineshaft, so to speak, and they are much less robust.'[34]

Notes

1 See Maia Szalavitz (2016), 'Autism – it's different in girls', Scientific American, 1 March.
2 See J. Gould and J. Ashton-Smith (2011), 'Missed diagnosis or misdiagnosis? Girls and women on the autism spectrum', Good Autism Practice (GAP), 12: 34–41.
3 It was Ami Klin, then director of the Yale Autism Programme. He is now at Emory University in Atlanta. See Emily Bazelon, 'What autistic girls are made of', The New York Times, 5 August 2007.
4 See P. Neighmond and J. Greenhalgh, 'Social camouflage may lead to underdiagnosis of autism in girls', www.npr.org/sections/health-shots/2017/07/31/539123377/social-camouflage-may-lead-to-underdiagnosis-of-autism-in-girls (accessed 31 July 2017).
5 Ibid.
6 Kevin Pelphrey in conversation with the author, 20 September 2017.
7 See Apoorva Mandavilli (2015), 'The invisible women with autism', The Atlantic, 22 October.
8 Kevin Pelphrey in conversation with the author, 20 September 3017.
9 Sharon Didrichsen in conversation with the author, 4 August 2017.
10 See Jonathan Andrews (undated), Autism and the Workplace: Common Myths and Untapped Talent.
11 See Apoorva Mandavilli, 'The invisible women with autism', The Atlantic, 22 October 2015.
12 Ibid.

13   Ibid.
14   See: www2.cipd.co.uk/pm/peoplemanagement/b/weblog/archive/2014/11/20/business-is-still-scared-of-autism.aspx (accessed 27 April 2018).
15   See Jessica Wright, 'New method aims to quantify "camouflaging" in autism', https://spectrumnews.org/news/new-method-aims-quantify-camouflaging-autism/ (accessed 19 January 2017).
16   See M.-C. Lai, M. V. Lombardo, A. N.V. Ruigrok et al. (2016), 'Quantifying and exploring camouflaging in men and women with autism', Autism, 29 November.
17   Ibid.
18   See Bargiela, S., Steward, R. and Mandy, W. (2016), 'The experiences of late-diagnosed women with autism spectrum conditions: An investigation of the female autism phenotype', Journal of Autism and Developmental Disorders, October, 46(10), 3281–3294.
19   Ibid.
20   Ibid.
21   Sarah Bargiela, in conversation with the author, 14 August 2017.
22   Ibid.
23   See Bargiela, S., Steward, R. and Mandy, W. (2016), 'The experiences of late-diagnosed women with autism spectrum conditions: An investigation of the female autism phenotype', Journal of Autism and Developmental Disorders, October, 46(10), 3281–3294.
24   Ibid.
25   Ibid.
26   Ibid.
27   Ibid.
28   Ibid.
29   See R. Loomes (2016), 'Gender differences in children and adolescents with high-functioning autism spectrum disorders', Doctoral thesis, UCL (University College London).
30   See Sarah Deweerdt, 'Autism characteristics differ by gender, studies find', https://spectrumnews.org/news/autism-characteristics-differ-by-gender-studies-find/ (accessed 27 March 2014).
31   See Apoorva Mandavilli (2015), 'The invisible women with autism', The Atlantic, 22 October.
32   Ibid.
33   S. Jacquemont, B. P. Coe, M. Hersch, M. H. Duyzend, N. Krumm, S. Bergmann, J. S. Beckmann, J. A. Rosenfeld and E. E. Eichler (2014), 'A higher mutational burden in females supports a "female protective model" in neurodevelopmental disorders', American Journal of Human Genetics, March 6, 94(3), 415–425.
34   See Jessica Wright (2014), 'Females are genetically protected from autism', Scientific American, 10 March.

Chapter 24

The implications for employment

Autism affects about 1 per cent of the world's population, and that figure includes many women, of course. But women with autism have historically been under-diagnosed. Currently, various studies put the sex ratio of men to women diagnosed with autism between 3–2:1. A lack of diagnosis can have a profound effect on autistic women's mental health and stack the odds against them when it comes to employment. And although those with diagnoses have better access to the support services which exist, there is little available for the undiagnosed to obtain and maintain long-term employment.

The Autism in Pink project, funded under the European Union's Lifelong Learning Programme to carry out research into autism in women, claims that autistic females have greater difficulties in gaining employment due to:

- Personal factors: negative self-perception, lack of social skills to face an interview, lack of training or education, passive attitude, mental rigidity, need for a structure, smaller social network.
- Social factors: social prejudice of the employers' 'typically female occupations' does not fit their features; their diagnosis limits their capacity actively to seek employment.
- Discrepancy between expectations based on their own cognitive and educational achievements and access to quality employment.[1]

The Autism in Pink report recommends the following actions:

- Create government assistance for business owners to employ them, taking into account gender and autism.
- Create specific programmes to increase skills of women with autism.
- Raise the subject of problems of women with autism in discussions with national parliaments so that [EU] Member States are encouraged to include their empowerment as a key element in the national strategies that seek to improve their overall condition.
- Promote a more integrated approach in the national strategies to combine education and employment areas.
- Raise awareness amongst professionals involved in early identification and diagnosis.
- Develop policies to ensure a deeper assessment, better understanding of real needs, and more appropriate support (for example, set an autism expert in each institution).[2]

A woman identifying herself online only as 'BJ' wrote the following:

> As a daughter of two Aspies, married to an Aspie and believing I am an Aspie ... it is clear that men and women experience and express Asperger's differently from men with Asperger's. However, like most medical diagnoses, the focus of research, so far, has been on the men. I think it is easy to miss these women because if they are disabled and cannot work, it is less atypical for women to be financially dependent on their husbands. Also, the traditionally male-dominated technical fields that the Aspergian brain gravitates to have only recently been available to women as an academic/professional option. I am 53 and at both high school and college level career counselling, I was still just being routed towards the more historically traditional fields for women: nursing and teaching. I was always at the top of my class academically and I could have pursued anything. I chose nursing and excelled academically, but the reality of the social aspects of the female-dominated aspects of the job with other female nurses proved to be very difficult for me ... It was very confusing and painful. My skills were always commended and I was routinely asked to train staff nurses to use new technical equipment because of my ability to understand the technology, and clearly articulate its function and use to others in a concise manner. But my lack of comfort in the clinical setting eventually drove me out of the employment realm altogether. Now, I am one of the extremely bright, embittered, Aspergerian assets of humanity that has fallen through the cracks.[3]

Auticon, the multinational social enterprise based in the UK, Germany and France, is looking to change this by going on a recruitment drive for autistic women. 'A lot of autistic women tell me they're trying to get a diagnosis, but the GP or psychiatrist says they can't be autistic because they are female,' says Auticon UK's chief operating officer, Viola Sommer. 'If GPs and psychiatrists are thinking that, it could also happen in the workplace.'[4] Sommer adds:

> All the diagnostic criteria for high-functioning autism are based on men. How are you going to fit a woman into those criteria? There's a shocking number of people out there who are struggling and they can't get a diagnosis and can't get support.[5]

The result of a woman with autism being told that they are neurotypical is troubling, because, as Sommer puts it, 'women tend to be better at ... acting like a non-autistic person'. And years spent meticulously observing, then mimicking, behaviours in order to fit in with neurotypical co-workers can have devastating psychological effects:

> It's exhausting for people [when] a huge chunk of your cognitive capacity is put towards acting 'normal'. But if everyone knows you're autistic, you don't have to worry about it, you can be yourself and focus on the actual work.[6]

Sommer also notes:

> Autistic people can have extreme hobbies and interests that they enjoy spending their time doing and are very good at doing. Parents and educators should facilitate and promote that and funnel it towards a productive career path. But sadly, perhaps if it's not agreeing with the gender role of the person, parents sometimes tend to shut it down.[7]

As Sommer told me: 'We are still very keen to employ more autistic women, but the vast majority of applications we receive are from men.'[8]

Richard Maguire, the Autism Oxford speaker, knows all too well about the difficulties women face when camouflaging their condition. He is married to Julie who, like him, is on the autism spectrum. She works long hours in her own business helping people with learning disabilities. 'Julie can appear to be coping,' Richard told me.

> All her conversational gambits run in a loop. Like me, she finds language very hard. I see her when the day is done and she is on the sofa, almost incoherent and semi-conscious, playing a game on her phone. People don't see that. If someone calls, she can snap back into work mode. She drives herself much too hard. When I'm knackered, I look at bikes and cars on e-bay![9]

❖ CASE STUDIES

- ROBYN STEWARD
- SOPHIA GRECH
- LAURA JAMES
- RACHEL ('CHASE') PATTERSON
- RACHAEL LUCAS
- EMILY SWIATEK
- CARLY JONES

ROBYN STEWARD is a woman diagnosed with Asperger's syndrome (at the age of 11) and cerebral palsy. Today, she is a well-known and successful speaker about autism. (She also participated in the pioneering UCL study cited in the previous chapter.) However, things did not begin so smoothly.

Her first encounter with employment was doing unpaid work experience at the High Street retailers, PC World, in Halesworth, Suffolk, fixing computers. Her

Figure 24.1 Robyn Steward

first paid job was working for Norwich Union insurance as a software tester. When she disclosed her Asperger's syndrome at Norwich City College, they sent a minder, Ant, to watch over her. 'I didn't like this at all, at first, but I eventually got to like him a lot. In fact, I even went to his wedding a couple of years ago!'[10]

Robyn began to research autism and realised that there could be a richly symbiotic process by which neurotypical people could teach people on the autism spectrum about the neurotypical world and vice versa. In 2004, she teamed up with two others and put on paid presentations at different departments of Norwich City College, which they called 'Dark Side of Autism' (after Pink Floyd's album, Dark Side of the Moon). 'People loved it. It was revolutionary – and well paid – for the time (£17.50 for 15 minutes' work).'[11]

At the age of 18, she began work at Norwich Union and, even though she was a popular employee, she herself hated it: 'It was completely the wrong environment for me. I went pale. Because of my CP, I couldn't sit down for long stretches of time. I quit after two months. My parents understood and fought my corner.'[12]

But she realised something: she enjoyed selling things! 'I like people – and helping them with their computer problems. I like being of use.'[13]

This is another example of the misguided generalisations which are constantly being drawn about the workplace. The thinking has been that as we move into the twenty-first century, and industry shifts further away from manufacturing towards services, this will represent bad news for people on the autism spectrum, who tend to find difficulties in interpersonal relations. We have already seen, in a number of telling cases – the Paddington information desk man, David Harris, and the counsellor, Ryan Tebbit – that autism is not necessarily any barrier at all to this kind of calm interaction with others. 'Being logical and unemotional works well – as long as you can turn on the charm!' says Robyn.[14]

She found another position working at PC World in Trafford, Manchester. Her CP again proved a problem – this time because she was standing up a lot and not moving around when things quietened down after Christmas. She also got into trouble because she was not willing to push customers when they said they were not interested in insurance. She found it impossible to deceive the customers: 'Lying is creating a parallel universe. I am capable of telling lies if they hurt no one.' In the end, she quit again, because the job was becoming too stressful.

She says she did not want to live off disability living allowance (DLA) – 'that didn't seem morally right for me'. So she went to Anglia Ruskin University in Cambridge to study creative design for a year. She then volunteered to do mentoring in schools. 'As a mentor, you are not a social worker. You care, but you do not get emotionally involved. You are there to listen.'[15]

It was at this point that Robyn became self-employed, giving talks to colleges and schools. She says self-employment can be really good for some people on the autism spectrum. 'You don't have to be a savant. It's important to enjoy your job – but talk to other self-employed people. All major towns have help to start up businesses.'[16]

As Temple Grandin has emphasised elsewhere in this book, however, self-employment 'is not for the faint-hearted'. There is a great deal of organisation and admin involved. Robyn finds it essential to use a mobile phone app, Xero, to arrange her invoices. She sends these, with the receipts, to her mother, who reconciles them and turns them into a spreadsheet. Her Mum enjoys the feeling of being helpful. Robyn also employs an accountant.

'A lot of evidence suggests that autistic women are better at masking their condition, but this means that people have expectations of what they can do,' Robyn told me.

> My experience, of the neurotypical world is that there is usually a very simple and direct way of doing things but that neurotypical rules complicate matters. You have to follow these neurotypical rules because this acts as a 'social lubricant'. Often, things like buying flowers seem foreign or manipulative to me, but you have to do them to smooth things over and avoid hassle.[17]

She agrees that it can be very tiring and stressful having to camouflage autism as a woman. 'But striving for perfection can also be exhausting. I have had to learn that things are not always perfect.'[18]

She now has her own rock band, called The Hatonauts. She says this has taught her to respect the views of others and to work as a team.

SOPHIA GRECH, the successful opera singer with Asperger's syndrome (see Chapter 3) told me:

> Camouflaging is one of the biggest problems for autistic women, and I would say it is one of the biggest problems for me because, as an adult, I 'mask' my autism so well that colleagues think I don't have autism, so they don't make allowances for situations I am clearly struggling with. This results in them thinking I'm 'thick', 'dizzy', 'not very bright'. I can't tell you the amount of humiliation I have suffered over my life.[19]

Sophia adds that,

> because I am hiding it, I become exhausted and can almost start to shake with stress, I can feel dizzy and sick. To make allowances for my autism, I can start to speak louder and louder, people then think you are super sociable and the life and sole of the party ... what a joke! I hate it! Inside, I am dying. A few years ago, I was away singing with an opera company. The director was a nice guy and because we were all living together in the middle of the countryside, he decided that he would allocate individuals certain responsibilities. Mine was 'Social Secretary'! This was the worst possible outcome imaginable for me: I had to arrange parties and social dinners. I lost nearly a stone in weight through the stress.[20]

Sophia's career has meant that she has had to socialise with, and meet, important people such as royalty, senior politicians and world leaders.

This causes me immense anxiety and stress, which internally is physically and mentally exhausting because I am using all my coping mechanisms. For example, the level of the conversations and the intellectual content leaves me standing there pretending I know what's going on when I really don't have a clue. As a result of having my career and having to fake social situations in the workplace, I don't mix with people outside of work. I can spend days and days alone at home without any social interaction and simply be myself without pretending. Just me and my dog, Thomas.[21]

LAURA JAMES, the well-known writer and journalist (see Chapter 3), told me:

I think women generally, autistic or not, often have to work harder on the fitting in thing in the workplace. I believe that it's harder for us all, that people are less forgiving of women and that we often have to work twice as hard in the same job for much less money! I don't think men and boys are expected to fit in, in the same way that women and girls are. Often men are seen as quirky or eccentric or passionate and driven, whereas women will be written off as weird, unsocial, unhelpful or – my least favourite word – strident.[22]

She added:

In terms of autistic women and masking, I think many of us learn to do it early on as a survival technique, often before we even realise what we're doing. I also agree completely that it takes a lot of energy and effort and can lead to burn-out. It's a bit like trying to do one's job in a country where you don't quite speak the language and you're having to translate in your head in real time. I think, right now, most of us have to mask to some extent to be able to succeed at work. I get lots of letters from women who say they are exhausted and feel broken by it.[23]

Laura says she is lucky

in that most of the time, I work from home, which means I control my environment and am not fighting against unwanted sensory input. I'm having a writing day and right now I'm sitting in the kitchen, with the window open and in utter silence. If I were doing this in an office, I would be assaulted by bright lights, air-con, people talking, phones ringing, the smell of other people's breakfasts etc. Each of those things would take up a little space in my brain and make me tense up against the world. A whole day of that can leave one feeling brittle and on the edge of a meltdown.[24]

RACHEL ('CHASE') PATTERSON, a woman with Asperger's syndrome, believes that autism is

too complicated for anyone to address any single area. People with autism, as a group, are unlikely to make any progress until someone

Figure 24.2 Rachel ('Chase') Patterson

acknowledges that they need to tackle all the problems at once. The three main areas that I think need to be addressed are housing, mental health and work environments, but they will only work for the majority of autistic people if they are seen as a single problem.[25]

Chase continues:

The world is scary. It's overwhelming. And autistic people need a 'safe space'. I live with my two very loving parents who do everything they can to support me and make things as easy as possible for me to live with. Living here is still torture. We live in a large semi-detached house in an expensive area of the country. I have severe sensory processing disorder, with sound being my most sensitive modality, and it's horrendous. I am woken up by other people rolling over in bed in other rooms. I am woken up by the neighbours' alarm through the wall. Other peoples' routines change without warning. They do unpredictable things. I live in constant fear because my housing is not suitable for me. The vast majority of what little processing power I have is taken up every day just trying to cope with where I live. But people outside the situation can't understand that. They see the big house and the loving parents …

Many autistic people who have the capacity to work may be able to do so only from home, so there would need to be a dedicated work space for that (since we have that paradoxical thing of being very focused and very easily distracted at the same time) … People as a species *need* to feel safe. It allows them to breathe for a second, away from whatever trouble is outside. Autistic people are a lot more scared. The world is a lot harder for them to deal with, and so their needs are much bigger. If you want autistic people to be able to work – to be able to contribute to society and be welcomed and valued – then you need to acknowledge the toll that will take on an autistic person's energy. You need to accept that they cannot perform those roles unless they have somewhere to escape to at the end of the day that feels safe. Somewhere they can process what's happened to them and recuperate for the next day.[26]

Chase was first referred to Community Mental Health (CMH) after a couple of years of private counselling. Very soon after she was diagnosed with Asperger's syndrome, she was discharged by CMH because

they said autism wasn't in their remit. So right now, it looks like I will have no mental health support. Which is ridiculous. It's already been proven time and time again that people with autism have astonishingly high levels of anxiety, depression, suicidal thoughts, issues with coping strategies, etc. We need professionals in place who can support us as we try to navigate our way through. We need people who have worked with us to set up a solid foundation before we can even think of adding the pressures of work, work environments and work colleagues on top of it.

Once we have a physical safe space, we need people who can help us establish a mental one that is robust enough to get by in the neurotypical world of work, and who can effectively support us when things in that new world go wrong. If we are struggling with something at work, or the anxiety is starting to overwhelm us again, we need someone who knows how to help us deal with that. Most people have friends and family to help them do that, and I'm sure family (less so friends – we don't all have many) would be valuable, but we may well need that expertise to stop us spiralling. We're very good at spiralling. Anxiety is such a consuming state. We need to know there are people who can rescue us.[27]

Chase says she has a high IQ and her language is good.

But my executive function is just awful. I can't make the simplest of decisions. My working memory is horrendous. My impulse and emotional control are that of a very small child. My ability to switch tasks is close to non-existent. I am severely disabled by my Asperger's, but because my language is good and my IQ is high, I am not seen as disabled by it (except by my psychologist, who has been a saviour in detailing how bad my problems are).

Until social services acknowledge that autism doesn't fit into their existing boxes, there is no hope of getting the necessary help to manage a life. If you can't manage your money or remember to pay bills or arrange insurance, you can't have a life. ... I am sure a lot of the depression in people like me is to do with a disconnection from the society around us. Being able to participate more in our communities and in places of work could well help to improve that. But it's not going to be possible without someone boosting us up and holding us in place until the glue starts to dry.[28]

Chase says that work environments are horrendous:

> There are so many obvious things like lighting and noise. Open-plan offices are a nightmare, and having my own office would be much more likely to get me to be productive. Most autistic people would be hugely better working from home. I am a strong believer in mentoring – if you put a nervous person in a new place, they need a single point of contact who they can feel safe asking endless questions for as long as it takes for them to get familiar with things. The mentors need to be very patient. But there are subtler things, too. Have you noticed that basically every single job advert wants someone who is outgoing? What's wrong with a quiet person who just gets on with their work? I'm unlikely to ever 'fit in seamlessly with our team'. That doesn't mean I can't do the job. And my particular favourite – 'must be good with phones/have a good telephone manner'. I'm awful with phones. They are not the way I can communicate effectively, but in this day and age with email being so widely used, that shouldn't be the barrier that it is. If I were deaf, no one would think twice about only emailing me. But because I can hear and speak, they think I must be brilliant with phones.[29]

Chase rightly points out that camouflaging

> isn't one thing. Some elements we choose to do, some our brain instigates without us knowing, and some our brain instigates whether we want to or not. All take a heavy toll on energy and confidence levels. It's widely accepted that women on the spectrum have a higher social drive. They desperately want to fit in and to get things right socially. We exhibit quite complex social mimicry to learn acceptable behaviours so that we can communicate more effectively with the people round us or to avoid situations we're not comfortable in, but it comes at a cost.

> If I'm stressed, I get agreeable! Being agreeable is the socially acceptable thing to do. Compromising with others is socially beneficial, so my brain has learnt enough that agreeing with the other person can be a way to establish social bonds and make progress on things. The problem is that I'll agree to anything, because my brain defaults into doing whatever it takes to stop discussion/fights/stalled progress. I have, in the past, agreed to things both at work and socially that I didn't want to do, or to things I knew would be counter-productive ...The only way to get round this is to let autistic people walk away and think about things before giving answers and ensuring that they have an environment where they feel safe enough to raise queries. Because we're 'the different ones' in most environments, it can be hard to have our questions listened to, because others don't see things from our perspective. We can be brushed off, so a supportive environment that will let an autistic person leave a discussion before they're forced into agreeing with things is vital. This kind of includes the fact that we process slower. Whilst it's not part of the camouflaging issue, if decisions need to be made on things, autistic people need time. We can agree to something in the moment, and have something occur to us a bit later that significantly impacts our decision,

and we need that acknowledged and allowed for. Time to think through all consequences and possible scenarios before a final decision is taken.[30]

She added that she never got into trouble at school.

But the second I got home, seven hours of intense distress, exhaustion, confusion, anxiety, all came flooding out. Autistic people need colleagues or bosses or teams who understand how autism works so that they can make sure the autistic employee's welfare is being cared for. An autistic person may say they're fine, but be completely the opposite. People need to know that can happen with us.[31]

Finally, Chase said, it was important to acknowledge how strong the urge was to avoid confrontation.

I have shops that I never go into any more because of one very slightly awkward experience. But lots of the confrontation has come from frustration at the above things: people who've forced answers out of me when I'm not ready, or rushed me into decisions I hadn't been given the chance to properly think through.[32]

After she quit her postgraduate degree at the University of Ulster, RACHAEL LUCAS took jobs in a number of areas, including as a horse trainer, a childcare specialist, teacher trainer, and an advertising salesperson. In each position, she would quickly become overwhelmed by the social elements of her job.

'I was good at the job,' Rachael recalled, 'but after six months walked out because I just couldn't cope with it.' She eventually turned to temping: 'I became very good at going into a situation and doing three or four months of very intense work and then being able to take a breather.' Choosing to work so infrequently was, she says, 'my own way of managing the autism'.[33]

It was only after two decades in work that Rachael was diagnosed with autism at the age of 44.

EMILY SWIATEK, 30, spent ten years working with autistic people before she realised she was one of them. Before that, she did her best to pass as a neurotypical person. She said 'masking' came easily to women because 'there are gendered expectations placed on women from a young age, based on ideas around: be nice, be sociable, make people feel comfortable, make people feel at ease'.[34]

The problems are below the surface – but not too far below: 'Women who mask often appear to be coping very well for a very long time,' says Emily.

That's because they'll be putting all their energy and effort into succeeding at work. But what won't be seen is the mental health difficulties that it can lead to; an autistic woman can reach a crisis point and it's a shock to her employers, because it's out of the pattern of her having been quite successful and high achieving.[35]

Emily found that being a personal assistant in marketing did not mesh with her interests, which include Arsenal Football Club players and her pet dogs. Neither did the office chatter expected of women:

> Some of the conversations around TV and fashion and what other people are doing and wearing can be quite difficult to navigate. If you struggle to understand the conversational rules and boundaries, you won't engage in those conversations.[36]

The isolation this causes might seem like a minor challenge, but it melds into a larger problem of how to deal with offices' expectations of female workers. Some autistic women with a special interest in fashion or beauty may easily navigate office dress codes, but for others, 'wearing something like tights or a tight blouse or high heels is going to be more challenging,' says Emily. This can be down to a simple inability to pick up on the unwritten rules maintaining what is work-appropriate, or a more complex difficulty to cope with the sensory stimuli of tight-fitting clothing.[37]

As Viola Sommer, of Auticon UK, puts it:

> Lots of autistic women would not be able to keep up with extreme beauty standards because of sensory issues, such as extreme sensitivities to tactile stimuli. Some people only feel comfortable wearing loose clothing, which is a challenge if you work in a corporate environment.[38]

Emily's mental health suffered as a result of constantly masking in the face of overwhelming social stimuli. Like Rachael Lucas (see case study above), she had to take intermittent stints of three to four months off work. Emily is now an employment training consultant with Britain's National Autistic Society.

Figure 24.3 Carly Jones
Source: Alex Harvey Brown (Savannah Photographic)

CARLY JONES is a prominent British autism advocate, filmmaker and speaker who was made an MBE in the 2018 Queen's Honours List. Apart from being the first British woman with autism to address the United Nations, Carly played a vital role in the creation of the international award-winning 2015 short film, *Epidemic of Knowledge* (which she directed under her other name of Olley Edwards), focusing on the under-diagnosis of autistic women.

Carly herself was not diagnosed with autism until she was 32, after two of her daughters were diagnosed. She found it a battle to get a diagnosis and started to notice a lack of understanding and resources when it came to autism and girls.

> 'My earliest memory is being the kid that couldn't go to preschool without my Mum staying. My Mum actually got a job at the preschool so I would go!' she recalled. 'I remember it seeming very noisy and busy. All the kids were playing but I wasn't. Then when I started school, that didn't change. I remember feeling very different then and things got even harder in secondary school. I was really anxious. I started realising that I never got invited to birthday parties. I couldn't cope with bright lights and they actually made me quite hyper. My teachers just thought I was naughty. I went to see an NHS psychologist who gave me a tick sheet with things like 'Do you prefer parties or museums?' – you know, one of those. I scored quite highly on it but then he asked: 'What are your hobbies?' and I said: 'I love acting' and he said: 'Oh, then you can't be on the autistic spectrum because autistic people can't act.'[39]

Carly was eventually diagnosed with Asperger's syndrome by the late Dr Lorna Wing, the psychiatrist who first coined that term in 1981.

> There was a mixture of emotions but overall it was complete elation. I had my answers and I could start rebuilding my life, understanding who I am. I always felt like a second-class 'normal' person and now I know that I'm a top class autistic, so I'm fine![40]

In 2008, Carly was informed by educational staff that it was impossible that she could have two autistic daughters 'because autism only happens to boys'. She believes that gender stereotypes are a major problem.

> Not only are there lots of women who are undiagnosed and unsupported; there are lots of men who present themselves in a more feminine way and they're not diagnosed and supported either, because they're not the stereotypical view of what autism is – they're not 'train-spotters' or like *Rain Man*. Also, female pain and female differences aren't always taken as seriously. It's always 'Oh they're probably hormonal'. Even my reaction to the sensory overload was seen as 'Oh she's in a bad mood' – and being autistic, I couldn't explain my discomfort to them.[41]

She also underlines the potency of what she calls the 'chameleon effect' – masking your differences and trying to blend in.

> We do this just to survive in a scary, unpredictable world. Things are changing but there are still pockets in the UK where this is happening and girls aren't being believed and supported. I want to make sure the girls in our country are protected and supported.[42]

Carly, who has set up the Olley Edwards Academy in Berkshire in a bid to end the isolation of home-educated autistic students, addressed the United Nations in Geneva in 2016 and spoke of the 'clinical misogyny' and 'misjudgements' that have led to autism being viewed as something that only affects white males, and of the violence and abuse experienced by autistic people.[43] Speaking at the UN Human Rights Council's annual Social Forum, Carly declared:

> Autistic females have suffered from a clinical misogyny past and that needs to be left in the past. Misjudgements have seen autism as a white male condition. I know from recent surveys that 100 per cent of [autistic] women in the black and Asian community have no autistic role models.[44]

Notes

1   Autism in Pink, 'Recognising needs of women with autism', EU Needs and Recommendations Lifelong Learning Programme.
2   Ibid.
3   See: www.dana.org/Cerebrum/2002/The_World_Needs_People_With_Asperger%E2%80%99s_ Syndrome/ (accessed 3 February 2015).
4   See Sophie Wilkinson, '"It's exhausting": The hidden struggle of working women with autism', https://broadly.vice.com/en_us/article/vb4d89/hidden-struggle-working-women-autism-auticon (accessed 9 May 2017).
5   Ibid.
6   Ibid.
7   Ibid.
8   Viola Sommer in communication with the author, 4 September 2017.
9   Richard Maguire in conversation with the author, 13 September 2017.
10 Robyn Steward in conversation with the author, 28 June 2017.
11 Ibid.
12 Ibid.
13 Ibid.
14 Ibid.
15 Ibid.
16 Ibid.
17 Ibid.
18 Ibid.
19 Sophia Grech in communication with the author, 22 July 2017.
20 Ibid.
21 Ibid.
22 Laura James in communication with the author, 24 July 2017.

23   Ibid.
24   Ibid.
25   Rachel ('Chase') Patterson in communication with the author, 21 August 2017.
26   Ibid.
27   Ibid.
28   Ibid.
29   Ibid.
30   Ibid.
31   Ibid.
32   Ibid.
33   See Sarah Wilkinson, '"It's exhausting": The hidden struggle of working women with autism', https://broadly.vice.com/en_us/article/vb4d89/hidden-struggle-working-women-autism-auticon (accessed 9 May 2017).
34   Ibid.
35   Ibid.
36   Ibid.
37   Ibid.
38   Ibid.
39   See: https://blog.scope.org.uk/2017/03/08/it-took-me-32-years-to-get-a-diagnosis-why-is-autism-in-girls-still-overlooked/ (accessed 8 March 2017).
40   Ibid.
41   Ibid.
42   Ibid.
43   See: www.disabilitynewsservice.com/disabled-campaigner-tells-un-of-discrimination-faced-by-autistic-females/ (accessed 6 October 2016).
44   Ibid.

Part VII

Employment schemes that work in the UK

Chapter 25

By way of introduction

There are various types of employment schemes available for people on the autism spectrum in the UK. These schemes, if successful, will, in turn, increase these individuals' independence and feelings of self-esteem:

- **Supported employment**
- **Sheltered workshops**
- **Consultancy services**
- **Mentoring**

Support must be made available to adults with autism regardless of their place on the autism spectrum. In general, supported employment is preferred to sheltered employment, because supported employment aims to introduce individuals into competitive, rather than sheltered work positions. Job placements are individualised, based on the person's specific strengths and previous work experience (if any). Instead of having to cope with stressful interview situations, individuals are supported in finding and applying for work.

Research shows that supported employment programmes are also superior to sheltered workshops because they promote greater financial gains, wider social integration, increased worker satisfaction, higher self-esteem and more independent living. The 2012 report by Britain's National Institute for Health and Care Excellence (NICE) stated:

> Research in individuals with learning disabilities has suggested that the outcomes of supported employment programmes appear to be superior to sheltered workshop or other day service options, in terms of financial gains for employees, wider social integration, increased worker satisfaction, higher self-esteem, and savings on service costs.[1]

Specialised supported employment schemes enable individuals with autism to secure and maintain a paid job in a regular work environment. These programmes involve: placing an emphasis on using individual strengths and interests, identifying appropriate work experience and jobs and ensuring the appropriate 'fit' between employment and employee; preparing individuals for employment using structured teaching techniques; using a job coach to provide individualised training and support for the supported employee in the workplace; and collaborating with families, caregivers, and employers in order to provide necessary long-term support. The key elements associated with successful schemes include careful job placement, prior job training, advocacy, follow-up monitoring and long-term support to ensure job retention.[2] The aim of supported employment programmes is to enable individuals with autism to be contributing members of the workforce through the provision of a stable and predictable work environment. Supported employment can increase feelings of self-worth for the individual on the spectrum, whilst also helping to increase public awareness and understanding of autism.[3]

Notes

1   S. Beyer and M. Kilsby (1996), 'The future of employment for people with learning disabilities: A keynote review', British Journal of Learning Disabilities, 24: 134–137; W. B. McCaughrin, W. K. Ellis, F. R. Rusch et al. (1993), 'Cost-effectiveness of supported employment', Mental Retardation, 31: 41–48; J. Noble, R. W. Conley, S. Banerjee et al. (1991), 'Supported employment in New York State: A comparison of benefits and costs', Journal of Disability Policy Studies 2: 39–73; L. Rhodes, K. Ramsing and M. Hill (1987), 'Economic evaluation of employment services: A review of applications', Journal of the Association for Persons with Severe Handicaps, 12: 175–181; P. Stevens and N. Martin (1999), 'Supporting individuals with intellectual disability and challenging behaviour in integrated work settings: An overview and a model for service provision', Journal of Intellectual Disability Research, 43(Pt 1), 19–29.

2   J. H. Keel, G. B. Mesibov and A. V. Woods (1997), 'TEACCH-supported employment program', Journal of Autism and Developmental Disorders, 27: 3–9; L. Mawhood and P. Howlin (1999), 'The outcome of a supported employment scheme for high functioning adults with autism or Asperger syndrome', Autism, 3: 229–254; J. R. Trach and F. R. Rusch (1989), 'Supported employment program evaluation: Evaluating degree of implementation and selected outcomes', American Journal of Mental Retardation, 94: 134–140; P. Wehman and J. Kregel (1985), 'A supported work approach to competitive employment for individuals with moderate and severe handicaps', Journal of the Association for Persons with Severe Handicaps, 10: 3–11.

3   See NAO, 2009.

Chapter 26

Where to go?

This section cannot, in any way, represent a complete guide to every available resource. Instead, I have indicated some of the most notable – and most successful – initiatives, with case studies in some instances illustrating their value to employees on the autism spectrum. Moreover, some organisations have already featured earlier in this book in greater detail.

Auticon

The German multinational company, AUTICON, launched its UK arm in April 2016. The company has more than 120 employees, and according to Viola Sommer, Operating Officer at Auticon in the UK, three-quarters of them are autistic. With investment from Richard Branson and from the UK charity, Esmée Fairbairn Foundation, the company is already turning a profit as it tries to help more autistic people get the most out of their skills. That goes for women, too. The modus operandi of this IT consultancy start-up, which now has offices across Germany, France and the UK, is permanently to employ autistic workers directly and then place them within other companies on a project basis while continuing to support them at work.

The company is explicitly modelled on the hugely successful Belgian company, Passwerk. The company prides itself in creating autism-friendly work environments as well as delivering outstanding quality to clients. The consultants are deployed in client projects which match their skills and expertise, and they work within the client's project team. Auticon has observed that having both autistic and non-autistic professionals in mixed project teams opens up new perspectives and will often significantly improve work output. All Auticon consultants (and clients) are offered the support of specially trained job coaches.

Viola Sommer explained to me that Auticon UK employs exclusively autistic adults full time at its London offices as IT consultants. Consultants are then deployed to complex quality assurance, data analytics, development or compliance projects across UK blue chip companies.

> We speak with universities, the National Health Service, clinics, charities, etc., but often candidates approach us directly. Some are recent graduates in computer sciences, maths or physics; others have already had careers but want an environment that is more suited to, and more understanding towards, autistic people,

says Sommer. Auticon UK has job coaches who inform clients about autism before the consultants arrive. 'There is one job coach on our pay roll for every six to eight autistic colleagues.'[1]

AS Mentoring

London-based AS MENTORING was launched by David Perkins in 2013 to provide specialist coaching and mentoring for people with Asperger's syndrome and other potentially exclusionary conditions. The company's aim is to help facilitate its clients' social inclusion through employment.

Perkins told me that he recruited people 'on the basis of their experience, enthusiasm and commitment'.[2] Since 2003, he and his colleagues have placed 65 people with Goldman Sachs and two at Bloomberg. Separately from such recruitment initiatives, some 50 per cent of AS Mentoring's funding comes from the UK Government's Access to Work Scheme for ongoing workplace support.

Perkins said that AS Mentoring asks:

> What does the client need? This may sometimes differ from what the client thinks he needs. For example, he may think he is ready for paid employment, when he needs to build up relevant experience elsewhere first. Autism can sometimes mean that a person has only limited insight into why an employer would not employ him.[3]

He added:

> We are *all* actors in the workplace. We *all* have to adjust. If employers think you have unrealistic expectations, they will run a mile. But employers *do* care that they can make a massive difference to someone's life. In fact, in my discussions with employers, they rarely mention the bottom line. What they care about is whether that particular person will be able to do the job in a specific team. And we want employees to succeed on merit, not on charity. Moreover, what's good practice for autism is generally true across the entire workplace.[4]

❖ CASE STUDY

- GOLDMAN SACHS

Since 2003, GOLDMAN SACHS has been offering work placements to candidates with Asperger's syndrome through a programme run in partnership with the National Autistic Society's now-defunct Prospects and more recently with AS Mentoring. It is a valuable opportunity for candidates to experience a professional office environment and aims to boost their confidence by enabling them to experience a 'safe' work atmosphere where their condition has been fully explained to their colleagues. A comprehensive Human Capital Management support programme is in place to help candidates and their managers.

Goldman Sachs works directly with AS Mentoring to monitor each placement, address any issues and allow the candidate to progress at his or her own pace. The bank says that it is thrilled with the continued success it brings to the business and all individuals involved.

The Autism Work Placement Programme at Goldman Sachs is innovative because of the unique partnership between the business, Human Capital Management and AS Mentoring. Goldman Sachs works closely with AS Mentoring when going through the interview process, providing the reasonable adjustments and the support which the candidates may need. AS Mentoring provides an awareness session for recruiters, Occupational Health, Administrators, Managers and the teams with which candidates will be working. This ensures that anyone who is connected to the candidate during the recruitment process or throughout the six-month placement has a certain level of knowledge and understanding of autism and eases the process for the candidates as they go through background-checks, a full occupational health assessment and their orientation as they begin their placement.

Action for Asperger's

ACTION FOR ASPERGER'S – a unique charity providing specialist counselling for lives affected by autism and Asperger's syndrome – was established in founder Elaine Nicholson's Northamptonshire home in 2008. It moved to offices in Barnwell four years later. In its first year as a formal charity, its number of clients increased from

Figure 26.1 Elaine Nicholson, MBE, founder of Action for Asperger's

20 to 480 and in 2015 it moved again, to larger, seven-roomed premises on the Corbygate Business Park.

Today, Action for Asperger's has more than 1,400 clients across the United Kingdom. The charity also runs outreach surgeries in North Yorkshire, North Wales and Birmingham. Around 5 per cent of its clientele come from overseas and receive counselling via Skype or Facetime. Action for Asperger's also provides school and college counselling for children and teenagers with autism and Asperger's syndrome.

Nicholson was 'delighted' when she was awarded an MBE for services to education and Asperger's syndrome in the 2016 Queen's Birthday Honours. The day before she heard about her MBE, Elaine was informed that she was to become the 551st 'Point of Light' – a title awarded by the British Prime Minister to outstanding individuals making a change to their community. The then-PM, David Cameron, wrote to Elaine to say:

> You have dedicated yourself to raising awareness and understanding of how best to support people with Asperger's syndrome and other variations of autism. It is wonderful that, through Action for Asperger's, you are using your considerable skills to support over a thousand people.

Autism Forward

AUTISM FORWARD, a London-based charity formed in 2017, provides grants for specialist mentoring for autistic adults to give them the support and advice they need to navigate the neurotypical world and find paid or voluntary employment.

It offers resources for employers, colleagues, friends and families of autistic adults to encourage them to listen, talk and accept their different way of seeing the world, so that adults on the spectrum are included and valued in communities and workplaces.

Step Into Work Plus

STEP INTO WORK PLUS is a specialist programme run by Autism Together (formerly the Wirral Autistic Society) in north-west England to help people with Asperger's syndrome prepare for the workplace. The 24-week programme includes a 12-week work placement, as well as numerous workshops and fieldtrips, where students have the chance to practise social skills. Students work together to develop new business ideas, play team games and work with IT programmes designed to aid concentration, memory and collaboration, On 'Smart Fridays', they have the opportunity to dress for business. The programme also helps employers to recognise that those with Asperger's can be capable, dependable members of staff.

The programme is funded by a Big Lottery grant and the funding stipulates that each student should have one 12-week work placement. In fact, a quarter of the students have had two or three placements, and to date six remain as volunteers and 11 have accepted permanent paid roles.

The programme's manager, Beverley Green, said:

We've had inquiries from as far afield as Kent, Northampton, Wales, Cheshire and Lancashire ... We've had some great outcomes at Step into Work Plus and our students are steady, reliable and trustworthy people who take such pride in what they do and, by working together, we aim to help employers to see their value too.[5]

❖ CASE STUDY

- CHRIS BIRSS

One of those the Step Into Work Plus programme has helped is CHRIS BIRSS, from Birkenhead, who took up a work placement at the Light Cinema in New Brighton, where he did unpaid work as part of the front-of-the-house team and has since been rewarded with a permanent part-time paid role.

Chris said: 'I have been thrilled to participate and have surprised myself with how much I have been able to achieve.' For her part, Jane Woodason, the cinema's education manager said:

We are pleased to be giving him – and his warm and pleasant personality – a chance to shine here and have been impressed by the way he has developed skills and adapted to his tasks. We've watched his confidence grow and grow and he's working really well with our customers and staff.[6]

North East Autism Society

A pioneering new employment scheme, Employment Futures, was launched by the NORTH EAST AUTISM SOCIETY in Gateshead in September 2016. According to the NEAS's chief executive, John Phillipson, 'our ambition is to establish a committed but open employment network, made up of employers large and small, across a range of industries, so we can place "trainees" in environments uniquely matched to their skill sets and interests.'[7]

The scheme aims to help remove barriers to meaningful employment for adults with autism and other disabilities. This service has been designed to support both the individual and the employer. It claims to be 'not only a package of support services [but] also the positive assertion we hope to achieve from all adults on the autism spectrum who want to succeed in the workplace'.[8]

Specifically for people already in work, Employment Futures offers coaching for the individual in the workplace: an assessment of the workplace, suggesting reasonable adjustments and practical guidance to support both the individual and also their employer, and specialist training.

Other elements of Employment Futures, aided by the Access to Work scheme, could see the NEAS providing in-work support for employees and guidance for companies (when employees identify themselves as being autistic), as well as coaching, mentoring and bespoke training on autism awareness. Access to Work is the British Government-funded employment support programme that aims to help more disabled people start or stay in work. It can provide practical and financial support for people who have a disability or long-term physical or mental health condition. However, deep financial cuts have weakened its role and efficacy.

John Phillipson has been dealing directly with Britain's Department of Work and Pensions. In view of the fact that many people with ASD are unable to cope in person with the noisy environment of the Job Centre and prefer to handle job seeking by telephone, Phillipson has proposed training one person in autism at every single one of the 750 job centres in England, Scotland and Wales. This has already happened in Wales and is currently taking place in England. Phillipson and his team have launched a number of employment schemes in North East England, including a farm in Country Durham and a micro-brewery. 'We want to allow employees with autism to spread their wings,' Phillipson told me.[9] More than 280 companies in the region have signed up to an Autism Charter pledging to support adults on the spectrum in a number of ways.

Phillipson said that the emphasis must be on persuading businesses that employing people with autism was not an act of philanthropy but was beneficial to the company.[10]

❖ CASE STUDY

- AILSA RIDDEL

AILSA RIDDEL, 31, is one of the most popular staff members at the Beamish Museum in County Durham. She cheerfully serves customers in the old Co-op, answering questions from a steady stream of visitors, polishing the brass railings, and generally being a Beamish ambassador. And all this wearing the broadest of smiles – as well as her blue and green straw boater and a long Edwardian frock: it is her job to fit in with the authentic sense of history that has made Beamish Museum a world-famous tourist attraction.

Ailsa grew up in Peterborough, the eldest of four children. Despite her autism, she was able to go through mainstream education, completing her GCSEs before embarking on a college course in IT and business. However, she needed more support – and it was not available in Peterborough. In 2004, after her family's research indicated that the North East had a lofty reputation for autism support, she moved to Sunderland and turned to the North East Autism Society.

Ailsa began working at Beamish as a volunteer, initially in the resource centre's library and assisting with school visits. She was then given experience of rural life on the Beamish farm, and her confidence grew to the point at which, in 2016, she was asked whether she would like to become a paid member of staff, working in the 1900s town and pit village. 'I couldn't believe it,' she says. 'I was so proud.'[11]

Today, she does two six-hour shifts a week and makes her way independently by bus from the Sunderland care home where she lives to the museum in north Durham. 'I love working here and the people I work with are so nice,' she says. 'Dealing with the public has made me so much more confident and every day is interesting.'[12]

Richard Evans, the director of the Beamish Museum, emphasises that he is lucky to have Ailsa on his staff: 'She has become a real asset,' he says.

> We could see how her self-esteem and confidence developed while she was volunteering, and she has the qualities we need. She has a lovely personality, a flexible attitude, she fits in well as part of a team, and she interacts so well with the visitors. It made sense to make her part of the staff.[13]

In fact, Ailsa is one of a number of Beamish employees who are on the autism spectrum, and the museum is one of the many businesses across Britain to have signed up to the Autism Charter, which provides free staff training in how to make reasonable adjustments for employees with autism.

Ailsa hopes to move into her own flat shortly, and she has no doubt that being in employment has prompted her new level of independence. 'It's just helped me to cope better. I've learned to be more organised and I think I'm happier than I've ever been,' she says.[14]

She met her boyfriend, James, at Beamish. He was a customer who strolled into the tea room and she served him an elderflower cordial. She tracked him down on Facebook, thanks to a friend who knew his name, and they have been together for two years.

Autism Plus

AUTISM PLUS, based in Sheffield, Doncaster and nearby Thorne, provides nation-wide consultancy services, including individual staff assessment. They are themselves sponsored by Jobcentre Plus and Access to Work.

The charity now has six social enterprise businesses in Yorkshire, whose ethos is to support people with disabilities on a 'whole life' basis to gain more control over their lives. Their conviction is that somewhere to live, access to a job, the right support, holidays, leisure and sport activities are prerequisites to leading a normal and healthy life.

The Ampleforth Abbey Trust owned a collection of redundant farm buildings which they agreed to lease to Autism Plus on a 99-year peppercorn lease, along with an adjacent five-acre field. In return, Autism Plus agreed to refurbish the buildings and bring them back into use by establishing a number of social enterprise businesses in the buildings and on the land, to produce goods and services which the Abbey and college committed to purchasing. The refurbishment work was divided into two phases: Phase One commenced in August 2014 and reached completion in June 2015. Autism Plus is currently fundraising for Phase Two.

Autism Plus's declared aim is to

create unique, vibrant and welcoming environments, where adults with autism and associated disabilities are given the opportunity to experience work in real life commercial businesses. We are creating businesses to teach transferable skills to prepare for the future, while at the same time individuals are helping create and develop successful enterprises that they can feel part of. Our key objective is to secure employment for co-workers either within the enterprise or within the local business community. Each enterprise is designed in such a way as to present a variety of roles that require different levels of ability. This enables individuals to access meaningful employment that fits with their level of ability.[15]

Autism Plus's specialist employment service, First Routes, is designed to help increase confidence and employability skills of individuals with autism or Asperger's syndrome. It provides tailored, one-to-one support to help increase employability skills, explore opportunities, complete CVs and application forms, as well as helping to understand expectations in the workplace.

The derelict farm buildings on the Ampleforth estate were carefully renovated into a chocolate factory, along with five acres of land for a horticulture project, known as Beanstalk Gardens. The chocolate business was successfully launched at the Great Yorkshire Show and the Skills and Training Chocolatier, Linda Jameson, made a chocolate plaque to commemorate the 100th anniversary of the Women's Institute, which was presented during the show.

In the autumn of 2015, Autism Plus was awarded grants from the Woodland Trust and the Howardian Hills AONB [Areas of Outstanding Natural Beauty] Project Fund to purchase 1,740 trees and hedging plants to screen the field. The charity then began the process of creating 30 allotment-style plots which will allow ownership to co-workers who wish to grow their own crops and aid progression into employment.

In another impressive move, Autism Plus has taken over the specialist instrument manufacturers, Mayfield Lyres of Sheffield. The workshop is now based at Autism Plus's head office, The Exchange Brewery in Sheffield, where people on the autism spectrum produce the much-praised Mayfield Bell Lyre and other marching band instruments. All Mayfield instruments are hand-made with beech wood, polished aluminium and steel back plates and each one is electronically tuned to ensure it is musically perfect.

Projects under consideration include more horticulture schemes, with the potential to develop the Beanstalk Gardens business even further, with the production and sale of veggie, salad and chocolate boxes to Autism Plus's own care homes, the local community and beyond, and a classic car hire business — which is currently being test-marketed externally.

Philip Bartey, chief executive of Autism Plus, told me:

Traditional day services have been closed down across the UK. We have retained them across our enterprises in support of service users with complex needs, some of whom will find it difficult to progress into employment. Our model is then to move them across from day service into employment.[16]

He said the belief of his company was:

Most people are capable of doing something. There are many people with autism who have been wrongly sectioned. Working with the Transforming Care Programme, Autism Plus is helping to move people out of hospitals into community settings.[17]

❖ CASE STUDIES

- FABIAN HARPER
- ALEX HARRIS

FABIAN HARPER has been receiving Autism Plus community support for some time now. In 2017, he started talking about the potential of getting into work. Personal Contract Purchase (PCP), team leaders and First Routes all worked together to ensure Fabian could split the eight hours of support he received every week between Community support and First Routes. First Routes worked with Fabian to identify the types of work in which he was interested. The team supported him to update his CV and helped highlight his positive attributes for potential employers.

The First Routes consultancy service team spent time in identifying jobs, practising filling in application forms and interview questions. Within just four weeks, Fabian was invited to four interviews. He said he could not believe how quickly it was all happening. One was a group interview, which unnerved Fabian a little, so a member of the team met him beforehand for a coffee and a chat, providing last-minute guidance and reassurance. The next day, after another interview, Fabian contacted First Routes to say: 'Do employers offer you jobs on the spot? Because I've just been offered a job before I left the interview.'

Fabian was absolutely overwhelmed but of course accepted the job, and he is due to begin work shortly at Pizza Express. First Routes is now working with Fabian and his employer to ensure he has support in place once he starts work. The employer commented: 'We would be delighted if you could work in our team. It is obvious what a lovely personality you have.'[18]

ALEX HARRIS first began receiving support from Autism Plus's First Routes service in October 2015. Since then, he has become involved in many projects which have helped him to increase his confidence, gain work experience, build up his CV and move into his own flat.

First Routes has helped Alex to engage in a multitude of activities, including creative writing through Ignite Imaginations, where Alex was paired with a professional writer to mentor him and encourage him to start creative writing. Alex has now written a story that had been developing in his mind for more than a decade. He is also completing a CISCO-certified network associate course (for early-career computer networking professionals). This placed him outside his 'comfort zone' but he has been working towards his qualification throughout 2016.

Alex initially attended Mayfield Lyres, which embraced his interest in science, technology and machinery. This boosted his confidence and, in turn, his attention to detail proved a valuable asset to Mayfield. However, he remained unsure as to what he wanted to do. First Routes then supported him in engaging in the Royal Horticulture Society-accredited course, Grow to Sell, at Beanstalks Gardens. On this course, Alex not only made his own creative planter to sell, but actually designed the product and made it from scratch out of recycled materials. He designed two herb planters which were sold at the Harlow Carr RHS show. Alex developed a real interest in woodwork design and his creativity shone through.

He has now started working with Top Notch, a company in Thorne, where he can take full advantage of his creativity and interest in woodwork. On his first session at Top Notch, Alex astounded the team by producing two different designs and plans for a bespoke rabbit hutch.

As Autism Plus puts it:

> We are certain that Alex will prove extremely valuable to the team over at Top Notch. We are so pleased for Alex and the progress he has made since starting at First Routes. Alex is also now settled in his own flat, and is fully embracing living independently, from cooking new meals for himself to hosting evenings with friends. Alex really is gaining more confidence in himself and his own ability every day and we are delighted to be able to continue to support Alex as he moves closer to securing paid work.[19]

Specialist Autism Services

Bradford-based **Specialist Autism Services**, a non-profit-making organisation, has worked exclusively for and with adults (of eighteen years of age upwards) on the autism spectrum and their families across the Yorkshire region since 1999.

❖ **CASE STUDIES**

(PLEASE NOTE THAT THE NAMES HAVE BEEN CHANGED TO PROTECT THEIR IDENTITIES)

- EMILY
- DAVE

EMILY, 19, was diagnosed with Asperger's syndrome at the age of eight. Throughout school, she was bullied but still managed, with help from her school's support staff, to leave with both GCSEs and A-Levels.

In September 2006, she was referred to Specialist Autism Services and initially chose the Arts and Crafts and Money Matters workshops. With Specialist Autism Services' support, she enrolled on a scheme run by Bradford Council called Workable, which provides work experience for adults with disabilities. One of these work experience placements involved working in the busy office of a housing association. She was initially supported by Specialist Autism Services' employment staff but gradually, as her confidence and ability in the job grew, the support was withdrawn and she was able to work independently.

Emily says that, after her placement at the housing association ended, she was very keen to find work in a public service area,

> so I refined my search for job opportunities in this area. I received support from Specialist Autism Services for filling in application forms and also attending the interviews, as these situations cause me a great deal of anxiety. Specialist Autism Services helped in these situations by providing me with lots of preparation, for example running through the types of questions that could be asked and how I would respond.[20]

After a few months of interviews, Emily was offered a position within the National Health Service.

> But I did not want to lose my momentum so I applied, and was successful, in obtaining a post at a council as a full-time mailing clerk. After being at the council for a while, I requested that Specialist Autism Services provide some training regarding autism spectrum conditions, as none of the staff had experience of working with someone with an ASC, except for one colleague who had had a negative experience. The training was provided and I found this to be very positive in that the number of situations which created anxiety have been reduced in the workplace and colleagues feel more confident asking me to do tasks.[21]

DAVE first started at Specialist Autism Services in October 2004 after the Disability Employment Advisor at his local Job Centre Plus recommended it. He had previously gained a little experience of employment through a volunteering placement in a charity shop in 2003. 'I had hoped that this placement would assist me in increasing my confidence,' says Dave.

> However, the opposite happened. A lack of structured support and awareness led to me feeling clueless. I had originally wanted to volunteer at a supermarket but, due to my condition, it was decided that it would be better if I did a placement where working with others wasn't much of a concern – hence my placement working in the charity shop's storeroom. After three months, I left the placement feeling I had achieved little.[22]

During the initial stages at Specialist Autism Services, Dave attended Social Skills, Arts and Crafts and Music workshops: 'To begin with, I thought that I would be shy but the workshops offered me a welcoming environment and I ended up speaking my mind, offering my opinions and ideas to the group.'[23]

In May 2005, he decided to participate in the Preparing for Work workshop, where discussions included coping strategies at work and appropriate conversations in the workplace.

> We also did role plays of interviews, which sparked my interest in drama and led to me writing a play about disproving the misconceptions about autism which was performed in 2006. I found Preparing for Work useful, as it raised my confidence and made me feel more positive about my ability to work.[24]

It was not until January 2007 that Dave was officially diagnosed with Asperger's syndrome:

> I had, through the Preparing for Work workshop, gained enough confidence to consider another placement. Specialist Autism Services' Employment Officer found me a volunteering role at the Christian African Relief Trust packing clothes to be sent to Africa. I was working with other people, involved as part of a team, and began to use many new skills. I noticed that many of the books needed sorting and so I used my own initiative of sorting them into alphabetical order. Also, as I don't like to leave tasks unfinished, I requested to volunteer for longer to make sure I completed all my jobs that day. From this placement, I realised that I enjoyed filing books and I spoke to Specialist Autism Services' Employment Officer about sourcing a role which would include these duties more.[25]

Specialist Autism Services' Employment Officer found him a volunteering role in the library at the University of Huddersfield and supported him until he was used to the environment and the other staff. His duties included filing medical books and journals and cataloguing them.

Eventually, a restructuring of the library's staff team meant that Dave's placement was no longer available. Specialist Autism Services' Employment Officer then helped him to find another at Batley Library. This was similar to his placement at Huddersfield, except that he also had to work on the reception desk doing customer service.

> I found this difficult, as I did not know what types of questions customers would ask me. Once, someone asked me for a train timetable, which I found confusing because the train station would be more appropriate to ring for this kind of request. At this point, I realised customer service was not for me![26]

Whilst at Batley Library, Specialist Autism Services' Employment Officer told Dave about an employability scheme being run by his local hospital. Specialist Autism Services supported him at the interview, during which he found out about the European Computer Driving Licence (ECDL) Foundation – an international organisation dedicated to raising digital competence standards in the workforce, education and society – for which he qualified in 2010.

> After completing my ECDL, I was keen to find a volunteering placement in which I could use my new computer skills. I had talks with my Employment Officer about this and was offered a voluntary place at the Nerve Centre, an organisation which helps those with mental health issues. Specialist Autism Services' Employment Officer found the placement and supported me on the first two sessions. However, I was keen to become more independent and requested to attend the placement alone. I was asked to update members' databases, research mental health issues on the Internet and make sure all information was kept up-to-date.

His next job was working for an organisation called SCARD, which helps people who have been involved in road traffic accidents. SCARD insisted that he attend the interview alone, without support. 'I was nervous at the interview but it went well, as I had done some preparation with my Employment Officer beforehand and I had lots to talk about.' The job was shortlisted down from 12 people and Dave was offered a month-long work trial, after which he was offered a permanent, paid position as an administrator/personal assistant.

'I have now been at SCARD for nearly two years and enjoy my role,' says Dave. 'I feel I can communicate with other staff, am part of a team and am interested in the work SCARD carries out. It is very important to me to work.'[27]

Evenbreak

EVENBREAK, an award-winning, not-for-profit social enterprise run for and by disabled people, was founded by Jane Hatton in 2011 to achieve three aims:

- To help inclusive employers attract more talented disabled people;
- To help disabled job seekers find work with employers who will value their skills;
- To promote the business benefits of employing disabled people.

Hatton herself has a degenerative spinal condition which means that she works lying down, with her laptop suspended in the air. Long before she became disabled, she was a Diversity Trainer, travelling up and down the UK helping employers understand how they could benefit through having a more diverse workforce.

Evenbreak works with employers such as EY, Network Rail, John Lewis, the Wellcome Trust and many others to help them attract talented disabled applicants when they advertise their roles. It also works with disabled candidates and with organisations who support them. 'As ... eight out of 10 disabled people acquired their disability during the course of their working life, the chances are that disability is an issue that you will come across in your company,' says Hatton.

In business, as in society, there are many misconceptions about disabled people, mainly driven by the negative image of us in the media. As employers, we are all concerned about saving money, and employing disabled people can feel like an expensive luxury. However, the reality is somewhat different and, interestingly, company surveys consistently conclude that organisations who have successfully employed disabled people are keen to employ more ... Many studies show that, on average, disabled employees are just as productive as their non-disabled colleagues (sometimes more so), have less time off sick, fewer workplace accidents and stay with their employers longer, increasing retention and saving money on recruiting and training new staff. Showing a positive approach towards disability also tends to foster good relations with other staff and generally enhances your reputation as an employer of choice.[28]

Hatton told me she had set up Evenbreak because 'there had been so many years of non-disabled people telling everyone what disabled people can and cannot do. So we are very authentic – although we don't have all the answers, either.'[29]

Evenbreak has an online portal – again led by disabled people – with useful information about workplace strengths and challenges. 'Employers are becoming more interested,' says Hatton. 'They are starting to see autism as an advantage, rather than a disability, and to consider employing them as a commercially sensible thing to do rather than a charitable act.'[30]

Nevertheless, as noted in Chapter 18, Hatton does not believe that either the Autism Act or the Equality Act has sufficient teeth to force employers to introduce reasonable adjustments in the workplace, even though these adjustments 'are not rocket science and and they don't cost a fortune.'[31]

❖ CASE STUDY

• OWEN

OWEN (not his real name) is an exceedingly bright man with Asperger's syndrome and several degrees. Yet he has not worked for ten years. He would love to work for a Left-wing think-tank. Jane Hatton says that it is her 'life's ambition' to see Owen employed, even though he is just one of 20,000 Evenbreak candidates.

Owen's main problem comes in the interview process. Whenever he is asked: 'Tell us something about yourself,' he either answers: 'I'm 5ft 10 tall ...' or he replies: 'That's a fucking silly question.' The ten-year-hiatus on his CV is a major hurdle, of course. 'We've started sending out his CV without dates in it, so that the gap is not obvious. But the employers also come back to us asking where the years are.'[32]

The most frustrating thing, says Hatton, is that Owen often gives talks about autism and about autistic strengths in the workplace, and employers are very impressed with what they hear – but still they don't offer him a job. 'He's very articulate – but he talks like an academic textbook.'[33]

Autism Oxford

AUTISM OXFORD, founded by Kathy Erangey in 2009, employs a team of nine autistic speakers on the autism spectrum to teach audiences about the realities of life on the autism spectrum. The team gives a range of unique powerful insights and strategies tried and tested by autistic men and women. The speakers are paid to speak at Autism Oxford events and the proceeds of these events pay their supported employment costs as trainers.

More than 2,000 people have so far benefited from hearing its speakers at its events. Erangey, herself the mother of an adult autistic son, says that, in all, she has taken on over 20 motivational, and inspirational, speakers on the autism spectrum. She recruits when someone asks to do training or speaking work – or she receives requests from support workers. 'If we have capacity, we invite them to come along for a training session.' Erangey told me.[34] Once they are employed, they are paid per session.

She produces a careful communication and sensory profile of each employee. They use natural lighting wherever possible and endeavour to ensure that the venues

Figure 26.2 The Autism Oxford team during training at Thames Valley police headquarters in Kidlington, Oxford. (Left to right: Kathy Erangey, Richard Maguire, Ann Memmott and James Hoodless)

for the presentations do not have strong patterns or colour schemes or loud noises. Noise-cancelling headphones are provided and there are individualised 'coping kits'. 'I myself avoid wearing patterned clothes or any perfume at all,' says Erangey.[35] The trainers always visit the venues beforehand. As one speaker put it: 'It's great not having to explain my sensory issues or anxieties to colleagues. They already understand, and pre-empt them. I can relax and enjoy working.'[36]

Other speakers were also quick to praise Autism Oxford:

'All my other jobs were horrid, in fact some were complete hell! With Autism Oxford, I feel at home, I feel safe, I feel happy.'

'It is great to be part of a team which is educating people so the next generation can get more effective support than we did.'

'This is the first job where I haven't been bullied, teased, manipulated by peers – I'm respected.'

'My mental health has improved. I earn money doing work I enjoy, which benefits others.'

'I have a career now, not just a series of unhappy jobs.'

'It's enormously empowering to have the experience of being someone worth listening to.'[37]

There are usually a maximum of eight people presenting at any one session.

Sometimes, one of them may fall out of a session. But even though they do not like change, one of them happily takes over that person's Powerpoint slides. On the other hand, a couple of Autism Oxford trainers have told the audience: 'My natural state is non-verbal. I'd prefer not to speak.'[38]

One of the trainers had gone on to work at a local garden centre. Kathy and her team helped him to prepare for the interview.

One of the Autism Oxford speakers, Tilus Clark, told me:

In other jobs, I have felt like I am under constant supervision and that there is an expectation for me to be 'busy' for every minute I am there. Breaks were always too short and I was not allowed to go outside or find somewhere quiet where I could de-stress. The Autism Oxford team is very friendly and easy-going. Working with them is easier and more informal than other teams I have worked with and they care about my needs and try to help with difficulties.[39]

Remploy – Marks & Spencer

REMPLOY describes itself as 'the UK's leading provider of specialist employment services to people who experience complex barriers to work'.

Since May 2011 when Marks & Spencer appointed Remploy as its official disability partner, Remploy has supported more than a thousand candidates into employment at M&S stores nationwide and in its logistics business at its national distribution centre at Castle Donington. Remploy was chosen to recruit, retain and sustain talented individuals who face barriers getting into work both through its direct hire service and M&S's Marks & Start work placement programme. The Marks & Start programme is designed to help people with disabilities or health conditions, young people, single parents and people who are homeless or at risk of homelessness. It is a highly effective partnership between Marks & Spencer and four delivery partners: Remploy, Gingerbread, The Prince's Trust and Business in the Community.

When a candidate is offered a job, Remploy then provides store managers with all the support needed to help their new employee settle in and progress. Potential candidates on the Marks & Start programme are taken through comprehensive pre-employment modules developed by Remploy. Those who successfully complete the modules take part in a two or four-week placement in an M&S store or the retailer's national distribution centre. They are helped on site by a Marks & Spencer buddy as they learn the ropes and this is complemented by follow-up support. Individuals who complete the programme and meet the criteria M&S is looking for are then accredited, which enables them to take up any suitable vacancy that is available without going through the normal recruitment process.

'We are striving to become the world's most sustainable major retailer, so doing the right thing is part of Marks & Spencer's DNA,' says Sophie Brooks, Senior Employee Engagement Manager at Marks & Spencer. 'But apart from this, any organisation that doesn't actively employ people with disabilities is missing out on a huge pool of talented people who, with the right support, have a lot to offer.'

❖ CASE STUDIES

- RACHAEL COVERY
- HOLLY WILKINSON
- AARON SMITH

RACHAEL COVERY, 24, from Airdrie in Scotland, thought she was a 'misfit' before finally being diagnosed with Asperger's syndrome eight years ago. With support and encouragement from Remploy, she secured a placement in the construction industry.

'People with Asperger's can often be misdiagnosed or are viewed as being a little bit slower than everyone else, which is what happened to me, as I was only diagnosed with Asperger's when I was 17,' says Rachael.

> Having Asperger's is normal to me now, but living with it means that I sometimes don't know what to do or say in certain situations, or how to read emotions on other people's faces. Being diagnosed with Asperger's really cleared things up for me; I thought I was just a misfit, so I felt relieved to know this wasn't the case.[40]

Rachael gained a 'Certificate of Work Readiness' in 2015 through Skills Development Scotland. Rachael, who has an HNC qualification in Administration from Coatbridge College in Lanarkshire, also completed a Lloyd's Bank placement before being supported by her adviser at Remploy's Airdie branch on to the 'Think Differently' work placement with Mitie Property Services.

Rachael began her Administration work placement within Mitie's Maintenance and Repairs department in September 2016. Her duties included filing and helping with the day-to-day running of the Mitie Maintenance and Repairs office.

She says: 'Everyone at Mitie is really friendly and patient with me. This is good, as sometimes my stress levels can increase dramatically without much warning and my colleagues at Mitie have been very understanding about this.'[41]

HOLLY WILKINSON, a 21-year-old autistic woman from North Yorkshire, who had been job hunting ever since she left school, was finally given the career start she craved, thanks to Remploy and the Marks & Spencer store in Northallerton. Holly, who had been unemployed for two years, was referred to Remploy who then helped her secure a work placement with M&S through its Marks & Start initiative.

'Before starting with M&S, I spent most of my time at home feeling very low and demoralised,' she said. 'Most people of my age want a job and I was no exception. However, I thought I would never get the chance to prove that I'm just as capable as anybody else.' During her four-week placement at M&S, Holly made such a great impression that her month-long placement turned into a temporary three-month job. Then the store manager, Vicky Stephenson, offered her a permanent job as a customer assistant.

'Employing Holly was an easy decision to make,' said Stephenson. 'She developed from a shy and introverted individual into somebody who is confident and really wants to do well, and these are exactly the qualities we look for.'

For her part, Holly says:

> Having a job means everything to me. I have a reason to get out of the house and I'm proud to tell others that I have a job. Finally, I have a future to look forward to, and that means more than anything.[42]

AARON SMITH, 25, a young man from Sheffield who has autism, recently lost his warehousing job and his family home. It had been his first job for many years and he had pinned all his hopes for his and his family's future on it being successful. He desperately wanted to provide a home for his partner and two young children.

He was eventually given the break he needed, thanks to a partnership between Remploy and Marks & Spencer. 'My working experience has been very limited because I need time to grasp what is required of me, and employers have just not been able to give me that chance,' said Aaron. 'My Dad, who is a plumber, understands perfectly, and over the years he has given me odd tasks to do but I really wanted a job and a life of my own.'

The local Jobcentre Plus office referred Aaron to Remploy, who then helped him secure a work placement on the Marks & Start programme. 'I gained on-the-job experience in the food department and learnt a lot about retailing,' said Aaron. 'I worked alongside a buddy – somebody who stood by me, had endless patience and who offered just the kind of support I needed.'

Aaron's abilities were recognised by his bosses at M&S and his position was soon converted into a part-time job. He was recently offered full-time employment at the Simply Food store, whose manager, Damien Wood, says:

> Whilst he has a disability, Aaron is treated no differently from anybody else – he is expected to do a good job, and he does. He also brings commitment and enthusiasm, and these are the key qualities we seek when looking for new people. He is one of five colleagues in this store alone to have benefited from the Marks & Start initiative, and we hope many others will follow in his footsteps.[43]

Project Search

PROJECT SEARCH is an international supported internship programme for young people with disabilities, including learning disabilities and autism. Each year, trainees undertake work experience in various regions of the UK. They are supported by the Project Search team while on their placements and to find employment after the placements.

The premise of Project Search, an initiative originally developed by Cincinnati Children's Hospital Medical Center in the United States, is to provide practical work experience and prepare young people with learning disabilities for the world of work. The programme typically consists of three work placements per year for each person (see Chapter 3).

Access All Areas

ACCESS ALL AREAS, which began life as the Rainbow Drama Group in 1976, is a London-based company which trains people on the autism spectrum to become actors. According to its director, Nick Llewellyn, there is a tremendously talented and under-used pool of potential and highly motivated performers among the autistic community. Llewellyn told me that people with autism actually have a better recall for their lines than 'neurotypical' actors, so learning a part is not a problem.[44]
Its most successful recruits have included Julius Robertson, a young man with Asperger's syndrome who plays a person with Asperger's in the British TV soap opera, Holby City, and Cian Binchy, who was employed as a consultant to the original National Theatre production of The Curious Incident of the Dog in the Night-Time and now tours the UK giving an illuminating and entertaining one-man show, The Misfit Analysis, about living with Asperger's, including at the Edinburgh Festival Fringe (see Chapter 6).

Llewellyn says that confidence is crucial for the actors he supports:

Figure 26.3 Nick Llewellyn, the director of Access All Areas: 'Confidence is crucial'
Source: Richard Davenport

> It's about enabling people to feel confident about who they are as a person and not just trying to fit in with everybody else, to embrace their difference, to use it within their work and to inspire other people to see that difference is interesting, that difference is complicated.[45]

He emphasises that there needs to be 'a balance between providing our artists and explaining that they need support. We should not be embarrassed to say they need support but not put people off.'[46]

Access All Areas runs an acting course culminating in a Performance Making Diploma for Adults with Learning Disabilities from the Royal Central School of Speech and Drama, which aims to help its students carve out legitimate careers in the arts. As Llewellyn puts it,

> there is a two-pronged approach. You have Cian on the one side creating his own show and actually making a market for that, as well. He's creating his own style of performance and his own aesthetic. And then Jules on the other side, breaking down doors in places like the BBC. There has been a closed shop for far too long.[47]

Llewellyn adds:

> As a society, we've really struggled to think about the potential of people with learning disabilities. What's great about the arts is that people with learning disabilities don't feel they're getting it wrong. Obviously, they learn acting skills, but there's not this restriction around their ability. There's a freedom in their expression.[48]

Access All Areas is all about devising ways of giving people voices. It teaches not just acting but social skills. As Llewellyn points out, it is important that the students with autism have people around them whom they can trust. This familiarity is critical.

Its latest project, Madhouse, in partnership with London's Barbican Centre and the Open University, looks at Britain's now-defunct series of long-stay hospitals, which used to house people with learning disabilities.

'What's great about the arts is that people with learning disabilities don't feel they're getting it wrong,' says Llewellyn.

> Obviously they learn acting skills, but there's not this restriction around their ability: there's a freedom in their expression. People can go and become all different things in their life, whereas people with learning disabilities are quite limited. So we're saying: 'Let's try to work with some of these really talented people and bring them into the public consciousness.'[49]

Heart n Soul

HEART N SOUL was established in Deptford, south-east London in 1987 by Pino Frumiento and Mark Williams – both of whom received an MBE in the Queen's New Year's Honours list in 2010. It was an organisation whose principal objective was to inspire people with learning disabilities – including autism – to be creative.

'The aim is to build up a pallet of possibility – because if you don't offer people a choice, they can't tell you what they want,' Williams told me.

> Our vision is a fun world for everybody, and that happens when you start including people who see the world differently. It is the opposite of the deficit model: we show people what we *can* do, not what we can't.[50]

One of the undoubted stars of Heart n Soul (featured in Chapter 6 of this book) is Dean Rodney, the singer with autism. But Williams does not actually know how many people at Heart n Soul are on the autism spectrum because he does not care about labels.[51]

None of the people with learning disabilities working at Heart n Soul is paid. Is this an issue? Pino Frumiento told me: 'Some artists at Heart n Soul would like to get paid, of course, and we do discuss this issue with them. But the problem is that if I and others get paid, then our benefits stop.'[52]

Heart n Soul's general manager, Sarah Ewans, says the basic motivation behind the charity is not to be employed but to produce creative, original material. We don't present what we do as therapy, either, although when it comes to funding applications we do speak about therapeutic outcomes – for example, overcoming social isolation. We use the language at that point – but not within the organisation.[53]

Autism Exchange Programme (Ambitious about Autism)

AMBITIOUS ABOUT AUTISM, the national charity for children and young people with autism, launched the AUTISM EXCHANGE PROGRAMME in 2014. It was first piloted with the Civil Service, and later with Santander and Deutsche Bank, and aims to get more unemployed young people with autism into the workplace by providing them with employability skills and work experience so they are better placed to get a job.

Working with their colleagues in education, such as University College London, the programme has three core elements – work experience, coaching and awareness sessions. Coaching is provided for the young people participating in the scheme and all receive a tailored development plan. Along with broader confidence-building and career planning guidance, sessions also focus on strategies for completing online tests, application forms, and attending job assessment centres.

Employers become 'autism-confident' through the training and support provided by the charity. Every manager receives basic autism awareness training to support them during the programme.

Thomas Kingston, Youth Patron at Ambitious about Autism, who took part in the Department of Work and Pensions pilot in July 2015, said:

> Throughout the two-week placement, I found that my health had improved. My anxiety was reduced, because I had a stable routine and I felt like I had accomplished something. I also feel like I've had a massive boost in self-confidence.[54]

The programme is gaining momentum and is being recognised for its success and innovation. The charity, together with the Civil Service, were nominated and won the Extending Reach award at the RIDI (Recruitment Industry Disability Initiative) Awards in the summer of 2017. The charity is currently working to extend this pro-gramme to more government departments and corporate organisations with the aim of supporting even more young people with autism into work.

Kevin Filby, Deputy Director of Service Development at Ambitious about Autism, said:

> Young people with autism have many of the same hopes and aspirations as everyone else. They want to be part of their community and, for many young people, this means employment and the chance to make a positive contribution to their society. As the Autism Exchange Programme has clearly demonstrated, with the right support, planning and opportunities from employers, young people with autism can learn, achieve and thrive. Evidence shows that with just a little support, enormous benefits can be gained by bringing young people with autism into the workplace and employers would see the positive impacts to their bottom line. It is in all of our

interests to work together to give young people with autism a chance to achieve what so many of us take for granted: having a job.[55]

Care Trade

CARE TRADE runs the Autism Project at Guy's and St Thomas' Hospitals in London. This project is a full-time, 36-week employability programme for young people on the autism spectrum who would like to work but need more confidence, support and experience to start applying for their first job. Students are given real work experience placements within Guy's and St Thomas' Hospitals four days a week, and they attend a classroom one day a week where they are taught valuable employability skills.

Care Trade began in 2010 with an evaluation of Project Search, the above-mentioned internship programme. Care Trade led one of these internships. It went on to develop its own autism-specific supported internship, The Autism Project, to help young people with autism to become work-ready and then proceeded to develop Employment Opportunities, a shorter programme to help people become independent job seekers and to secure the paid employment of their choice.

The Autism Project is a full-time, two-year employment programme for young people on the autism spectrum who would like work but need more confidence, support, skills and experience. The programme uses a module-based learning system so that students can start at the beginning of any term and can progress at a pace that best meets their individual needs. All students follow the supported internship curriculum for their first term and typically students will spend three terms (their first year) following this: they will learn within real work experience placements at either Guy's or St. Thomas' Hospitals four days a week, supported by workplace mentors and specialist job coaches, and attend class once a week, where they learn valuable employability and independent living skills and work towards City & Guilds qualifications. The objective is for young people to become 'work-ready' and to have gained a reference from their workplace. Students progress to the Year Two curriculum once 'work-ready', typically in Term 4, where the focus is on greater independence in the workplace (with a wider range of employers). Students are supported to develop their interview and communication skills and actively to seek and gain paid employment, a paid apprenticeship or further vocational training of their choice.

Since it was established in 2010, Care Trade has benefited more than 74 Londoners with autism. Around 20 of these young people have completed both The Autism Project and Employment Opportunities and of these, over 55 per cent gained sustained paid employment of their choice.

Care Trade's development director, Judith Kerem, has worked in the field of autism since 1998, with both children and adults at Treehouse School (now part of Ambitious about Autism), the National Autistic Society and the Autism Education Trust.

Mi.Life Limited

MI.LIFE LIMITED is another scheme providing training, consultancy and project management for those who help adults and young people with autism and other disabilities to find solutions allowing them to meet their full potential.

Mi.Life's managing director, Andrew Billings, has over 20 years' experience in supported employment working with people with autism and learning disabilities and training within both the private and public sectors. He works with SEN educational providers and local authorities and supports individuals and families through the process of obtaining paid employment and independence in natural settings.

One of those people with autism helped into employment by Mi.Life says:

> I had no clear idea on the type of work [I wanted to do] or whether I had good skills to get a job. But I did want to get a paid job. My job coach got to know me at school and home. We worked on my travel skills to youth club and school. Finding me a holiday job, my job coach supported me on my travel and at work, until I was OK on my own. This was in the summer for five weeks in admin support for the local council. It was my first paid job. From my profile, my job coach saw I had excellent understanding and memory for numbers. With this knowledge, my job coach looked at jobs at the local hospital. So in my last year of school, I joined the supported internship programme in the outpatients department, where my job involved collating patient files, data recording and filing patient records away in a very large storage room ... I had this job for about three years. The hospital went through a few changes and my job ended. I got in touch with my job coach; we met and discussed new jobs. After a few months, we found another job. It is as an administration assistant at a school.[56]

Another autistic job seeker was eased into self-employment by Mi.Life:

> I always like to draw and make storyboards. At my end-of-school review, I drew pictures of the meeting. A person from the supported employment team came up with the idea of my own business: maybe I could use my drawing skills to explain other meetings that were in words for people who needed easy-to-read information? After some research by my job coach, we had a talk about me being my own boss. With my Dad and the job coach, we set up my own graphic facilitation business with support. Inspired Animations now translates the written word into pictures enabling those who cannot read very well to understand information.[57]

Little Gate Farm

The impressive LITTLE GATE FARM near Rye has featured elsewhere in this book. It has so far found work for 20 people on the autism spectrum in local companies. Among its many achievements is the Little Gate Farm Charcoal social enterprise. As the farm points out, the vast majority of charcoal consumed in the UK is imported from countries such as Brazil and Namibia and it is frequently of poor quality, requiring chemical lighting fluids to get it to burn. Only a small percentage of Britain's coppice woodlands are properly managed, but the reinstatement of the Little Gate Farm coppice cycle — meaning cutting different areas of the woodland or 'cants' in different years and then allowing them to regrow — is having many ecological benefits. Moreover, the charcoal will be produced as part of a social enterprise programme, providing employment opportunities for adults with autism.

❖ CASE STUDIES

- ANGELA DELLOW
- PATRICK BIRMINGHAM
- DAVID CHEGWIDDEN

ANGELA DELLOW, 22, has been working in an Italian restaurant in Bexhill for the past three years. She has learned to make tiramisu a systematic way, so that every single dessert meets the same exacting standard. Although she has autism, both the restaurant's owners and its customers have high expectations. Indeed, Angela produces perfect desserts, and this year the staff at the Trattoria told Little Gate Farm that in the 10 years they have been open, no one makes the tiramisu as well as Angela does, not even the pastry chef!

Angela enjoys a good relationship with colleagues and no longer needs the support of her job coach, although Little Gate staff often visit the restaurant to see how she is getting on.

Figure 26.4 Angela Dellow displaying her justly celebrated tiramisu
Source: Georgie Scott

This is Angela's first job. It is also the first time that this employer has hired an adult with autism. 'Changing employer attitudes to learning disability is an important part of what we do,' says Little Gate.[58]

PATRICK BIRMINGHAM, a 21-year-old man with autism has attended a mainstream school and was awarded a Merit in Mechanical Engineering at Sussex Coast College. He recently started work at the Source Skate Park in Hastings but he also has a paid job at Little Gate Farm, managing the charcoal retort and charcoal production. He works independently and can be relied on to operate the charcoal retort to a high standard. He is responsible for making enough charcoal to fulfil the orders generated by his colleague, Emma. In the long term, Patrick would like to be able to use his knowledge of engineering, and is sensibly gaining valuable paid work experience.[59]

DAVID CHEGWIDDEN, 34, came to Little Gate Farm in 2016. He is autistic and had never been in paid employment but had a strong desire to work. He is bright and very able but finds social interaction challenging at times, and works hard to manage his own stress levels.

David was offered a data entry job in a highly pressured tax office and, with the support of his job coach, he excelled for the first six months and enjoyed the challenges of the work. The senior managers at the tax firm were very impressed with him and wanted him to go full-time. David's hours were indeed increased and his role expanded but, as Little Gate itself concedes, even with the support of a job coach, this was, in hindsight, a mistake: after three months, it was decided that the role was not right for David and he is no longer working at the tax firm. According to Little Gate, David's confidence was knocked initially but he immediately wanted to find another job.

> The lesson for us was that the staff at the tax office were too busy to take up our offer of autism training, the environment was too pressured to be supportive, and the natural supports kept changing as staff came and went,

says Little Gate. 'Despite this setback, David is committed to finding another job and we will help him find one. He will be an asset to any business.'[60]

Autism Centre for Research on Employment (ACRE)

The AUTISM CENTRE FOR RESEARCH ON EMPLOYMENT (ACRE), formerly the Autism Centre for Employment, is run by Dr Beatriz López at the University of Portsmouth's Department of Psychology. ACRE was developed, first of all, to address the gap in provision for autistic adults in terms of employment and, second, to facilitate job retention by developing tools to support employers in the process of making work adaptations tailored to their employees with autism. The National Autistic Society honoured it with its award for Outstanding Adult Services in 2016.

Figure 26.5 Dr Beatriz López, of the University of Portsmouth, director of the Autism Centre for Research on Employment

ACRE's proclaimed aim is 'to empower and support autistic people to help them realise their full employment potential'. It believes that autistic people have a right to contribute to society and that support for autistic adults needs to be tailored to their individual strengths and needs.

The centre offers a comprehensive assessment service to autistic people in employment or actively seeking employment. The assessment tools have been developed by the ACRE team specifically for work settings. The Individual Employment Profile report resulting from the assessment process offers information about the individual profile of the autistic individual and also offers specific recommendations to employers regarding strengths and adaptations required in the workplace.

ACRE also provides specialist training for professionals from employment agencies, local authorities and charitable organisations, as well as person-centred training to employers with the aim of creating a supportive and productive working environment and helping to overcome any potential challenges which may arise in the initial stages of employment.

Its current research project aims to identify the factors which may influence employment prospects in autistic undergraduate students. Specifically, the study will explore how the cognitive profile associated with autism links to factors known to enhance employment success so the centre can develop employability workshops tailored to students with autism. This project is a collaboration between Portsmouth Business School and the University of Portsmouth's Department of Psychology.

Another of ACRE's projects aims to open the pathway to employment for autistic job seekers and ensure that Hampshire is a leader for much-needed change in the area of employment support for autistic adults. The programme's focus is to inform, inspire and connect local employers, organisations who provide volunteer opportunities and training, employment agencies (providers) and autistic job seekers.

The SPACE Initiative

The newly formed Glyn Hopkin Charitable Foundation has teamed up with a British autism charity, Sycamore Trust UK, to help people from Barking and Dagenham, Redbridge and Havering into long-term employment with local businesses.

THE SPACE INITIATIVE – which stands for Supporting People with Autism into Continued Employment – offers support to employers to help them sustain full-time job placements for young people. It also offers help with job searches and interview preparation and provides a personal helpline to offer continuing guidance for people once they are employed. The scheme was officially launched at the House of Commons in 2017 and is set to expand across neighbouring London boroughs in the future.

Sycamore Trust UK's chief executive officer, Chris Gillbanks, welcomed the programme's launch and said:

> We know there are many young people who are desperate to prove that they are talented and loyal workers. The funding and support from the Glyn Hopkin Charitable Foundation will enable us to change lives through the SPACE programme by delivering a much-needed service to local people.[61]

For his part, Glyn Hopkin, who owns a series of car dealerships bearing his name as well as being director of Dagenham and Redbridge Football Club, said:

> As chairman of a local business that employs hundreds of people, I recognised vacancies could more readily be taken on by people with autism if more guidance and support was offered to potential employers. Since the programme was launched, we have helped individuals with autism secure positions across the Glyn Hopkin motor retail business, and we look forward to welcoming many more young people into our company as the programme develops.[62]

ASPIeRATIONS

ASPIeRATIONS was founded by Laurel Herman with the aim of easing people with Asperger's syndrome into the workplace It has received high levels of interest from potential employers – JPMorgan, National Grid, BP, BAESystems, Co-op, EY etc. – although the recruitment strand of ASPIeRATIONS was due to launch only in October 2017.

The ASPIeRATIONS Recruitment Workgroup consists of professionals in recruitment, human resources, employment law, autism, etc. to ensure it is responsible, robust and using best practice. It has already placed two candidates into employment: Jonathan Silver, at Hyperion, and Jonty Reid, at Royal Mail.

❖ **CASE STUDIES**

- JONATHAN SILVER
- JONTY REID

JONATHAN SILVER, a graduate of Brunel University, was taken on by Hyperion Insurance Group in July 2016, initially on a three-month contract. He has since been made a permanent employee, working on the IT service desk. Hyperion Insurance Group has been working closely with ASPIeRATIONS to offer individuals on the high end of the Autistic Spectrum opportunities within the IT Service desk.

Jonathan heard about ASPIeRATIONS through the Positive Presence website and emailed the team. He was then interviewed by Skype on two occasions.

> This gave me a chance to explain my disability, demonstrate my interest in the scheme and explain my skill set and IT knowledge through previous work experience. The team then sent me two vacancies at a city-based insurance company which matched my interest. I wrote a letter of application for a second-line service desk role with the company,

he said.[63] He felt very relaxed at the interview at Hyperion, which was very informal.

> I could be myself and this allowed me to perform better than I would usually perform in an interview. I was given plenty of time to expand upon my application and demonstrate my technical knowledge by giving examples. In a normal interview setting, someone on the autistic spectrum can often feel nervous and may stumble on words in this type of setting.[64]

ASPIeRATIONS offered Jonathan comprehensive written instructions and accompanying material before the interview to ease any anxiety and he then met face-to-face with the recruiting consultant, who gave him interview tips and allowed him to practise sample interview questions.

He says Hyperion has been very helpful in the workplace: 'My manager has met with me regularly to discuss best practices – for example, working style – and has connected me with other colleagues to get me exposure to many other live projects in our IT department.' One of the biggest challenges Jonathan has encountered is knowing whom to approach with a question and also the ability to assess the urgency of the issue.

His manager, Dave Dickson, is pleased with the quality of his work. One email read:

> As is always the case with your work, the document is very well-constructed and flows easily when reading through it. You should be very proud of your achievements in your first year at Hyperion. You have

impressed a number of our key stakeholders throughout the business and this carries so much weight, especially when we are going through the challenges of an aggressive change and improvements programme. I expect that this next year will see you continue to make a positive difference to IT's business contribution.[65]

JONATHAN (JONTY) REID, a law undergraduate at the University of Kent, was recruited by Royal Mail for their summer internship scheme. Darren Heilig, of Royal Mail has said:

Jonathan's energy and enthusiasm was clear; that makes hosting all the more engaging. He completed some legal tasks well and showed a real desire to learn more. Jonathan's Asperger's syndrome wasn't evident; we were particularly focused on making clear to Jonathan the plans for each day in advance, but this is something we try to do for all candidates in any case. There didn't seem to be any impediment to Jonathan's participation in the scheme; not only that, but it was great to have Jonathan around; a very lively, dynamic character ... From a disability point of view, we did not feel that we needed to make any particular adjustments for Jonathan and some participants commented that if they had not been informed of the Asperger's element, they would have been none the wiser.

Jonty himself calls his internship with Royal Mail

a truly rewarding experience ... I was shown the new and unfamiliar environment of an in-house setting, where I was given the opportunity to get to know the inner workings of the company and how aspects like competition law and employment law played their part in a commercial setting ... [Later], I was shown the entire archive for Royal Mail and its services, which was mind-blowing, before being passed on to a junior lawyer working within the administrative section and another lawyer working within the anti-bribery department who helped me work through my CV and learn about the core values of RM's anti-bribery and fair competition policy. Overall, it was a lovely and enlightening experience and I more than received the opportunity to test the limits of my Asperger's, as well as explore how it would impact my working life in a legal environment.[66]

ASpire

ASPIRE is a small voluntary sector project in Brighton and Hove, Sussex, run by Sarah Hendrickx, offering training to organisations and long-term mentoring in life skills for adults with Asperger's syndrome and high-functioning autism. ASpire encourages voluntary work as a first step into employment. An independent evaluation in 2007 showed that half of those who used its service reported improvements in practical areas, including employment.

Figure 26.6 Autistic workers cheerfully employed at Harry Specters

Harry Specters

HARRY SPECTERS is an award-winning chocolate company based in Ely, Cambridgeshire, which offers free work experience, training and employment opportunities to young people on the autism spectrum who are either completing, or have just left, full-time education. The company was launched by Shaz and Mona Shah after their son, Ash, was diagnosed with autism. While visiting a chocolate shop on a holiday in Scotland in 2011, Mona discovered a perfect way of combining her passion for creating positive change for people with autism with her love for chocolate. Harry Specters was born a year later (Shaz Shah told me that his son came up with the name.)[67]

The company is dedicated to crafting the most delicious chocolates, while creating employment for young people with autism, involving them in every aspect of the business, from making and packaging the products to administration, design and photography. Every lovingly hand-crafted bar of chocolate helps improve the lives of people with autism. In the three years the firm has been going, it has worked with 100 students from a local special needs school and provided work experience to 40 students. There are both part-time and contract workers helping in the production and packaging of chocolates, photography and graphic design, and back office work.

Harry Specters first started out in the couple's kitchen but now operates a full-scale production line supplying beautiful bespoke chocolate gifts directly to corporate groups such as BT, PwC, Lloyds Bank, Santander, Microsoft and Hogan Lovells. Over the next year, the company plans to supply hotels, as well as Waitrose and other premium stores, as well as have a factory outlet. People buy from them not only because they offer high-quality products and excellent customer service, but because they want to support the company in its social cause. (As a social enterprise, Harry

Specters has committed 60 per cent of its profits to improving the lives of people with autism.) When the company was launched, it received considerable support from the School for Social Entrepreneurs (SSE) programme.

Shaz Shah said:

> We have a son with autism and when he was 12 we started to get worried about what he would do when he grows up, so then we started looking at some of the statistics and what we found was that 85 per cent of teenage adults with autism in the UK are unemployed and are desperate to work, so that got us a bit more worried. We wanted to open up something with people with autism but we were not sure exactly what we would need.
>
> We went on a family holiday to Scotland and my wife Mona was in love with chocolate. We went to that shop, a highland chocolatier called the Inverness. It was a very beautiful shop ... Mona went on a course after the holiday and she had an epiphany: namely, that chocolate making is a structured and routine work, so something suitable for people with autism.[68]

Mona Shah says that government support plays an important role in scaling the business's social impact: 'We welcome the possibility that more funds could be unlocked to help make a difference to the work we do in creating employment for young adults with autism.'[69]

Harry Specters – which has provided training and work experience to 183 autistic people – has already won more than 22 awards, including from the Guild of Fine Food and the Academy of Chocolate. In December 2017, it was named one of the 16 'most promising microenterprises in the UK'.

The Vault

THE VAULT – the former River's Edge Hotel in Gateshead, north-east England – is a unique enterprise. However, special mention must also go to the excellent Foxes Academy specialist catering college and training hotel for young adults with learning disabilities at the other end of the UK, in Minehead, Somerset. Foxes also runs the Cream Café in the town. (Among Foxes' many success stories is Patrick, a young autistic man who works two days a week at Tesco as a kitchen assistant and also washes up and cleans at the charity, Age UK.) Owned and operated by the St. Camillus Care Group, The Vault's mission is to hire people on the autism spectrum as well as others with learning disabilities. These paid positions will focus on the different hospitality services offered by the hotel, including computer literacy, art, design and those skills needed to work in a restaurant.

Each employee receives comprehensive training and support. The aim is to train up to 28 employees through the programme each year. Rooms at The Vault are currently being revamped to accommodate the needs of those on the spectrum. The Vault is open to visitors who wish to eat at the establishment's American-themed diner, designed by people with autism, or visit their entertainment facilities – both of which make accommodations for people with special needs.

The £2 million project was granted planning permission in August 2016. The current group of trainees has been learning a variety of skills, from manning the reception to preparing food and serving in the hotel's diner. A statement said 10 of the trainees would be working at the hotel in jobs which include bar staff, kitchen, reception and as general assistants, while a further three have earned posts with Key Developments, the company which is currently carrying out the refurbishment on the property.

Holly Kelleher, centre manager at The Vault, said:

> This is exactly what we are here to do. The trainees are getting valuable training and experience to ensure that they are eventually able to get paid employment in the hospitality industry and to prove they are a real asset to any workforce. We are delighted that we have been able to offer so many of them a proper job which will give them even more experience which can only help them going forward.[70]

The St Camillus Care Group is also looking at a number of other sites to expand its operation which will offer a range of traineeships and internships for 18- to 24-year-olds with a range of learning difficulties.

The cornerstone of The Vault's mission is to offer jobs to people on the autism spectrum as well as others with learning disabilities. 'Our overall goal is to have potential employees assessed so that we are able to meet their employability needs,' says Darren Wilson, The Vault's director of housing, health and care.[71] These paid positions will focus on the different hospitality services offered by the hotel, including computer literacy, art, design and those skills required to work in a restaurant.

Prior's Court Bakery

In 2017, PRIOR'S COURT School in Thatcham, Berkshire, announced ambitious plans to launch a commercial, self-sustaining BAKERY providing real employment opportunities for young people with severe autism.

The project – the first of its kind in the UK – will be located on the school site and will be led by a Master Baker, Steve Fudge, with a workforce of Prior's Court young people. Fudge is a trained confectioner with a passion for biscuits, having been part of the successful family bakery, Thomas J. Fudge.

Prior's Court, which was founded by Dame Stephanie Shirley in 1999, has always had a commitment to building work skills and currently 75 per cent of its 16–25 age group have at least one work placement onsite or offsite with the support of the local community.

Mike Robinson, Chief Executive of Prior's Court, said:

> We work to unlock the potential of our young people by being ambitious in our aims and in the strategies we use to ensure they achieve in every area of their lives, but this project is our most ambitious yet. Through the bakery, we will provide real jobs and build skills for life and we hope this will enable us to increase the number of people with autism in employment. We have been in consultation with experts in the baking industry to research not just the financial viability but also the suitability of the baking processes to the strengths, interests and needs of young people with autism. The bakery can accommodate a wide range of skills. Our young people respond positively to practical, routine tasks and they find baking and food preparation motivating and rewarding.[72]

According to Prior's Court, the bakery will use its unique combination of specialist knowledge and best practice in both the baking and autism fields to establish a structured, autism-friendly environment producing high-quality, organic baked produce. Initially for sale in the local community, the charity's aim is to go beyond this with bread on the shelves of national supermarkets and a model that can be replicated.

'We want to create a team of bakers with real skills and a product that tastes great,' said Robinson. 'We want to challenge perceptions and raise the bar for autism employment.'[73]

SCOTLAND

The 2009 Autism Act does not apply in Scotland. A number of initiatives have sprung up there over the past few years to encourage people on the autism spectrum into work.

IWork4Me

Edinburgh-based IWORK4ME promotes supported self-employment for people on the autism spectrum. Among their success stories is a new radio station run by and for people with autism in Edinburgh and a woman snake-breeder (who works part-time as a lifeguard). Sue Hope, IWork4Me's development manager, told me that sustainability (long-term funding) was a major problem, as it is in so many of these admirable projects across the UK.[74]

However, money is not the main driver for most of her clients. 'They want to achieve a level of financial independence they can cope with, but more than that, they want to contribute meaningfully to society,' Hope told me.[75] The other self-employment business ideas IWork4Me has supported in Edinburgh, Ayrshire, Perth and Stirling include translators, soap manufacturers, jewellers, a genealogist, photographers and ceramicists.

IWork4Me was founded in 2009 in response to research findings recommending the creation of a charity to focus on supporting people with autism to consider self-employment as a realistic and achievable employment solution. The model of self-employment support that IWork4Me has developed is entirely unique. All clients receive personally tailored support within their individual business advice sessions and are then encouraged to move forward at their own pace. Where appropriate, the organisation initiates contact between service users to offer peer-to-peer support. Through its most recent scheme, Autism Voices, they facilitate paid opportunities for self-employed people with autism to share their experiences and insights into autism through a wide range of media, including the spoken word, art, photography and writing. This initiative grew out of a recognised need for more people with autism to contribute to conferences and training events, providing a fresh insight into the impact of autism.

IWork4Me is convinced that everyone with autism has the potential to be an effective, contributing and happily productive member of society but that many need support to achieve the outcome that is right for them. As a direct result of its support, 50 per cent of individuals have become registered as self-employed, which is the organisation's key performance indicator.

Although based in Edinburgh, it has supported individuals from Ayrshire, Perth, and Stirling as well as throughout Edinburgh and the Lothian regions. Working within a small budget, with grants from the Scottish Government, National Lottery and a couple of trust funds, IWork4Me delivers its unique service through two part-time employees who are supported by a committed small group of volunteers and volunteer trustees. The charity says its long-term objective is to influence the providers of generic self-employment advice to be able, as far as possible, to meet the needs of people with autism.

Sue Hope also runs her own consultancy. One of her clients – Scottish Outdoor Education Centres (SOEC) – has piloted a programme in partnership with the Lothian Autistic Society designed to use the outdoors both as a therapeutic learning environment to increase life skills such as resilience, communication skills, etc., and also to enhance 'transition to employment' skills. Its twin objectives are: to explore the therapeutic value of the outdoors and to develop the qualities and skills to enhance employability.

❖ CASE STUDY

- FIONA

FIONA, a ceramicist and mosaicist, 47, approached IWork4Me on completion of her artist apprenticeship at a gallery in Edinburgh. She is highly articulate and held down a career in law prior to her Asperger's syndrome diagnosis. When the IWork4Me team first met her, she was particularly anxious about what the future held. Fiona suffers from a number of health issues, many relating to anxiety, and the IWork4Me team worked with Fiona in taking small manageable steps in considering the best way forward.

Fiona wished to sell her original ceramic and mosaic work but had, in the past, suffered a sense of loss following sales. This loss caused her considerable anxiety and made her unsure how to proceed with her plans. By taking time and listening to her concerns and aspirations, the IWork4Me team were able to suggest that, as Fiona retained the rights to the images of past completed and sold works, these images could form the basis of a range of merchandise (greetings cards, coasters, mugs, prints, etc.) which she might sell to retail outlets and online via the ETSY e-commerce shopping portal. This suggestion appealed to Fiona as she considered it a means to keep in touch with past artworks and keep them 'alive' for her.

Together, the team worked with Fiona to discuss the most logical way to progress her plans. Once she had decided on her range, the team supported her to research and compare manufacturers and ultimately negotiate supply contracts. Successful sales resulted in a growth in confidence and self-belief which, in turn, led to a period of refreshed creativity; her creativity had hitherto been stagnant for a number of months. Fiona chose to further broaden her range of crafting skills by taking up new classes.

Helping her draw up and observe an expenditure budget and timeline meant she was able to launch her range of merchandise in time for Christmas

2015. With each successful decision, Fiona's confidence improved, as did her general mood and demeanour which the team logged at each meeting. Her new-found self-confidence and belief in her products enabled Fiona to take on the major task of setting up sales pitches with potential retail outlets. The team helped with preparation for these meetings and advised on presentation skills and how to word appropriate business emails for each step of the sales process. Successfully organised business meetings led to Fiona managing her anxiety and experimenting with 'door-stepping' sales techniques – that is, making spontaneous sales calls to potential outlets and subsequently building relationships with shop-owners and learning about supply chains. This proved to be a most imaginative solution.

Fiona says:

> IWork4Me has been invaluable to me. Sue and Bryce [Potter] are incredibly knowledgeable and helpful and it's been great to have their support with trying to establish a name and a market for my artwork. This can otherwise be a lonely and challenging endeavour. It was great having them in the background, encouraging me and always pointing me in the right direction.[76]

IntoWork

Also in Scotland, INTOWORK is a specialised employment support service for disabled job seekers, including those with autism, across Edinburgh, and East- and Mid-Lothian. The organisation works with employers, organising autism awareness training.

IntoWork's employment advisers work closely with local employers to help them recruit and retain people with disabilities. They also provide advice and practical assistance with enhancing employers' recruitment practices to make them accessible to more people with disabilities, and helping them to adjust the interview process to ensure disabled people are given the best possible chance to shine. The company offers specific disability awareness training for staff and advises on appropriate workplace adjustments to ensure that an employee on the autism spectrum enjoys a smooth transition into the workplace.

Moving Forward

Still in Scotland, The National Autistic Society Scotland's MOVING FORWARD project is helping 16- to 24-year-olds with autism in Glasgow to develop skills for the workplace and find employment, thanks to funding from the Scottish government's Cashback for Communities initiative.

> Jim Doherty, project manager at The National Autistic Society Scotland, said: We know that autistic young people can have difficulty finding work because of challenges they experience around social interaction and the fact that many employers still have negative perceptions of autism. [Our project] helps them to build self-esteem and practical skills through a combination of one-to-one mentoring, group work, and placements with employers who understand autism.[77]

In a recent survey, 80 per cent of young people involved in the Moving Forward project stated they felt more confident about their future as a result of taking part. And an impressive 91 per cent of employers said that they felt more confident about employing autistic people as a result of engaging with the project and learning about the condition.

NORTHERN IRELAND

Specialisterne NI

SPECIALISTERNE NI is a not-for-private-profit, community interest company which opened in 2014 as the local expression of the Specialisterne Foundation.

Its chief executive, Sharon Didrichsen, told me that each country where Specialisterne is based encounters country-specific challenges and opportunities. For example, in Northern Ireland autistic adults travel to the Specialisterne offices in Belfast from across Northern Ireland, and transport makes this feasible. Country specific challenges include the current uncertainty regarding Stormont, and Brexit, which can limit or place uncertainty over available funding streams.[78]

Over the past year, Specialisterne NI has trained 600 managers in 'social communication difference'. While referring to autism, the broader term of social communication difference is used to include those who may find communication at work challenging and do not have – or choose not to pursue – a diagnosis. Didrichsen emphasises:

> out of the 400 people on the spectrum on Specialisterne NI's register, the unifying feature is that so many really want to work. A strong work ethic is particularly appreciated in Northern Ireland. We work across sectors, as talent does not fit into stereotypes. Our strategy is 'bottom-up', supporting autistic people to utilise their strengths to achieve the things they want. We want autistic people to develop autistic strategies, and support our clients to become confident autistic people. Autistic people can possess amazing originality, and

Figure 26.7 Sharon Didrichsen, chief executive of Specialisterne NI

when matched to a job that utilises an individual's skills, an autistic employee can really flourish. One person, for example, who had a lovely steady approach to work, was referred to by his employer as being like a drum – not missing a beat in the workplace. This has led to the employee implementing new business improvements across the UK. Another person on the spectrum loves innovation, and has channelled this love into different workstreams and opportunities in the workplace.[79]

Didrichsen has established the CR8 programme, designed to exploit creativity to the full. 'If people want to work in the areas of make-up artists, or in film direction, animation, travel writing, we support the person on the spectrum and the mentor. It's all about taking away the middleman between employee and employer.'[80]

Stepping Stones NI

STEPPING STONES NI is a social enterprise organisation which permits people with learning difficulties and disabilities the opportunity to access accredited training and employment. The project is part-funded through the Northern Ireland European Social Fund Programme 2014–2020 and the Department for the Economy.

Stepping Stones NI runs a number of social enterprises, including four coffee shops, a bespoke wedding stationery business and a Guild-commended picture framing business. The organisation won Social Enterprise of the Year at the 2016 Lisburn and Castlereagh City Business Awards and its Chief Officer, Paula Jennings, was named Business Person of the Year.

In April 2017, it launched a new campaign to encourage people with autism in the province to seek paid employment and realise their full potential in the workplace. 'We have a very dedicated team that works with each individual at their own pace,' said Ciara Brennan, from the organisation. 'So it's very important that we understand everyone's individual needs and look at what their goals and dreams are for a job.'[81]

❖ CASE STUDY

• STEPHEN GILLESPIE

STEPHEN GILLESPIE, 32, who was diagnosed with autism as a young boy, works for Pink Elephant Cards in Lisburn producing bespoke wedding stationery. He has also been doing a paid job (four days a week) for the Danish company, Danske Bank, where he started work six years earlier after joining Stepping Stones NI.

'It feels pretty rewarding,' said Stephen. 'It has helped me build my confidence and my independence.' He added that he hoped to encourage others to realise that, although entering the world of work and holding down a job could be daunting, it had certainly been worth it.[82]

WALES

Engage to Change

Around a thousand young people in Wales with a learning disability or autism are to be offered work placements as part of a $10 million project, ENGAGE TO CHANGE, which will help participants with one-on-one job coaching, job matching and interview training. It was announced in 2017 that the project had received a grant from the Big Lottery Fund, in partnership with the Welsh government.

Engage to Change says that it will work with the 1,000 autistic youths aged 16–25 to help them to develop their work skills through paid work placements lasting 6–12 months with 800 employers across Wales.

❖ **CASE STUDY**

• JORDAN

After finishing school, JORDAN moved with his family from Essex to Newport to be closer to his extended family. After living in Newport for about a year, he decided that he wanted to find work. Engage to Change has supported Jordan since then, and in January 2017, he started work in a community centre in Newport called the Share Centre.

Jordan works for eight hours over two days per week, and his main tasks are to open up the centre in the morning and prepare refreshments for students and visitors to the centre. He also has various administration tasks, including updating the diary with any room bookings, and dealing with invoicing.

At the beginning of the placement, Engage to Change supported Jordan in completing work tasks. He needed assistance to remember in which order to do tasks and certain details of the tasks set. He required a great deal of support to interact with other members of staff in the workplace, as he was initially very shy. After a few weeks of job coaching, new tasks such as invoicing and filing were added, which demanded extended job training.

Jordan says that his favourite part of the job is the invoicing, as it is something over which he has a sense of control and command, and it is also a transferable skill, which can be of great benefit to the Share Centre. Moreover, as other members of Jordan's family do jobs that involve invoicing, he feels that this gives him something in common with them, work-wise. Jordan feels that this placement has taught him to have confidence in his own abilities, to communicate with various people comfortably, and to use SAGE accounting software and handle the invoicing process.

Jordan gets on very well with the staff at the Share Centre and with the trustees of the organisation when he sees them. After working at the centre for a few months, he now says that he feels far more confident and is able to interact well with visitors. He is able to answer most questions put to him and is comfortable in seeking assistance when this is required. Jordan is now considered part of the team.

His family are delighted with the progress he has made. They have noticed that he has gained confidence in many areas of life, including day-to-day tasks like going shopping and catching the bus. They say that, whereas Jordan would never have previously initiated a conversation, he is now approaching others and starting conversations of his own accord. Since beginning work on the Engage to Change project, he has also stopped exhibiting signs of depression. His stress levels have also greatly diminished, if not disappeared.

Jordan would like to continue developing his skills and confidence. He has recently started to drive again and is due to take part in a production with his drama group. In time, Jordan would like to look for full-time work.[83]

Do-IT Solutions

Professor Amanda Kirby, who has a chair at the University of South Wales and is the CEO of DO-IT SOLUTIONS, has developed an online workplace assessment package aimed at unlocking the hidden talents in an employee's work and provide guidance for both employee and employer.

'The tool provides a means of asking questions in a format that suits the end user and their style, as well as being consistent in the information gathered,' Kirby told me.

We work with people right across the autism spectrum, including those who are non-verbal. And we deal with a whole variety of jobs. All people have some strengths and we want to harness these. Once we can understand this we can help them to maximise their skills and minimise challenges. Do not close down opportunities: open them up through their motivation and interests.[84]

Notes

1   Viola Sommer in conversation with the author, 19 July 2017.
2   David Perkins in conversation with the author, 22 June 2016.
3   Ibid.
4   Ibid.
5   See: http://enablemagazine.co.uk/wirral-autistic-society-achieves-national-recognition-for-helping-autistic-people-into-work/ (accessed 13 February 2014.
6   Ibid.
7   John Phillipson in conversation with the author, 19 May 2016.
8   Ibid.
9   Ibid.
10 Ibid.
11 The Northern Echo, 24 August 2016.
12 Ibid.
13 Ibid.
14 Ibid.
15 Information supplied by Autism Plus.

16   Philip Bartey in conversation with the author, 12 July 2017.
17   Ibid.
18   Information supplied by Autism Plus.
19   Ibid.
20   Information supplied by Specialist Autism Services.
21   Ibid.
22   Ibid.
23   Ibid.
24   Ibid.
25   Ibid.
26   Ibid.
27   Ibid.
28   See: https://hireserve.com/benefits-employing-disabled-people (accessed 24 November 2015).
29   Jane Hatton in conversation with the author, 18 August 2017.
30   Ibid.
31   Ibid.
32   Ibid.
33   Ibid.
34   Kathy Erangey in conversation with the author, 25 May 2016.
35   Ibid.
36   Autism and Asperger's Conference, Royal College of Psychiatrists, London, 13 September 2016.
37   Ibid.
38   Ibid.
39   Tilus Clark in communication with the author, 13 September 2017.
40   Information provided by Remploy.
41   Ibid.
42   Ibid.
43   Ibid.
44   Nick Llewellyn in conversation with the author, 11 August 2016.
45   Ibid.
46   Ibid.
47   Ibid.
48   Ibid.
49   *Hackney Gazette*, 4 December 2015.
50   Mark Williams in conversation with the author, 12 June 2017.
51   Ibid.
52   Sarah Ewans in conversation with the author, 18 April 2017.
53   Pino Frumento in conversation with the author, 18 April 2017.
54   Information supplied by Ambitious About Autism.
55   Ibid.
56   Information supplied by Mi.Life Limited.
57   Ibid.
58   Information supplied by Little Gate Farm.
59   Ibid.
60   Ibid.
61   *Barking and Dagenham Post*, 4 September 2017.
62   Ibid.
63   Information supplied by ASPIeRATIONS.
64   Ibid.
65   Ibid.
66   Ibid.
67   Shaz Shah in conversation with the author, 19 February 2016.
68   See: www.cambridge-news.co.uk/news/local-news/how-funding-boost-help-autistic-12719676 (accessed 9 March 2017).
69   Ibid.

70 See: www.hotelowner.co.uk/8669-uks-first-hotel-children-autism-hires-first-group-staff/ (accessed 22 March 2017).

71 See: www.upworthy.com/this-hotel-designed-for-people-with-autism-is-one-of-the-first-of-its-kind (accessed 16 September 2016).

72 See: www.priorscourt.org.uk/news/bakery-launch (accessed 27 April 2018).

73 Ibid.

74 Sue Hope in conversation with the author, 29 July 2016.

75 Ibid.

76 Information supplied by IWORK4ME.

77 See: www.glasgowlive.co.uk/news/glasgow-news/autistic-young-people-glasgow-offered-13035299 (accessed 27 April 2018).

78 Sharon Didrichsen in conversation with the author, 4 August 2017.

79 Ibid.

80 Ibid.

81 ITV News, 31 March 2017.

82 Ibid.

83 Information supplied by Engage to Change.

84 Amanda Kirby in conversation with the author, 23 June 2016.

Bibliography

Books

Attwood, T. (1998) *Asperger's Syndrome: A Guide for Parents and Professionals* (London: Jessica Kingsley).

Beardon, L. (ed.) (2017) *Bittersweet on the Autism Spectrum* (London: Jessica Kingsley).

Bergemann, R. A. (2014) *An Asperger's Guide to Entrepreneurship – Setting Up Your Own Business for Professionals with Autism Spectrum Disorder* (London: Jessica Kingsley).

Bissonnette, B. (2012) *The Complete Guide to Getting a Job for People with Asperger's Syndrome – Find the Right Career and Get Hired* (London: Jessica Kingsley).

Bissonnette, B. (2013) *Asperger's Syndrome Workplace Survival Guide – A Neurotypical's Secrets for Success* (London: Jessica Kingsley).

Bissonnette, B. (2014) *Helping Adults with Asperger's Syndrome Get & Stay Hired – Career Coaching Strategies for Professionals and Parents of Adults on the Autism Spectrum* (London: Jessica Kingsley).

Bogdashina, O. (2013) *Autism and Spirituality – Psyche, Self and Spirit in People on the Autism Spectrum* (London: Jessica Kingsley).

Bogdashina, O. (2016) *Sensory Perceptual Issues in Autism and Asperger Syndrome* (London: Jessica Kingsley).

Booth, J. (2016) *Autism Equality in the Workplace – Removing Barriers and Challenging Discrimination* (London: Jessica Kingsley).

Carley, M. J. (2016) *Unemployed on the Autism Spectrum – How to Cope Productively with the Effects of Unemployment and Jobhunt with Confidence* (London: Jessica Kingsley).

Edmonds, G. and Beardon, L. (eds) (2008) *Asperger Syndrome and Employment – Adults Speak Out about Asperger Syndrome* (London: Jessica Kingsley).

Fast, Y. (2004) *Employment for Individuals with Asperger Syndrome or Non-Verbal Learning Disability – Stories and Strategies* (London: Jessica Kingsley).

Feinstein, A. (2010) *A History of Autism: Conversations with the Pioneers* (Chichester: Wiley-Blackwell).

Gallup, S. (2017) *Making Friends at Work – Learning to Make Positive Choices in Social Situations for People with Autism* (London: Jessica Kingsley).

Grandin, T. (2008) *Developing Talents: Careers for Individuals with Asperger Syndrome and High-Functioning Autism* (Shawnee, OH: AAPC Publishing).

Grandin, T. and Moore, D. (2015) *The Loving Push – How Parents and Professionals Can Help Spectrum Kids Become Successful Adults* (Arlington, TX: Future Horizons).

Hearst, C. (ed.) (2015) *Being Autistic: Nine Adults Share Their Journey from Discovery to Acceptance* (Reading: Autangel).

Hendrickx, S. (2008) *Asperger Syndrome and Employment – What People with Asperger Syndrome Really Really Want* (London: Jessica Kingsley).

Jackson, L. (2016) *Sex, Drugs and Asperger's Syndrome – A User's Guide to Adulthood* (London: Jessica Kingsley).

James, L. (2017) *Odd Girl Out* (London: Bluebird).

Jansen, H. and Rombout, B. (2013) *AutiPower! Successful Living and Working with an Autism Spectrum Disorder* (London: Jessica Kingsley).

Leach, S. (2002) *A Supported Employment Workbook Using Individual Profiling and Job Matching* (London: Jessica Kingsley).

Lundine, V. and Smith, C. (2006) *Career Training and Personal Planning for Students with Autism Spectrum Disorders – Practical Resource for Schools* (London: Jessica Kingsley).

Maguire, R. (2014) *I Dream in Autism* (CreateSpace Independent Publishing Platform).

McManmon, M. P., Kolarik, J. and Ramsay, M. (2002) *Mploy – A Job Readiness Workbook – Career Skills Development for Young Adults on the Autism Spectrum and with Learning Difficulties* (London: Jessica Kingsley).

Meyer, R. N. (2000) *Asperger Syndrome Employment Workbook – An Employment Workbook for Adults with Asperger Syndrome* (London: Jessica Kingsley).

Murray, D. (ed.) (2006) *Coming Out Asperger – Diagnosis, Disclosure and Self-Confidence* (London: Jessica Kingsley).

Rigler, M., Rutherford, A. and Quinn, E. (2015) *Turning Skills and Strengths into Careers for Young Adults with Autism Spectrum Disorder – The BASICS College Curriculum* (London: Jessica Kingsley).

Rigler, M., Rutherford, A. and Quinn, E. (2016) *Developing Workplace Skills for Young Adults with Autism Spectrum Disorder – The BASICS College Curriculum* (London: Jessica Kingsley).

Robison, J. E. *Look Me in the Eye – My Life with Aspergers* (London: Ebury Press).

Santomauro, J. (ed.) *Autism All-Stars: How We Use Our Autism and Asperger Traits to Shine in Life* (London: Jessica Kingsley).

Saperstein, J. A. (2014) *Getting a Life with Asperger's – Lessons Learned on the Bumpy Road to Adulthood* (New York: Perigree).

Scheiner, M. and Bogden, J. (2017) *An Employer's Guide to Managing Professionals on the Autism Spectrum* (London: Jessica Kingsley).

Silberman, S. (2015) *Neurotribes – The Legacy of Autism and the Future of Neurodiversity* (London: Penguin Publishing Group).

Simone, R. (2010) *Asperger's on the Job* (Arlington, TX: Future Horizons).

Smith Myles, B. (2004) *The Hidden Curriculum – Practical Solutions for Understanding Unstated Rules in Social Situations* (Shawnee, OH: Autism Asperger Publishing Company).

Stanford, A. (2011) *Business for Aspies – 42 Best Practices for Using Asperger Syndrome Traits at Work Successfully* (London: Jessica Kingsley).

Steward, R. (2014) *The Independent Woman's Handbook for Super Safe Living on the Autistic Spectrum* (London: Jessica Kingsley).

Wehman, P. and Smith S. C. (2009) *Autism and the Transition to Adulthood: Success Beyond the Classroom* (Baltimore, MD: Brookes Publishing Company).

Documents

Allard, A. (2009) Transition to Adulthood: Inquiry into Transition to Adulthood for Young People with Autism. London: The National Autistic Society.

American Psychiatric Association (2013) Diagnostic and Statistical Manual of Mental Disorders (5th edn) (Washington DC: American Psychiatric Association).

Andrews, J. (undated) Autism and the Workplace: Common Myths and Untapped Talent.

Autism in Pink, 'Recognising Needs of Women with Autism'..(2014) EU Needs and Recommendations Lifelong Learning Programme.

Beardon, L. and Edmonds, G. (2007) ASPECT Consultancy Report: A National Report on the Needs of Adults with Asperger Syndrome. Sheffield: The Autism Centre, Sheffield Hallam University.

Booth, J. (2014) Autism in the Workplace. Report for the Trades Union Congress.

Case Management Society UK (2015) Working Together to Promote Excellence in Case Management.

Cockayne, A. and Warburton, L. (2016) An Investigation of Asperger Syndrome in the Employment Context. Conference paper, CIPD Applied Research Conference on The shifting landscape of work and working lives (Conference paper number: CIPD/ARC/2016/5).

Deweerdt, S. (2014) 'Autism characteristics differ by gender, studies find', posted on 27 March and available at https://spectrumnews.org/news/autism-characteristics-differ-by-gender-studies-find/ (accessed 14 May 2018).

Forsythe, L., Rahim, N. and Bell, L. (2008) Benefits and Employment Support Schemes to Meet the Needs of People with an Autistic Spectrum Disorder. London: National Audit Office.

Hendrie, D., Falkmer, M. and Falkmer, T. et al. (2016) Autism in the workplace: Maximising the Potential of Employees on the Autistic Spectrum. Curtin, Western Australia: Bankwest Curtin Economics Centre.

Iemmi, V., Knapp, M. and Ragan, I. (2017) The Autism Dividend: Reaping the Rewards of Better Investment, on behalf of the National Autism Project.

Kenyon, S. (2014) 'Autism in Pink: Qualitative Research Report', available at http://autisminpink.net (accessed 14 May 2018).

Loomes, R. (2016) Gender Differences in Children and Adolescents with High-functioning Autism Spectrum Disorders. Doctoral thesis, UCL (University College London).

López, B. and Keenan, L. (2015) Barriers to Employment in Autism: Future Challenges to Implementing the Adult Autism Strategy, Autism Research Network, First Edition.

National Audit Office (2009) Supporting People with Autism through Adulthood (London: National Audit Office).

National Autistic Society (2016) 'Too much information', available at www.autism.org.uk/get-involved/tmi.aspx (accessed 14 May 2018).

Shirley, Dame Stephanie (2016) 'The Issues and Challenges around Autism Employment', presentation to the North East Autism Society's 'Employment Futures' conference in Gateshead, UK, 16 September.

Standifer, S. (2011) 'Fact Sheet on Autism and Employment', Paper presented at Autism Works: National Conference on Autism and Employment, St. Louis, MO, available at www.autismhandbook.org/images/5/5d/AutismFactSheet2011.pdf (accessed 14 May 2018).

Tebbit, R. (undated) An Autoethnographic Inquiry Into My Experiences and Journey of Autism and Becoming a Counsellor.

Townsley, R., Robinson, C., Williams, V. et al. (2014) Employment and Young People with Autistic Spectrum Disorders: An Evidence Review (Cardiff: Welsh Government).

Wiles, D. 'Square Holes for Square Pegs: Current Practice in Employment and Autism'. Report for the Business Disability Forum, available at https://members.businessdisabilityforum.org.uk/media_manager/public/86/Resources/Square%20Pegs_Final_GF.PDF (accessed 14 May 2018).

Xu, Q., Samson Cheung, S. and Soares, N. (2015) LittleHelper: An Augmented Reality Glass Application to Assist Individuals with Autism in Job Interview. Proceedings of the Asia-Pacific Signal and Information Processing Association Annual Summit and Conference (APSIPA). 1276–1279.

Articles

Asperger, H. (1979) 'Problems of infantile autism', *Communication*, 13: 45–52.

Asperger, H. ([1944] 1991) 'Autistic psychopathy in childhood', in U. Frith (ed.), *Autism and Asperger Syndrome* (Cambridge: Cambridge University Press), 37–92.

Austin, R. D. and Pisano, G. P. (2017) 'Neurodiversity as a competitive advantage', *Harvard Business Review*, May–June, 96–103.

Baldwin, S. and Costley, D. (2015) 'The experiences and needs of female adults with high-functioning autism spectrum disorder', *Autism*, 25 June.

Baldwin, S., Costley, D. and Warren, A. (2014) 'Employment activities and experiences of adults with high-functioning autism and Asperger's Disorder', *Journal of Autism and Developmental Disorders*, 44(10): 2440–2449.

Bargiela, S., Steward, R. and Williams, M. (2016) 'The experiences of late-diagnosed women with autism spectrum conditions: An investigation of the female autism phenotype', *Journal of Autism and Developmental Disorders*, 46(10): 1573–3432.

Bazelon, E. (2007) 'What autistic girls are made of', *The New York Times*, 5 August.

Bernick, M. (2017) 'Increasing autism employment: An anthropologist's perspective', *Forbes* 9 May.

Best, C., Arora, S., Porter, F., and Doherty, M. (2015) 'The relationship between subthreshold autistic traits, ambiguous figure perception and divergent thinking', *Journal of Autism and Developmental Disorders*, 45(12): 4064–4073.

Beyer, S. and Kilsby, M. (1996) 'The future of employment for people with learning disabilities: a keynote review', *British Journal of Learning Disabilities*, 24: 134–137.

Booth, J. interviewed by Damian Milton on the JKP Blog, 15 July 2016, available at www.jkp.com/jkpblog/2016/04/autism-equality-workplace-interview-janine-booth/ (accessed 27 April 2018).

Buescher, A. V., Cidav, Z., Knapp, M. and Mandell, D. S. (2014) 'Costs of autism spectrum disorders in the United Kingdom and the United States', *JAMA Pediatrics*, 168, 721–728.

Burke, R. V., Andersen, M. N., Bowen, S. L., Howard, M. R. and Allen, K. D. (2010) 'Evaluation of two instruction methods to increase employment options for young adults with autism spectrum disorders', *Research in Developmental Disabilities*, 31(6): 1223–1233.

Burt, D. B., Fuller, S. and Lewis, K. R. (1991) 'Competitive employment of adults with autism', *Journal of Autism and Developmental Disorders*, 21: 237–242.

Capo, L. C. (2000) 'Autism, employment and the role of occupational therapy', *Work*, 16: 201–207.

Chadsey-Rusch, J. (1992) 'Toward defining and measuring social skills in employment settings', *American Journal of Mental Retardation*, 96, 405–418.

Chen, J. L. et al. (2015) 'Trends in employment for individuals with autism spectrum disorder: A review of the research literature', *Review Journal of Autism and Developmental Disorders*, 2(June, 2): 115–127.

Chiang, H. M., Cheung, Y. K., Li, H. and Tsai, L. Y. (2013) 'Factors associated with participation in employment for high school leavers with autism', *Journal of Autism and Developmental Disorders*, 43, 1832–1842.

Cimera, R. E. and Burgess, S. (2011) 'Do adults with autism benefit monetarily from working in their communities?' *Journal of Vocational Rehabilitation*, 34: 173–180.

Cimera, R. E. (2012) 'The economics of supported employment: What new data tell us', *Journal of Vocational Rehabilitation*, 37: 109–117.

CRAE (the Centre for Research in Autism and Education, London), 2 April 2015, available at http://crae.ioe.ac.uk/post/115301526093/interview-with-daniel-lightwing-who-inspired-the (accessed 14 May 2018).

Creed, P. A. and Macintyre, S. R. (2001) 'The relative effects of deprivation of the latent and manifest benefits of employment on the well-being of unemployed people', *Journal of Occupational Health Psychology*, 6(4): 324–331.

Deweerdt, S. 'Autism characteristics differ by gender, studies find', available at https://spectrumnews.org/news/autism-characteristics-differ-by-gender-studies-find/ (accessed 27 March 2014).

Dworzynski, K., Ronald, A., Bolton, P. and Happé, F. (2012) 'How different are girls and boys above and below the diagnostic threshold for autism spectrum disorders?' *Journal of the American Academy of Child and Adolescent Psychiatry*, 51(8): 788–797.

Eack, S. M. et al. (2018) 'Cognitive enhancement therapy for adult autism spectrum disorder: Results of an 18-month randomised clinical trial', *Autism Research*, 11(March, 3): 519–530.

Farley, M. et al. (2017) 'Mid-life social outcomes for a population-based sample of adults with ASD', *Autism Research*, 11(1): 142–152.

Feather, N. T. and O'Brien, G. E. (1986) 'A longitudinal analysis of the effects of different patterns of employment and unemployment on school-leavers', *British Journal of Psychology*, 77(November, 4): 459–479.

Feinstein, A. (ed.) (2011) *Looking Up*, 5(6): 24.

Frood, A. 'Games plus group therapy may help adults with autism find jobs', available at https://spectrumnews.org/news/games-plus-group-therapy-may-help-adults-autism-find-jobs/ (accessed 7 February 2018).

Furfaro, H. 'Jobs, relationships elude adults with autism', available at https://spectrumnews.org/news/jobs-relationships-elude-adults-autism/ (accessed 15 February 2018).

García-Villamisar, D. and Hughes, C. (2007) 'Supported employment improves cognitive performance in adults with autism', *Journal of Intellectual Disability Research*, 51: 142–150.

García-Villamisar, D., Wehman, P. and Diaz Navarro, M. (2002) 'Changes in the quality of autistic people's life that work in supported and sheltered employment: A 5-year follow-up study', *Journal of Vocational Rehabilitation*, 17, 309–312.

Gould, J. and Ashton-Smith, J. (2011) 'Missed diagnosis or misdiagnosis? Girls and women on the autism spectrum', *Good Autism Practice (GAP)*, 12: 34–41.

Haertl, K., Callahan, D., Markovits, J. and Sheppard, S. S. (2013) 'Perspectives of adults living with autism spectrum disorder: Psychosocial and occupational implications', *Occupational Therapy in Mental Health*, 29(1): 27–41.

Hagner, D. and Cooney, B. (2003) 'Building employer capacity to support employees with severe disabilities in the workplace', *Journal of Prevention, Assessment and Rehabilitation*, 21(1).

Hagner, D. and Cooney, B. F. (2005) '"I do that for everybody": Supervising employees with autism', *Focus on Autism and Other Developmental Disabilities*, 20(2): 91–97.

Happé, F. and Frith, U. (2006) 'The weak coherence account: Detail-focused cognitive style in autism spectrum disorders', *Journal of Autism and Developmental Disorders*, 36(January, 1): 5–25.

Happé, F. and Vital, P. (2009) 'What aspects of autism predispose to talent?' *Philosophical Transactions of the Royal Society Biological Sciences*, 364: 1369–1375.

Hendricks, D. (2010) 'Employment and adults with autism spectrum disorders: Challenges and strategies for success', *Journal of Vocational Rehabilitation*, 32: 125–134.

Hill, E. (undated) 'Autism spectrum disorder and employment', available at www.gold.ac.uk/news/comment-autism-spectrum-disorder-and-employment/ (accessed 14 May 2018).

Hill, E. L. (2004) 'Evaluating the theory of executive dysfunction in autism', *Developmental Review*, 24: 189–233.

Hillier, A. et al. (2007) 'Two-year evaluation of a vocational support programme for adults on the autism spectrum', *Career Development and Transition for Exceptional Individuals*, 30(May, 1): 35–47.

Howlin, P. (2000) 'Outcome in adult life for more able individuals with autism or Asperger syndrome', *Autism*, 4, 63–83.

Howlin, P., Alcock, J. and Burkin, C. (2005) 'An 8-year follow-up of a specialist supported employment service for high-ability adults with autism or Asperger syndrome', *Autism*, 9, 533–549.

Howlin P., Goode S., Hutton J. and Rutter, M. (2009) 'Savant skills in autism: Psychometric approaches and parental reports', *Philosophical Transactions of the Royal Society of London, B: Biologial Sciences*, 364(May, 1522): 1359–1367.

Hurlbutt, K. and Chalmers, L. (2002) 'Adults with autism speak out: Perceptions of their life experiences', *Focus on Autism and Other Developmental Disabilities*, 17(2): 103–111.

Hurlbutt, K. K. and Chalmers, L. (2004) 'Employment and adults with Asperger syndrome', *Focus on Autism and Other Developmental Disabilities*, 19, 215–222.

Jacquemont, S., Coe, B. P., Hersch, M., Duyzend, M. H., Krumm, N., Bergmann, S., Beckmann, J. S., Rosenfeld, J. A. and Eichler, E. E. (2014) 'A higher mutational burden in females supports a "female protective model" in neurodevelopmental disorders', *American Journal of Human Genetics*, 94(March, 3): 415–425.

Jammaers, E. et al. (2016) 'Constructing positive identities in ableist workplaces: Disabled employees' discursive practices engaging with the discourse of lower productivity', *Human Relations*, 69(June, 6): 1365–1386.

Johnson, T. D. and Joshi, A. (2016) 'Dark clouds or silver linings? A stigma threat perspective on the implications of an autism diagnosis for workplace well-being', *Journal of Applied Psychology, American Psychological Association*, 101(3): 430–449.

Kanner, L. (1971) 'Follow-up study of eleven autistic children originally reported in 1943', *Journal of Autism and Childhood Schizophrenia*, 1(April–June, 2): 119–145.

Keel, J. H., Mesibov, G. B. and Woods, A. V. (1997) 'TEACCH-supported employment programme', *Journal of Autism and Developmental Disorders*, 27: 3–9.

Kenyon, L. (2015) 'How to manage autism in the workplace', *Personnel Today*, 21 August.

Kim, C. 'Musings of an Aspie', available at https://musingsofanaspie.com/2013/08/09/the-challenges-of-being-a-self-employed-aspie/ (accessed 27 April 2018).

Knapp, M., Patel, A., Curran, C. et al. (2013) 'Supported employment: Cost-effectiveness across six European sites', *World Psychiatry*, 12: 60–68.

Knapp, M., Romeo, R. and Beecham, J. (2009) 'Economic cost of autism in the UK', *Autism*, 13: 317–336.

Kopp, S. I. and Gillberg, C. (2011) 'The Autism Spectrum Screening Questionnaire (ASSQ)-Revised Extended Version (ASSQ-REV): An instrument for better capturing the autism phenotype in girls? A preliminary study involving 191 clinical cases and community controls', *Research in Developmental Disabilities*, 32(November–December, 6): 2875–2888.

Krieger, B., Kinebanian, A., Prodinger, B. and Heigl, F. (2012) 'Becoming a member of the work force: Perceptions of adults with Asperger Syndrome', *Work*, 43(2): 141–157.

Lai, M.-C., Lombardo, M. V., Auyeung, B., Chakrabarti, B. and Baron-Cohen, S. (2015) 'Sex/gender differences and autism: Setting the scene for future research', *Journal of the American Academy of Child and Adolescent Psychiatry*, 54(1): 11–24.

Lai, M.-C., Lombardo, M. V., Ruigrok, A. N. V. et al. (2016) 'Quantifying and exploring camouflaging in men and women with autism', *Autism*, November 29.

Mandavilli, A. (2015) 'The invisible women with autism', *The Atlantic*, 22 October.

Mavranezouli, I., Megnin-Viggars, O., Cheema, N. et al. (2014) 'The cost-effectiveness of supported employment for adults with autism in the United Kingdom', *Autism*, 18, 975–984.

Mawhood, L. and Howlin, P. (1999) 'The outcome of a supported employment scheme for high functioning adults with autism or Asperger syndrome', *Autism*, 3: 229–254.

McCaughrin, W. B., Ellis, W. K., Rusch, F. R. et al. (1993) 'Cost-effectiveness of supported employment', *Mental Retardation*, 31: 41–48.

Mostafa, M. (2007) 'An architecture for autism: Concepts of design intervention for the autistic user', *International Journal of Architectural Research*, 2(1): 189–211.

Müller, E. A., Schuler, B. A. and Yates, G. B. (2003) 'Meeting the vocational support needs of individuals with Asperger syndrome and other autism spectrum disabilities', *Journal of Vocational Rehabilitation*, 18, 163–175.

Neighmond, P. and Greenhalgh, J. 'Social camouflage may lead to underdiagnosis of autism in girls', available at www.npr.org/sections/health-shots/2017/07/31/539123377/social-camouflage-may-lead-to-underdiagnosis-of-autism-in-girls (accessed 31 July 2017).

Nicholas, D. B., Attridge, M., Zwaigenbaum, L. and Clarke, M. (2014) 'Vocational support approaches in autism spectrum disorder: A synthesis review of the literature', *Autism*, 1–11.

Noble, J., Conley, R. W., Banerjee, S. et al. (1991) 'Supported employment in New York State: A comparison of benefits and costs', *Journal of Disability Policy Studies*, 2: 39–73.

Ozonoff, S. and McEvoy, R. E. (1994) 'A longitudinal study of executive function and theory of mind development in autism', *Development and Psychopathology*, 6: 415–431.

Pierce, J. L. and Gardner, D. G. (2004) 'Self-esteem within the work and organisational context: A review of the organisation-based self-esteem literature', *Journal of Management*, 30, 591–622.

Ragins, B. R. and Cornwell, J. M. (2001) 'Pink triangles: Antecedents and consequences of perceived workplace discrimination against gay and lesbian employees', *Journal of Applied Psychology*, 86, 1244–1261.

Rhodes, L., Ramsing, K. and Hill, M. (1987) 'Economic evaluation of employment services: A review of applications', *Journal of the Association for Persons with Severe Handicaps*, 12: 175–181.

Richards, J. (2012) 'Examining the exclusion of employees with Asperger syndrome from the workplace', *Personnel Review*, 41: 630–646.

Richards, J. (2015) 'Asperger syndrome and employment inclusion: Towards practices informed by theories of contemporary employment', *Interdisciplinary Perspectives on Equality and Diversity*, 1(1).

Ritvo, E. R. et al. (1989) 'The UCLA-University of Utah epidemiologic survey of autism: Recurrence risk estimates and genetic counselling', *American Journal of Psychiatry*, 146(August, 8): 1032–1036.

Robertson, S. M. (2010) 'Neurodiversity, quality of life and autistic adults: Shifting research and professional focuses on to real-life challenges', *Disability Studies Quarterly*, 30.

Robison, J. E. (2013) 'What is Neurodiversity?' *Psychology Today*, 7 October.

Romoser, M. (2000) 'Malemployment in autism', *Focus on Autism and Other Developmental Disabilities*, 15: 246–247.

Roux, A. M., Shattuck, P. T., Cooper, B. P., Anderson, K. A., Wagner, M. and Narendorf, S. C. (2013) 'Post-secondary employment experiences among young adults with an autism spectrum disorder', *Journal of the American Academy of Child & Adolescent Psychiatry*, 52: 931–939.

Rynkiewicz, A., Schuller, B., Marchi, E., Piana, S., Camurri, A., Lassalle, A. et al. (2016) 'An investigation of the "female camouflage effect" in autism using a computerized ADOS-2 and a test of sex/gender differences', *Molecular Autism*, 7(10).

Schall, C. M. (2010) 'Positive behaviour support: Supporting adults with autism spectrum disorders in the workplace', *Journal of Vocational Rehabilitation*, 32(2): 109–111.

Schall, C. M., Wehman, P., Brooke, V. et al. (2015) 'Employment interventions for individuals with ASD: The relative efficacy of supported employment with or without prior Project SEARCH training', *Journal of Autism and Developmental Disorders*, 45: 3990–4001.

Splatt, A. J. and Weedon, D. (1981) 'The urethral syndrome: Morphological studies', *British Journal of Urology*, 53(June, 3): 263–265.

Stevens, P. and Martin, N. (1999) 'Supporting individuals with intellectual disability and challenging behaviour in integrated work settings: An overview and a model for service provision', *Journal of Intellectual Disability Research*, 43(Pt 1): 19–29.

Strickland, D. C., Coles, C. D. and Southern, L. B (2013) 'JobTIPS: A transition to employment programme for individuals with autism spectrum disorders', *Journal of Autism and Developmental Disorders*, 43: 2472–2483.

Szalavitz, M. (2016) 'Autism – it's different in girls', *Scientific American*, 1 March.

Taylor, J. L. and Seltzer, M. M. (2011) 'Employment and post-secondary educational activities for young adults with autism spectrum disorders during the transition to adulthood', *Journal of Autism and Developmental Disorders*, 41: 566–574.

Trach, J. R. and Rusch, F. R. (1989) 'Supported employment program evaluation: Evaluating degree of implementation and selected outcomes', *American Journal of Mental Retardation*, 94: 134–140.

Wagner, M. and Taylor, J. L. (2012) 'Post-secondary education and employment among youth with an autism spectrum disorder', *Pediatrics*, 129: 1042–1049.

Walsh, L., Lydon, S. and Healy, O. (2014) 'Employment and vocational skills among individuals with autism spectrum disorder: Predictors, impact and interventions', *Journal of Autism and Developmental Disorders*, 1: 266–275.

Wehman, P. and Kregel, J. (1985) 'A supported work approach to competitive employment for individuals with moderate and severe handicaps', *Journal of the Association for Persons with Severe Handicaps*, 10: 3–11.

Wehman, P. H., Schall, C. M., McDonough, J. et al. (2014) 'Competitive employment for youth with autism spectrum disorders: Early results from a randomised clinical trial', *Journal of Autism and Developmental Disorders*, 44: 487–500.

Wertheim, J. and Apstein, S. 'Defying expectations, people with autism are participating and excelling in sports', available at www.si.com/sports-illustrated/2016/11/01/people-with-autism-spectrum-disorder-embrace-sports-athletics (accessed 1 November 2016).

Westbrook, J. D., Nye, C., Fong, C. J. et al. (2012) 'Effectiveness of adult employment assistance services for persons with autism spectrum disorders', *Campbell Systematic Review*, 5: 1–67.

Whetzel, M. (2014) 'Interviewing tips for applicants with autism spectrum disorder (ASD)', *Journal of Vocational Rehabilitation*, 40: 155–159.

Wilkinson, S (2017) ' "It's exhausting": The hidden struggle of working women with autism', posted on 9 May and available at https://broadly.vice.com/en_us/article/vb4d89/hidden-struggle-working-women-autism-auticon (accessed 14 May 2018).

Wing, L. (1981) 'Asperger's syndrome: A clinical account', *Psychological Medicine*, 11(1): 115–129.

Wright, J. (2014) 'Females are genetically protected from autism', *Scientific American*, 10 March.

Wright, J. (2017) 'New method aims to quantify "camouflaging" in autism', posted on 19 January and available at https://spectrumnews.org/news/new-method-aims-quantify-camouflaging-autism/ (accessed 14 May 2018).

Index